The Mediterranean Connection

The Mediterranean Connection

Criminal Networks and Illicit Economies in North Africa

Phil Williams,
Jason M. Blazakis,
and Colin P. Clarke

LYNNE RIENNER PUBLISHERS
BOULDER
LONDON

Published in the United States of America in 2024 by
Lynne Rienner Publishers, Inc.
1800 30th Street, Suite 314, Boulder, Colorado 80301
www.rienner.com

and in the United Kingdom by
Lynne Rienner Publishers, Inc.
1 Bedford Row, London WC1R 4BU
www.eurospanbookstore.com/rienner

Library of Congress Cataloging-in-Publication Data
Names: Williams, Phil, 1948– author. | Blazakis, Jason M., 1975– author. | Clarke, Colin P., author.
Title: The Mediterranean connection : criminal networks and illicit economies in North Africa / Phil Williams, Jason M. Blazakis, Colin P. Clarke.
Description: Boulder, Colorado : Lynne Rienner Publishers, Inc., [2024] | Includes bibliographical references and index. | Summary: "Ranging from antiquities smuggling to human trafficking, the authors explore the nature of the widespread illicit flows of goods and people across North Africa and beyond"— Provided by publisher.
Identifiers: LCCN 2024012823 (print) | LCCN 2024012824 (ebook) | ISBN 9781685859978 (hardcover) | ISBN 9781962551366 (ebook)
Subjects: LCSH: Smuggling—Africa, North. | Human trafficking—Africa, North.
Classification: LCC HJ7094.5.Z5 W55 2024 (print) | LCC HJ7094.5.Z5 (ebook) | DDC 364.1060961—dc23/eng/20240515
LC record available at https://lccn.loc.gov/2024012823
LC ebook record available at https://lccn.loc.gov/2024012824

British Cataloguing in Publication Data
A Cataloguing in Publication record for this book
is available from the British Library.

Printed and bound in the United States of America

∞ The paper used in this publication meets the requirements of the American National Standard for Permanence of Paper for Printed Library Materials Z39.48-1992.

5 4 3 2 1

Contents

Acknowledgments

THE AUTHORS THANK PMI IMPACT FOR PROVIDING RESEARCH SUPPORT, AND they also thank the Soufan Group, where Colin P. Clarke and Jason M. Blazakis both work. Phil Williams would like to thank his two dogs, Daisy and Maggie, who drive him crazy and keep him sane. He also thanks the Global Initiative Against Transnational Organized Crime for the incredibly useful Organized Crime Index, as well as for the impressive research done by many of its outstanding scholars, especially Matthew Herbert, Max Gallien, and Mark Micallef, whose pioneering work on North Africa helped to shape and inform this book. He would like to thank, too, Sharad Joshi for going above and beyond in providing invaluable help in research and referencing for the initial draft of the book. Jason M. Blazakis dedicates his portion of the work to John W. Winkle III, who passed in 2022. John was a great mentor and friend. He will be missed. Jason also thanks Judy Wyatt for her research support. Colin P. Clarke would like to thank his colleagues at the Soufan Group and the Soufan Center, but mostly his family for dealing with his long hours at work. Finally, the authors thank Marie-Claire Antoine for her steadfast support and encouragement.

1

Criminal and Illicit Networks in North Africa

THE UPWELLING OF DISCONTENT THAT GRIPPED COUNTRIES THROUGHOUT North Africa and the Middle East, which was simplistically and optimistically termed the "Arab Spring," disrupted social, political, and economic life. Images from Tahrir Square in 2011 and those of the food vendor in Tunisia whose self-immolation sparked the revolution remain vivid. Political reform in North Africa may still be just out of reach, but the desire for political change in the region remains steadfast—making North Africa a relevant region for a wide range of studies and analysis.

More than a decade ago, North Africa was at the center of a maelstrom of dramatic political upheaval. Assuming center stage in the world's imagination is not new to the region. Indeed, throughout history, ancient empires, imperialists, colonialists, and locally powerful fiefdoms vied for the region's rich natural resources and strategic locations fundamental to securing geopolitical dominance. The Vandals, Byzantines, Carthaginians, Ottomans, Romans, and many other conquerors, like locusts, feasted on North Africa's landscape. For the Romans, North Africa was the granary of its empire. Yet, North Africa is far more than its land produces or the imports and exports that move through its ports. Culturally, linguistically, and historically, North Africa is an important crossroads that has indelibly shaped and contributed to the development of Western civilization. Ancient land and sea trade routes that link the Sahara to the Mediterranean Sea and into Europe remain extant and quite vibrant. These routes allowed for the transmission of knowledge, goods, and culture that would shape the world for centuries to come. Today, these routes pass through the modern North African states of Morocco, Algeria, Tunisia, Libya, and Egypt, allowing the flow of people, including irregular migrants, and both licit and illicit goods.

Some may object to the inclusion of Egypt in a book on North Africa. But Egypt is critical to any discourse on North Africa, especially one that examines the illicit economies of the region. Egypt is the sinew that unites western Asia, North Africa, and Europe. Indeed, Napoleon once observed that Egypt was the most strategic country in the world. At the very least, its political, economic, social, cultural, and historical significance is difficult to overstate. And it remains a critical waypoint for illicit economies.

Popular examination of illicit economies is often shaped by hyperbole, simplicity, and at times even conspiracy theories that have little relevance to reality. Sadly, these tendencies obscure the real challenge of illicit economies that often prey on society's most vulnerable people. The legitimate challenges of criminal networks engaged in illicit activity also occur far beyond US borders and, for this reason, often escape Washington's bandwidth to address in a meaningful way. Yet, the reverberations of illicit economies wash upon distant shores. Moreover, they are part of the sordid underbelly of a world that, despite some pushback and reversals, is still highly globalized, linked, and interconnected.

As a region, North Africa is vitally important to the study of illicit economies and criminal networks. These challenges are historic and relevant to geographic locations noncontiguous to the region. For example, privateering, piracy, and frequent deployment of corsairs to plunder US commercial vessels engaged in legitimate commercial exchange resulted in the rapid expansion of the US Navy in the early 1800s. Today, the challenges associated with illicit economies in North Africa are significant, with profound impact beyond the geographic contours of the five countries this book examines. Individuals like Mokhtar Belmokhtar, an arch-terrorist who became known by the sobriquet "Marlboro Man" because of his engagement in cigarette smuggling, and organized criminal enterprises like the Italian mafia are key players and critical nodes in the story of illicit economies. Criminal networks and pioneering terrorists like Belmokhtar have financed their deadly operations by engaging in illicit trafficking and smuggling. Yet, as transnational crime scholars Matthew Herbert and Max Gallien have written, the challenge associated with illicit activity plagues both the hinterlands and borderlands of the North African states. Scholars like Herbert and Gallien have pointed to a hierarchical stratification in North African society that has contributed to human misery, resulting in well-meaning individuals turning to smuggling to make ends meet. This instinct to survive by engaging in illicit activity as a coping mechanism emerges throughout this book and is frequently revisited. Moreover, we would be remiss not to mention that politicians in Algiers, Tunis, Cairo, Rabat, and Tripoli often fail to administer to the needs of those who live precariously at the periphery of society and the economy. As a result, people who have been marginalized and forgotten by their capitals have no resort other than to put their lives at risk by engaging in dangerous and illicit markets and activities. In this sense, organized crime and illicit markets provide a safety net and even a safety valve where economic marginalization and social exclusion are pervasive features of society.

This book is intended to inform a wide readership, especially scholars, government practitioners, journalists, regional experts, and the attentive public who want to learn more about criminal networks and illicit economies in North Africa. Written during and after the Covid-19 pandemic, the book also considers, to the extent possible, how Covid-19 affected the criminal networks and illicit trading practices and patterns in North Africa. Although they underwent short-term disruption, both networks and the illicit economies in which they operated proved highly resilient, adapting through new routes and makeshift hubs, enabled by the rapid advance of digital communications and highly sophisticated information technologies.

Purpose and Scope

In this book we examine the scale, scope, and impact of criminal networks and illicit economies in five North African states: Morocco, Algeria, Tunisia, Libya, and Egypt. We look at various forms of trafficking and smuggling, ranging from drugs and arms to human beings—some of whom are engaged in what is sometimes termed irregular migration and some of whom are being trafficked into a life of sexual servitude or forced labor. We identify not only the routes that are used but also the key hubs where routes converge and where there is also, in some cases at least, a concentration of criminal services and criminal activities. In other words, the aim is to map the illicit flows in and through the five North African countries that are being examined.

Each country section study is structured similarly, with an introductory overview that analyzes state capacity and resilience and provides a foundation for understanding both the inhibitors to and the facilitators of smuggling and trafficking activities. This process is made somewhat easier by the ENACT Organized Crime Index of 2019 and the Global Organized Crime Index that was published in 2021 and refined and updated in 2023. The latter index, which is produced by the Global

Initiative Against Transnational Organized Crime, is a major game changer as it massively strengthens the knowledge base about organized crime and illicit economies not only in Africa but globally. Furthermore, the iterative nature of the index both facilitates the understanding of criminal trends and informs policies that can more effectively respond to the challenges of criminality.[1]

> The Index measures criminality and resilience for each country on a scale of 1 to 10. Countries' criminality scores are made up of the average scores of ten criminal markets and four criminal actor types. Criminal market scores consider the scope, scale, value, and reach (i.e. non-monetary impact) of each illicit economy. Criminal actor scores consider the structure, control, and influence of each criminal actor type. The higher the criminality score a country has, the more severe its criminality conditions are.[2]

In September 2023, ENACT and the Global Initiative Against Transnational Organized Crime released a new version of the Index. This not only updated the country assessments, but also extended the categories to encompass fifteen different criminal markets and five different criminal types—mafia-style groups, criminal networks, state-embedded actors, foreign actors, and private-sector actors. The new criminal markets added to the index are financial fraud, cyber-dependent crimes, counterfeiting, the illicit trade in excisable goods, and extortion and protection-racketeering. The surprise was that financial fraud emerged as the largest criminal market.

Both the original index and the 2023 update identified twelve dimensions of resilience—defined as the "ability to withstand and disrupt organized criminal activities as a whole . . . through political, economic, legal and social measures."[3] These included factors such as political leadership and governance; transparency and accountability; law enforcement, policies, and laws; the judicial system; and nonstate actors.

The index—supplemented by observations about the quality of governance, the effectiveness of the rule of law, and recent political and economic developments—provides the basis for the introductory section of each country study. The analysis then moves from the general to the specific. It recognizes that while the five North African countries face some common challenges in terms of organized crime and illicit economies, there are also important variations in terms of which illegal markets are most prominent, the commodities that are smuggled or trafficked, the extent to which corruption is an important facilitator, as well as the capacity and even the desire of the governments concerned to combat these activities.[4]

As always, when examining the illicit and the covert, a degree of caution is in order. Research on illicit economies attempts to shed light on conduct, transactions, and flows that, by their very nature, deliberately reside in the shadows. Too many studies of illicit activity attempt to quantify what is inherently unquantifiable. Many of the figures that are typically used are based on law enforcement and interdiction successes, but it is almost impossible to determine the percentage of illicit flows that are intercepted, whether trends are moving in a favorable or unfavorable direction, and whether law enforcement agencies were particularly efficient, or the criminals simply failed to develop effective risk management strategies. Such difficulties notwithstanding, this study makes use of a wide variety of sources ranging from those produced by international organizations and specialized nongovernmental organizations (NGOs) to scholarly ethnographic research conducted at the national and local levels. It also makes good use of community access to detailed news articles reporting from on the ground. In effect, we have tried to piece together a kaleidoscope that provides insight and understanding of the complex drivers, facilitators, and inhibitors of criminal behaviors and illicit economies.

Smuggling and Trafficking: The Challenges

Although the terms *smuggling* and *trafficking* are often used interchangeably, they have slightly different meanings. These have been captured succinctly in the comment by Mark Shaw and Tuesday Reitano that

> the term 'trafficking' represents those activities involved in moving . . . illegal commodities (drugs or guns or people against their will). 'Smuggling' denotes the movement of commodities that are not themselves illegal (food, fuel, cigarettes, or people who consent), but their sourcing or the activity of moving them across borders contravenes the law of at least one government, such as in relation to the payment of tax or customs duties. This latter category of smuggling overlaps significantly with a substantial and growing informal (or grey) economy.[5]

This is a helpful distinction despite an inevitable degree of fuzziness at the edges. Some criminal organizations, for example, might be engaged in both smuggling and trafficking at the same time. Moreover, when the focus is on human beings, it appears that those engaged in irregular migration—and are being smuggled voluntarily—can also become victims of human traffickers who use coercion or deception and force women into sexual servitude and men into forced labor. The analysis here looks at both smuggling and trafficking.

Even if governments have both the will and significant capabilities to combat smuggling and trafficking, the task remains formidable partly because illicit markets develop where the legal market is not functioning properly, and partly because of the skill, sophistication, and capacity for adaptation of criminal organizations and networks. The most effective criminals are highly opportunistic and able to take advantages of global phenomena—for example, new markets created by the Covid-19 pandemic. In this connection, it is useful to look at what can be termed the smuggling and trafficking toolkit. The toolkit not only highlights methods that are common to both but also explains why smuggling and trafficking are so difficult to counter. The toolkit consists of four major techniques and methods, but these can be mixed and matched in ways that create positive synergies for the perpetrators and additional complications for those trying to combat their activities.

Method 1. Concealment of goods is designed to ensure that they are, in effect, moved covertly. The degree of sophistication varies greatly from simply hiding the commodities under something else in a truck or container, through sealed compartments in cars or trucks, to what might be termed deep concealment. Southern Colombia-based Cali drug trafficking organizations were particularly good at deep concealment, hiding cocaine in cement posts, while more recent drug traffickers from Latin America have used canned goods supposedly containing fruits or vegetables to hide cocaine and heroin moving to the United States and Europe.[6] Concealment works because it is relatively easy to hide illicit commodities within the vast shipments of licit goods that both contribute to and are a product of globalization. In effect, illicit trade is a parasite on the back of the transnational flows of goods and services that have become a critical component of the contemporary global economy.

Method 2. Deception obviously overlaps with concealment but typically involves portraying the commodities that are being moved as something they are not—through papers such as false bills of lading, counterfeit passports, or falsified end-user certificates. In a fascinating account, a *sistemista* (an experienced cocaine smuggler) who arranged shipments of cocaine from Colombia to Europe highlighted the importance of deception as an additional safeguard against discovery and seizure. He emphasized the need to ensure that "the stuff travels in shipments of big-name firms, world-famous and above suspicion" as this significantly reduces the probability that the container will be scanned or searched.[7] "What you need is a reliable name, a respectable firm—well-known and trusted. Precisely because thousands of containers cross borders every day and the traffic of goods is continuous, those that tend to go through the arch belong to little-known or suspect companies, provenances that give cause for doubt."[8]

Method 3. Circumvention involves the avoidance of formal ports of entry or other locations where regulatory measures might be in place, or intrusive inspections might occur. In many borderland regions, there are well-established and traditional crossing points that are far from checkpoints, require no inspections, and are part of integrated local and regional cross-border economies. Purchases in such regions are often based on arbitrage opportunities resulting from price differentials between the two sides of the border.[9] The result is a thriving cross-border trade, sometimes involving barter, that benefits populations but not governments.

Method 4. Facilitation involves the use of bribery and corruption to ensure that authorities with the responsibility to combat smuggling and trafficking fail to do their job and are neither efficient nor effective at interdicting smuggled or trafficked commodities. In some instances, all that is required is passivity or simply looking the other way, while in others, more active participation is necessary. Whatever the case, close and enduring relations between criminals and government officials often play a critical role in the success of smuggling and trafficking activities and provide a slew of benefits for criminal enterprises. In this connection, there are two distinct if interrelated conceptions of corruption: first is corruption as a condition that permeates to some degree or another the public administration of a country; second is corruption as an instrument that can be used by criminal organizations to neutralize the coercive and punitive powers of the state, to undermine legal and regulatory measures, and to facilitate the flows of prohibited, regulated, stolen, or counterfeit commodities.

As suggested above, these four methods can be combined in different ways. Yet it is not simply about skill or sophistication. It is also about exploiting the sheer volume of licit flows that has become a deeply embedded characteristic of contemporary globalization. Although this volume declined precipitously during the Covid-19 pandemic, it bounced back relatively quickly. The 2022 DHL Global Connectedness Index, for example, noted that "international trade, capital, and information flows" had all surpassed those prior to the pandemic.[10] The challenge for governments, therefore, is not so much to find a needle in a haystack but to find a specific needle in a very large stack of needles. More broadly it is to exploit the benefits of globalization while inhibiting or constricting the flows of prohibited, regulated, stolen, or counterfeit commodities and limiting the power of the criminal enterprises that manage these flows.

At the same time, it is important not to characterize illegal activities as only imposing harms—which they obviously do—on societies, economies, and, even more significantly, on human security. They also provide benefits that need to be acknowledged. Without widespread benefits, organized crime and illicit economies would be relatively easy to deal with. Moreover, the emergence and expansion of criminal organizations and activities can be understood in large part as a symptom of deeper problems connected to globalization, neoliberalism, and what can best be described as a global crisis of governance at the national level.[11] With the massive expansion of global trade facilitated by the invention and widespread adoption of the intermodal container, the rise of global financial markets, the end of the Cold War, and the emergence of deeply interconnected computer and information systems resulting in the growth of cyberspace, the opportunities for both traditional and new forms of organized crime increased exponentially. The technologies have been user-friendly, thereby lowering the barriers for entry.

The rise of transnational organized crime and the expansion of illicit economies were also facilitated by weak states and by the dominant ethos of neoliberalism, with its preference for markets over regulation, for the limited role of government, and for the reduction or withdrawal of social safety nets. The rise of massive economic inequalities both between nations and within them, the dominance of entrenched elites seeking only to maintain their preferential status, the social and economic exclusion of key segments of the population, and the gap between aspirations and opportunities for young people all fed into the growing attractiveness of the illicit economy as a coping mechanism and safety net and of organized crime as the only available ladder for economic and social mobility. This downside of globalization has been effectively captured by Thomas Friedman. An avowed champion of globalization, Friedman is also sensitive to its adverse effects, acknowledging that it has also produced "a powerful backlash from those brutalized or left behind by the new system."[12] In effect, Friedman recognizes that globalization has winners and losers—and the pain for the losers can be enormous. In a similar vein, two books have been published with the title *The Dark Side of Globalization.* In one of them Jorge Heine and Ramesh Thakur note that global governance mechanisms have lagged far behind globalization itself, and this has "let loose the infrastructure of uncivil society and accelerated the transnational flows" of crime, terrorism, and disease.[13] In the other, edited by Leila Talani and Roberto Roccu, the dark side is seen in terms of "purposive actions" by criminal networks to exploit the illicit opportunities that are the inevitable accompaniment to globalization.[14]

Seen in this context, the focus on the five nations of North Africa can be understood as a subset of these global problems and one which highlights the way they are manifested at the regional level and at the level of the states within the region. Accordingly, this analysis starts from the presumption that, whether exploring illicit organizations and activities within a single state or a small group of states, it is crucial to examine the broader neighborhood. This neighborhood provides context, opportunities, and threats. It can be a source of instability that creates the possibility of exogenous shocks leading to population outflows, a source of inspiration that encourages population inflows, or a source of stability that helps to dampen endogenous shocks within the North Africa region.

North Africa's Neighborhood

North Africa has two very different neighborhoods. During the colonial era, the European neighborhood was a source of control; it now offers an attractive vision of employment opportunities, democratic participation, and social safety nets, as well as an aging population. The neighborhood to the south is very different, with some endemically weak states, the increased virulence and reach of Islamist extremists, insurgencies and civil wars, high levels of poverty, and continuing and rapid population growth. Concomitantly, North Africa itself has a form of dual identity: it is part of the Mediterranean littoral but is also a part of Africa, albeit a relatively prosperous and developed part. The Mediterranean component highlights the links to Europe, links that were part of the colonial experience but also, and at times more importantly, reflect the impact of geographical proximity—especially in the cases of Morocco and Spain and Libya and Italy, respectively. It is therefore then hardly surprising that, as Mehdi Lahlou has emphasized, the Mediterranean has been crucial in shaping a "shared history" of Europe and North Africa.[15] Other observers focus more on the African component of North Africa's complex identity. The land borders are more immediately and directly shared; there is a common experience of colonialism—even though its manifestations differed significantly from country to country—and the Berbers, the indigenous people in the Maghreb, extend not only through Morocco and Algeria but into Mali, Mauritania, and Niger. Moreover, as Algerian commentator Iman Amrani noted, the countries of North Africa and those of sub-Saharan Africa "have had shared struggles" during both the colonial era and the fractious period of decolonization.[16] She also suggested that although the economic attraction of the Middle East is important, in the final analysis, "Morocco, Algeria, Tunisia, Libya, and Egypt share not only a colonial past with the rest of Africa but also a physical continent."[17]

Accordingly, it bears emphasis that both the Mediterranean/European and the African components of the neighborhood are crucial to understanding the activities of criminal networks and smuggling and trafficking throughout North Africa. It is also worth emphasizing that the five countries of North Africa—while sharing a regional identity and other common attributes—possess unique characteristics that differentiate each one of them from its neighbors. Egypt also has the distinction of being part of the Middle East as well as North Africa with all the geopolitical complexities and other complications that are involved. Further, all five countries were impacted to a greater or lesser degree by the Arab Spring.[18] Regime changes occurred in Egypt, Libya, and Tunisia, while Morocco and Algeria, although not impervious to the profound changes taking place, did not suffer from the same levels of economic and political dislocation. While the differences will be discussed in the country sections, this introduction focuses primarily on the Mediterranean and African environments within which North Africa functions. It then considers the flows through the five countries and identifies ways in which these countries converge and diverge.

The Mediterranean Context

The Mediterranean has traditionally been a connector—a maritime superhighway for trade, cultural exchanges, movements of people, and transfers of knowledge and ideas—between North Africa and Europe. The North African coastline—which starts from the Atlantic Ocean and goes to the Eastern Mediterranean and the Red Sea—extends 9,311 kilometers and hosts a significant number of ports, large and small. As one description noted: "The Mediterranean Sea region . . . is surrounded by 22 countries, which together share a coastline of 46,000 km. It is also home to around 480 million people living across three continents: Africa, Asia, and Europe. It is still one of the world's busiest shipping routes with about one-third of the world's total merchant shipping crossing the sea each year."[19]

Dynamar, a commercial company based in the Netherlands and focused on maritime trade, produced a series of enormously valuable reports about trends and developments in "the intra-Mediterranean container trade as it daily unfolds between the two outlets of Gibraltar Straits and the Suez Canal."[20] Its 2014 report noted that "about 170 intra-Mediterranean shipping services carrying containers call at total 100 ports large and small spread all over mare nostrum. Combined, these services offer nearly . . . 170 sailings per week, an average of 90 departures every day from each port."[21] In terms of the percentages of containers being transshipped through the port—as opposed to the port being the point of origin or final destination—Gioia Tauro in Italy and Tanger Med port, a Moroccan industrial port complex, had the highest shares.[22] Indeed, Tanger Med port has emerged as the premier container port in the Mediterranean. In 2020, its throughput of 5.77 million twenty-foot equivalent units (TEU)—up from 2.6 million TEU in 2013—surpassed that of Piraeus in Greece and Valencia in Spain.[23] In 2021, Tanger Med handled over 7.17 million TEU, with Valencia around 5.6 million and Piraeus around 5.3 million TEU.[24] When the important Egyptian ports, especially Port Said and Alexandria, are also considered, it is clear there continues to be enormous dynamism in shipping and commerce throughout the Mediterranean, with North African countries playing an important role in this activity. Although Covid-19 had a significant impact on intra-Mediterranean trade in the first half of 2020, the trade rebounded somewhat in the second half of the year and has continued to flourish since then.

In a speech in 2019, Angelino Alfano, then Italian minister for foreign affairs and international cooperation, emphasized that the Mediterranean was "a sea of many opportunities, with a huge proportion of the world's economic activity and maritime traffic."[25] He also noted, however, that "the region could retain its historic significance as a meeting place of nations, trading freely and cross-fertilizing cultures, or it could descend to a place where insecurity overshadowed all such activity."[26] The reason for this ambivalence had been identified more than a decade earlier in a special issue of *Mediterranean Politics*. The editor, Bradford Dillman, noted that "the countries bordering the Mediterranean are connected through a dense set of trade, capital, cultural, and people flows. Globalization, liberalization, and the end of the Cold War have accelerated integration and relationships of mutual gain. However, these same processes have produced what can be called 'shadow globalization'" with the "illegal flows of goods, services, capital, and people."[27] Significantly, he also noted that "shadow economies are not peripheral, residual phenomena" but are "inherent components of global capitalism and globalization."[28]

These shadows are also particularly salient in ports and port cities. Historically, organized crime has typically developed and flourished in many port cities: Shanghai, Hong Kong, Marseilles, New York, and Naples are among the most obvious cases. "Round up the usual suspects" might be most memorable as a line from the movie *Casablanca*, but it also captures part of the reality of many ports and littoral cities throughout the world—including those in North Africa. The ways in which organized crime operates in ports has been succinctly captured by Anna Sergi. Noting the pervasiveness of "criminality on the waterfront," Sergi argued that "organized crime manifests across three trajectories in seaports: trafficking through the port, infiltration in the port economy, and governance of the port management."[29] She observed that corruption of dock workers as well as "government agents and port employees, including border agents and terminals' employees are also persistent factors."[30] This fully accords with the notion of facilitation discussed above as part of the smugglers' toolkit. In this connection, it also bears emphasis that North Africa has a wide variety of ports—small and large—mostly on the Mediterranean, but with some on Morocco's Atlantic coast, and some Egyptian ports on the Red Sea. According to the World Port Source, Morocco has fifteen ports, Algeria has eighteen, Libya has fifteen, Tunisia has eight, and Egypt has twenty-eight ports with one large port, three medium, and the rest—including those on the Red Sea—being small and very small.[31]

Ports have always been highly cosmopolitan. They are also border regions. When we think of borders, we typically think of land demarcations where countries abut one another. Yet ports can also be understood as part of a country's border. They are points of entry and exit to a country and are key nodes in the network of licit global commerce. As Sergi has noted, "ports are unique environments; they are universes of processes and meanings. Ports are border zones, liminal areas across different juridical systems. Even morphologically, they are in flux, being places of arrival and places of transit and departures, in between economic processes and political decisions."[32] They are also enormously complex and very busy, serving as the engines of global trade, making it extremely difficult to find anomalies or detect overt indicators of illicit activity. Efforts to combat illicit activity will invariably stymie the trade flow of licit goods, presenting a difficult cost-benefit equation to state authorities seeking to thread this needle.

Ports are, first and foremost, about commerce. Consequently, the emphasis is on movement. Container ports, especially, are enormously important in facilitating the easy movement of goods from sea to land

and vice versa. Inspection of the contents of ships or containers slows down this movement. When the tradeoff is between rapid throughput of high volumes of goods and thorough scrutiny and inspection, therefore, inspection typically comes second. As Interpol noted, "with high competition, African ports are under a lot of pressure to maintain throughput metrics and reduce turnaround times, which in turn compromises law enforcement oversight processes."[33] In sum, speed and efficiency often trump security. Moreover, even when and where inspection occurs, it is often difficult to differentiate between licit and illicit commodities. As Interpol once again noted, "the sheer volume of the shipping industry presents organized crime with an ideal opportunity to hide illegal activities in plain sight."[34]

These are inherent challenges for regulatory and law enforcement agencies responsible for detecting and interdicting smuggling and trafficking. The challenge becomes even more formidable when the smugglers' toolkit outlined above and criminal sophistication and adaptation are added to the equation. Bills of lading, for example, which are central to the shipping process, can be "altered to hide the true origin/route/destination of the shipping container, and filled with inadequate or incomplete information concerning the consignor, consignee, ownership and business activities of the shipment."[35] Another evasion technique noted by Interpol is "trafficking illicit goods via Free Trade Zones in the Middle East before arriving in, or after departure from, African ports and airports. They are believed to take advantage of the flexible regulation environment . . . to better conceal the origin and/or destination of the illicit goods."[36] Indeed, Free Trade Zones are used to move a wide variety of counterfeit goods. Their opacity also allows transfers of goods between containers as well as the introduction of illicit goods into licit shipments. In effect, they do for illicit trade what offshore financial centers have done for money laundering since the 1990s. Another challenge identified by Interpol is that cargo and container scanners are sometimes deliberately disabled. This can create freight traffic backlogs, because of which trucks are then simply waved through without inspection to make up for lost time.[37]

Not all illicit activity is confined to ports of course. Long stretches of deserted or rugged coastline provide opportunities to circumvent the formal checks and inspections that are an integral—if often cursory—part of port operations. In one way or another, therefore, the North African coast is inherently vulnerable to smuggling and trafficking. Yet, this is not the only criminogenic factor in the Mediterranean. Southern Europe has several criminal hubs that contribute significantly to illicit activities in North Africa. The idea of criminal hubs in Europe, initially discussed in Europol's 2007 Organized Crime Threat Assessment, emphasized two different facets of hubs: one was the concentration of groups and activities; the other was a center for logistics and distribution.[38] Europol's 2011 Organized Crime Threat Assessment, however, focused more heavily on the latter and defined criminal hubs as "concentrations of criminal logistics which receive illicit flows from numerous sources, and whose influence extends throughout the EU. Such concentrations facilitate not only the trafficking of illicit commodities but also the forging of new criminal markets, providing new opportunities for criminal groups."[39] Europol also suggested that the key attributes of these hubs included close "proximity to major destination markets, commercial and transport infrastructure, prevalence of criminal groups and opportunities for criminal migration."[40]

The logistic focus is very important and was highlighted by Patrick Radden Keefe, who astutely noted the parallels between transportation and delivery patterns in licit and illicit commodities. As he stated, "in the same way Continental Airlines, Amazon.com, and United Parcel Service (UPS) construct their delivery routes around a handful of critical hubs, black marketeers come to rely on some locations more than others."[41] In some instances, this may be a matter of targeted corruption to ensure that illicit goods avoid interdiction. "But in other cases, criminal actors will come to base a large part of their business in these hubs, staging their shipments there, sourcing otherwise hard-to-come-by documentation, or laundering their money." [42] This suggests that hubs can be much more than logistical or distribution centers, especially if there is a concentration of diverse criminal organizations and activities in a particular location. It is useful, therefore, to delineate three distinct kinds of hubs: (1) a concentration-of-crime hub, (2) a logistical hub, and (3) a super-hub that has multiple, influential criminal organizations and activities while also operating as a logistics center.

Efforts to delineate spaces in terms of any one of these hubs, however, run into a level-of-analysis problem and the issue of whether the focus should be a city, a region within a state, a state itself, a region encompassing several states, or even areas where several borders come together. In fact, hubs can exist at multiple levels since they are highly scalable. One way to think about hubs is to think about fractals, described as "infinitely complex patterns that are self-similar across different scales."[43] In other words, we can look for hubs at the global level, the national level, the city level, and so on. Here, the focus is on criminal hubs in the broad Mediterranean region. Still, when we move to the study of illegal activities and criminal flows in the five North African countries under consideration, we will also be able to identify hubs at the subnational level, whether logistical hubs or hubs that provide a concentration of criminal organizations and activities. In some cases, we might even find what can be understood as mini super-hubs, with a very localized concentration of logistics, criminals, and activities. The notion of preferential attachments might also be relevant as criminal services spring up to provide documents that facilitate irregular migration or other forms of illicit activities.

Three countries bordering the Mediterranean can legitimately be described as criminal hubs or even super-hubs: Spain, Italy, and Turkey. In addition, some of the countries in the Balkans have easy access to the Mediterranean and are also home to powerful criminal organizations, which further emphasizes the salience of criminal markets in the region. Perhaps equally significant and often overlooked, Malta has emerged as an important mini hub facilitating organized crime, people smuggling, financial crimes, and sanctions evasion.

Spain is host to diverse sets of criminals from Russia, Ireland, Mexico, and Colombia as well as gangs from Central America, Italian mafia organizations, Balkan criminals, and criminals from Britain and the Netherlands. Spain is attractive to transnational organized crime because of its location as an entry point to Western Europe, its proximity to North Africa, its 4,200-kilometer coastline, the importance of the tourist and construction sectors of the economy, and its large immigrant and tourist populations, as well as nightlife hot spots like Ibiza, which draws hordes of young revelers and pleasure seekers from across the world to its infamous bacchanals.[44] Moreover, Spain's location close "to the logistical bases of powerful criminal organizations, such as the Marseilles clans or the Sicilian Cosa Nostra" as well as its role as a transshipment country for Moroccan hashish being smuggled to Europe and its status as a natural southern entry point to the open market of the European Union add to its attractiveness—and vulnerability—to transnational criminal organizations.[45] As if this were not enough, the coast of Galicia is remote and offers multiple opportunities for smuggling. Market dynamics reinforce the attractiveness of Spain to criminals: "Spain remains one of Europe's biggest cocaine consumers and among the top three consumers of cannabis."[46] Colombians and other Latin American drug traffickers can operate in Spain relatively easily because of cultural and linguistic affinity, while North African criminals benefit from proximity and ease of access. In addition, the infrastructure is adequate, air travel is buttressed by tourism, and there are multiple ports through which smuggling can occur.

The attractions of Spain far outweigh the few offsetting risks or inhibitors that might act as a deterrent. Spain has been easy for transnational criminal organizations to penetrate because of "weaknesses or inefficiencies in some state institutions and systems . . . political (and other types of) corruption, particularly surrounding urban planning; a lack of public and political attention given to the problem of organized crime and a lack of political will to fight it; deficiencies in the legal and judicial spheres; and complexities surrounding the Spanish law enforcement and policing structures."[47] As a criminal hub, Spain has added significance because of the country's proximity to Morocco. In addition, Spain has two enclaves in Morocco—Ceuta and Melilla, both autonomous cities—that are still deemed to be Spanish territory and are sometimes described as Europe's only direct land border with Africa. These cities are a bone of contention between Spain and Morocco but have also become destinations for migrants seeking access to Europe. In addition, Spain maintains jurisdiction over the Canary Islands, an archipelago that at its closest is only about 70 miles away from the North African coast. Not surprisingly, the Canaries have increasingly been seen as another migrant route to Europe.

Italy is another major criminal hub, with a concentration of three large homegrown mafias—the 'Ndrangheta, the Camorra, and the Sicilian Mafia (Cosa Nostra)—and a less significant mafia, Sacra Corona Unita.[48] In addition, Italy has become host to Albanian criminal networks and to Nigerian criminal gangs such as the Vikings and the Black Axe.[49] The latter organization is highly active in Palermo but has engaged in criminal activities in at least fourteen Italian provinces.[50] The town of Castel Volturno, about 25 miles north of Naples, is the epicenter of Nigerian organized crime in Italy, although it seems that Nigerian organizations operating there still pay tribute to the Camorra. This is hardly surprising given the deeply entrenched power of the Camorra clans in the coastal city of Naples and the surrounding region of Campagna. Even so, Roberto Saviano's characterization of Castel Volturno as an "African city in Europe . . . culturally African"[51] appears to be compelling.

The 'Ndrangheta, which is based in Calabria but is active in other major cities such as Milan and Genoa, is even more powerful than the Camorra. Indeed, the 'Ndrangheta, which also has a presence in Australia, Canada, the United States, and Latin America, is now widely accepted as Italy's most powerful mafia.[52] One reason for this is 'Ndrangheta's involvement in cocaine trafficking to and across Europe.[53] This is closely linked to the development of the port of Gioia Tauro, which began operating in 1995. Indeed, the use of the port for the importation of drugs into Italy reflected the 'Ndrangheta's two dimensions as "a power syndicate"—with control over the territory (including the port)—and as an "enterprise syndicate" engaged in various forms of trafficking.[54] The 'Ndrangheta also seems to have a significant presence in the port of Genoa. As Sergi noted, the prevalence of various forms of smuggling and trafficking through the port reflects the proximity to both France and Switzerland as well as Northern European markets.[55] Moreover, "drug trafficking is particularly effective in Liguria thanks to the ports—not only Genoa but also the smaller ones of Imperia and Ligure, where both mafia organizations and other criminal groups have different connections and prolific businesses.[56] Besides drugs coming in, waste disposal shipments go out to North and West Africa.[57] The port of Genoa hosts a variety of criminals, ranging from loose networks and ethnic groups to mafia organizations."[58] The 'Ndrangheta, however, stands out as particularly important and powerful.

The Sicilian Mafia, which was once Italy's premier mafia organization, has declined in importance partly because it seriously overplayed its hand in the early 1990s with the killing of judges Giovanni Falcone and Paolo Borsellino and partly as the result of a leadership vacuum. Letizia Paoli observed in 2008 that "Cosa Nostra has seen all of its high-ranking members of the 1980s and 1990s arrested, has been excluded from most international trafficking and has lost political power nationally."[59] At the same time, the Sicilian Mafia has exploited new opportunities, especially in relation to irregular migrants and the need for reception centers and accommodation facilities.[60] Misappropriation of funds and exploitation of migrants has provided an alternative but lucrative source of income when more traditional criminal opportunities were no longer as readily available to the Sicilian Mafia. Whatever the trajectories of the specific mafia organizations in Italy, organized crime remains deeply entrenched in the society, politics, and economy of the country, thus elevating its status as a major criminal hub.

Turkey—although closer to the Middle East than North Africa—can also be understood as a criminal hub. Part of this is simply Turkey's geographic location. Connecting both Asia and the Middle East to Europe, Turkey has long coastlines in both the Mediterranean and the Black Sea, is close to the Balkans and the Caucasus, and has borders with Iran, Iraq, and Syria. All these factors make Turkey a major transshipment hub for both licit and illicit goods. Although Turkey banned opium poppy cultivation in 1972, as opium and heroin production increased in Afghanistan during the 1990s, the country developed into an important transshipment country for heroin—much of which is smuggled across the border from Iran.[61] Once heroin is in Turkey, some of it is trafficked by couriers on commercial air flights to airports in the Netherlands, the UK, and Germany, while much of it goes out via land routes through the Balkans.[62] Drug trafficking is not confined to criminal organizations, and the Kurdistan Workers' Party (PKK), which is designated as a Foreign Terrorist Organization (FTO) by the US Department of State, has also been deeply involved.[63] Yet drugs represent only one of many illicit commodities that are moved into Turkey and then widely distributed to a variety of other countries.[64]

In this connection, "Turkey's proximity to conflict zones has also fed illicit trade into and through the country. Conflict zones transform markets as they create a new opportunity structure for participation."[65] As a result of the insurgency in Iraq that followed the US intervention in 2003 and the subsequent rise of the Islamic State in Iraq and Syria (ISIS), Turkey also developed into a major hub for the oil smuggling and antiquities trafficking. Oil smuggling opportunities, initially identified by Saddam Hussein as part of sanctions evasion, were subsequently exploited by al-Qaeda in Iraq (AQI) and ISIS, often working closely with families in the borderlands who had been engaged in cross-border smuggling to Turkey for decades, if not centuries. Even today, Turkey remains a crucial hub for ISIS money launderers, logisticians, and facilitators.[66] Other illicit markets in Turkey include counterfeit cigarettes, looted antiquities, contraband liquor, and stolen cars. Turkey has also become a transshipment country for nuclear materials trafficking—although the destination country is usually unknown.[67] It has also become a destination for human trafficking and a target country for human smuggling.

In sum, Turkey has a wide range of organized crime activities. The proceeds from these activities created a housing boom and have been invested in hotel construction and the tourism sector.[68] The prevalence of illicit markets also reflects the concentration of organized crime in Turkey—a concentration that is a mix of domestic organizations and groups from elsewhere. Russian criminals have a well-established presence, while Georgian and Albanian criminals have traditionally had close links to Turkish groups. The same can be said about Bulgarian and Romanian criminals. Indeed, Turkey has become a favorite destination for foreign criminals, with Georgians and Russians involved in armed robbery; Pakistanis in kidnapping; Russians, Moldovans, and Ukrainians in controlling prostitution; Iranians in scams; and various African nationalities involved in passing counterfeit money.[69] The situation has been worsened by the war in Ukraine and sanctions on Russia. Not surprisingly, Turkey has become a super-hub of organized crime and has a large and sophisticated illicit economy.

The other Mediterranean country that requires attention is Malta. With a population of just over half a million, the nation of Malta is an archipelago located south of Sicily, east of Tunisia, and north of Libya. While it is not in the same league as Italy, Spain, and Turkey in terms of being a criminal hub, it is strategically located in a key part of the Mediterranean and one that has witnessed a surge of irregular migration. Small as it is, Malta has managed to carve out a litany of corrupt and criminal activities, with government figures playing a large role. In fact, the Organized Crime and Corruption Reporting Project (OCCRP) named Maltese prime minister Joseph Muscat as its 2019 Person of the Year in Organized Crime and Corruption. As the OCCRP wrote, "Under Muscat's leadership, criminality and corruption have flourished—and in many cases gone unpunished—in the small Mediterranean archipelago of Malta, creating an environment that led to the 2017 murder of investigative journalist Daphne Caruana Galizia."[70] Malta has displayed enormously high levels of corruption, buttressed by a climate of impunity, which attracts more criminals seeking illicit profits.[71] The island's Pilatus Bank was involved in sanctions evasion for money paid by Venezuela to Iran for a massive housing construction project. Malta has also facilitated the sale of golden passports and the creation of shell companies. "Vessels change names and ownership with ease, swapping national flags from Togo to Tanzania to Belize."[72] An Italian law enforcement official has described Malta, unsurprisingly, as "a crossroad of illegal trafficking."[73] Reportedly, a "network of smugglers" has built "a stronghold on the docks."[74] These smugglers "have been linked to trafficking in illegal drugs and migrants; smuggling cigarettes; illegal fishing; and spiriting fuel stolen from Libya's poorly protected stockpiles to avid customers."[75] They are highly innovative, "scouting new routes and implementing new techniques, from masquerading as fishermen to interspersing legitimate cargo with illegal wares. The trade crosses many borders around the Mediterranean, from the ports of Spain all the way east to the island of Cyprus."[76]

In sum, North Africa belongs to a Mediterranean neighborhood that is highly criminogenic. Yet another crucial factor feeds into this: the demographic divergence between Europe, with an aging and declining population, and Africa, which continues to have high birth rates, even though these have leveled off somewhat in recent years. The upshot is labor shortages in Europe and a surfeit of workers in Africa. The initial

European response to this involved guest worker programs, but these have given way to a much more hostile approach to immigration. As one scholar noted, the Mediterranean has been turned "into a defensive moat to stop the flow of unwanted migrants. Contrary to the popular vision of the Mediterranean Sea as a homogeneous and lawless expanse lying outside the reach of state power, this maritime territory is, in fact, crisscrossed by variegated and at times conflicting jurisdictional regimes. . . . In this techno-political moat, the communication networks of 'Fortress Europe' have established a buffer zone surrounding EU territorial waters."[77] Moreover, even though some of the antimigrant rhetoric abated slightly after the 2014–2015 surge in irregular migration, Western governments continue to be restrictive, "especially with regard to those illegalized by state policies: the unauthorized entrant, the asylum seeker, and the victim of trafficking."[78] Although Covid-19 provided a short-term lull in illegal or irregular migration, the issue came back to the fore in 2022 and 2023. The result is that North Africa remains caught between the restrictive policies of Fortress Europe and the inexorable drivers of poverty—violence, conflict, and repression—that continue to push many Africans toward the Mediterranean coast and to Europe. These drivers can only be explored by looking at the conditions and challenges facing North Africa's southern neighbors.

The African Context

Although all five North African countries experienced considerable—albeit varying—levels of turbulence during the Arab Spring, they now (with the glaring exception of Libya) seem to enjoy a higher level of stability and security than many, if not most, of their southern counterparts. Whether focused on the Sahel, the Horn of Africa, or West Africa, kleptocratic leaders, corrupt bureaucracies, jihadist extremists, and violent conflict are endemic. Moreover, throughout much of sub-Saharan Africa, the state—which is typically weak or repressive—remains the prize of politics, with those in power distributing favors to family, cronies, and expansive patronage networks. Many are excluded from economic opportunity. With continued, if gradually slowing population growth and global climate change, conditions are certain to deteriorate further.

State weakness has also had significant consequences in sub-Saharan Africa, perhaps nowhere more poignantly than in the Sahel region. And what happens in the Sahel rarely stays in the Sahel; instead, it spills over into North African states. Over the past decade, the Sahel, a vast semiarid region of western and north-central Africa, has fallen to a range of transnational terrorist groups, including the Islamic State in the Greater Sahara, Boko Haram, and Jama'at Nusrat al-Islam wal-Muslimin. Operation Barkhane, France's eight-year military campaign geared toward stabilizing the region, ended in failure in the fall of 2022, leaving a security vacuum that was quickly filled by jihadists and Wagner mercenaries.[79] Some of the violent nonstate actors in the region have benefited from Libyan weapons trafficked across multiple borders. And while the Wagner Group was brought in to help "coup-proof" various junta regimes while protecting warlords, the byproduct has been more chaos. Wagner's arrival has energized jihadist groups, while the mercenaries' draconian approach has pushed civilians into the arms of terrorist and insurgent groups.

Wagner has deployed mercenaries to Mali and Libya, as well as to the Central African Republic and Sudan. Since first sending troops to Africa in 2017, the group has embedded itself in these fragile states and siphoned valuable resources—a quid pro quo that offers military muscle in exchange for mining contracts that allow Wagner subsidiaries to extract gold, diamonds, and other commodities that pad Russia's coffers.[80] Their operations have frequently resulted in the deaths of civilians, with credible accusations of sexual violence, torture, and extrajudicial killings. The arrangements boil down to simple supply and demand: African leaders need the security that Wagner can provide, and the Kremlin needs the funding stream to soften the blow from biting Western sanctions. But for Wagner, business in the Sahel is good and made better by what Declan Walsh has labeled Africa's "coup corridor." Beginning in the west with Guinea and extending across nearly the width of the continent, there have been coups in Burkina Faso, Mali, Niger, Chad, and Sudan.[81] This belt of failing states is directly south of the five countries analyzed in this book, and the Sahel's instability impacts each of them to one degree or another. Conversely, upheaval in North Africa can send shock waves through the Sahel, as occurred with the collapse of Muammar Gaddafi and the dispersion of Libyan weapons.

If state weakness and restrictions of economic opportunity are an important part of the context for contemporary organized crime and illicit economies, there are several additional drivers that are particularly relevant to North Africa. One of these is migration. Mobility and migration, of course, are nothing new. It is arguable, however, that more of the world is on the move than ever before, with over 108 million displaced people.[82] Partly this reflects a growing population and the unprecedented ease and speed of transportation that was dislocated, but only temporarily, by the Covid-19 pandemic. In the long term, many destination countries, particularly in the Global North, allow only strictly limited legal immigration. Yet this demand side response has done little to contain the supply side. Indeed, flows of irregular migrants (that is, those who have not been granted legal permission to reside in the host country), refugees, and internally displaced persons (IDPs) are still seeking entrance into Europe, the United States, Canada, and elsewhere. Much of the movement of particular concern in this study is from the Middle East and West, Central, and East Africa through North Africa into Southern Europe and, in many cases, upward to Northern Europe, including Scandinavia. There are some pull factors—with the lure of a better life being the most obvious—contributing to this phenomenon, but the push factors are often more compelling and play a large part in migration spikes. While poverty is important, pervasive violence in countries that are unstable or deeply oppressive seems to be a huge driver, whether the violence is from civil wars, from insurgencies, or perpetrated by ruthless criminal enterprises.

Although some migrants have unrealistic expectations about both the journey and the destination country, the decisions of many others can be understood in terms of prospect theory. Developed by Daniel Kahneman and Amos Tversky, this theory notes that "people underweight outcomes that are merely probable in comparison with outcomes that are obtained with certainty. This tendency, called the certainty effect, contributes to risk aversion in choices involving sure gains and to risk seeking in choices involving sure losses."[83] In other words, the greater the risk involved in staying at home amidst violent conflict, the more likely it is that people will be prepared to risk the perils involved in irregular migration. In some cases, of course, the issue is not violence but simply despair at the lack of opportunities—something that makes the status quo untenable.

It is tempting, partly because of the importance of violence and instability as drivers, to ignore the multifaceted nature of migration and, indeed, the caustic debate that often surrounds it. One author, for example, has noted that migration, is best understood as "a permanent structural phenomenon that—precisely because of the kind of characteristics driving it—can only ebb and flow, and never ceases completely."[84] From this perspective, demographic factors cannot be ignored. Much of Africa is undergoing a "demographic transition" with "declines in mortality and birth rates accompanied by a middle transition phase characterized by intense population growth and likely higher out-migration rates."[85] The birth rate decline remains slow with an average of 4.7 children per woman.[86] As a result, Africa is on course to become "a population giant: a quarter of the world's people will live there by 2050 (it was less than 10% in 1950). Africa's population was half that of Europe during the 1960s; today it is close to 1.3 billion while the European population is less than 750 million. In the next two decades, the African population will reach over 2.5 billion, more than three times that of Europe."[87] Moreover, Nigeria is on course to become the third most populous country in the world by 2050, surpassing the United States.[88]

This helps to illuminate two things. First, it is not surprising that so many Africans move to Europe. "After all, the continent with the largest population growth in the world—the African population will double in the next thirty years—sits next door to the continent where population growth is in decline. Demographic imbalances tend toward a natural 'readjustment' of the population through the influx of new people from the most populous to the least populous countries."[89] Second, large migration flows will continue for the foreseeable future.[90] There are good reasons to expect that these flows will intensify rather than abate. One reason for this is that as sub-Saharan countries develop further, then migration is likely to increase as more people will have the resources to allow increased mobility. Indeed, "the largest flows do not start from the poorest countries, but from those with a development process" already underway.[91] A "certain degree of economic and social development" is necessary "to trigger aspirations for improvement, availability of resources and knowledge necessary to implement the decision to emigrate."[92] Yet, even in expanding economies, employment opportunities fail to keep pace with the growing labor market. Against this background, one analysis even suggested that in West Africa the choice many young people face is between emigration and radicalization.[93] The former offers better prospects, while the latter helps to create a sense of belonging and status and, in some instances, provides financial support.

Another important push factor is climate change, which is having a significant impact on the Sahel and is resulting in "galloping desertification, increasingly scarce rainfall, recurrent cycles of drought, famine and food crisis, and the difficulties in accessing water and cultivable land. These challenges combine to produce a lethal cocktail for the survival of local populations, driven by unsustainable practices like deforestation (wood for household use) and land- and water-grabbings."[94] The impact of climate change will undoubtedly become even more important in the years ahead, creating significant hardship and disruption and exacerbating both internal conflict and migration, resulting in the mass movement of "climate refugees." Climate-related violence in the Sahel, for example, is sometimes mischaracterized as jihadist violence, when the initial trigger has nothing to do with extremism and everything to do with a competition for scarce resources, including grazing land and access to potable water.

It is also worth emphasizing that African and Middle Eastern migration to Europe did not start with the Arab Spring and the Syrian civil war. These two developments simply intensified trends that were already underway. A study by the UN Office on Drugs and Crime (UNODC) in 2006 noted that because it was "difficult for young Africans to work in Europe legally, every year tens of thousands attempt to cross the borders illegally."[95] It also observed, somewhat presciently, that a study by the Real Instituto Elcano had warned that this was "only the beginning of an immigration phenomenon that could evolve into one of the largest in history."[96] The study also suggested that "at least 200,000 Africans enter Europe illegally annually, while another 100,000 try and are intercepted."[97] Many are sent back. Some never make it in the arduous land journey north, while others perish crossing the Mediterranean. Significantly, Spain's North African enclaves of Ceuta and Melilla were popular routes, although stronger enforcement efforts have led to "alternative routings, including attempts via the Canary Islands from West Africa, and attempts to reach Italy from Libya and Tunisia."[98] The study also noted that most of the migrants of the 1990s were from North Africa but these began to decline, while from 2002 onward, increased numbers came from sub-Saharan Africa, especially Eritrea, Ethiopia, Somalia, and Sudan.[99] It was subsequently reported that the number of illegal immigrants entering Spain via the Canary Islands increased from 4,715 to 31,678 in 2006.[100] The 2006 UNODC study also focused on the role of organized crime, noting that more sophisticated organizations offered "full packet solutions" from point of departure to destination, while more localized and opportunist groups adopted a modular approach, taking migrants part of the way and then handing them off to other smugglers or simply abandoning them at various points along the journey.[101]

In 2010, UNODC offered another study, reviewing some of the specialized literature. One of the most important observations focused on the fact that North African countries were no longer "only points of departure for irregular migration directed towards Europe (outgoing flows), but . . . also areas of destination and transit for international migration coming from the South, in particular sub-Saharan Africa."[102] The concern over transit to Europe was reflected in pressure from the European Union and southern European countries on North African governments to take a tougher approach to the migrants from sub-Saharan Africa.[103] Some of this was successful. At that time, sea routes from

Tunisia, which had been active during the 1990s, were no longer used, partly because of agreements with Italy, and also because of the passage and enforcement of new laws. Similarly, maritime movement of migrants across the Mediterranean decreased during this period. For its part, Algeria arrested 65,000 foreigners and 70,000 Algerian nationals for activities related to irregular migration from 2000 to 2007, and in 2007 alone there were "35,000 police incidents" related to migration.[104] Meanwhile, a reported 145,000 irregular migrants were expelled from Libya between 2003 and 2005.[105] Morocco arrested 36,000 migrants in 2003 but only 30,000 in 2005 and under 15,000 in 2007.[106]

All of this suggests that the European Union was already de facto extending its borders into North Africa, in effect, demanding that the countries of North Africa play a key interdiction role to stop the flow of migrants across the Mediterranean. As the UNODC report noted, however, national, and international migration controls provoke "a constant redefinition of the geography of routes. More precisely, the geography of irregular migration is the result of the countermeasures of authorities, on the one hand, and the efforts of smugglers and migrants to contravene them on the other."[107] The impact was not to stop the smuggling but to create a new Darwinian dynamism in the smuggling process demanding adaptation, innovation, and greater sophistication by the smugglers. This was reflected in a 2018 European Union report reiterating that a "large majority" of irregular migrants from Africa to Europe in previous years were from Sub-Saharan Africa.[108]

Two other related points about migrants and refugees need to be emphasized: first, there are far more of them in developing countries than in countries of the Global North; second, for a surprising number of migrants, what were initially viewed merely as transit countries become their final destinations. In this connection, it is worth noting that "only a small fraction of international migration in Africa results in journeys to Europe. This particularly applies to sub-Saharan Africa, where most movement is intra-regional."[109] Moreover, when it goes beyond this, many irregular migrants only make it as far as North Africa. Often described as transit migrants, many of these simply become permanently stranded there, while others desperately seek work to finance the next stage of the journey. Against this background, North Africa can be understood for some migrants as the space between their homes and Europe but for others as their new homes.

Having established the context within which North Africa can best be understood, it is necessary to look at the region itself before moving on to the individual countries. This is done initially in terms of North

Africa as a space of flows, as a microcosm of illicit or shadow globalization. Second, it is important to highlight the commonalities among the five countries in the region as well as their distinctive features. In effect, our analysis focuses on what might be termed pentagonal symmetries and asymmetries.

The North African Space of Flows

One way of thinking about North Africa is as "a space of flows." Developed by Manuel Castells, the idea of a space of flows has been increasingly used in relation to globalization.[110] David Held, for example, one of the most perceptive analysts of globalization, has emphasized the flows—of people, money, commodities, information, messages, digital signals, and services—around the world as one of its central features.[111] In today's modern world, the "space of flows" is now a global space.[112] This is as true of trade and finance as it is of the internet, which facilitates the almost instantaneous flow of information and messages. In one sense, of course, there is nothing new about flows. During the medieval crusades, there were considerable flows to and from Europe to the holy land, while the slave trade of the eighteenth and nineteenth centuries rested upon the flow of people—albeit involuntarily—from Africa to Europe and the United States. In the nineteenth century, as one author observed, "Tripoli was the swinging door that connected the Mediterranean countries with the interior of Africa. Merchandise from Europe entered through the city's busy port. Goods from Africa's interior—ivory, gold, indigo, cotton cloth, animal skins, ostrich feathers, leather goods, kola nuts—left the city for Europe and the Ottoman countries. But the main export moving through Tripoli was slaves."[113]

The difference in contemporary flows is their scale and diversity as well as the speed and relative fluidity with which they occur. As several analysts have noted, there has been "an intensification of flows and networks of interaction and interconnectedness that transcend nation-states."[114] Increased density has been accompanied by increased speed and decreased costs. Global flows ranging from commodities to communications have long been feasible—but the time and the associated transportation and transaction costs have been considerably compressed. This is certainly true in North Africa, which remains the lynchpin between the African Continent and Europe. This is not to suggest that the region is simply a transshipment funnel for flows moving through. Some flows originate in North Africa while other flows terminate there.

In considering flows, it is important to emphasize points of origin, direction, putative and actual destinations, and whether these flows are constant or intermittent. Flows themselves can surge and recede. Moreover, flows are typically multidirectional. It is tempting, for example to see all the flows through North Africa as coming from the south and moving inexorably and directly toward Europe. This is certainly true of many of these flows, but even these are characterized by horizontal movements and displacements, as constraints and opportunities vary and those controlling the flows adapt. In addition, some flows—including illicit flows—move north to south. It is also important to consider horizontal flows from east to west and west to east throughout North Arica. In this connection, Gallien has argued that "if we observe the central nodes of smuggling routes in the region, another geography of regional trade emerges. At its heart are places like Nador, Tamanrasset, Zuwara, or Ben Gardane—medium-sized cities in the geographic and economic periphery of their respective nation-states, and logistical centers of commercial networks that include strong East-West links across the region, alongside connections to Europe and the wider global economy."[115] Indeed, some flows also move diagonally, while routes can shift slowly and incrementally or radically and quickly. Flows can cross one border or multiple borders. They can be interrupted, diverted, or in some cases halted altogether. What is intended as transit zones or way stations sometimes become interim or even permanent destinations. Yet flows are like water—they usually find a way. Sometimes, flows are even reversed. As noted above, in the early stages of the Libyan revolution, many weapons left Libya, creating contagion effects in neighboring countries such as Niger and Chad and even as far away as Mali. Subsequently, weapons have been flooding into Libya as external powers seek to sponsor various proxy groups and directly influence the outcome of the ongoing civil war.

Many of these flows are driven by sound economic principles. Some of the illicit flows, however, are driven by what Nikos Passas termed criminogenic asymmetries.[116] Whether it is price differentials in different countries, differences in laws and regulations, or variations in state capacity, particularly in the areas of law enforcement and customs enforcement, such asymmetries provide attractive and often lucrative opportunities for criminal exploitation. Criminal organizations and networks typically take advantage of these variations, engaging in a form of jurisdictional arbitrage that minimizes risk and maximizes opportunities and profits. We trace the scale, as well as the movements and directions of these flows, more fully in the country sections.

One question that obviously arises concerns the role of borders in all this. Once again, however, there is no simple answer. Borders or boundaries can be understood, in the words of one book subtitle, as barriers, conduits, and opportunities.[117] They are barriers in the sense that the state at least formally tries to determine what comes in and out, which of these products are permissible and which are prohibited or regulated, and what, if any, monetary costs should be imposed for entry or exit. Borders have often become the focus of security forces, particularly in the era of global Islamist terrorism that so dramatically impacted the world on September 11, 2001. Nevertheless, borders vary significantly in terms of how strictly or permissively the flows are dealt with—and this often changes over time at the same border, depending on a variety of domestic and external factors. Borders are conduits for both licit and illicit trade, and it is significant that, for prohibited products in particular, a border crossing will often result in higher prices. For licit goods, in contrast, smuggling from one jurisdiction to another is attractive because prices of illegally imported commodities are often lower for consumers than the domestic equivalents. Opportunities for smuggling also often reflect the commonality of communities on each side of the national border, a commonality that is often tribal or familial in nature. In effect, borders divide, but tribal and kinship links transcend divisions, creating a sharp discrepancy between the fictions of border control and the realities of cross-border movements. Both borderland and diaspora communities are clear evidence of this. Even though the borders among the North African countries themselves vary significantly, the commonalities of the borderlands across the region are, in fact, very striking, as will become evident from the analyses of the individual countries. In the next section, we seek to identify more broadly similarities and differences among the five nations across the region.

North African Pentagonal Asymmetries

It used to be said that when one looked at the big three powers in Europe, there was always an odd one out: Britain and France were nuclear powers, Germany was not; Britain and Germany were members of North Atlantic Treaty Organization (NATO), France under General Charles de Gaulle had left the organization; Germany and France were both members of the European Economic Community (EEC) and then the European Union, Britain was much slower to join the EEC and then the first country to leave the European Union following Brexit. A British military officer described this phenomenon in terms of triangular asymmetries and suggested that it was an important reason that Western Europe had not developed a stronger and more coherent common defense and security strategy. It can be argued that similar kinds of asymmetries exist in the five countries of North Africa. On some dimensions, there is an odd one out; on others, the split is three and two. Whatever the constellation, however, there is rarely uniformity among all five countries. This means that it is difficult for the five countries to develop a coherent and coordinated response to common challenges, such as the spread of extremism and terrorist attacks or the expansion of various forms of trafficking and smuggling and the growing power of organized crime. Against this background, it is necessary to understand the diversity of the five countries in terms of physical factors such as size of the country, the extent of both maritime and land borders, the contiguous countries, and the degree of urbanization. These are summarized in Table 1.1.

In terms of land mass, Algeria is by far the biggest country, with Libya in second place, followed by Egypt and Morocco. Tunisia is the smallest country in the region with a land mass that is less than one-quarter of the size of Morocco and one-tenth the size of Libya. Regarding urbanization, Egypt with 43 percent is a major outlier with by far the lowest level, while both Algeria and Libya have over 75 percent of their populations in cities, and Tunisia has around 70 percent and Morocco just over 65 percent of its population living in urban areas.

Algeria and Libya each have six contiguous neighbors. Ironically, the longest common land border in North Africa is that between Algeria and Morocco. It is also the most contentious and has been formally closed since 1994. A poorly delineated border with rich mineral deposits in the disputed areas combined with Moroccan aspirations for a "Greater Morocco" provided the background for the fighting in September and October 1963. Almost 700 Cuban troops or "volunteers" were deployed to Algeria to help defend the country against what was seen as Moroccan aggression. This helped to level the playing field, and after considerable diplomatic pressure a truce was reached on October 30, 1963. A formal peace treaty was signed in February 1964, but in 1975 when Spain relinquished control over the Western Sahara, Algeria supported the Polisario Front for the Sahrawi people, which resisted Moroccan claims of sovereignty—thereby contributing to the continued tensions between the neighbors. These tensions were exacerbated more recently by allegations in each country that the other was facilitating drug trafficking. More important, a ceasefire between the Polisario Front and Morocco that had lasted for several decades broke down in November 2020 when Moroccan soldiers dispersed a Sahrawi protest,

Table 1.1. Physical Attributes

Country	Total Area (square kilometers)	Coastline Length (kilometers)	Land Border Length (kilometers)	Neighboring Countries and Length of Borders (kilometers)	Urban population 2023 (%)
Morocco	716,550	2,945	3,523.5	Algeria: 1,941 Mauritania: 1,564 Spain: 0 Ceuta: 8 Melilla: 10.5	65.1
Algeria	2,381,740	998	6,734	Libya: 989 Mali: 1,359 Mauritania: 460 Morocco: 1,941 Niger: 951 Tunisia: 1,034	75.3
Tunisia	163,610	1,148	1,495	Algeria: 1,034 Libya: 461	70.5
Libya	1,759,540	1,770	4,339	Algeria: 989 Chad: 1,050 Egypt: 1,115 Niger: 342 Sudan: 382 Tunisia: 461	81.6
Egypt	1,001,450	2,450	2,612	Gaza Strip: 13 Israel: 208 Libya: 1,115 Sudan: 1,276	43.1

Source: Central Intelligence Agency, *The World Factbook*, https://www.cia.gov/the-world-factbook/.

provoking the Polisario Front into renewed attacks and reigniting a conflict that has been described as "decolonization's last stand."[118]

If Algeria continues to provide support for the Polisario Front, the prospects for a formal reopening of the border between Morocco and Algeria will remain poor. On the other hand, the closure of the border—as will be discussed more fully—has not completely stopped illicit flows in either direction. Indeed, a salient feature of North Africa is its excessively permeable land and maritime borders. Consequently, horizontal illicit flows across the region continue to thrive despite efforts to strengthen border controls.

The other dimensions that need to be considered are governance and stability. During the 1990s, four of the countries seemed to exhibit a relatively high degree of stability, wheras the Algerian government fought a civil war with Islamist extremists that lasted from 1991 to 2002. More recently, national trajectories have become even more diverse. During the Arab Spring, three countries—Egypt, Libya, and Tunisia—underwent regime change, while Algeria and Morocco simply made some constitutional reforms and adjustments.

After the toppling of longtime strongman Hosni Mubarak, Egypt enjoyed short-lived democratically elected government, but the military then reestablished control. The international community looked the other way as Abdel Fattah al-Sisi usurped the leadership of Mohamed Morsi of the Muslim Brotherhood. Moreover, there has been little or no movement toward democracy. On the contrary, the Bertelsmann Transformation Index (BTI) published by Bertelsmann Stiftung has consistently noted that in Egypt, the trend toward authoritarianism and state control has been unwavering. Sisi was reconfirmed as president in "an unfair and unfree election" in March 2018.[119] Moreover, "policymaking remained dominated by anti-democratic veto actors, with the military and intelligence agencies playing a particularly prominent role."[120] The regime also strengthened control over the judiciary, neutralized anticorruption agencies, and continued to strengthen the power of the presidency.[121] The 2022 report described more of the same, while also noting that Covid-19 had been "particularly damaging for lower income segments and vulnerable groups such as day laborers in the informal sector."[122] In retrospect, the continuity from Mubarak to Sisi is remarkable. It is almost as if the Arab Spring never happened.

Following the overthrow and death of longtime Libyan dictator Muammar Gaddafi, the country disintegrated into chaos, with competing militias and warlords and what appears to be an enduring instability. In spite of the ceasefire agreement in October 2020, in 2023 Libya still suffered from pervasive violence and insecurity that continued to have ripple effects of one kind or another throughout North Africa and the Sahel.[123] The 2020 BTI report was unflinching, noting that "Libya has experienced an unprecedented process of state collapse and violent disintegration," with over 1.1 million people requiring humanitarian assistance and "the Libyan health care system . . . on the brink of collapse."[124] Libya had become anarchic with multiple militias and the targeting of civilians, including sexual violence against women. Migrants were at particularly high risk of being held in detention centers, where they were exploited for commercial sex and forced labor. Despite the 2020 road map and the formation of a Government of National Unity, the country continued to suffer from rival claims of authority. Indeed, in 2022 another new government was formed, this time called the Government of National Stability. In both cases, the names represented little more than overly optimistic aspirations in a country that had no semblance of unity and remained a long way from stability.

In contrast, Tunisia's Jasmine revolution was widely hailed as a success. Yet the poster child for the Arab Spring has not aged well. The Economist Group's Democracy Index 2020 called Tunisia a "flawed democracy" but acknowledged it was the only state resembling a democracy in North Africa.[125] This assessment increasingly appears to have been overly optimistic. The youth bulge, extensive unemployment, and the gap between the wealthy coastal areas and the marginalized hinterland and borderlands increasingly created profound disillusionment with the transition and a realization that the economic future remained dismal. Moreover, after a period in which Tunisia's politics were gridlocked, the president in effect launched an internal coup that was subsequently given spurious legitimacy by a referendum on the revised constitution. The judiciary has lost its independence, crackdowns on protesters have been fierce, and dissent or criticism of the regime has become dangerous. More than a decade after the toppling of the regime of Zine El Abidine Ben Ali, the revolution has been replaced by resurgent authoritarianism. In short, expectations of large-scale change and improvement have disappeared, and Tunisia has ceased to be the poster child for democracy.

For Algeria, there was a belated and rather modest "Arab spring" when, in 2019, widespread protests against an aged and infirm president seeking another term in office led to his removal by the military. This followed and upheld the constitution adopted in 2016 that imposed term limits on the president and strengthened the legislature. Yet there are continued tendencies toward stifling freedom of association and limiting the freedom of the press. In addition, "sluggish decision-making and a failure to push forward on governance reforms, as well as the continued crisis associated with falling oil prices weakened Algeria's previously strong financial standing" at a time when there are increased demands for government public service provision.[126] Connected to this, the 2020 BTI commented that "massive urbanization over the last 20 years has put pressure on Algeria's public services such as education, health, housing and transport. Resulting social unrest also contributes to rash political decisions, such as subsidizing prices, giving out grants to ensure social calm, or as is often suggested, to 'buy the peace.'"[127] It is not entirely clear why these subsidies are rash, since they have a stabilizing effect. Moreover, Algerian subsidies, particularly on oil, have typically provided opportunities for arbitrage that contributed to commodity smuggling across borders, but in ways that reduced the prospects for social and political instability. Although Covid-19 contributed to a further deterioration of the economy and public health, the subsequent rebound increased prices and demand for oil and gas. Not surprisingly, therefore, Algeria increased production from 175.9 million tons of oil equivalent (toe) in 2020 to 185.2 million toe in 2021. Over the same period, hydrocarbon export revenues rose from $20 billion to $34.5 billion, providing the Algerian government with increased "breathing room."[128]

In some respects, Morocco is the most traditional regime in North Africa, with a monarchical constitutional republic. However, Morocco's king, Mohammed VI, initiated "a reform program that included a new constitution, passed by popular referendum in July 2011, under which some new powers were extended to parliament and the prime minister, but ultimate authority remains in the hands of the monarch."[129] This seemed to have some impact in maintaining stability and minimizing demands for regime change. According to the BTI, however, "reforms undertaken in the wake of the Arab Spring in 2011 have done nothing to alter the distribution of power in Morocco."[130] Moreover, the last few years have witnessed some regression, with the arrests of journalists and human rights activists—yet nothing as severe as in Tunisia. Morocco is criticized for its tacitly permissive approach to hashish production in the northern Rif region, although serious efforts to suppress this would increase disaffection and instability.[131] One area of promise, however, is Rabat's environmental policies that aim to provide over 50 percent of Morocco's energy needs by 2030 through renewable sources such as solar power.

In sum, pentagonal asymmetries were evident in the Arab Spring, with three countries—Egypt, Libya, and Tunisia—experiencing regime change, while Morocco and Algeria avoided it. Two of these three countries have suffered from the reimposition of authoritarian rule, while the third remains dominated by turmoil and civil strife. There are also three countries—Algeria, Libya, and to a much lesser extent Egypt—where oil has been the dominant source of wealth. In terms of illicit markets, there are significant variations. In some countries in the region, there is clearly a dominant commodity: cannabis resin in Morocco, fuel in Algeria, antiquities in Egypt, and arms in Libya. Migrants were also important in Libya, but as migrant smuggling temporarily declined in Libya, drug trafficking increased. Morocco is the only major producer of drugs, but Libya has also become more important as a consumer country for illicit pharmaceuticals. Egypt is important because of its vast store of antiquities and the extent to which, in recent years, these have been widely looted.

The formal economy and demographics in the five countries are summarized in Table 1.2.

As this table reveals, there are some asymmetries along with a significant commonality: in all five countries in the region, the youth bulge will get larger for some years before it gets smaller. When this is combined with the unemployment figures for the 15 to 24 age group, it suggests that regardless of divergent political systems there is a structural demographic tsunami that could seriously challenge stability in the five North African countries. Coming on top of the Covid-19 pandemic and the economic, social, and public health damage so widely inflicted, the politically destabilizing consequences could make the turbulence of the Arab Spring appear insignificant. On the other hand, in the short term, the resurgent authoritarian governments in Egypt and Tunisia will likely prove difficult to dislodge, while both Algeria and Morocco have maintained a surprising level of stability.

Table 1.2 Economic and Demographic Data

Country	Population (2023 est.)	Real Gross Domestic Product (2021 est.)	Real Gross Domestic Product per Capita (2021 est.)	Percentage of Population 14 or under (2023)	Percentage of Population Aged 15 to 24 (2021)	Percentage of Unemployment Among 15–24 Age Group (2023)
Morocco	37,067,420	$303.36 billion	$8,100	26.01%	16.55	27.2
Algeria	44,758,398	$487.716 billion	$11,000	28.78% (2023)	13.93	31.9
Tunisia	11,976,182	$127.509 billion	$10,400	24.77% (2023)	12.9	38.3
Libya	7,252,573	$147.942 billion	$22,000	32.81% (2023)	15.21	50.5
Egypt	109,546,720	$1.264 trillion	$11,600	34.37%	18.01	24.3

Source: All data from Central Intelligence Agency, *The World Factbook*, for 2021 and 2023, as of October 10, 2023.

When it comes to political economies of the five countries, there is a similar mix of commonalities and variations. The commonalities include significant inequalities—often combined with regional variations—in each country. As suggested above, coastal areas are typically more prosperous than the hinterlands, while border economies offer significant arbitrage opportunities through smuggling. There are also large informal economic sectors in all five countries.

Definitions of the informal economy typically note that it is an economy that is neither taxed nor monitored by the government. It often acts as a safety valve and generally provides employment for a significant portion of the economy. In Morocco, for example, two-thirds of all jobs are in the informal economy, which deprives the government of $3.4 billion in tax revenues and limits expenditure on public goods. In the agricultural sector 97 percent of the jobs are informal. According to the Moroccan statistics agency, the informal economy is about 44 percent of the size of the gross domestic product (GDP).[132] World Economics estimates the informal economy as 36.6 percent of Morocco's GDP.[133] Indeed, informal economies are difficult to measure, with different analysts using different methodologies and often coming up with divergent assessments. An assessment by World Economics in 2023, for example, estimated the size of Algeria's informal economy as 17.4 percent of GDP, which represented approximately $103 billion. A few years earlier, assessments had been much higher at about 40 percent of GDP. Moreover, one detailed scholarly study in 2022 noted that several assessments had estimated the informal economy as well above 40 percent.[134] The study also set out to explain the high level by examining "institutional settings" that create "incentives that drive economic agents to conceal their activities."[135] This is an important theme throughout North African countries. It helps, for example, to explain a World Bank report on Morocco, noting that job creation was not keeping pace with population growth, identifying the shortage of good jobs in high-productivity industries, and highlighting the exclusion of women and youth from the labor market.[136] A similar situation exists in Tunisia, albeit with a pronounced divide between urban and rural areas. The informal economy in urban areas is only 26 percent of all jobs, whereas in the western and southern regions of the country it ranges from 44 to 68 percent.[137] The overall situation, however, is like that in Morocco, with youth and women, especially in rural areas, restricted in their job opportunities. And when they do get jobs in the informal sector, they face conditions of real hardship amidst an absence of labor standards. According to World Economics the overall size of Tunisia's informal economy is 30.4 percent of the GDP, although this seems to be low given that many observers believe that the informal economy has been expanding in recent years.

If assessing informal economies is almost invariably difficult, these difficulties are especially pronounced in Libya where the political and military competition for power remains both acute and indeterminate. Moreover, since the fall of Gaddafi, Libya has had a war economy in which the informal and illicit are largely indistinguishable from one another. Nevertheless, the Libyan informal economy has been estimated by World Economics as 35.3 percent of the country's GDP. A 2018 doctoral thesis even suggested that Libya enjoyed a vibrant informal economy in the food sector that provided a high level of food security even as the country endured protracted civil strife.[138] The author concluded not only that the sector provided "food to the poor at affordable prices" but also that it created employment and even business opportunities for people who otherwise would find it difficult to earn a livelihood.[139] In Egypt, the informal economy has grown over time, with an estimated 63 percent of all Egypt's labor working outside the formal sector. Moreover, the informal economy "accounts for almost 50 percent of all non-agricultural employment and a staggering 30–40 percent of the country's economy."[140]

In other words, despite national variations, for all five countries of North Africa, the informal economy is large, sprawling, and an important—albeit imperfect—social and economic safety net. Yet at the same time, it also acts as a drag on economic growth and development. Consequently, it is necessary to explore the reasons for both the emergence and the persistence of these informal economies.

Informal economies result from a mixture of excessive regulations and tax burdens. They also reflect poor governance of the economy. As an International Monetary Fund (IMF) blog pointed out in 2011, weak institutions and poor governance limit access to public services, foster corruption, and make access to the formal sector unavailable.[141] In addition, "restrictive product market regulations and high tax burdens raise compliance and entry costs," making entry into the formal economy unattractive.[142]

In all five countries, these barriers are substantial and, hitherto, endemic. Yet the inhibitions to a greater degree of entrepreneurial activity in the formal economy provide only one part of the story.

Another dimension that needs to be examined is the control of the economy. In Libya, the economy, like the state itself, is highly contested. The prize is control of both the state apparatus and the economy, especially the oil, which would simultaneously provide an amalgamation of power and wealth. Yet, this remains a long way from fulfillment for all the warring factions. In Egypt, in contrast, the military under Sisi has not only reestablished an upgraded authoritarianism but has also facilitated military control over much of the economy. According to one analysis, "military entrepreneurs have replaced private capital as the leading force in the government and the market. The state apparatus is increasingly constituted of retired officers who also occupy top government positions controlling the economy. They foster the military institution's monopolies in sectors of civilian production and services" and have relegated the traditional business elite to subcontracting or irrelevance.[143]

In Morocco, too, there is a concentration of economic wealth in the hands of the king and his key advisors and associates. At the same time, the king appears to have a long-term strategy of modernization that is linked to both a transition to green energy and a shift of focus from Europe to Africa. The Moroccan economy is becoming increasingly diversified as exemplified in the increasing importance of the Tanger Med port, domestic transportation improvements, and the external role of Moroccan banks—in particular Attijariwafa Bank, Banque Centrale Populaire, and Bank of Africa—in a variety of countries in Africa, especially West Africa.[144] Yet if there are highly positive developments in Morocco's economic modernization, it is still a work in progress. Illiteracy remains high and the economy is very uneven. There is a recognition in the palace and elsewhere in the government that "much more is needed to deliver a sustainable better life for the majority of Moroccans," but the goal remains elusive.[145] Much the same could be said of Morocco's neighbor. Algeria, although a rentier state dependent on oil revenues, also has a largely centralized economy. Algeria's bloody civil war in the 1990s was followed by "another centralized state structure, blending nationalist control with the promotion of new business classes linked to the ruling, military-security-dominated establishment, widely known as *le pouvoir*."[146] The Bouteflika clan emerged as the dominant force within this structure, but continued levels of cronyism and corruption provoked widespread sentiment that the family and its allies were enriching themselves at the expense of the country. The Hirak protest movement that began in February 2019—and consisted largely of unemployed youth—eventually led the military to withdraw its support. As a result, the president was compelled to resign. As one analysis observed, the movement "was sudden, spontaneous, and overwhelming. It caught a complacent and sclerotic regime completely off-guard."[147] Yet, much of the deep state structure remains intact, and Algeria continues to be a difficult and unattractive place for foreign investment. *Le pouvoir*, "the power," might have taken on a different form, but it has not gone away—and the increase in oil prices since the Covid-19 pandemic has provided it with an unexpected breathing space. Tunisia, in contrast, has not only seen widespread political disillusionment since the promise of the 2011 revolution but also experienced more than a decade of deterioration of its economy. One World Bank commentary even described the years after the revolution as "a lost decade of growth."[148] Much of this is attributable to overregulation and limited investment and innovation. The reliance on the welfare state, public employment, and subsidies proved insufficient; it also led to an increase in public debt, which by 2022 stood at 79.3 percent of GDP.[149]

The chapters that follow will elaborate on these themes and further explore the asymmetries and commonalities as we investigate the scale, scope, and impact of criminal networks and illicit economies of the five North African countries. Chapter 2 examines North Africa's last monarchy, Morocco, and the impact illicit economies and activities have had on the country itself as well as its neighbors. Chapter 3 explores Algeria, a country that has long faced threats by transnational terrorists and now also faces a broad array of challenges stemming from illegal economies on the one hand and government corruption on the other. Chapter 4 focuses on Tunisia, a country that, despite its central role in the Arab Spring, has not fared as well as might have been expected. Moreover, Tunisia's efforts to curb illicit economies remain a work in progress. In Chapter 5, we see that Libya, a country still reeling from its second civil war, continues to see its progress stifled by a mash-up of criminal profiteers who hinder the development of the country. Chapter 6 looks at Egypt's persistent criminal underbelly, which inflicts damage to the country's economy. Finally, Chapter 7 highlights how criminal networks continue to thrive and prosper throughout North Africa, placing this firmly within a context of inadequate and corrupt governance.

In each chapter, we follow a common format, to the extent possible given the variations in the criminal landscapes and illicit economies in the five North African countries. For example, Egypt has a section on organ trafficking that is not discussed elsewhere, while only Egypt and Libya have major problems with antiquities trafficking. Each chapter has a scene-setting introduction that is followed by analyses of drug trafficking, human smuggling, human trafficking (treated separately where possible and together when necessary), arms trafficking, and cigarette smuggling. This is typically followed by natural resource exploitation or contraband smuggling, depending on the country. A section on corruption, money laundering, and illicit financial flows rounds off each chapter and is followed by a short assessment.

Notes

1. See ENACT, "Organised Crime Index—Africa 2019." See the Global Organized Crime Index, "ENACT Index—Africa," for the 2021 and 2023 reports.
2. Global Organized Crime Index, "About the Index,"—ENACT, https://ocindex.net/about.
3. Dandurand, "Thinking Globally, Acting Locally."
4. See for example, Price, "Illicit Financial Flows."
5. Shaw and Reitano, *Political Economy of Trafficking*, p. 4.
6. See for example, Woody, "Police in Peru"; Guarascio, "Europe Flooded with Cocaine."
7. Rastello, *I Am the Market*, p. 138.
8. Ibid., p. 146.
9. For more on arbitrage opportunities, see for example, Eaton et al., *Conflict Economies*, pp. 39–41.
10. Altman and Bastian, *DHL Global Connectedness Index 2022*, p. 5.
11. Williams, "The Global Crisis of Governance," pp. 21–45; Passas, "Global Anomie, Dysnomie," pp. 16–44.
12. Friedman, *Lexus and the Olive Tree*, pp. 7–8.
13. Heine and Thakur, *Dark Side of Globalization*, p. 4.
14. Talani and Roccu, *Dark Side of Globalisation*, pp. 10–11.
15. Lahlou, "Migration Dynamics in Play in Morocco," p. 2.
16. Amrani, "Why Don't We Think?"
17. Ibid.
18. See, for example, Khan and Mezran, "Aftermath of the Arab Spring."
19. European Environment Agency, "Mediterranean Sea Region Briefing."
20. Fonseca, "'Intra-Mediterranean Container Trades' Update."
21. Ibid.
22. Ibid.
23. Hand, "Mediterranean Top Container Port Crown."
24. Pacific Logistics Group, "Top 5: Busiest Container Ports."
25. UN Security Council, "Violence, Hatred, Piracy."
26. Ibid.
27. Dillman, "Introduction: Shining Light on the Shadows," p. 125.
28. Ibid., p. 127.
29. Sergi, "Policing the Port, Watching the City," p. 639.
30. Sergi, *Port-Crime Interface*, p. 21.
31. World Port Source, "World Ports by Country."
32. Sergi, *Port-Crime Interface*, p. 24.
33. Interpol and ENACT, "Illicit Goods Trafficking," p. 17.
34. Ibid., p. 5.
35. Ibid., p. 25.
36. Ibid., p. 4.
37. Ibid., p. 21.
38. Europol, *OCTA 2007*, pp. 23–27.
39. Europol, *OCTA 2011*, p. 50.

40. Ibid.
41. Keefe, "The Geography of Badness," p. 99.
42. Ibid.
43. New Mexico Museum of Natural History and Science, "What Are Fractals?" n.d. https://nmnaturalhistory.org/events/first-friday-fractals.
44. Sands, "Organized Crime and Illicit Activities."
45. Resa-Nestares, "Transnational Organized Crime in Spain," p. 57.
46. Gómez-Céspedes, "Spain: A Criminal Hub," p. 175.
47. Sands, "Organized Crime and Illicit Activities," pp. 211–212.
48. See for example, Tondo, "Puglia Crimewave Points to Emergence."
49. See for example, Sergi, "Nigerian Gangs Partner with Mafia"; Klein, "Italy Arrests Dozens"; Mackie, "Italian Police: Mafia and Nigerian."
50. BBC News, "Black Axe Mafia"; Meers, "Italy: After Cosa Nostra."
51. Quoted in Alberici and Sirignani, "In a Ruined City."
52. France 24, "Five Things to Know."
53. Recent reporting includes Anesi, Bettoni, and Rubino, "'Armed and Dangerous'"; Anesi, Bettoni, and Rubino, "The 'Ndrangheta's 'Little Kiss.'"
54. Calandra, "Between Local and Global," footnote 3, p. 79.
55. Sergi, "Policing the Port, Watching the City," p. 639.
56. Ibid., p. 640.
57. Europol, "Trash Worth Millions of Euros"; Interpol, "Hazardous Materials Seized"; Interpol, "Operation Targets Illegal Trade."
58. Sergi, "Policing the Port, Watching the City," p. 644.
59. Paoli, "Decline of the Italian Mafia," p. 27.
60. Orsini and Sergi, "Emergency Business: Migrants Reception."
61. Cengiz, "Amped in Ankara," p. 3; European Monitoring Centre for Drugs and Drug Addiction, "Opioid Trafficking Routes."
62. See also, Kemp, *Transnational Tentacles: Global Hotspots*, pp. 30, 45.
63. Levitt, "Contending with the PKK's Narco-Terrorism"; US Department of the Treasury, "Treasury Sanctions Supporters of the PKK."
64. See for example, Kemp, *Transnational Tentacles: Global Hotspots*, pp. 40–49.
65. McGrath, "Conflict and Crime: Smuggling to Turkey," p. 105.
66. US Department of State, "United States Designates ISIS Financial Facilitators."
67. Zaitseva, "Illicit Trafficking in the Southern Tier" 168–182; BBC News, "Turkish Police Seize Radioactive Material"; Sabrihomuglu, "Turkey Detects Nuclear Material"; Nuclear Threat Initiative, "Eight Persons Caught Smuggling Nuclear Materials."
68. Cengiz and Karademir, "Impacts of Authoritarianism on Organized Crime"; Shelley, "Money Laundering into Real Estate," p. 135.
69. *Daily Sabah*, "Turkey Becomes Favorite Destination."
70. Organized Crime and Corruption Reporting Project, "Joseph Muscat."
71. Euronews, "Malta's Government Responsible for Murder."
72. Anesi, Bagnoli, and Rubino, "Malta, a Modern Smugglers' Hideout."
73. *Times of Malta*, "'Malta Has Become a Crossroad.'"
74. Anesi, Bagnoli, and Rubino, "Malta, a Modern Smugglers' Hideout."
75. Ibid.
76. Ibid.
77. Jacquemet, "Transidioma Afloat: Communication, Power," p. 138.
78. Mainwaring, *At Europe's Edge*, p. 26.
79. Clarke, "If Your Country Is Falling Apart."

80. Arieff et al., *Russia's Wagner Group in Africa.*
81. Walsh, "Coast to Coast."
82. UNHCR, "Key Facts and Figures."
83. Kahneman and Tversky, "Prospect Theory: An Analysis," p. 263.
84. Torelli, "Introduction," p. 12.
85. Impicciatore and Rosina, "Europe and Africa: Demographic Dynamics," p. 19.
86. Ibid.
87. Ibid., p. 21.
88. Carbone, "Nigeria and Contemporary African Migration," p. 51.
89. Torelli, "Introduction," p. 13.
90. See also UNDP, "Scaling Fences."
91. Impicciatore and Rosina, "Europe and Africa: Demographic Dynamics," p. 28.
92. Ibid.
93. De Georgio, "West Africa: Economic and Socio-Political Dynamics," p. 64.
94. Ibid., p. 60.
95. UNODC, "Organized Crime and Irregular Migration," p. 1.
96. Ibid.
97. Ibid., p. 5.
98. Ibid., p. 8.
99. Ibid., p. 9.
100. UNODC, "Transnational Organized Crime in West Africa," p. 31.
101. UNODC, "Organized Crime and Irregular Migration," pp. 13–16.
102. Monzini, *Smuggling of Migrants*, p. 6.
103. De Haas, *Irregular Migration from West Africa.* More recent reporting on this aspect includes the following: Coggio, "Europe's Tackling of 'Root Causes'"; Mbiyozo, "Pressure Grows on Africa."
104. Monzini, *Smuggling of Migrants*, p. 7.
105. Ibid.
106. Ibid., pp. 7–8.
107. Ibid., p. 35.
108. Fabrizio, Migali, and Münz, *Many More to Come?* p. 16.
109. Impicciatore and Rosina, "Europe and Africa: Demographic Dynamics," p. 26.
110. Castells, "Grassrooting the Space of Flows."
111. Cochrane and Pain, "A Globalizing Society?" in Held, ed., *A Globalizing World?* p. 16.
112. Castells, "Grassrooting the Space of Flows."
113. Kemper, *Labyrinth of Kingdoms: 10,000 Miles*, p. 22.
114. Cochrane and Pain, "A Globalizing Society?" p. 16.
115. Gallien, "Smugglers and States: Illegal Trade," p. 70.
116. Passas, "Globalization, Criminogenic Asymmetries."
117. Nugent and Asiwaju, *African Boundaries.*
118. Bianchi and Magid, "Decolonization's Last Stand in the Sahara."
119. Bertelsmann Transformation Index (BTI), *BTI 2020 Country Report: Egypt.*
120. Ibid.
121. Ibid.
122. Bertelsmann Transformation Index (BTI), *Egypt Country Report 2022.*
123. For a balanced assessment, see International Crisis Group, *Libya Turns the Page.*
124. Bertelsmann Transformation Index (BTI), *Libya Country Report 2020.* See also Brahimi, "Libya's Political Impasse."

125. Economist Intelligence Unit, *Democracy Index 2020*, pp. 27, 40.
126. Bertelsmann Transformation Index (BTI), *Algeria Country Report 2020.*
127. Ibid.
128. Serrano, "Higher Oil Prices."
129. Central Intelligence Agency, *The World Factbook,* "Morocco."
130. Bertelsmann Transformation Index (BTI), *Morocco Country Report 2020.*
131. See for example, Blickman, *Morocco and Cannabis: Reduction, Containment*; Eljechtimi, "Morocco's Bill to Legalise Cannabis"; Deutsche Welle, "Should EU Help Legalize Cannabis?"
132. Eljechtimi, "Informal Labour."
133. World Economics, www.worldeconomics.com.
134. Bouanani and Bounoua, "Analyzing the Informal Economy."
135. Ibid.
136. Lopez-Acevedo et al., *Morocco's Jobs Landscape*.
137. Dridi, "Tunisia's Informal Employment Crisis."
138. Tika, "Role of the Informal Economy."
139. Ibid.
140. Mabrouk, "Egypt's Sizeable Informal Economy."
141. Ahmed, "Bringing the Informal Sector into the Fold."
142. Ibid.
143. Beinin, Haddad, and Seikaly, *Critical Political Economy*, p. 66.
144. Rahhou, "Moroccan Banks Dominated."
145. See Marks, "The Maghrib Economies," p. 578.
146. Ibid., p. 571.
147. McDougall, "Fall of Abdelaziz Bouteflika."
148. See World Bank, "World Bank in Tunisia."
149. Ibid.

2

Morocco: Drugs, Migrants, and Money

MOROCCO IS UNIQUE AMONG NORTH AFRICAN COUNTRIES IN SEVERAL ways: it remains the only monarchical system in North Africa, albeit one that operates within a broader political framework; it is the only country in the region that is both a major drug producer and exporter; it is the only country with an Atlantic as well as Mediterranean coast; and it is the only country directly bordering a European country, through the Spanish enclaves of Ceuta and Melilla. Morocco is also party to a frozen conflict in the Western Sahara; this continues to be a source of serious contention with Algeria, which supports the Polisario Front, an insurgent group fighting for independence. Although the common border between Algeria and Morocco is settled, it is also carefully policed and, in some areas, heavily militarized.

In political terms Morocco is far from qualifying as a democracy. Still, the Arab Spring did lead to some constitutional reforms and to an early election in which the opposition party, the Justice and Development Party (PJD), obtained a plurality of seats in government.[1] The February 20 Movement encompassed a broad political spectrum ranging from "reformist-monarchists" to "revolutionary-republicans."[2] King Mohammed VI's willingness to compromise by enacting some constitutional reforms rather than remaining intransigent shifted momentum to the reformists and marginalized the revolutionaries.[3] Indeed, the king seemed to have a reformist impulse: he improved the legal status of women and created a commission to provide compensation for victims of human rights abuses. Moreover, the Moroccan regime lacked "some of the sclerotic and aging features of many of its neighbors."[4] Political intermediaries acted as "links between the center of power and society," and this helped to manage change and reduce crises.[5]

At the same time, the king was reluctant to permit measures that would in any way undermine the political authority or legitimacy of the monarchy, and he has done nothing that would change what the Bertelsmann Transformation Index (BTI) termed the "the underlying configuration of power."[6] Reforms have been more than cosmetic but a long way from having large-scale impact on politics. For example, it was acknowledged, as part of the constitutional reform, that the king was no longer "sacred," but the persona of the king was "inviolable."[7] Moreover, the king's religious authority buttressed the legitimacy of the monarchy.[8] It is hardly surprising then that BTI remains critical of the continued power and authority of the monarchy and consistently laments the lack of checks and balances, transparency, and accountability.[9] In its 2022 report it noted that "Morocco is a liberalized authoritarian monarchy in which the regime uses democratic institutions to sustain an authoritarian regime and undemocratic practices."[10] During 2022 and 2023, however, criticisms of the king also emerged domestically, largely because he spent considerable time out of the country, especially in Paris, and kept a low profile even when in Morocco.[11] His friendship with "a younger, German-born Moroccan mixed martial arts fighter, Abubakr Abu Azaitar . . . and his two brothers" also raised concerns, not least because Abu Azaitar was believed to "be driving a wedge between the king and his advisers."[12] In addition, the king's absences led to "the emergence of a new actor on the Moroccan political stage, one that might be called the 'Security Alliance.' This alliance comprises security and intelligence agencies, businessmen benefiting from the rentier economy, and other stakeholders, including politicians and senior officials in state institutions."[13] Even prior to all this, BTI had noted that "levels of political disaffection remain high among the general population," with low turnout at elections and "low levels of trust in parliament and political parties."[14] The Hirak Rif movement's protests and boycotts demonstrated widespread disaffection with current socioeconomic conditions and increasing impatience with poor governance and endemic corruption.[15]

Nevertheless, Morocco and many Moroccans pride themselves on the level of stability that the country has maintained not only since the Arab Spring, but over the past several decades. There is also a sense of moderation and judiciousness in Morocco that is quietly impressive. The country legitimately projects a moderate vision of Islam, and for all the criticisms that are directed at the monarchy it rarely acts in an overly heavy-handed manner.[16] Moreover, the king, regardless of all the recent concerns, appears to make the correct moves at times of crisis.

His visit to a hospital in Marrakesh soon after the earthquake of September 8, 2023, as well as photographs of him giving blood, were generally well received—despite criticisms that he had been slow returning from France to Morocco in the immediate aftermath of the earthquake.

The Covid-19 pandemic posed a new set of challenges to Morocco, and levels of satisfaction with the government have declined as they did in many other countries. The weaknesses of Morocco's health-care system were certainly laid bare by the pandemic. In October 2020, the king announced a plan "to revive the country's economy with the help of a major universal social security project which will reform public establishments. Another . . . focus will be determining how to revive and prioritize key sectors that were harshly affected by the Covid-19 pandemic, such as tourism, transport, hospitality, and the private sector."[17] In the aftermath of the pandemic, however, the challenges have become even more formidable with postpandemic inflation and growing inequality. Moreover, as one commentary noted, for the first time the king has not been immune to the criticism that he has failed "to alleviate the country's economic crisis, especially the unprecedented rise in food and petroleum prices."[18] As a result, Morocco might be heading toward a "crisis of governance."[19] Even if such a crisis is avoided, Morocco will have to overcome many hurdles, including its limited resource base. One possible outcome is that some people will find themselves being relegated from the formal economy to the informal sector, while others might be lured into criminality because of the lack of viable alternatives.

As noted in Chapter 1, assessment of organized crime and illicit economies in North Africa has been facilitated by successive reports providing an index of both organized criminality and resilience. ENACT's 2019 African Organized Crime Index gave Morocco a score of 4.88 in terms of criminality, which placed it third in North Africa and twenty-seventh of fifty-four African countries.[20] The Global Organized Crime Index released by ENACT and the Global Initiative Against Transnational Organized Crime in September 2021 saw criminality at 4.79, an assessment that reflected high scores for the cannabis and cocaine trades as well as human smuggling and human trafficking.[21] The 2023 edition saw a similar criminality score with 4.80, which placed it fourth in North Africa.[22] Morocco is a major producer, consumer, and exporter of cannabis, while cocaine and synthetic drugs are becoming more prevalent. The 2023 index also highlighted the heroin trade as "a significant problem in the northern regions of Morocco, particularly Nador, Tetouan, and Tangier."[23] The heroin comes primarily from Europe and is reportedly bartered for cannabis.[24] Human smuggling is also a significant activity, with Morocco acting as both a transit country and a country of origin.

Morocco scores higher in terms of criminal markets than it does in criminal actors. Even so, as the 2019 report noted, "criminal networks, state-embedded actors and foreign actors all exert significant influence in organized crime."[25] State-embedded actors scored 7 in 2021 and 7.50 in 2023. They are regarded as the criminal actor type with the greatest influence and involvement in various forms of corruption. The collusion of law enforcement with drug traffickers is also a problem. There are consolidated linkages between Moroccan drug trafficking networks and cocaine trafficking organizations from Latin America, but according to the 2023 index the latter have not had "a significant impact on violence or government corruption."[26] Financial crimes, the trade in counterfeit goods, and extortion and protection racketeering were all prominent among the criminal markets in 2023.

Concerning Morocco's capacity to respond to organized crime, or what the organized crime index terms *resilience*, the country scores well, the second highest in North Africa in 2021 and the highest in 2023. Morocco has a highly appropriate legal framework to combat organized crime, a robust judiciary, and its international cooperation, particularly with Spain, is impressive. Arrangements for helping victims and protecting witnesses are reasonable but not robust. The lowest-scoring resilience indicator in the 2019 report was the economic regulatory environment. The score of 5.5 reflected "the culture of patronage, nepotism, corruption and *wasta* that hinders legitimate businesses in the country."[27] In 2023 the economic regulatory capacity was 4.50, while the category of government transparency and accountability was even lower at 3.50. The index also noted that civil society was robust but had been weakened by crackdowns on journalists.

Drug Trafficking

When it comes to narcotics, Morocco is the six-hundred-pound gorilla in North Africa, especially regarding cannabis and cocaine. Morocco is the major producer of cannabis in North Africa and has become the North African transshipment country of choice for cocaine from Latin America. In addition, somewhat ironically, Morocco is also the destination for synthetic drugs from the Netherlands, some of which have seriously dangerous consequences.

Production of Cannabis

Morocco is one of the largest producers of cannabis resin, also known as hash, in the world. The majority of its output is destined for Europe, but significant shipments also transit to and through other North African countries.[28] As Herbert and Gallien noted, "By the mid-1990s, Moroccan producers had come to dominate the market for cannabis resin, supplying 70–80% of the drug imported from outside into Europe."[29] Although the authors suggest that Morocco was able to establish "a quasi-monopolistic supply position to the European market," Morocco's cannabis production has shifted over time, with periods of decline followed by resurgence.[30] Reports of the poor quality of Moroccan cannabis were accompanied by a decline in cultivation areas. Indeed, sources suggest that in 2003, Morocco reached its apex with 134,000 hectares under cultivation.[31] As Pierre-Arnaud Chouvy noted in a background paper for the European Monitoring Centre for Drugs and Drug Addiction (EMCDDA), the crop had decreased to 47,196 hectares in 2013.[32] Inconsistencies between "the dramatic fall in estimated cannabis resin production in Morocco" and seizure data, however, compelled a closer look.[33] It emerged that Morocco's traditional landrace was "being replaced by cannabis hybrids of various origins and pedigrees displaying radically different physical aspects and allowing for much higher resin yields and THC contents."[34] Some of them have names like Pakistana, Amnesia, and Gorilla, but in the Ketana region of the Rif the dominant strain is Critical, which sells for 230 euro per kilogram while the traditional Beldiya sells for four times as much.[35] There are some disadvantages to the hybrids, particularly the requirements for improved irrigation and more intensive fertilization, which in the long term will likely have an adverse environmental impact.[36] Overall though, the hybrids have helped to revitalize the business. As more countries legalize medical and recreational cannabis, however, competition will become more intense, and Morocco is likely to decline in terms of market share.

The impact of these new hybrids—many from the Netherlands—was intensified by more efficient extraction and production methods. According to a recent assessment, "Moroccan cultivators are estimated to be able to generate roughly 35,000 metric tonnes of cannabis annually, which, when processed, accounts for 713–714 tonnes of resin. The value of this is estimated at up to US$23 billion per year, representing a two-fold increase over the last decade."[37] Moreover, although production has become more efficient, it remains labor intensive, providing unique employment opportunities in disadvantaged areas (see Figure 2.1).[38]

Figure 2.1 Major Areas of Cannabis Production in Morocco

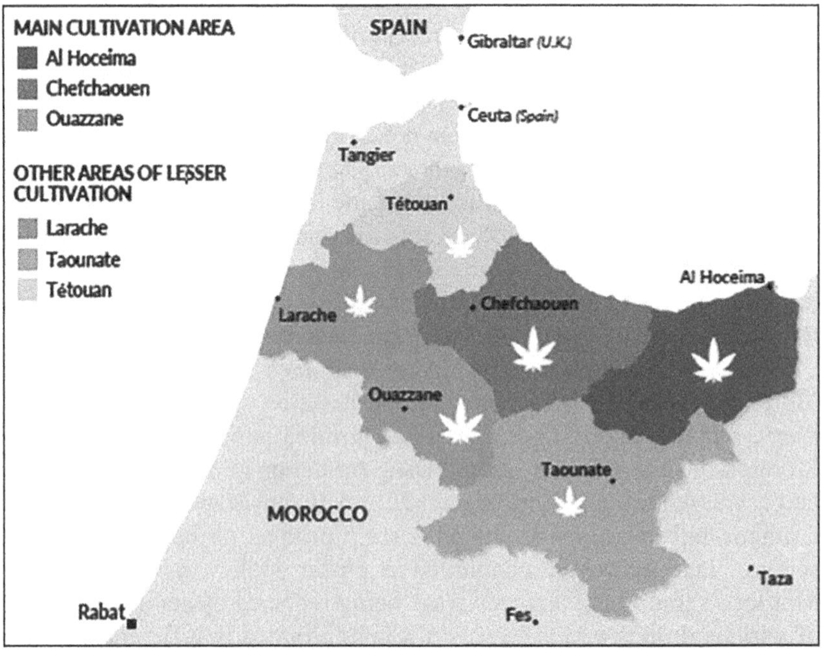

Source: Matt Herbert and Max Gallien, *A Rising Tide: Trends in Production, Trafficking and Consumption of Drugs in North Africa* (Geneva: Global Initiative Against Transnational Organized Crime, June 1, 2020).

Although cannabis production is still illegal in Morocco, it is widespread in the Rif mountains and "takes place on tens of thousands of farms across the northern Rif region, concentrated around the cities of Ouazzane, Al Hoceima and Chefchaouen, particularly in the Chefchaouen communes of Beni Ahmed, Bab Berred and Bab Taza."[39] According to one assessment, there are "between 96,000 and 140,000" growers, but the business is believed to support over 1 million people in a region that has few alternative sources of sustenance.[40] For many in the trade, cannabis production offers only limited income. Some farm laborers earn just between 100 and 150 dirhams (9.30–13.90 euros) a day.[41] In contrast, other aspects of the value chain are more lucrative. Larger farms, wholesalers, traffickers, and brokers command high profit margins.[42] The overall impact on the region is positive and, despite government rhetoric about cannabis being illegal, there seems to be tacit acceptance of its importance in providing livelihoods and maintaining stability in a region where the state has limited presence. This tacit reliance on illicit economies is also evident in other parts of the world. As one study pointed out, this likely explains "the recent decline in eradication and seizures in the Rif, as a prolonged protest movement based in the city of Al Hoceima has cautioned the Moroccan state from further antagonizing the population of the Rif region."[43] As mentioned above, however, Morocco more broadly and the Rif specifically will face greater competition from Europe as decriminalization proceeds. There are growing signs that Spain is becoming a legitimate competitor to Morocco. This could have serious economic consequences for the Rif and create a political challenge for the Moroccan government.

Cannabis Traffickers and Trafficking Routes

The routes for trafficking of cannabis to and through other countries in North Africa will be dealt with in the other sections of this book. The focus in this chapter, therefore, will be on cannabis trafficking to Europe and to South America. Many Moroccans have migrated to Europe, and two countries in particular stand out in relation to cannabis trafficking—Spain because of proximity, and the Netherlands because of its permissive attitudes toward cannabis. France has some importance too because of its historic relationship with Morocco.

One of the best explorations of the Moroccan cannabis trade was published in 2008 and described how "balls, blocks and packages of hashish and hashish oil are carried to Europe by speedboat, fishing boat, cargo ships, cars, vans, trucks, small aircraft, and individuals who carry the drug in their bags, their clothes or their bodies. Hashish is hidden beneath vegetables, fish, wood and any other commodities crossing the Strait."[44] Significantly in terms of the timeline for Morocco's involvement in cocaine trafficking, the analysis added that "lately, Moroccan hashish and Latin American cocaine have been smuggled together."[45] The study also examined 1,370 operational cases and identified more than "800 regional distributors and importers."[46] Almost all of those arrested with over 500 kilograms (or kilos) of hashish were smugglers or large-scale distributors; 430 groups imported between 1 and 36 tonnes.[47] On average, 3.4 tonnes were seized in these operations, and 7.4 people were arrested by project or police raid.[48] One case led to the arrest of nearly 100 individuals from across Europe connected to a wide transnational ring of smugglers, distributors, and money launderers.[49] The study also identified the nationality of those arrested in 757 cases.[50] Thirty-eight percent of groups were formed by Spaniards working with Spaniards, while 19 percent were Moroccans working with each other.[51] When people from different nationalities cooperated within range of Spanish police, the most frequent combination was that of Spanish and Moroccan nationals (8 percent of all groups arrested).[52] Gender was specified in 280 cases and about 19 percent were women, although for the most part, they operated in small groups and with small amounts of cannabis.[53]

In terms of size and sophistication, the participants in this criminal market—and this is true of almost all other illicit markets—varied enormously. They ranged from individuals or small groups of two or three people who carry the drug or hide it in body cavities to higher-level echelons of the hashish import-export industry which primarily consisted of groups dealing with dozens of tonnes at a time, coordinating and managing sophisticated, industrial-scale operations.[54] A lot of the smaller hashish smuggling and distributing firms were informal, decentralized, and ad hoc, while many of the brokers or entrepreneurs worked on the periphery of formal criminal organizations, relying instead on "legal enterprise for a more permanent business structure and stable contractual relationships for some of their associates."[55] Although this description was offered back in 2008, it captured a complex reality that has increasingly become the norm.

In terms of routes, Spain's proximity to Morocco makes it almost axiomatic that Spain is, and will remain, *the* major gateway for Moroccan cannabis to Europe. It is also the oldest trafficking route in the region, first emerging in the 1960s. By the early 2000s, however, "Spain deployed a surveillance system in the western Mediterranean that proved vastly more effective at spotting and tracking the transport boats and planes used by the smugglers."[56] In turn, this led traffickers to adapt their efforts to circumvent or neutralize the surveillance system, prompting innovations with helicopters and light aircraft.[57] Nevertheless, maritime trafficking into Spain and Portugal across the Strait of Gibraltar and the Alboran Sea remains the preferred route for Moroccan cannabis traffickers to reach Europe. Spain regularly seizes some of the largest quantities of cannabis resin in the world.[58] "As enforcement has increased, so too has the profitability of the trafficking networks and their ability to invest in high-end equipment."[59] In recent years, there have been some large seizures and multiple arrests. These include the following sample:

- In January 2017, traffickers on five inflatable boats in the Bay of Gibraltar were spotted by authorities and threw overboard twenty-seven bales of hashish weighing about 800 kilos and worth 4.7 million euros before evading both the Royal Gibraltar Police and Spain's Guardia Civil.[60]

- In February 2017, the Spanish civil guard seized 900 kilos after a car chase in La Linea.[61]
- In February 2017, Gibraltar police agencies recovered 2.4 tonnes of cannabis resin in seventy-nine bales and worth about 12 million pounds.[62]
- In February 2019, a 40-foot rigid-hulled inflatable boat was floundering, and the Royal Gibraltar Police who rescued it found 3 tonnes of cannabis in eighty-four bales with an estimated street value of 14 million pounds.[63]
- In March 2019, police seized 1.675 tonnes of cannabis resin in Fez.[64]
- In April 2019, the Central Bureau of Judicial Investigations seized 7 tonnes of cannabis in Casablanca.[65]
- In July 2019, Moroccan police seized 27.3 tonnes in one haul.[66]
- In late October 2019, police and customs made separate seizures of 8 tonnes and 4 tonnes of cannabis resin in trucks going through the Tanger Med port on consecutive days.[67]
- In February 2020, French law enforcement in Villepinte, in the suburbs of Paris, seized 4.8 tonnes of cannabis resin that had been trafficked from Morocco via Spain to France.[68]
- On January 12, 2021, a Spaniard and a Portuguese national were arrested after 825 kilos of hashish was found on their boat.[69] A search by customs authorities from Gibraltar found the hashish—which was reportedly worth 4 million pounds—in a secret hydraulic compartment.[70]
- In April 2021, Spanish police arrested 100 members of a drug trafficking organization called Monparlet, which had been using speedboats to move cannabis from Morocco to Spain.[71] The drugs were transported inland via the Guadalquivir River and then driven in food trucks to a warehouse in Dos Hermanos, from where they could be smuggled into France.[72]
- In June 2021, Spanish authorities seized over 20 tonnes of cannabis resin "when a large shipping vessel from Morocco was boarded approximately 90 nautical miles off the coast of the Canary Islands."[73] Reportedly, the seizure resulted from a tip by Irish intelligence, and the drugs were being moved to Europe by a transnational criminal organization.[74]

The seizures continued throughout 2022. In April, Moroccan police seized over 31 tonnes of cannabis resin in a warehouse near Tangier.

The cannabis was reportedly "packaged and stuffed in fruit and vegetable figurines" designed to provide concealment during the export process.[75] In June, over 3 tonnes were seized from a container in Casablanca port.[76] This pattern of seizures in ports and port cities continued, with Moroccan authorities seizing 5.4 tonnes of cannabis resin from an international freight truck in Tangier port in April 2023.[77]

While these were examples of individual seizures, the composite figures are even more illuminating, not least because in the last several years there has been a significant decline in seizures by the Moroccan authorities. In 2020, the General Directorate of National Security (DGSN) seized over 217 tonnes of cannabis and arrested 97,564 people for offenses related to drugs.[78] Ironically, arrests were down by 23 percent from the previous year, while the seizures increased by 37 tonnes. In 2021, over 191 tonnes of cannabis resin were seized—a reduction of 12 percent from 2020.[79] In 2022, however, seizures fell to 98 tonnes.[80] The difficulty, of course, is knowing what percentage of production is being seized and what the trend line really looks like.

There is an additional consideration. In July 2021 the Moroccan government legalized production of cannabis "for industrial, medicinal and cosmetic uses in the three provinces of the Rif while also creating a National Regulation Agency for Cannabis Activities (ANRAC) to monitor the production of legal cannabis."[81] According to reports, however, there is still great uncertainty in the Rif, with many cannabis farmers concerned that the profits from legal production and sales of marijuana will be lower than those accrued from the illicit market. Such concerns have inhibited registrations allowing farmers to function as licit producers and sellers.[82]

Whatever the case—and even allowing for Spanish cannabis—the Morocco to Spain cannabis trade remains robust. According to one report, in July 2020, drug trafficking across the 14 kilometers of the Strait of Gibraltar remained pervasive, with an estimated 280 tonnes of drugs moved through each month.[83] The authors also claimed that about 80 percent of the hash consumed in Europe was imported via this route.[84] The report concluded that both the authorities and traffickers agreed that "the Strait remains uncontrollable."[85] A report later in 2020, however, suggested that Covid-19 and the resulting restrictions on movements had accomplished—at least temporarily—what law enforcement agencies and interdiction efforts had been unable to achieve, interrupting air routes, making land transportation more difficult, and forcing traffickers to take longer more indirect routes.[86] In effect, Moroccan trafficking networks had been forced to travel south before they could go north. The new route involved "transporting drugs for hours from the Rif to the remote beaches of Sidi Abed, 217 kilometers (135 miles) south of Rabat, using food trucks whose drivers have permits to travel during confinement."[87] The cannabis resin was then loaded on fishing boats, which traveled north through the Atlantic to Spain. This was criminal adaptation par excellence and shows why drug trafficking is so hard to prevent.

During the last several years and predating Covid-19, the central Mediterranean route from Libya has become an additional means of importing cannabis to Europe. As with smuggled oil from Libya, the Hurd Bank, an anchorage just outside Maltese waters, has become a transshipment point for cannabis. Some drug shipments are transferred from ship to ship before being sent to Europe, while others are shipped straight to disembarkation points in either southern Italy or the western Balkans.[88] Trafficking networks typically use "small craft, including Maltese and Italian fishing boats," although there have also been some examples of "small and medium cargo ships" transporting cannabis from Morocco via Libya to various locations in Europe.[89] Malta seized 591 kilos of cannabis resin in 2017, but in 2018, authorities seized over 17 tonnes, placing the country in fifth place in Europe for seizures behind Spain, France, Italy, and Turkey.[90] Much of this came from a single container in Malta's Freeport that was in transit from Syria to Libya with the cannabis likely originating in Lebanon rather than Morocco.[91] In 2019 only 118 kilos were seized, while in 2020, largely as a result of Covid-19 lockdowns, the figure was a minuscule 0.36 kilos.[92] Although it has gone back up since 2020, as of this writing, there has been nothing in Malta comparable to the 2018 figure, suggesting that this was an anomaly. Moreover, in 2022 Malta changed its laws to allow recreational use of cannabis.

The implication is that most cannabis resin originating in Morocco and passing through the central Mediterranean goes directly to the European mainland. The waters around Malta are far more important for transshipment than the island itself. As for the route from Morocco to Italy, a law enforcement study noted that it is direct: "the port of Tangiers . . . is a major departing point for hashish trafficking to Italy, notably to ports on the Tyrrhenian Sea, such as Genoa, Civitavecchia, and Porto Torres in Sardinia."[93] The implication is that the role of Malta in drug smuggling is far less important than its role in oil smuggling—which is discussed more fully in Chapter 5 in connection with Libya.

Another important development appears to be an emerging barter system between Moroccan cannabis traffickers and Colombian cocaine trafficking organizations. As an Interpol assessment noted, the "increase in bulk sea shipments of cocaine arriving in and/or transitioning through Morocco, coincides with the emerging trend reported by the United States Department of State of cannabis resin being smuggled to South America and the Caribbean where it is being exchanged for cocaine."[94] Similarly, a UNODC study in 2023 noted that while cocaine was coming east to Europe, cannabis resin was being shipped to South America, especially Brazil. Some of this was done by sailing boats that often docked at the Canary Islands or Cabo Verde en route. As a UNODC report noted, in June 2021, a vessel with 4.3 tons of cannabis resin was intercepted 420 kilometers from the port of Recife in Brazil.[95] The boat, travelling from Portugal, had picked up the drugs in Morocco. In some instances—and with a nod to increased efficiency—the same vessels sometimes moved cannabis resin to South America and cocaine from South America back to Europe or North Africa. It is to these cocaine shipments that attention must now be given.

Morocco as a Cocaine Transshipment Country

During the 2000s, in response to Spanish interdiction of cocaine shipments in the Atlantic, Colombian and Venezuelan trafficking networks began to move drugs through West Africa and especially Guinea Bissau, and from there into North Africa and Europe.[96] Some land routes passed "through northern Mali, Niger and on through Algeria, Libya and Egypt."[97] Another route followed "the West African coast, moving through Mauritania and Morocco to the northern cities of Nador or Al Hoceima," from where shipments were moved "into Spain by boat or helicopter."[98] Moroccan cannabis trafficking networks seem to have diversified and emerged as serious players in cocaine transshipment to Europe. Relationships increasingly overlapped and intersected as cocaine traffickers relied on both "cannabis-resin smugglers and European organized-crime networks" to move shipments "across the Mediterranean into Europe."[99] Instability in the Sahel seems to have encouraged a shift from West Africa to North Africa, with Morocco—partly because of its attractive location and its Atlantic and Mediterranean coastline and ports, and partly because of the smuggling expertise developed in the cannabis trade—being pivotal to this shift. Moreover, in terms of Morocco as an arrival zone, the overland route through Mauritania mentioned above took on increasing importance because of the risks associated with conflict and instability in Libya. According to UNODC this was corroborated by reporting from Morocco, which revealed that in 2021, 23 percent of the cocaine entering Morocco came in via land.[100]

One of the key figures in deepening Morocco's involvement in the cocaine business was Ridoaun Taghi—aided by Saïd Razzouki—who had become a consummate smuggler of cannabis into the Netherlands and would soon become a serious player in the cocaine trafficking business. As one commentary noted, in 2008 when many South American drug trafficking organizations "decided to shift their trafficking operations from the US to Europe, using north-western Africa as a jumping-off point, Taghi was ready to accommodate them. He shipped a fleet of high-powered speedboats to Morocco to scale up deliveries, hired fishermen to receive shipments of cocaine and built out his empire."[101] Against this background, it is tempting to look at the Mocro Maffia—which operates in the Netherlands and Belgium—as an extension of drug trafficking in and from Morocco. Although this is only part of a complex story, there are few, if any, scholarly studies of the Mocro Maffia in English, so knowledge remains incomplete.[102] Having said that, the Mocro Maffia has at least ten major clans and organizations, which are often in conflict with one another. They have developed their own identities, involving conflicts and alliances, the extensive use of violence and assassinations, and their connections with criminal and drug trafficking organizations in Latin America, the Balkans, and Eastern Europe more generally.[103] Given that many members of the Mocro Maffia or their parents were part of what is sometime termed the Riffian diaspora, the links with Moroccan drug traffickers are likely to be both strong and enduring, facilitating the flows of drugs in both directions. Even so, the center of gravity of the Mocro Maffia is in the Netherlands and Belgium, not Morocco itself. Furthermore, the members of the clans and organizations seem increasingly focused on cocaine coming in through Rotterdam and Antwerp.[104] Nevertheless, Morocco remains an important transshipment country for cocaine moving to Europe. It is also emerging as a destination country.

Seizures provide at least some glimpses into the routes and modes of trafficking. In December 2016, Spanish and Moroccan authorities working together and using a helicopter and two patrol boats seized 2,575 kilos (5,677 pounds) of cocaine on a ship "about 100 miles off the coast of Dakhla in Western Sahara."[105] They arrested eighteen Moroccans as well as two Colombians, and two Spaniards in Galicia.[106] One of the Colombians was believed to be the leader of the organization, which was described as "the 'most active' group operating in Europe, Africa, and South America."[107] The trafficking organization reportedly "had a significant logistical and economic capacity allowing it to deploy a number of ships to move cocaine" and to break up the shipments into smaller loads as a method of risk mitigation.[108]

In October 2017, Moroccan police made a cocaine seizure of almost 2.39 tonnes, while arresting thirteen people including "Spanish and Dutch nationals of Moroccan origin."[109] They also confiscated "105 kilograms of hashish, 394,520 euro ($463,572) and 172,000 dirhams ($18,215) in cash, eight vehicles three with Spanish registration two hunting rifles and a satellite phone."[110] The two men directing the trafficking network had been in prison in Morocco since 2014 when the investigation started.[111] The network had been exporting cocaine to Spain, the Netherlands, and Germany.[112] The cocaine had been shipped from Brazil and "was recovered from storage sites in and around Rabat and in the northern city of Nador."[113] A few months later, in February 2018, Moroccan authorities seized 541 kilos of cocaine being moved through Casablanca in a container.[114] Six people, including the Brazilian leader of the operation, were arrested, while five cars and large sums of currencies were also confiscated.[115] The importance of the maritime route was further underlined in early 2019 when a ship with a Russian crew sailing from Panama to Morocco had to stop in Cabo Verde. The local authorities searched the ship and found 9.5 tonnes of cocaine. By any measure, this was a large seizure and underlined the continued role of Morocco as a transshipment country for cocaine trafficking.

There were also seizures that seemed to be linked to a burgeoning domestic market for cocaine. In July 2020, for example, Moroccan law enforcement in Marrakesh, Rabat, and Tangiers, seized 6 kilos of cocaine and arrested four people, including one woman and a Frenchman of Moroccan origin.[116] In another case, three drug dealers using rental cars were arrested after delivering 5 kilos of cocaine. This led to a subsequent seizure of $100,000 in cash and several mobile phones.[117] Similarly, in October 2023 Moroccan police seized 1.37 tonnes of cocaine in Casablanca. The cocaine was hidden in a shipment of frozen fish and was believed to have come from Latin America via Spain.[118] On January 1, 2024, National Security and Customs intercepted a shipment of 362.95 kilograms of cocaine at the El Guergarate border crossing, south of Dakhla. Authorities searched a truck that had arrived from a sub-Saharan African country and discovered bundles concealed "in the cab and bodywork. The lorry was registered in Morocco."[119] The truck driver and his assistant were arrested. The implication of these arrests was that Morocco was moving from simply being a transshipment state to also becoming a cocaine consumer country, albeit one in the early stages of this transition. This was reinforced when civil society groups highlighted the increasing abuse of a form of crack cocaine called pouf. Apparently, this was concocted from a mix of cocaine residue and various chemicals, and users often experienced hallucinations and behaved unpredictably and violently.[120]

In their brilliant and comprehensive 2020 assessment of the drug trade in and through North Africa, Herbert and Gallien noted that "many recent seizures have involved commercial shipping operations, in which the drugs are loaded in shipping containers and hidden among otherwise licit cargo."[121] They were absolutely correct in identifying the trend of exploiting container shipping. This was dramatically reaffirmed on January 3, 2024, when authorities announced that Moroccan law enforcement, working with Spanish security services, had seized 1,488 kilograms of cocaine at the Tanger Med port; the load had 1,277 bricks of cocaine concealed within bananas on a container ship that had embarked from South America and was sailing to Turkey.[122]

Herbert and Gallien not only identified the importance of intermodal containers for drug trafficking but also observed that there might be an air route into southern Morocco.[123] Subsequently, evidence suggested the existence of a nascent air route from Morocco to Spain. In July 2021, Spanish police put on display a large drone with a 4.5-meter wingspan and a capacity to carry 150 kilos of cargo, including drugs.[124] The Chinese-made drone could go up to a height of 7,000 feet (2,134 meters), had a speed of up to 170 kilometers per hour, and could fly for seven hours. It had four electric motors and a small combustion engine and cost somewhere between 30,000 and 150,000 euros.[125] Although the report suggested that it had been used to carry cocaine, no evidence was provided to substantiate this. Nevertheless, it is striking that it involved a French drug trafficking organization that was using the drone to fly drugs from Morocco to Spain.[126] Other evidence of increased diversity of routes and methods came from a Spanish police discovery in March 2021 that a warehouse in Malaga hosted a small submarine that was designed to carry up to 2 tonnes of narcotics and transport cocaine across the Strait of Gibraltar.[127] It is also worth noting that in 2016 a conversion laboratory was found in Oujda along with Peruvian chemists and 250 kilograms of refined cocaine.[128] This is a fascinating development, that follows a pattern evident in West Africa several years earlier when Venezuelan, Mexican, and Colombian methamphetamine cooks visited Nigeria and provided training and assistance in creating production laboratories.

Although most drug flows are going north from Morocco to Spain, Italy, the Netherlands, and elsewhere in Europe, there are also flows from Europe south to Morocco and indeed other North African countries. As the US Department of State's 2021 International Narcotics Control Strategy Report (INCSR) noted, "MDMA (ecstasy), originating in Belgium and the Netherlands, continues to be smuggled into northern Morocco and is sold on the domestic market."[129] It is worth noting though that "closed borders and increased border controls during the Covid-19 pandemic significantly affected the trafficking of MDMA, as evidenced by 116,122 tablets seized in 2020 versus 917,675 reported in 2019."[130] In 2021, only 55,000 MDMA tablets were seized.[131]

One of the drugs that does flow south is "Karkoubi," which is "a mixture of psychotropic drugs, hashish, and sometimes alcohol or glue, which causes hallucinations and psychotic behavior. The psychotropic substances such as Rivotril or Valium used in the fabrication of the Karkoubi are trafficked at international and regional levels."[132] The raw materials have historically been smuggled to Algeria, turned into hallucinogenic pills, and moved into Morocco.[133] Morocco's response was to strengthen border control, but criminals simply adapted. In 2017, they began to use "a new supply route bringing the psychotropic substance necessary for the manufacture of Karkoubi directly from Spain to Morocco."[134] Diverted pharmaceuticals that include amphetamines from Spain are now shipped directly to Morocco, where they are mixed in local laboratories and sold as pills. Unfortunately, they have what has been termed a "Rambo effect," inducing rage and violent behavior, and creating what has been described as a "spectacular upsurge in aggression and barbaric crimes."[135]

Most of these seizures, arrests, and even the highly disturbing trends pale into insignificance when compared to the scandal that emerged in December 2023. The case was set apart by the prominence of some of those involved in both politics and business. "Around 20 individuals have been arrested. They include policemen, government officials, company directors, a notary and a tourism promoter," as well as Said Naciri, owner of Morocco's most successful football club, and Abdenbi Bioui, a major businessman involved in construction and real estate.[136] According to *Le Monde*, both Naciri and Bioui are also members of a major political party that participates in government.[137] They have been charged with drug trafficking, the formation of a criminal gang, money laundering, and the falsification of official documents.[138] It appears that they were implicated by El Hadj Ahmed Ben Ibrahim—also known as "the Malian" and "the Escobar of the Desert"—who has been in prison since 2019.[139] Reportedly, the three men have been collaborating in drug trafficking adventures since 2010 and the two politicians seized some of the Malian's property after he was imprisoned in 2016.[140] Where this story will lead is uncertain, but it highlights the ways in which supposedly legitimate entrepreneurs are often simultaneously involved in criminal activities. Whether this is simply the result of greed or was necessary to maintain their licit enterprises remains uncertain. What is certain though is that there will be significant ramifications of the case in Morocco.

Human Smuggling

Morocco is a transit country, a destination country for many migrants, and a point of origin for Moroccans seeking to migrate to Europe. As is the case throughout North Africa, there is a sense of frustration—and frequently desperation—about economic and social advancement that drives a resurgent wave of Moroccans trying to reach Spain and elsewhere in Europe. For migrants from sub-Saharan Africa, Morocco has long been a transit and sometimes a destination country. To get there, however, is rarely easy. Although a 2010 study noted that 13 percent of migrants had arrived in Morocco by air, the rest came through various land routes, the vast majority—73.5 percent—entering via Algeria, with 55.9 percent moving from Maghnia to Oujda and 17 percent crossing the southern borders into Morocco.[141] Moreover, an estimated 87 percent of migrants from sub-Saharan Africa had used the services of smugglers.[142] This is hardly surprising given the difficulties and dangers of traversing these routes. Since then, however, entry into Morocco has become more difficult due to increased border controls. As discussed further in the Algeria chapter, the Maghnia to Oujda crossing has become much more difficult. Moreover, both Algerian and Moroccan authorities have increasingly hardened their policies toward irregular or illegal migrants. The Moroccan government has engaged in occasional deportations and has also moved migrants away from coastal regions within the country itself.

At the same time, there has been an interesting development whereby Morocco has established closer links with sub-Saharan Africa and opened new opportunities for migrants to transit Morocco.[143] Royal Air Maroc has expanded its flights to African countries and established Casablanca as a regional hub. A policy of visa exemptions for nationals from Algeria, Tunisia, Mali, Niger, Senegal, Guinea Conakry, Congo, Gabon, and Côte d'Ivoire encouraged irregular migration flows, although Morocco subsequently put in place preregistration requirements for citizens of Congo,

Guinea Conakry, and Mali.[144] Nevertheless, the ease of access to Morocco without a hazardous and arduous land journey helped to create "a new dynamic . . . whereby middle-class and qualified African migrants are transported to Europe through Morocco to fill labor-market gaps in European countries."[145] Moreover, as Arezo Malakooti and Chiara Fall explain, there is "a 'door-to-door service' that includes flying into Casablanca . . . and then being moved to the coast immediately to board speed boats to Spain. The entire journey is completed in a matter of days."[146] The migrants then move from Spain to France and Germany, where they have jobs lined up with employers who assist with the regularization process.[147] Examples include Ivorian nurses going to Paris to work in the health-care sector and Gambian engineers being taken to Germany.[148] Migrants who do not benefit from visa exemptions have typically obtained counterfeit passports from countries with these waivers.[149]

Routes from Morocco

In 2020, there were over 41,000 arrivals in Spain recorded on what is termed the Western Mediterranean route, which also incorporates a subset of departures from Morocco's Atlantic coast.[150] Indeed, the migration from Morocco, the Western Sahara, Mauritania, and Senegal has appropriately been termed the Atlantic route by Alarm Phone, an NGO that monitors the flows—and the human rights violations—in irregular migration from Africa to Europe.[151] The importance of this route can be seen in Table 2.1 highlighting the number of irregular migrants arriving in Spain—including the Canary Islands in the Atlantic and the Balearic Islands in the Mediterranean as well as the enclaves of Ceuta and Melilla—between 2015 and 2022.

Table 2.1 Irregular Migrants Arriving in Spain

Year	Sea Arrials	Land Arrivals	Dead and Missing
2022	29,895	1,868	1,221
2021	41,979	1,218	1,571
2020	40,326	1,535	821
2019	26,168	6,345	685
2018	58,569	6,814	811
2017	22,103	6,246	209
2016	8,162	6,443	102
2015	5,312	11,624	67

Source: UNHCR Operational Data Portal, Spain, https://data.unhcr.org/en/country/esp.

Within this, however, the Atlantic route has become particularly important. According to the UN High Commissioner for Refugees (UNHCR), of the migrants seeking to reach Spain in 2020, 71 percent traveled to the Canary Islands, 22 percent to the Spanish Peninsula itself, and 7 percent to the Balearic Islands.[152] If the Atlantic route to the Canary Islands has increased in popularity, however, it has also increased in precariousness. The migrants take enormous risks, and it has been claimed that one in every twelve people heading for the Canary Islands drowns en route.[153] While this is not confirmed in the table above, the UNHCR figures for the dead and missing are likely a significant underestimation. In this connection, the Spanish aid organization Caminando Fronteras recorded 4,404 dead or missing while trying to reach the Canary Islands in 2021.[154] Although this is more than double the UNHCR figure, it is probably a far more accurate assessment given that Caminando Fronteras has excellent networks in migrant communities and provides an unrivaled level of granularity.

The Canary Islands experienced a significant upsurge of irregular migrants arriving in 2020 and 2021, with boats leaving from Morocco, the Western Sahara, Senegal, and Mauritania. Perhaps surprisingly, Moroccans "constitute around half of all arrivals on the Canary Islands. They flee the country because of unemployment and lack of opportunities, or because of political persecution and because they cannot speak freely."[155] While the sense of limited opportunities might be slightly less stifling than in Algeria and Tunisia, similar dynamics appear to be at work. Indeed, the impetus to migrate was intensified by the Covid-19 shutdown and the loss of jobs in the tourist sector and the informal economy. The situation was exacerbated by postpandemic inflation, the increased food prices caused by the war between Russia and Ukraine, and a drought in Morocco itself. Lucia Bird Ruiz-Benitez De Lugo—in a brilliant and multifaceted analysis—confirms that much of the recent upsurge in irregular migration has been driven by Moroccans: "between January 2020 and June 2022, 42% of the 55,067 migrants intercepted by Spanish authorities were Moroccan nationals, with most embarking from points in southern Morocco or northern and central areas of the Moroccan-administered Western Sahara."[156] These points of embarkation were less subject to surveillance and avoided the controls on mobility in the north of Morocco. The smuggling networks are headed by Moroccans with considerable experience in smuggling contraband and narcotics. The top smugglers are "reportedly well-connected to state authorities but are not part of state apparatus" and are often referred to by migrants as Hajj, a term of respect in Arabic.[157] One smuggler who did an interview with a Spanish newspaper claimed that he earned 60,000 to 70,000 euros in October and November 2020 and that he "paid a high-ranking police officer €10,000 per boat to make sure that maritime surveillance" was absent "the night of departures."[158] Local smugglers in Dakhla were often Sahrawi, but Moroccan smugglers from the north were also involved, especially in the recruitment of migrants.[159] The existence of embarkation points as far north as Safi also suggests that smugglers from the north have extended their activities southward.[160] Captains of migrant vessels can earn about 6,000 euros—which makes the position very attractive.[161] "In early 2022, sea crossings from southern Morocco and Western Sahara to the Canary Islands cost between €1900 and €2830, with sub-Saharan and foreign migrants" paying the most.[162] The problem, of course, is that—as with most illicit markets—there is no quality control and considerable opportunity for deception, with migrants often misinformed about "the number of motors, captains and people travelling on the boat."[163]

In 2023, the dynamics changed somewhat. Senegalese citizens—pushed by climate change, depleted fisheries, and large-scale unemployment—have been part of irregular migration since the early 2000s with a peak of over 31,000 migrants arriving in the Canary Islands in 2006. In 2023, however, political instability and associated violence in Senegal precipitated another massive surge of irregular migrants seeking security and better opportunities in Spain. According to UNHCR, as of November 5, 2023, just over 46,000 irregular migrants had arrived in Spain since the beginning of the year—with 32,047 arriving in the Canary Islands and just under 14,000 going through the Western Mediterranean route.[164] The vast majority of those going to the Canary Islands were from Senegal.

For those who survive the dangers and arrive intact in the Canary Islands, the situation is not great. Things have improved since 2020 when thousands of people were living in "makeshift tents on some stretches of tarmac" and the harbor of Arguineguín (Gran Canaria) was described as the 'dock of shame.'"[165] The Spanish government has subsequently built new emergency centers, but many locals remain hostile to the migrants and have even created vigilante groups.[166] Moreover, bickering between authorities in Madrid and those in the Canaries has complicated the management of the new arrivals. With so many different stakeholders and continuing climate change, the irregular migrant problem in the Canary Islands will only get worse, likely becoming a "wicked problem" that is resistant to solution.[167]

The Enclaves of Ceuta and Melilla

Another major route into Spain is through the Spanish enclaves of Ceuta and Melilla on the Moroccan coast. In 2020, relatively modest numbers were able to enter the two Spanish cities from Morocco. Between the end of September and December 27, "513 travelers had reached the enclaves (299 to Ceuta, 214 to Melilla), adding up to a total of 856 arrivals to Ceuta and 1,485 arrivals to Melilla in 2020."[168] In 2019, most travelers had reached Ceuta by land, but in 2020, the border crossings took place primarily by sea. The following year, this stream turned into a river that in May 2021 flooded its banks. In two days more than 8,000 people, many of them minors, swam from Morocco to Ceuta.[169]

This created twin crises—both a migratory crisis and a diplomatic crisis between Spain and Morocco. The root of the crisis, however, dated to 1975 when Western Sahara, under Spanish jurisdiction, was seized by Morocco after 300,000 Moroccans participated in what was called the Green March into the Western Sahara. The claim of sovereign territory by Morocco is challenged by the Sahrawi independence movement, the Polisario Front. In February 2021, Morocco had proposed to Spain that it would grant the Western Sahara autonomy under the sovereignty of the King of Morocco. This was seemingly overtaken by events when in April it was revealed that the leader of the Front was being treated for Covid-19 in a Spanish hospital—and that Morocco had not been formally informed.[170] In response, the Moroccan authorities not only allowed but also encouraged would-be migrants to move into Ceuta. Much of the Moroccan security presence was removed, and it became common knowledge in the migrant community that restrictions would be eased. As one commentary noted, "Morocco appears to have used unaccompanied minors to pile more pressure on Spanish prime minister Pedro Sanchez. The NGO Fundacion Raices says children as young as six from Moroccan villages surrounding the enclaves and teenagers from West African countries and as far away as Yemen were among those who crossed over."[171] In some ways, Morocco was playing a variant of the Turkey card, by using the possibility of uncontrolled migration to obtain concessions from a member of the European Union. In the case of Turkey, the prize was an increased aid package in return for continuing to host migrants and refugees from Syria and elsewhere. In the Moroccan case, however, it seems, initially at least, to have been retaliation for Spain supporting Morocco's enemy. Yet, it also acted as a warning to Spain that Morocco was willing and able to ease restrictions on irregular migration.

A month and a half after the "migratory" and diplomatic "crises" between Rabat and Madrid, Moroccan authorities reinforced security along the border with Ceuta. The Royal Gendarmerie installed new barbed wire along the coastal area near Tarajal beach, an area through which almost 12,000 migrants passed illegally on May 17 and 18.[172] In late July 2021, however, attention turned to the other enclave, Melilla, as over 300 migrants tried to climb over the border fence into the city, and 238 of them were successful.[173] A few days later, Moroccan authorities prevented another crossing into Melilla. In effect, Morocco had shown Spain what it could do by reducing border controls into the enclaves and what it could accomplish by reimposing more stringent security. Nevertheless, the enclaves again became the focus of attention in early March 2022. Against a background of migrants sheltering in poor weather conditions, migrants, many of them Sudanese, stormed the barriers into Melilla, with 500 getting through on March 2, and another 350, the following day.[174] On March 8, a thousand migrants tried to move into the city, but few succeeded.[175] It was against this background that, on March 18, Morocco announced that Spain had changed its position on the Western Sahara and was supporting Morocco's proposal of autonomy under sovereignty. Although there had been considerable commentary in Spain decrying Morocco's attempts at blackmail, Spain had made the necessary payoff. This was underlined on June 25 when 1,700 migrants tried to storm their way into Melilla. They were met with strong resistance from both Moroccan and Spanish border guards, and at least 37 people died—most of them trampled—and 73 are unaccounted for.[176] The June 2022 Melilla massacre, as it became known, was the antithesis of the events in May 2021 when 8,000 migrants were allowed to swim into Ceuta.

In many respects, this represents a harder line by the authorities in Rabat. Although Morocco, for some years, was regarded as being relatively progressive in its attitudes toward migrants, it is now colluding with the European Union's "Fortress Europe" approach and working closely with Madrid to restrict migrants traveling to Spain, whether their origin is Morocco or sub-Saharan Africa.

From Morocco to the Spanish Peninsula

Unlike departures to the Canary Islands, the sailing time to Spain from the north coast of Morocco is much shorter, especially with the use of speedboats. There have been numerous occasions where smugglers have used speedboats to carry mixed loads of migrants and drugs—a form of what Marina Mancuso and Francesca Maldi term crime convergence.[177] There also seem to have been elements of adaptation, diversification, and emulation as some of the smugglers began to use speedboats that had hitherto been employed for drug trafficking for migrant smuggling.[178] Spanish police "identified groups of African migrants arriving in the rubber inflatable boats, known as RIB or 'narcoboats,' which have previously been used to ship stashes of marijuana resin, or hash, from Morocco."[179] In March 2020, Spanish authorities arrested 89 people who had used eleven speed boats to carry "269 people and over 10,000 kilograms of hashish. The ring used radar systems and lookouts on the coast to avoid detection."[180] The smugglers also held the migrants in Spain "until their families paid 5,000 euros ($5,600)."[181] Another 39 suspects were under investigation.[182] In addition to the drugs, police confiscated "26 boats, 29 vehicles, 250,000 euros ($282,000) in cash and 12 firearms."[183] A feasible conclusion is that this reflects the diversification of cannabis smugglers and their involvement in human smuggling. Given the use of the same routes and the acquired skill in evading the authorities, this seems like a natural and logical progression.

Several crossing points have been identified as part of the Western Mediterranean route. Many migrants going into southern Spain disembark in Andalusia after crossing either the Strait of Gibraltar from Tangier or the Alboran Sea from the coast between Tangier and Nador. Typically, it is more expensive to embark from Nador (2,500 euros) than it is from Tangier (300 euros).[184] "To the west of the strait, south of Tangier, migrants depart from points between Salé and Larache and arrive in Cadiz province in southern Spain."[185] Most of the crossings occur with wooden or inflatable boats. "Migrants who depart from points between Tangier and Ceuta arrive between Tarifa and Algeciras in Spain. In this area, migrants depart from beaches such as Misrat or Kankouch and typically use inflatable boats or dinghies. There are also movements by jet ski in this area, as the distance to be traversed is quite small and can be done quickly with a jet ski."[186]

Some of the migrants use smugglers for the journey, but there has also been a trend toward self-organization or do-it-yourself smuggling. For these voyages, communities pool together their financial resources and their skills and expertise in what is truly a collective effort.[187] This was also evident in Algeria and Tunisia but typically involved a single nationality. This is not surprising since, as one study noted, "these journeys are assembled primarily by groups of friends known to each other, extended families or neighbors relying on the skill and knowledge of others in the group. It was not uncommon to find fishermen among the passengers, whose navigational knowledge and insight were critical for the journey."[188]

It is more difficult for migrants from sub-Saharan Africa to do this given that they must keep a low profile and around Nador they typically hide from the authorities in the forests.[189] Yet, occasionally they are able to organize some kind of crossing. One study also suggested that "a hybrid approach has emerged since 2017. This approach sees migrants choosing to arrange their own journeys, but then paying a smuggler for a particular contribution, such as paying bribes or dealing with authorities."[190]

It also appears that some of this smuggling from Morocco to Spain is controlled by a rudimentary hierarchy particularly within the existing migrant community. "Smugglers in Morocco, referred to as chairmen, tend to operate in small networks with few Moroccans visible at the top of the hierarchy. The chairmen are typically West African."[191] Moroccans provide logistic support, act as drivers, supply cars and dinghies, and deal with the police if they appear. They are also known as the "taxi-mafia" since they transport migrants in Oujda and in the forest in Nador.[192] Crossings seem to have doubled in price since 2017 and typically cost around 2,500 euros for a boat with an engine, although far less for rowboats.[193] According to one report, in early 2022 prices ranged from 944 euros to 1,900, but by June 2022 they were over 2,000 euros (with the cost of speedboats double that) during the summer months.[194]

The Western Mediterranean voyage is typically not as dangerous for the migrants as the Central Mediterranean route nor the route to the Canary Islands. The route across the strait, however, became a lot more restrictive initially because of Covid-19 and subsequently because of the rapprochement between Morocco and Spain and the agreement to work together in combating the smuggling. Indeed, "Moroccan authorities systematically clamped down on irregular migration, including tightening border controls along the country's coastline and forcibly moving foreign irregular migrants away from coastal cities and embarkation zones."[195] If the journey has become harder, however, one response has likely been bribery of officials; another has been changing the points of embarkation. And even with the restrictions in place, over 14,000 irregular migrants arrived on the Spanish Peninsula and the Balearic Islands between January 1, 2023, and November 12, 2023.[196] Together with the flow to the Canary Islands, this suggests that human smugglers are continuing to make substantial profits from the aspirations of migrants for a better life in Europe. So long as these aspirations remain, the business will continue to thrive.

Human Trafficking

The media in Europe often fail to distinguish between human smuggling and human trafficking, preferring to use the term *traffickers* to apply to all those involved in the people-moving business. While some of those involved in human smuggling are indeed extremely predatory and seek to exploit those being smuggled, others are simply in the transportation business. Human trafficking though invariably involves ruthless exploitation through deception, coercion, or a mix of both. In 2023, as in 2021, the US Department of State Trafficking in Persons (TIP) Report noted that Morocco has made serious, if still inadequate, efforts to counter human trafficking and remains on Tier 2 in this report.[197] In 2021, one of the biggest shortcomings was that Morocco did not differentiate clearly enough between trafficking and smuggling, with the result that it likely inflated its actions against trafficking by including human smugglers among those who were being prosecuted.[198] This also distorted countermeasures and how to respond. This was not the only area in which the Moroccan government failed to meet minimum standards. In 2020, "investigations, prosecutions, and convictions of trafficking cases decreased, with the government reporting it investigated 79 alleged trafficking cases involving 138 alleged traffickers and prosecuted 69 cases."[199] Partly this reflected the diversion of resources to enforce Covid-19 restrictions. Other shortcomings included a lack of international cooperation in this area as well as inadequacies in victim protection—although the government did identify "441 trafficking victims—including 426 Moroccans and 15 foreigners—and referred them to Ministry of Justice (MOJ) protection units and civil society organizations for assistance. Of the 441 identified victims, 245 were female, 196 male, 398 were adults, and 43 were children."[200]

The 2023 TIP Report, however, acknowledged Morocco's efforts to disaggregate trafficking and smuggling cases. It also highlighted stronger and more vigorous efforts against trafficking. Law 27.14 criminalized both sex and labor trafficking, with five to ten years of imprisonment for trafficking of adults and twenty to thirty years in cases involving children.[201] The government prosecuted 149 traffickers in 2022, and 101 traffickers were convicted—a big increase on the 54 convictions in 2021.[202] Only 22 of the convictions, however, came with sentences of over five years.[203] Significantly though, Morocco was involved in Interpol's Weka II Operation, which rescued nearly 700 victims of human trafficking and succeeded in arresting a thirty-four-year-old man who trafficked women from Nigeria via Morocco "to Spain and other European destinations, where they were forced into prostitution."[204]

If Morocco had stepped up its law enforcement activities, its prevention and protection policies remained partial and inadequate. Undocumented migrants primarily from sub-Saharan Africa remained vulnerable to sex trafficking and forced labor. The women were often "exploited sexually at the frontiers by Moroccan police and immigration authorities as payment to enter into Morocco."[205] This is not surprising: border guards can rape sub-Saharan women with impunity since irregular migrants have no legal status and no recourse to law enforcement.[206] This pattern of abuse is often continued within the country as sub-Saharan women migrants find themselves in sexual servitude or in a situation of forced labor acting as domestic servants with no protections. Some women and children in the migrant communities are also coerced into organized street begging networks.[207] Nigerian women in Morocco are likely to be particularly vulnerable given the longstanding practice of trafficking Nigerian women to Europe, particularly Italy, where they have gone on to work in the commercial sex trade. For its part, the Fondation Scelles, a French NGO working to fight prostitution, claimed that "powerful Nigerian, Cameroonian, and Malian criminal networks throughout Morocco . . . traffic women by forcing them into prostitution."[208] The 2023 TIP Report was less specific about the nationality of trafficking networks, but more specific about at least some of the locations in which they operated. The report identified Oujda on the Algerian border and northern coastal cities, such as Nador, as places where undocumented migrant women and even children were exploited for sex trafficking and forced begging.[209]

Perhaps the most critical problem in Morocco is that human trafficking, even of minors, is often not recognized as such even though it has a long history. A 2021 article exploring the problem observed that the Moroccan Health Ministry had noted in 2008 that 36 percent of domestic workers were children.[210] Some of them escape domestic servitude only to find themselves even more vulnerable. As the study noted, "it is in this moment, in which these Moroccan minors lack protection and are invisible to the system, that they are recruited by trafficking networks for the purpose of sexual exploitation in Morocco, Spain or even other countries" including the Gulf states.[211] Those who find themselves single mothers are particularly vulnerable to being trafficked.[212] Although there is a lack of data, it seems clear that the study has identified a serious, if largely invisible problem—and that much more needs to be done in terms of research, raising awareness, and policy initiatives. Based on interviews with officials and NGOS, the most striking feature of the research was the lack of visibility and lack of understanding of the problem. It was only during the interviews that the respondents recognized that those particular cases might involve not only prostitution but also human trafficking and sexual exploitation.[213] The initial focus was on *petites bonnes*, or young housemaids, typically girls from eight to fifteen who come from poor and rural areas and are often "sold, forced, coerced or deceived into domestic work by richer families at private houses, which are usually located in larger cities. These girls . . . are exposed to significant discrimination; isolation; malnutrition; contempt; verbal, physical, emotional, and sexual abuse; sexual harassment and other violations of children's rights with devastating health consequences."[214] Most of them had come from rural areas, and 30 percent of them had never attended school while 49 percent had dropped out.[215] In many cases they had been sold by their families and were often forced to work up to twelve or even sixteen hours a day.[216]

Nor are the problems of abuse confined to girls. The renowned network of civil society organizations, End Child Prostitution in Asian Tourism (ECPAT International), issued a study in November 2022 that highlighted the problem of sexual abuse of boys in Morocco.[217] Noting that sex abuse occurred across genders, the study also emphasized that "boys are exploited in trafficking for sexual purposes and prostitution, particularly in the context of travel and tourism."[218] In this connection, it is worth noting that the Fondation Scelles has claimed that "sex tourism is a prosperous industry in Morocco" but one that the government, concerned about reputation, refuses to recognize.[219] Such allegations have been strengthened by an Israeli press report that since the normalization of Israel's relations with Rabat, there has been an upsurge of Israeli citizens engaged in sex tourism to Morocco. The epicenter for this seems to be Marrakesh, but other Moroccan tourist cities have witnessed the same phenomenon, albeit on a smaller scale.[220] The dilemma for the government is that sex tourism has become a major driver of revenue at the very time that the government is seeking to develop and implement strategies to combat human trafficking.

For all its shortcomings, the Moroccan government has moved significantly to develop more effective and encompassing policies to combat human trafficking, including the use of a hotline for tips from the public. It has also developed a 2023–2030 national strategy to combat human trafficking as well as an accompanying 2023–2026 implementation plan. Increased resources, a concerted effort to overcome blind spots in relation to child trafficking and abuse, enhanced protection for victims, and—most fundamentally—an acknowledgment of the scale and scope of the problem are all essential if the Moroccan government is to combat human trafficking successfully. For all the hurdles, the promise is still there. Indeed, despite its shortcomings in combating human trafficking, Morocco could well be doing better than other countries in North Africa. This irony is perhaps best captured by Naima Benlarabi, whose highly compelling analysis of sub-Saharan women in Morocco includes unforgettable accounts of the harrowing experiences of individual women.[221] Despite this, Benlarabi concludes that "migrants, who are stuck in Morocco because of the European border tightening, consider Morocco a comfortable stopped destination based on its peaceful nature and its warm cultural virtue of accommodating foreigners. . . . Morocco is the most receptive and accommodating Arab country, which is why most of the migrants who are stuck at the frontier take refuge or seek asylum in Morocco."[222]

Arms Trafficking

In considering arms trafficking, an abundance of caution is required. As Rahma Ouled Cherif acknowledged, the "figures can only represent a fraction of the actual arms that are trafficked because trafficking is multidimensional. Firearms are manufactured and traded both legally and illicitly, making the tracing of illegally trafficked firearms complex."[223] Even bearing this in mind, it appears likely that Morocco was spared from the massive flows of weapons originating from Libya during the 2011 to 2013 period that followed Gaddafi's ouster. Part of the reason for this was that Algeria and, to a lesser extent, Tunisia, served as important buffers. As the country furthest away from Libya, it was only natural that Morocco was impacted less than Libya's immediate neighbors. The steps that Algeria and Morocco have taken to strengthen their common border has also had a beneficial impact for Morocco.

At the same time, there are several reasons that Morocco should not be overly sanguine about the situation. First, there have been claims by reputable sources that drug traffickers are much better armed than in the past.[224] Second, reports in January 2017 revealed that Morocco's Central Bureau of Judicial Investigation (BCIJ) had not only dismantled a terrorist cell in El Jadida, about 100 kilometers south of Casablanca, but also had confiscated "several weapons" that had been "smuggled into Morocco from Libya via Algeria."[225] This seems largely consistent with a Flemish Peace Institute study, which concluded that "violence and gun smuggling in Morocco are mostly connected to Polisario or ISIS."[226] Indeed, the Polisario Front has "enough weapons of its own to be able to sell some and to supply the regional market."[227] Third, and perhaps most significant, the Stockholm International Peace Research Institute (SIPRI), in a report published in March 2019, noted that in terms of weapons trafficking, Morocco ranked sixth in the Middle East and North Africa (MENA) region and seventeenth in the world for the period 2009–2018.[228] Reportedly, "Morocco received 485 trafficked guns in 2017 and 387 in 2018, representing 15% of the guns trafficked into the MENA region in the two years."[229] Fourth, the Norwegian Initiative on Small Arms Transfers observed that in 2019 Morocco had imported 2,702 sporting and hunting shotguns worth US$1,289,403, 157 sporting rifles worth over US$97,000, and 752 pistols and revolvers worth US$393,948.[230] It is worth emphasizing that these were not trafficked into Morocco but represent arms that were legitimately purchased and transferred. There is always the possibility, however, that some of these will be diverted or stolen and end up on the arms black market.

In sum, arms trafficking is not a major problem in Morocco, but neither is it something that can be dismissed. There is also a possibility that as Algeria and Morocco ratchet up their arms race, they will acquire not only more heavy weapons, but also more small arms and light weapons that can be stolen or diverted.

Cigarette Smuggling

In terms of both arms trafficking and cigarette smuggling there is a sense that Morocco is slightly sheltered and that neither phenomenon is as pervasive as in other North African countries. While there is something to this argument, the patterns in cigarette smuggling are not that different from elsewhere in the region. As with the rest of North Africa, the problem stems in part from the Jebel Ali Free Trade Zone in the United Arab Emirates, where there are large cigarette production facilities.[231] Some of the cigarettes produced there are moved to the Nouadhibou Free Trade Zone in Mauritania from where they are moved through Dakhla in Western Sahara and Tan-Tan in Morocco.[232] From a Moroccan perspective, however, the heavyweight producer is Mauritania and, according to a Transcrime report, "approximately 1 billion illicit cigarettes produced in Mauritania were smoked in Morocco in 2017."[233] The report also estimated that one-third of these came through Western Sahara, while the other two-thirds were transshipped through Algeria and into Morocco.[234]

Despite the closed border, the tensions between the two countries, and the reinforced border controls, cigarette flows from Algeria into Morocco remain steady, with estimates suggesting that "cigarette illicit flows from Algeria to Morocco decreased by only about 4% between 2008–2012 (average of the five years) and 2017 (from 1.64 billion to 1.57 billion)."[235] A possible explanation is that the Algerian-Moroccan frontier includes rugged terrain such as mountains and deserts that are difficult to control.[236] Another possible reason is that interdiction efforts are much less stringent when it comes to cigarette smuggling than with more harmful commodities such as drugs and weapons. A third factor is corruption of customs agents. Although Morocco has fewer cigarettes coming into the country, the total illicit outflows have increased from about 1 billion per year in the earlier period of 2008–2012 to 1.6 billion in 2017.[237] As with other illicit products, proximity to Spain is a major advantage for Moroccan traffickers. In Morocco itself, illicit cigarettes account for only 13 percent of the total consumption of cigarettes; 41 percent of these are contraband cigarettes that have been smuggled in to evade taxes, while 45 percent are what are known as "illicit whites" that are legally produced for smuggling into foreign markets.[238]

Environmental Crime and Resource Extraction in Morocco

Morocco does not have a great deal of environmental crime, with rather modest fauna and flora smuggling. There is some smuggling of the goldfinch and the barbary macaque, but this too appears to be limited.[239] Illegal logging of cedar trees in Morocco's Atlas Mountains, in contrast, is a serious challenge.[240] The most far-reaching natural resource exploitation in Morocco though—and one that gets very little attention—is sand extraction. This is not unique to Morocco. Mozambique and Sierra Leone face similar challenges, while illicit sand mining has also become widespread in the Caribbean, in India, and in Indonesia.[241] In Morocco, however, illegal sand extraction is a major problem. As a major component of concrete, sand is critical to the construction industry, whether for roads and other infrastructure or for houses and hotels.[242] An estimated 30 million tonnes of sand is extracted every year in Morocco, and it is believed that half of this is illegally extracted, either by regulated construction companies that breach regulations governing locations and amounts, or by criminal groups.[243] According to one assessment, "the illegal sand extraction business is run by a syndicate second in size only to Morocco's drug mafia. The latter are also believed to be involved in sand trafficking, especially in the northern Rif region where hashish is grown."[244] There is also an important transnational dimension, that once again emphasizes the connections between North Africa and southern Europe, in this case, between Morocco and Spain. Spanish construction companies, particularly those in the south, use Moroccan sand when building new hotels and restaurants.[245] According to one estimate, about a billion dollars' worth of sand is shipped out of Morocco each year, with Spain as the primary destination.[246] In addition, companies in "the Spanish enclave of Melilla . . . use sand illegally extracted from the nearby Moroccan province of Nador," under the auspices of politicians and government officials.[247] Official complicity and corruption provide a high degree of impunity for those involved. Perhaps not surprisingly, it has been estimated that Morocco mines a larger volume of beach and coastal dune sands than any other country in Africa.[248]

Ironically, a 2017 decree intended to regulate and limit sand extraction has had unexpected consequences that have exacerbated rather than alleviated the problem. By covering only registered companies and quantities of extraction, it created incentives "for unregistered sand businesses to either extract sand from zones that registered companies cannot exploit, or to accept 'sub-contracts' from the same registered companies."[249] In other words, ostensibly licit companies engage in illicit activities, while criminal groups engage in ostensible licit activities. Moreover, it seems likely that there is collusion between these companies and the National Ports Agency.[250] The irony in all this is that sand extraction is designed to enhance the short-term viability of the infrastructure for the tourism industry, but in the long term will make the Moroccan coast far less attractive to tourists as sandy beaches are transformed into bedrock and moonscapes.

Corruption, Money Laundering, and Illicit Financial Flows

Most notions of illicit financial flows have two key components: financial transfers across national borders and a linkage to illegal or criminal activity. In this connection, organized crime scholar Peter Reuter identified five major sources for illicit financial flows: bribery and corruption, tax evasion, the proceeds of crime, corporate profit shifting, and currency regulation evasion.[251] It could be argued that there is a sixth dimension, although it can subsume some of these others and be subsumed by them—and that is capital flight.

In terms of corruption, Morocco does not score as well as it needs to, but it does not score as badly as might be expected. In the 2022 Corruption Perception Index it ranks 94 out of 180 states and has a score of 34 out of 100.[252] This is readily explicable. The strong centralized authority of the king and his top officials, and the lack of both transparency and accountability accords closely with Robert Klitgaard's well-known formulation that corruption results from monopoly plus discretion minus accountability.[253] Moreover, a WikiLeaks cable from a US official that was among a trove of material released in 2010 highlighted "the influence and commercial interest of the king and some of his advisers in virtually every major real estate project."[254] Another US official noted "the appalling greed of those close to King Mohammed VI" and claimed that this undermined "the good governance that the Moroccan government is working hard to promote."[255] In some respects, though, there was little that was new. Although it was a sensitive topic, the monarchy was already known for its wealth, for its involvement in business, and for its far-reaching political and economic influence. Partly because of this, the leaks did not seriously dent the prestige and legitimacy of the king.

More recent developments included details about the king's sister in the Pandora Papers. The leaks revealed Princess Lalla Hasnaa's ownership of a shell company in the British Virgin Islands, and that she had used it to buy a home in Britain worth US$11 million. The funds were listed as belonging to the royal family.[256] The Covid-19 pandemic also led to allegations of favoritism and cronyism as contracts were awarded with little oversight or transparency. Despite this, the king provided visible and decisive leadership, and according to a survey by the Moroccan Institute for Policy Analyses, 77 percent of those polled were satisfied with the steps taken by the government to counter the spread of the virus.[257]

Although allegations of corruption have had limited impact, another scandal broke in December 2022 centered around Pier Antonio Parenzi, an Italian former member of the European Parliament. Parenzi had reportedly taken money and gifts from both Qatar and Morocco (the latter through the Moroccan ambassador in Poland) and in return had promoted positive images of both countries.[258] This was important for Morocco because the European Union had typically been critical of Rabat's position on the Western Sahara. More members of the European Parliament have been caught up in the Belgian investigation, however, and in January 2023, the European Parliament overwhelmingly passed a resolution urging "the Moroccan authorities to respect freedom of expression and media freedom."[259] This was clearly a shot across the bow, and although the Moroccan government has pushed back, it clearly needs to take stronger measures against corruption, including vigorously implementing the National Anti-Corruption Strategy that was approved in December 2015 but has been largely dormant.

Although capital flight is often linked to high-level political and bureaucratic corruption, it can also stem from corporate activities, either because of corporate malfeasance or because the country environment is inhospitable. In terms of highlighting the problems of capital flight from Africa, Global Financial Integrity, a Washington-based think tank founded by Raymond Baker, has been exemplary. For Morocco, capital flight has been linked to the electrical machinery and equipment sector and to the apparel market.[260] One assessment suggested that over a ten-year period, Morocco had lost an estimated US$88 billion in capital flight.[261] A more recent UN Conference on Trade and Development report published in 2020 estimated illicit financial flows out of Morocco in 2013–2014 as US$16.6 billion, a figure that is highly consistent with the earlier losses.[262]

Of more immediate concern is that Moroccan criminal enterprises—especially those involving cannabis production and trafficking, and human smuggling—generate such a large stream of criminal proceeds that the money must be laundered to ensure that it appears to have come from legitimate sources and not the proceeds of crime. There are myriad ways this can be achieved, including the movement of bulk cash, the use of front companies that can move money through the formal financial system without necessarily arousing suspicion, hawalas and other informal value transfer systems, and trade-based money laundering—something that has emerged as particularly prominent because of the increased scrutiny of banks and other financial institutions. According to the 2021 INCSR, published by the US Department of State, Morocco is vulnerable to money laundering as a result of "the prevalence of cash-based transactions, geographic location, established trafficking networks, a high volume of remittances, and public corruption. Morocco serves as an integration point into the legitimate economy for illicit drug money, with an estimated hundreds of millions of dollars laundered through Morocco annually."[263] Much of this was reiterated in the 2023 INCSR, although the estimate of the cash-based economy was reduced significantly from 20 to 30 percent of GDP to 11 percent.[264] The 2023 INCSR noted that money transfer services continued to present a vulnerability due to their volume.[265] Most remittances simply come from Moroccans in Europe sending money back to their families; the fact that Europe is also the major market for Moroccan cannabis inevitably raises red flags.

Nevertheless, it is hard to find cases of money laundering linked to Morocco apart from the charges the government has made against Maati Monjib, a professor, journalist, and human rights activist, after an investigation that began in October 2020.[266] The charges have been vigorously denounced by human right advocates, including Amnesty International. There are, however, two money laundering cases, both involving Moroccans, that give at least some glimpses into a significant challenge for the government of Morocco as well as those of Spain and France.

The first case, which occurred in May 2013 when Spanish police dismantled a network of Moroccan and Chinese, was quite sophisticated and provided an example of trade-based money laundering. According to a contemporary report, "the network sold hashish that was smuggled from Morocco to Spain, distributing it to Britain, France, and other countries, and laundered the money via wholesale purchases of clothes and jewelry. The police said they seized 21 million items of clothing worth more than 100 million euros ($131 million) as well as luxury cars and jewels and watches worth four million euros."[267] The group was reportedly laundering half a million euros each week and specialized in integrating criminal proceeds into the legal economy through commercial transactions of clothing, jewels and other designer goods.[268] The money launderers worked out of "the industrial estate of Cobo Calleja, considered the biggest Chinese wholesale hub in Europe."[269]

The second case began in 2018 when investigators in Lyon, France, which somewhat ironically also happens to be the home of Interpol, "discovered a structured criminal network involved in an important collection of cash generated by narcotic dealers known to law enforcement."[270] The proceeds of drug trafficking were collected in various locations in France and Spain and then—in a textbook example of bulk cash smuggling—"dirty money was transported across borders from France to Morocco and via Spain by concealing it in transportation trucks and vehicles. Overall investigators seized EUR 2.5 million in cash, three apartments, three trucks, six vehicles and several bank accounts, 37kg of cannabis and 5kg of cocaine, and two shotguns and one automatic pistol."[271] The network, which was dismantled in 2019, was believed to have been laundering approximately 90 million euros a year.[272] Eighteen people were arrested, and the cash and other assets seized were valued at approximately 4 million euros.[273]

This paucity of data is not entirely surprising as there were only eight convictions for money laundering in Morocco from 2008 to 2018.[274] During the last several years, however, Morocco has devoted more attention and resources to combating money laundering. This resulted in thirty criminal cases in 2019 and 193 in 2020, although during the two years only sixty-two convictions were obtained.[275] By September 2021 an additional thirteen convictions had been obtained. The difficulty, according to the US assessment, is that "these cases involve relatively simple money laundering, integrating drug proceeds into buildings and businesses, and do not include more complex cases involving professional money launderers or organized crime; officials claim complex money laundering and organized crime do not exist in Morocco."[276] While this is wishful thinking, it is worth considering that most of the profits in the cannabis trade accrue after the drugs have been exported from Morocco. Even so, to dismiss the possibility of sophisticated money laundering occurring in Morocco is a mistake. It also helps to explain why Morocco's record in combating money laundering and terrorist finance is checkered and inconsistent.

In February 2021, Morocco was placed on the Financial Action Task Force's (FATF's) gray list of countries that had deficiencies in their efforts to prevent money laundering and counter terrorism financing. This was not the first time Morocco had fallen afoul of the FATF. The organization identified critical deficiencies in Morocco's policies and strategies in 2010 and it was not until 2013 that the country was removed from the compliance monitoring process.[277] In 2019 it was assessed again, and although there were high levels of compliance in meeting many FATF requirements, there were gaps and deficiencies in some areas. It was claimed that Morocco did not fully understand money laundering risks, lacked a comprehensive framework for cooperation and coordination, and needed stronger investigative capabilities to link money laundering more closely to predicate crimes. In addition, the government needed to strengthen the effort to counter terrorist finances and establish a legal basis to combat proliferation finance.[278]

As a result, Morocco, to the chagrin of the government, was placed in the same category as Syria, Yemen, and Pakistan.[279] This was partly a reflection of frustration with the slow pace of anti-money-laundering legislation, which had been stalled in the Parliament of Morocco, and was perhaps reinforced by a rather critical report from Transparency International.[280] The response was mixed. *Morocco World News* wrote a scathing critique of both FATF and Transparency International suggesting that "the FATF's designation of Morocco is based on a minimal noncompliant rating, making the whole thing counterproductive or needlessly punitive at best, and highly politicized or ill-intentioned at worst."[281] Parliament, however, finally adopted new measures in May 2021.[282] In July, an FATF plenary meeting noted that "Morocco should continue to implement its action plan to address its strategic deficiencies."[283] By February 2023, Morocco had clearly done this and the FATF removed the country from the gray list.

Conclusion

This list of criminal activities and illicit markets is not complete. It is believed, for example, that Morocco's port of Tangier is a conduit for stolen cars from Europe. "They are usually smuggled on passenger ships and on cargo ships and then driven to West and Central African countries where they are introduced into the licit market."[284] Yet this is simply using Morocco as a convenient transshipment country, and although it likely involves operational corruption at ports and border crossing, it is relatively minor in relation to the drug business. In this connection, although Morocco's cannabis industry appears to be thriving, this could change. Not only has Spain become a major producer of marijuana and therefore, a competitor to Morocco, but this competition, ironically might become more intense as some European states and Morocco move—albeit tentatively and hesitantly—toward decriminalization and even in some instances legalization. Morocco will also take time to recover fully from Covid-19. Yet in some ways, it appears to be the most stable—or perhaps more accurately, least unstable—country in North Africa. There are political problems to be sure, and real democracy remains a chimera, but Morocco's citizens do not seem to share the deep ennui and despair that is so pervasive in Tunisia and Algeria—at least not to the same extent. The increasing question marks and concerns about the king, however, suggest that storm clouds could be on the horizon.

Notes

1. BBC News, "Islamist PJD Party Wins"; Bertelsmann Transformation Index (BTI), *BTI 2020 Country Report: Morocco*, p. 3.
2. Badran, "Demobilising the February 20 Movement."
3. Ibid.
4. Molina, "Monarchy vs. the 20 February Movement," p. 436.
5. Ibid.
6. Bertelsmann Transformation Index (BTI), *BTI 2020 Country Report: Morocco*, p. 5.
7. Ibid., p. 7.
8. Ibid.
9. Ibid., p. 11.

10. Bertelsmann Transformation Index (BTI), *BTI 2022 Country Report: Morocco*, p. 15.
11. See Hamamouchi, "Morocco: Brewing Crisis of Governance."
12. Erlanger, "Morocco's Elusive King in Spotlight." See also Pelham, "Mystery of Morocco's Missing King."
13. Hamamouchi, "Morocco: Brewing Crisis of Governance."
14. Bertelsmann Transformation Index (BTI), *BTI 2020 Country Report: Morocco*, p. 3.
15. Ibid., p. 3.
16. Ibid., p. 16.
17. Abouzzohour, "Coping with COVID-19's Cost."
18. Hamamouchi, "Morocco: Brewing Crisis of Governance."
19. Ibid.
20. ENACT, *Organized Crime Index 2019—Morocco*, p. 1.
21. Global Initiative Against Transnational Organized Crime, *Africa Organized Crime Index 2021—Morocco*, p. 1.
22. *Global Organized Crime Index 2023—Morocco*, p. 1. https://ocindex.net/assets/downloads/2023/english/ocindex_profile_morocco_2023.pdf.
23. Ibid., p. 3.
24. Ibid.
25. ENACT, *Organized Crime Index 2019—Morocco*, p. 3.
26. Global Organized Crime Index, *Morocco 2023*, p. 4.
27. ENACT, *Organized Crime Index 2019—Morocco*, p. 4.
28. Herbert and Gallien, *A Rising Tide*, p. 5.
29. Ibid., p. 5.
30. Ibid., p. 6.
31. Blickman, *Morocco and Cannabis: Reduction, Containment*, pp. 2 and 6.
32. Chouvy, *Supply of Hashish to Europe*, p. 6.
33. Ibid., p. 7.
34. Ibid., p. 9.
35. Middle East Online, "Foreign Cannabis."
36. Ibid.
37. Herbert and Gallien, *A Rising Tide*, p. 6.
38. Ibid.
39. Ibid.
40. Ibid., p. 7.
41. Ibid.
42. Ibid.
43. Ibid., p. 8.
44. Gamella and Rodrigo, "Multinational Export-Import Ventures," p. 272.
45. Ibid.
46. Ibid., p. 275.
47. Ibid.
48. Ibid., p. 276.
49. Ibid.
50. Ibid.
51. Ibid.
52. Ibid.
53. Ibid., p. 278.
54. Ibid., p. 281.
55. Ibid., p. 286.

56. Herbert and Gallien, *A Rising Tide*, p. 12.
57. Ibid.
58. Ibid.
59. Ibid.
60. Summers, "You Dopes!"
61. *China Daily*, "Spain Seizes Over 900 Kilos."
62. *Gibraltar Chronicle*, "Police and Customs Fish 2.4 Tonnes."
63. Gulraj, "Cannabis Bales Worth £14m."
64. *Morocco World News*, "Police in Fez Seize 1.675 Tons of Cannabis Resin."
65. Kasraoui, "Morocco's BCIJ Seizes 7 Tons."
66. Adimoha. "Moroccan Police Seize 27.3 Tonnes."
67. Kasraoui, "12 Tons of Cannabis Resin Seized."
68. Government of France, "Two Operations Against Drug Trafficking."
69. Web24.news, "Gibraltar Detains a Spanish and a Portuguese."
70. Ibid.
71. BBC News, "Spain Drug Bust."
72. Ibid.
73. Reynolds, "Over 20 Tonnes of Cannabis Resin."
74. Ibid.
75. AfricaNews, "Record Seizure of Over 31 Tonnes."
76. Zouiten, "Police Abort."
77. Al Arabiya News, "Morocco Police Seizes 5.4 Tonnes."
78. Kasraoui, "DGSN Annual Report."
79. AfricaNews, "Record Seizure of Over 31 Tonnes."
80. Kasraoui, "Moroccan Police Seize 3 Tonnes."
81. Mahyou, "'Outlaws': Morocco's Rif."
82. Collas, "Morocco: Two Years After."
83. Morris, Guerard, and Perez Mas, "Strait of Gibraltar: A Gateway."
84. Ibid.
85. Ibid.
86. *Maritime Herald*, "New Drug Route from Morocco."
87. Ibid.
88. Herbert and Gallien, *A Rising Tide*, p. 16.
89. Ibid.
90. Delia, "Just Four EU Countries."
91. Vella, "Customs' Drug Bust."
92. Malta National Focal Point for Drugs and Drug Addiction, *National Report on the Drug Situation*, p. 11.
93. Interpol and ENACT, *Illicit Goods Trafficking*," p. 36.
94. Ibid., p. 18.
95. UNODC, *Global Report on Cocaine 2023*, p. 115.
96. Herbert and Gallien, *A Rising Tide*, p. 17.
97. Ibid., p. 18.
98. Ibid.
99. Ibid.
100. UNODC, *Global Report on Cocaine 2023*, p. 111.
101. Loudis, "Cartel, the Journalist and the Gangland Killings."
102. The only comprehensive account in English, and one that relies almost exclusively on a wide range of Dutch sources, is the Wikipedia entry "Moroccan Mafia" at https://en.wikipedia.org/wiki/Moroccan_mafia.
103. Gormezano, "Dutch PM Under."

104. Preussen, "Record Amount of Cocaine Seized."
105. Woody, "Spanish and Moroccan Police."
106. Ibid.
107. Ibid.
108. Ibid.
109. Agencia EFE, "Spaniards Arrested."
110. Ibid.
111. Ibid.
112. Ibid.
113. Herbert and Gallien, *A Rising Tide*, p. 18.
114. Kisambe, "Morocco: Massive Cocaine Smuggling."
115. Ibid.
116. *North Africa Post*, "Morocco's Police Seize Over 4.8 Tons."
117. Ibid.
118. Reuters, "Morocco Seizes 1.37 Tons of Cocaine."
119. Simpara, "Morocco Seizes Nearly 363 Kilograms."
120. Amezian, "Morocco's Civil Society."
121. Herbert and Gallien, *A Rising Tide*, p. 18.
122. Ganot, "Morocco Intercepts Over 1.4 Tons."
123. Herbert and Gallien, *A Rising Tide*, p. 18.
124. Sanchez, "Spanish Police Seize Large Drone."
125. Ibid.
126. Ibid.
127. Tyson, "Spanish Police Uncover Submarine."
128. Herbert and Gallien, *A Rising Tide*, p. 18.
129. US Department of State, *International Narcotics Control Strategy Report*, Volume 1 (March 2021), p. 184.
130. Ibid.
131. US Department of State, *International Narcotics Control Strategy Report*, Volume 1 (March 2022), p. 171.
132. Interpol and ENACT, *Overview of Serious and Organized Crime*, p. 13.
133. Ibid., pp. 13–14.
134. Ibid., p. 14.
135. Hekking, "From Fuel to Amphetamines."
136. Aublanc, "Moroccan Political and Business Leaders."
137. Ibid.
138. Ibid.
139. For a fuller discussion of El Hadj Ahmed ben Ibrahim, see Kasraoui, "Tale of the Desert Escobar Case."
140. Aublanc, "Moroccan Political and Business Leaders."
141. Monzini, *Smuggling of Migrants*, pp. 9 and 15.
142. Ibid., p. 5.
143. Malakooti and Fall, *Migration Trends Across Mediterranean*, pp. 30–31.
144. Ibid., p. 31.
145. Ibid., p. 33.
146. Ibid.
147. Ibid.
148. Ibid., p. 34.
149. Ibid.
150. Alarm Phone, "Shocking Number of Deaths."
151. Ibid.

152. Ibid.
153. Ibid.
154. News Desk, "NGO Report Claims."
155. Alarm Phone, "Shocking Number of Deaths."
156. De Lugo, *North-West Passage*, p. 7.
157. Ibid., p. 12.
158. Ibid.
159. Ibid.
160. Ibid.
161. Ibid., p. 13.
162. Ibid.
163. Ibid., p. 15.
164. UNHCR Operational Data Portal, Spain, https://data.unhcr.org/en/country/esp.
165. Alarm Phone, "Shocking Number of Deaths."
166. Martin and Perez, "Tensions Rising in Canary Islands."
167. Alarm Phone, "Shocking Number of Deaths."
168. Ibid.
169. Ritter, "Explainer: Spain's Migrant Crisis."
170. Al Jazeera, "Morocco Scolds Spain."
171. Devereux, "Trouble in Spanish Africa."
172. Kozlowski, "Spain Plans to End Crisis."
173. Reuters, "Over 200 Migrants Scale Fence."
174. Reuters, "Hundreds of Migrants Scale Fence."
175. Euro News with AP, "Hundreds of Migrants Attempt in Vain."
176. Bremner, "The Melilla Massacre."
177. Mancuso and Maldi, "Does Human Smuggling Converge?"
178. Associated Press, "Spain to Ban Speedboats."
179. Ibid.
180. Associated Press, "Spain Arrests 89 for Speedboat Smuggling."
181. Ibid.
182. Ibid.
183. Ibid.
184. Malakooti and Fall, *Migration Trends Across Mediterranean*, p. 43.
185. Ibid., p. 45.
186. Ibid.
187. Sanchez et al., *Beyond Networks, Militias and Tribes*, p. 82.
188. Ibid.
189. Malakooti and Fall, *Migration Trends Across Mediterranean*, p. 46.
190. Ibid., p. 48.
191. Ibid.
192. Ibid.
193. Ibid., p. 49.
194. Abderrahim, *Morocco: Irregular Migration Ebbs*, p. 15.
195. Ibid., p. 3.
196. UNHCR, "Operational Data Portal, Spain."
197. US Department of State, "2021 Trafficking in Persons Report: Morocco."
198. Ibid., p. 1.
199. Ibid.
200. Ibid., p. 3.
201. US Department of State, "Trafficking in Persons Report 2023: Morocco."
202. Ibid.

203. Ibid.
204. Ibid. and Interpol, "Operation Weka II."
205. Benlarabi, "Human Trafficking in African Women," p. 176.
206. Ibid.
207. For a fuller discussion see ibid.
208. Fondation Scelles, "Morocco," p. 5.
209. US Department of State, "Trafficking in Persons Report 2023: Morocco."
210. Melgar et al., "'Petites Bonnes' Minors," p. 3.
211. Ibid., p. 5.
212. Ibid.
213. Ibid., p. 4.
214. Ibid., p. 3.
215. Ibid.
216. Ibid.
217. ECPAT International and Amane, *Sexual Exploitation of Boys*.
218. Ibid., p. 5.
219. Fondation Scelles, "Morocco," p. 3.
220. Kutub, "What Happens in Morocco."
221. Benlarabi, "Human Trafficking in African Women."
222. Ibid., p. 196.
223. Cherif, "SIPRI: Morocco."
224. Herbert and Gallien, *A Rising Tide*, p. 13.
225. Interpol and ENACT, "*Overview of Serious and Organized Crime*, p. 17.
226. Cherif, "SIPRI: Morocco."
227. Strazzari and Zampagni, "Illicit Firearms Circulation," p. 451.
228. Cherif, "SIPRI: Morocco."
229. Ibid.
230. NISAT, "Researcher's Database: Imports to Morocco."
231. Meneghini and Milani, "Maghreb Route," p. 12.
232. Ibid.
233. Ibid.
234. Ibid.
235. Ibid., p. 15.
236. Ibid.
237. Ibid., p. 25.
238. Ibid., p. 16.
239. Global Organized Crime Index—*Morocco 2023*.
240. Ibid.
241. For further details see Pilkey et al., *Vanishing Sands*.
242. Abderrahmane, "Illegal Sand Extraction."
243. Ibid.
244. Ibid.
245. Ibid.
246. Pilkey et al., *Vanishing Sands*, p. 169.
247. Abderrahmane, "Illegal Sand Extraction."
248. Pilkey et al., *Vanishing Sands*, p. 171.
249. Abderrahmane, "Illegal Sand Extraction."
250. Pilkey et al., *Vanishing Sands*, p. 173.
251. Quoted in Price, "Illicit Financial Flows," p. 4.
252. Transparency International, "Our Work in Morocco," 2022, https://www.transparency.org/en/countries/morocco.

253. See, for example, Klitgaard, "International Cooperation Against Corruption."
254. Black, "WikiLeaks Cables Accuse Moroccan Royals."
255. Ibid.
256. Middle East Eye, "Pandora Papers."
257. Masbah and Aourraz, *COVID-19: How Moroccans View*, p. 19.
258. For a good overview see Bencharif, "EU Parliament Scandal."
259. Bobin and Jacqué, "In the European Parliament."
260. Price, "Illicit Financial Flows," p. 7.
261. Ibid., p. 9.
262. UNCTAD, *Tackling Illicit Financial Flows*, p. 46.
263. US Department of State, *International Narcotics Control Strategy Report*, Volume 2 (March 2021), p. 138.
264. Ibid., p. 138. See also US Department of State, *International Narcotics Control Strategy Report*, Volume 2 (March 2023), p. 138.
265. Ibid., p. 139.
266. AfricaNews, "Moroccan Opponent Maati Monjib."
267. Dunya News, "Spain Busts Money Laundering."
268. Ibid.
269. Ibid.
270. The Paypers, "EUR 4 Million Seized."
271. Ibid.
272. Ibid.
273. Ibid.
274. US Department of State, *International Narcotics Control Strategy Report*, Volume 2 (March 2021), p. 140.
275. Ibid.
276. Ibid.
277. See KnowYourCountry, "Morocco: Risk & Compliance Report."
278. MENAFATF, *Kingdom of Morocco Mutual Evaluation Report*.
279. Hamann, "Morocco Accused."
280. Transparency International, "Morocco: Glaring Gaps Revealed."
281. Hamann, "Morocco Accused."
282. Agence de Presse Africaine, "Moroccan Parliament."
283. Babchinetskaya, "FATF Concludes Fourth Plenary."
284. Interpol and ENACT, *Illicit Goods Trafficking*," p. 36.

3

Algeria: The Rentier State and Illicit Economies

ALGERIA TODAY IS A POSTCONFLICT STATE THAT HAS BEEN UNDERGOING A belated and minimalist version of the Arab Spring but that also is faced with some serious challenges from both an antiquated state-run economy and a variety of illicit economies. Military forces continue to play an outsized role in politics and the state has not fully come to terms with its past. From 1991 to 2002, Algeria was torn apart by a bloody civil war characterized by mass slaughters and horrific acts of mutilation. The conflict, which came after a period of liberalization, was precipitated by the government canceling elections to prevent the Islamic Salvation Front (FIS), the likely winner, from taking power.[1] The civil war featured displays of anomic violence that went far beyond the bounds of normal conflict: massacres and mutilations occurred with remarkable frequency. As Jacob Mundy noted, "the primary tools of war" became "terror, mass atrocities, ethnic cleansing, and genocide."[2] Since the civil war, however, and perhaps as a direct result of its horrors, Algeria has maintained a high degree of stability—most notably during the Arab Spring.[3] Because of the extremely tumultuous experience Algeria had in the 1990s, its leaders were well prepared when the Arab Spring erupted in 2011. The government responded with an overwhelming security presence and by repeatedly reminding the population that democracy was invariably accompanied by chaos. It also relied on petrodollars to provide subsidies that other Arab Spring countries, bereft of oil wealth, could not afford to offer. All of this resulted in what one observer labeled "the Algerian exception."[4]

The ruling party, the National Liberation Front (FLN), "relentlessly concentrated political power within the country's ruling military and administrative bodies, sculpting a state with near-total institutional controls linked to party machinery or FLN politicians."[5] Despite poor health after suffering a debilitating stroke in April 2013, President Abdelaziz Bouteflika won reelection in 2014. This was followed by a period of drift and decay with absent leadership and a declining economy resulting from falling oil prices. Against this background of political and economic stagnation, Bouteflika's announcement in February 2019 that he intended to run for a fifth term provoked widespread dismay and mass protests, leading to what has been called the Hirak movement.[6] Although the movement was largely peaceful and restrained, it resulted in a military intervention that ousted Bouteflika, who subsequently died in September 2021.

The election was postponed from its original date of April 19 to July 2019 and then to December 12, 2019. In the event, many protesters boycotted the elections largely because the five candidates for president had all been closely tied to the Bouteflika clan. The result was a turnout of just under 40 percent. In the event, Abdelmadjid Tebboune was elected with 58 percent of the votes cast. With many Algerians unhappy about the outcome, the Hirak continued until 2020 when the Covid-19 lockdown along with repressive actions by the new government created a hiatus. In the aftermath of the pandemic, protests reemerged, albeit on a smaller scale and with far less energy and enthusiasm. Tebboune had initiated the drafting of a new constitution, but when this was presented in a constitutional referendum on November 1, 2020, the voting was a desultory 23 percent. The new constitution, however, strengthened the president's prerogatives and established that the army could intervene in politics when necessary to "save the interests of the nation."[7] Not surprisingly, the prodemocratic movement targeted the military's influence in politics and demanded fundamental reforms, including greater freedom of expression and an end to corruption. In May 2021, however, the Hirak movement was banned from protests.[8] In the June 2021 parliamentary elections, the ruling party, the FLN, had the largest number of seats but was far from a majority in an election that had a meager turnout of just 30 percent—the lowest in twenty years.[9] The Tebboune administration seems intent on reform, albeit under duress, but it is not clear that it has the will or the capacity to break the impasse. Claus Leggewie and Rachid Ouaissa encapsulated this impasse as a "Gramscian" situation in which "the old world is dying, and the new world struggles to be born."[10]

Closely linked with its political challenges, Algeria faced major economic challenges. As a rentier state, it has benefited disproportionately from oil and gas extraction—often at the expense of the agricultural sector and the service industry—distributing largesse to its population partly through a generous program of subsidies.[11] Although this program has encouraged the growth of smuggling in the borderlands with Algeria's neighbors, during the past two decades it has also contributed to stability—or at least succeeded in postponing another period of upheaval. Yet serious economic problems accumulated due to the decline in oil prices from 2014. This decline "upset Algeria's enormous hydrocarbon industry, threatening financial shortages that could rupture national supply lines and prevent basic resources from reaching everyday Algerians."[12] With Algeria importing 70 percent of its consumption needs, its financial reserves also declined.[13] Moreover, oil production declined partly because of what one commentary described as "years of mismanagement and a lack of investment."[14] Production of liquid natural gas has also fallen while gas consumption is going up.[15] In addition, "the housing crisis . . . worsened and the pandemic . . . revealed glaring deficiencies in health care. Most foods and consumer goods must be imported, and a large share of Algerian families remain dependent on remittances."[16]

Covid-19 also had a significant impact on the political situation. In the short term, lockdown restricted protests, with the result that much of the energy and momentum of the Hirak was lost. Moreover, as a Chatham House commentary noted, the pandemic "magnified and exacerbated the numerous inequalities and failures of the Bouteflika regime to sufficiently invest in human security (economic, food, health, environmental, personal, community, and political)."[17] Predictably, Algeria's resilience also seemed to be diminishing significantly as its foreign exchange reserves fell from almost $122 billion in October 2016 to $42 billion by March 2021.[18] This had serious implications not only for Algeria's financial foundation but also for political stability. As one analyst noted, "Algeria has one of the largest welfare budgets per capita of its OPEC peers."[19] Any major change in this could rekindle protests in the country and fundamentally challenge the stability of the regime.

Yet just as things seemed at their gloomiest, Algeria was able to get at least a temporary reprieve. The economic rebound in 2021 after the Covid-19 pandemic combined with logistical bottlenecks to increase oil prices. The concomitant was a rise in Algerian oil production of almost 10 million tons of oil equivalent from 2020 to 2021. Increased oil revenues also created political and economic breathing room. Concern that inflation of food prices might spark further protests led Tebboune to freeze tax increases on certain food products. Geopolitics gave Algeria a further boost. Algeria was one of the primary beneficiaries of Russia's invasion of Ukraine in February 2022. Many countries, particularly in Europe, wanted to wean their economies off Russian energy and Algeria was identified as a country that could step in and potentially serve as an alternative supplier of energy, especially natural gas.[20] Some of the increased revenues from oil prices were used to subsidize sugar and cooking oil. In addition, projected tax increases on some foods were frozen, while provision was made for unemployment support to 900,000 Algerians between the ages of eighteen and forty.[21]

The problem for Algeria is that it is so dependent on oil and gas that the economy remains highly vulnerable to price changes. If oil prices fall again, social welfare payments would likely be unsustainable. Cutbacks in the welfare system would likely lead to an expansion of organized crime and the illicit economy. In this connection, ENACT's Organized Crime Index in 2019 noted that Algeria ranked fortieth in Africa and fifth "out of the six countries in North Africa, placing it in the bottom third of the criminality ranking for Africa overall."[22] In the 2021 index, Algeria had moved up to thirty-seventh in Africa and fourth in North Africa. In 2023 it was thirty-first and third respectively. Its criminality score, which was 4.21 in 2019, had edged up to 4.51 in 2021 and continued to increase to 4.88 in 2023. The trend was not a positive one for Algeria, although the challenges posed by organized crime remained moderate rather than high.

In 2019, non-renewable-resource crimes like oil smuggling and illegal gold mining were the most important criminal markets, followed by the cannabis trade, human smuggling, and arms trafficking.[23] By 2023, criminal markets related to human smuggling, resource crimes (oil and gold), and the cannabis trade were all assessed at 7.0, while financial crime—a new category for the index—was the highest of all with an 8.0 rating.[24] In terms of criminal actors, state-embedded groups—that is criminal networks and organizations that are integrated into government agencies and institutions—are at the top followed by criminal networks, with foreign groups increasingly evident in the south, especially in gold mining, human smuggling and trafficking, arms trafficking, and contraband smuggling.[25]

On resilience, Algeria was ranked fifteenth in Africa in 2019, but was twenty-second in 2023.[26] The country had significant capacity against organized crime with a powerful military apparatus and law enforcement but suffered from lack of transparency, a poor judicial system, inadequate victim and witness support services, and the absence of a robust anti-money-laundering system.[27] This last point was also emphasized in the US State Department's International Narcotics Control Strategy Report (INCSR) 2021. The problem, as it noted, is not in the banking system as such, but in "a large informal, cash-based economy, estimated at 40 percent of GDP" that "is vulnerable to abuse by criminals. The real estate market is particularly vulnerable to money laundering."[28] The challenge of combating money laundering was further underlined in the 2023 Organized Crime Index, which noted that while the banking system was robust, the real estate sector remained highly vulnerable as "transactions are mainly conducted in cash with no requirement to prove their origin."[29]

In sum, the Organized Crime Index highlighted significant but not overly dramatic problems with organized crime and illicit economies. Yet, given that Algeria has the potential for enormous economic and political instability, criminality will likely continue to increase, and quite possibly—given the resource constraints on the government that would result from another significant downturn in oil prices—resilience will continue to decline. As state largesse contracts, criminal activities and illicit economies will likely expand to fill the void. In sum, the prognosis is that, in terms of criminality, things will get worse before they get better.

Drug Trafficking

Algeria has a growing drug problem with increasing arrests for drug trafficking, possession, and use.[30] The drugs are varied and range from cannabis resin, which goes through the Maghreb from Morocco; cocaine for local use and for transshipment to Europe; synthetic drugs and diverted pharmaceuticals; and small amounts of heroin. Given Algeria's proximity to major producer Morocco, it is hardly surprising that cannabis is widespread, with an estimated 200,000 users, which—as Matthew Herbert and Max Gallien note—could well be an underestimate.[31] A major trend in recent years, has also been the increasing popularity of synthetics and pharmaceuticals. Indeed, "the number of people arrested per year for the consumption or possession of prescription and synthetic drugs has grown faster than the cannabis consumption."[32] Between 2014 and 2019, arrests more than quadrupled.

Despite a closed border between Algeria and Morocco, cannabis resin is smuggled into Algeria through several distinct routes. These have been clearly identified and elucidated by Herbert and Gallien.[33]

- The northern route "starts along the northern third of the Morocco–Algeria border, concentrated roughly between Figuig and Saidiyya," with frequent shipments in the 10 to 30 kilograms range, and some with 100 kilograms or more.[34] "Further south, in the border areas around Naâma and Béchar, larger shipments . . . of several hundred kilograms" are common.[35] Indeed, in two days in May 2019, "authorities intercepted over three tonnes of resin coming across the border near the city of Aïn Safra in Naâma."[36]

- A second route crosses central Algeria, "often through the cities of Ghardaïa, Ouargla and El Oued and sometimes Tébessa" and then into Tunisia.[37] Traffickers also move large shipments on this route from El Oued into Tunisia.[38] Moreover, "some of the cannabis resin moved along the central Algeria route is smuggled directly into Libya in and around the Algerian city of Debdeb and the Libyan city of Ghadames."[39]
- A third route "also goes from the area on the northern Morocco–Algeria border south to Béchar or Adrar and then east to Illizi province, where it crosses over into Libya."[40]

Typically, the major cannabis traffickers in Morocco move drugs to the border and then pass it onto to Algerian traffickers at the border who are locals or are based in Oran.[41] "These traffickers recruit youth from border towns to move the drugs across the frontier using backpacks or loaded on donkeys," thereby minimizing their own risk.[42] At the same time, "the local networks often have pre-existing relationships with local security officials and know which officials are willing to allow cross-border trafficking in exchange for payment."[43] If the strategy of facilitation or bribery is used at the border, the drugs are moved through Algeria using the concealment component of the traffickers' toolkit that was discussed in Chapter 1. "Smaller volumes are secreted within cars or pickup trucks, while large shipments often utilize trucks, with the drugs hidden underneath produce or other goods."[44] In addition, scout cars are used to identify checkpoints.[45] "Most shipments move along the East-West Highway towards Oran and Algiers."[46] Interdiction has some impact, with seizures during 2019 amounting to well over 50 tonnes, which is estimated to be between a fifth and a quarter of all flows into and through Algeria.[47] In June 2021, 200 kilograms of cannabis resin was reportedly seized by authorities in Oran, who also arrested four individuals.[48] According to the Algerian National Office Against Drugs and Drug Addiction, over 25 tonnes of cannabis resin was apprehended in the period January–April 2021, which reportedly reflected a decrease in cannabis seizures in comparison to the same time period in 2020.[49] The subsequent month, during a six-day period,

May 19–25, authorities seized 2,500 kilograms of cannabis (and 14,200 psychotropic tablets) and arrested nine drug traffickers.[50] Clearly the business remains profitable, and at least some cannabis trafficking groups in Algeria are well armed.[51]

If cannabis trafficking and use in Algeria is to be expected, the presence of large shipments of cocaine has been more surprising. Yet there is a clear trend, with several cocaine shipments being discovered in recent years.

- In January 2015, fishermen found over 81 kilograms of cocaine close to the Habibas Islands, about 10 kilometers from Oran.[52]
- Also in 2015, a 156-kilogram shipment of cocaine was recovered at the Baraki port, "concealed in a food container carrying powdered milk imported from New Zealand and transiting via Spain towards Algeria."[53]
- In May 2018, Algerian authorities, probably acting on a tip from Spain, confiscated a shipment of 701 kilograms of cocaine hidden in a container under frozen meat.[54] The cargo had arrived in Oran from Santos, Brazil, a known embarkation port for cocaine, via the ports of Las Palmas and Valencia in Spain.[55]
- In January 2019, 300 kilograms was found on the shore in Skikda in northeast Algeria. The cocaine was packed into sealed backpacks.[56]
- In June 2021, fishermen alerted authorities to "suspicious" packages floating in the waters off Arzew, on the country's northwestern coast, which turned out to be 490 kilograms of cocaine in 442 packages.[57] The packages were located 6 nautical miles (11 kilometers) from Oran's Cap Carbon.[58]

Even prior to the June 2021 seizure, there was considerable speculation that Algeria was somehow becoming part of the global cocaine distribution network. The 2018 shipment, in particular, led to a major investigation and the arrest of Kamel Chikhi, owner of Dounia Meat, and several of his business associates.[59] Chikhi, nicknamed "the butcher," was a real estate businessman and "the largest Algerian importer of frozen meat."[60] He was subsequently sentenced to eight years' imprisonment, but then the sentence was reduced to four years.[61] One of his associates was Khaled Tebboune, whose father, Abdelmadjid Tebboune, became president in December 2019.[62]

In some ways Algeria—along with Morocco—is a useful fallback as a drug transshipment country given its easy access to Europe as well as proximity to the Middle East. It also reflects the flexibility of drug trafficking organizations in response to interdiction. As the Spanish Navy has become more effective in interdicting shipments from Latin America to Spain, drug traffickers pivoted to West Africa as a transshipment point. Cocaine shipments were moved through the Sahel often under the (enforced) protection of groups such as al-Qaeda in the Islamic Maghreb (AQIM).[63] As this route became more dangerous, however, North Africa began to look increasingly attractive as an alternative. As suggested in Chapter 2, this was reinforced by links between cannabis traffickers in Morocco and cocaine traffickers in Latin America. Moreover, traffickers used cannabis trafficking routes for moving cocaine, a trend that seems likely to grow stronger rather than abate.[64] Since the June 2021 discovery of cocaine in the sea near Algeria's coast, however, maritime seizures seem to have been limited. The judicial police service seized 1.418 kilograms of cocaine and more than 40 kilograms of cannabis in Algiers and Annaba in October 2021, but this was a far cry from the earlier seizures and suggested that the traffickers have become more circumspect and adept or that they are increasingly shipping cocaine directly to Spain and the Netherlands rather than using Algeria as a transshipment country. The implication of several recent reports is that the former hypothesis is probably correct: traffickers are simply becoming more professional and careful. Indeed, in its 2023 global cocaine report, UNODC noted that cocaine still goes through Algeria to Europe.[65] This is reinforced by the 2023 Organized Crime Index report on Algeria, which contends that "Algeria is emerging as a new and significant hub for cocaine trafficking."[66] The report also claims that "large quantities of cocaine transit Algerian waters and port facilities, with corrupt security officials, local business, political elites, and overseas criminal organizations facilitating the trade through the country."[67]

This is not to ignore cocaine shipments for domestic consumption that come via West Africa and the Sahel. As UNODC has noted, however, "the cocaine seized destined to the domestic market in Algeria is typically trafficked in small quantities by occasional smugglers, in particular from Mali and Niger, as a means to finance accommodation, transport and false documents for illegal immigration to Europe."[68] This phenomenon of one kind of crime financing other criminal activities and markets is not new; criminal proceeds can be reinvested in the business, either for larger and more valuable drug shipments or for a more diversified criminal portfolio.[69] As regards the domestic market, the EMCDDA noted that in January 2021 a crack cocaine production facility was detected in Algeria; later that year, a drug trafficking network that had been selling cocaine and crack cocaine was dismantled by authorities.[70]

The other dimensions of the drug problem in Algeria involve synthetic drugs such as ecstasy and prescription pharmaceuticals. Unlike cannabis or cocaine, however, "there is no simple directionality to the smuggling in prescription medication and synthetic drugs in the Maghreb. There are multiple flows, some going east or north, others west or south. Some of the drugs are smuggled into the region hidden in bulk container ships, others body-carried in by plane, while many others are fraudulently sourced from pharmacies."[71] In terms of fraudulent sourcing and diversion, Algeria maintained an early edge over other countries because of its subsidized pricing of medications.[72] As a result, it grew to become the epicenter of the illicit trade.[73] Initially, this mostly involved "clonazepam (sold under the name Rivotril) an anti-seizure drug," but it subsequently included diazepam and tramadol.[74] Most of the ecstasy comes in from Europe.[75] In August 2021, Spanish police arrested twenty-one suspected traffickers who transported "large quantities of hashish and thousands of irregular migrants to Europe and then ecstasy on the return trip to Algeria, making over 2.5 million euros (US$2.94 million) in profits."[76]

In addition to tramadol and codeine, pregabalin (a prescription pharmaceutical used to treat nerve pain and seizures) has become more widely abused in Algeria.[77] Pregabalin was responsible for sixty-four (almost 50 percent) nonfatal acute toxicity emergencies in a center in Babl El Oued and seven cases (24.1 percent) in Oran.[78] In addition, there is some processing of methylone and butylone—both of which are part of the amphetamine family. Laboratories processing these drugs have appeared from 2016 onward, with production concentrated in Constantine, an important regional center in eastern Algeria.[79] "Some production of the drug, mainly for local markets, is believed to take place in small-scale processing laboratories located in low-income neighborhoods" not readily amenable to law enforcement crackdowns.[80] Given this competition and the plethora of cheap options, it is hardly surprising that heroin is one of the least consumed drugs in Algeria—although here too, the market could be growing.

Drug trafficking has become an additional source of discord between Morocco and Algeria. The Algerian government has strongly criticized the cannabis trade, while Moroccan authorities have been critical of Algeria's role in trafficking synthetic drugs and pharmaceuticals.[81] In the aftermath of the June 2021 cocaine seizure in Algeria, however, Moroccan press commentary was scathing. *Morocco Latest News* noted that the find was "revealing of the dynamism of drug traffickers thanks to the complicity of the regime and more particularly of the army which makes the rain and shine."[82] For good measure, it added that combating drugs was "not in the genes of the Algerian security services."[83]

Human Smuggling

The 2023 Organized Crime Index noted that "Algeria is a transit and destination country for human smuggling, which is a growing problem. A higher volume of migrants has been received by the country in recent years, some of whom have reached Algeria using smuggling routes. On the other hand, Spain has registered an increase in irregular entries of Algerians, who are the largest nationality recorded."[84] Although Algeria has experienced significant levels of human smuggling, historically it has been less important than Libya or even Tunisia in this illicit market. In the early 2000s—reflecting the end of the civil war as well as government development programs—there were changes to the pattern of irregular migrant settlement.[85] Whereas migrants had traditionally lived in southern cities such as Tamanrasset, Adrar, and Ourgla, they traveled further north to live in large cities such as Algiers, Oran, and Annaba.[86] During this period migrants were not seen as a major problem and seemed to be integrated into Algerian society. Attitudes toward migration and migrants, however, changed drastically in the aftermath of the Arab Spring.[87] In response to the overthrow of the Gaddafi regime and subsequent instability in Mali, Algeria closed its borders with Libya, Niger, and Mali.[88] Concerns about instability in neighboring countries also led the government to make border crossings more difficult with the construction of a large sand berm and increased border security patrols.[89] Yet, despite the difficulties in getting into and moving through Algeria as well as the significant risks of deportation, "Algeria continues to attract thousands of sub-Saharan migrants journeying north along the Central Sahara route."[90] Some of the key border locations that attract smugglers and migrants are shown in Figure 3.1.

Smugglers in Niger, concerned about the border patrols, drop migrants 1 to 5 kilometers from the border and force them to cross the sand berms by themselves.[91] Even once they are across, they must reach In Guezzam by themselves before they are once again picked up by smugglers and taken to Tamanrasset for around the equivalent of 40 euros per person.[92] On the Algeria-Mali border, "most smuggling occurs from In-Khalil east to Tinzaouatine. . . . West of In-Khalil, smuggling is limited, as Algerian military surveillance in the region is high and there are few services for migrants in the region of Taoudenni."[93] Tinzaouatine

Figure 3.1. Map of Southern Algeria, Mali, and Niger

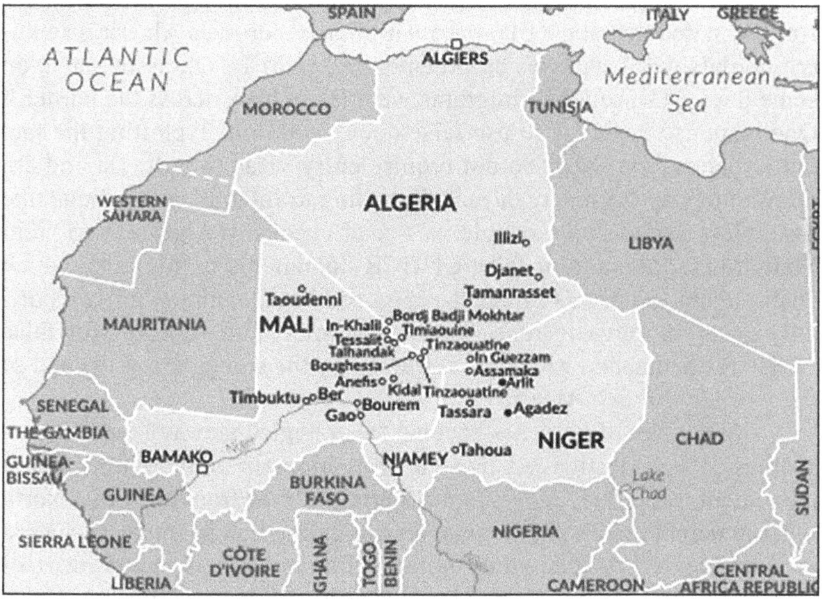

Source: Raouf Farrah, *Algeria's Migration Dilemma: Migration and Human Smuggling in Southern Algeria* (Geneva: Global Initiative Against Transnational Organized Crime, December 2020), p. 6.

is a village that straddles the Mali-Algeria border. Although the two parts of the village were already formally separated, in 2020 Algerian border officials installed barbed-wire fencing to reinforce the demarcation.[94] This was followed by protests in which at least one person was shot and killed. The fence is likely to have displaced the migrant route through the village(s), with migrants having to cross the border outside the village and then make their way to the Algerian side from which they can get transport to Tamanrasset.[95] The smugglers rely on multiple different strategies. They regularly monitor information related to the location of patrols and frequently shift their routes, moving through the desert near In Guezzam from Niger, and Bordj Badji Mokhtar, Timiaouine, and Tinzaouatine from Mali.[96]

Although the presence of migrants from Mali in Bordj Badji Mokhtar has declined, the town hosts a migrant community from Guinea.[97] In effect, Algeria's southern border remains permeable, even though crossings have become much more difficult than in the past. Moreover, getting into Algeria does not guarantee staying in Algeria. In 2018, it was estimated that about 500 irregular migrants crossed Algeria's southern borders daily; as a law enforcement agent in Tamanrasset noted, on some days, 200 would-be migrants were taken back across the border.[98] One response to this is to use false documentation, exploiting the fact that citizens from Mali do not require entry visas for Algeria and are allowed to stay for ninety days.[99] According to Interpol, a technique that smugglers use to move people past road checks in Algeria is to "rent Malian passports and/or false UNHCR documents to migrants, which enable them to pose as refugees registered in the country."[100] It reportedly costs 50 euros to rent a Malian passport and 10 euros for false UNHCR documents, which are retrieved by the smugglers at the end of the journey through Algeria.[101]

Algeria, unwillingly, has become "a strategic gateway" for migrants seeking it as a destination or as a transshipment country for onward movement to Europe, either from Algeria itself, or from one of its North African neighbors.[102] The key human smuggling hub in southern Algeria is Tamanrasset. As one study noted, "Tamanrasset is at the heart of southern Algeria's growing role as a destination point for migratory flows. In 60 years, it has been transformed from a tiny military post into a modern city of 120,000 inhabitants"[103] The population consists of Tuaregs and Arabs from the south, northern Algerians, and between 20,000 and 25,000 irregular migrants, who are concentrated primarily in three neighborhoods, Gat El Oued, Tahaggart, and Sersouf Ferraille, where many of them live in group houses known as *foyers*.[104] Some of the foyers are owned and operated by those involved in human smuggling.[105] This is not surprising because Tamanrasset has become "a strategic city for human-smuggling networks, from which they organize the logistics, lodging and transportation for migrants."[106] There are several options for migrant smugglers moving people to the Mediterranean coast from Tamanrasset: northwest to Morocco, north to the Algerian coast, and northeast to Libya and possibly from there to Tunisia. Morocco seems to have become the favored route for many. As a study by two geographers noted, Tamanrasset "represents the distribution point for migrants on the central route to Libya through the eastern Algerian border regions of Illizi, Djanet, Dabdab and then to Italy via the Mediterranean. Additionally, Tamanrasset is a transit hub on the western route to the north of Algeria, passing through Ouargla, Chardaia, Adrar, and Maghnia on the western Algerian-Moroccan borders and then towards Spain."[107]

For those migrants seeking to go to Morocco, which is seen as the major gateway to Spain, the key crossing point is the border-crossing from the Algerian town of Maghnia to the Moroccan town of Oujda.[108] The two towns are 27 kilometers apart, and tensions between the two countries add to the difficulties that migrants face. Indeed, the crossing is also the point at which "Moroccan and Algerian authorities deport irregular migrants from their territory. The border, however, has been closed since 1994, effectively making these deportations both illegal and hazardous for migrants when carried out, and the lives of migrants on both sides of the border extremely precarious."[109] Maghnia itself is highly militarized and under constant surveillance.[110] Yet it has also seen the development of illicit markets "and increased levels of criminal activity with the complicity of local authorities in both Algeria and Morocco, from smuggling of drugs or ordinary goods (from gas to olive oil, or goats) to human trafficking."[111]

Migrants can easily locate smugglers as well as migrant camps or ghettos that have been established in the countryside surrounding Maghnia, especially in the riverbeds in the Oued valleys.[112] Communities are generally based on nationality and are well organized with a clear hierarchy led by a chairman and several assistants including a censor, a secretary, and a superintendent.[113] "Migrants reaching Maghnia and planning to cross the border are taken directly to the camp by community officials. There they have to introduce themselves and pay their right to stay to the superintendent."[114] In 2012, the price was 15 euros for the stay and 50 euros for crossing the border.[115] Once eight migrants had assembled, a smuggler would take the migrants across the border into Morocco.[116] There they also faced the possibility of being sent back to Algeria. It was reported that "Moroccan and Algerian law enforcement officials play surreal ping pong games with migrants, each trying to push them to the other side by force—all the while taking advantage of these expulsions to help themselves to the migrants' money and other belongings."[117]

Migrants in Maghnia are often harassed, and in March 2018 a major migrant camp was burned down.[118] Moreover, both Algeria and Morocco have taken steps to harden the border. For example, in 2018, Algeria improved its border control mechanisms with Morocco as part of an effort to prevent the smuggling of gas and contraband.[119] Moreover, Morocco built fences along its border with Algeria as part of an initiative to stop border crossings by migrants between the two countries. Some crossings still occur, of course, but the price has increased significantly. According to Malakooti and Fall, crossing the border between Algeria and Oujda can cost sub-Saharan migrants between 100 and 200 euros; for Arabs crossing the border, the price spikes upward to 1,000 euros, particularly when they are moved directly to Nador.[120] The price structure further fluctuates, climbing to an additional 350 euros for a woman (especially if the woman is pregnant) seeking to cross the border. Malakooti and Fall explain that it is not uncommon for pregnant women migrants to seek to transit these regions, often to escape forced prostitution in Maghnia.[121]

The hardening of the border by both Algeria and Morocco is simultaneously based on convergent interests and mutual antipathy. Yet, for Algeria this is only the latest manifestation of its hardline stance on irregular migrants. The roots of its policy can be traced back to its free trade agreement with the European Union in April 2002. After a crisis in Ceuta and Melilla in summer 2005, the European Union pressed Algeria to become more involved in controlling migration through its territory. In the months that followed, Algeria expelled hundreds of sub-Saharan migrants, beginning a pattern that would be frequently repeated and periodically intensified. The Migration Act of 2008 empowered the government to expel those who had entered Algeria illegally—albeit with notice and a grace period to leave. When the crisis in Syria intensified the problem, Algerian responses became even more ruthless and included large-scale expulsions. "Since 2015, Algeria has expelled or repatriated an unprecedented number of migrants to Niger and, to a lesser extent, Mali. National and international advocacy groups and organizations have expressed grave concerns that these operations are tainted by human rights violations, such as physical violence and abuse during detention and deportation."[122] According to an Associated Press report in June 2018, the International Organization for Migration had estimated that 30,000 people had died in the desert since the repatriations began.[123] Moreover, in the previous fourteen months, 13,000 people had been sent back to Niger: these included "pregnant women and children, stranding them without food or water and forcing them to walk, sometimes at gunpoint, under temperatures of up to 48 degrees Celsius (118 degrees Fahrenheit)."[124] In October 2020, Human Rights Watch reported that 16,000 migrants had been expelled since the beginning of the year—despite Covid-19—with 3,400 removed from the country since early September.[125] The manner of the expulsions had also caused concern about arbitrary detentions and lack of due process for asylum seekers. Despite the protestations of NGOs concerned about human rights abuses, however, the expulsions have continued. According to one commentary, Doctors Without Borders recorded 27,208 deportees from Algeria in 2021 and 36,083 in 2022.[126]

Ironically, Algeria has increasingly been unwilling to cooperate with the European Union. Although Algeria's migration policy developed initially in parallel with the early moves toward Fortress Europe, its migration and border control policies subsequently evolved in ways that were not only autonomous but also antithetical to European Union preferences and policies.[127] Although there was a broad convergence on a highly restrictive approach, this did not result in cooperation. Algeria has marched to the beat of its own drum in devising a Fortress Algeria stance. Nevertheless, Algeria's preoccupation with securing its border, its implementation of hardline policies against irregular migration, and its willingness to deport migrants back across the southern borders with Mali and Niger have done little to dispel the problem. Indeed, the flow of migrants into and through Algeria increased as movement through Libya became more dangerous and difficult. In 2023, however, the pendulum started to swing back somewhat with irregular migration across the Mediterranean from Libya reaching its highest point since 2017.

An additional wrinkle in all this is that while some migrants from sub-Saharan Africa are content to stay in Algeria, as long as they can avoid the increased deportation activities by the authorities, an increasing number of Algerians are seeking to migrate illegally to Europe. In 2009 Algeria passed a law on "illegal exit," and those who violated it faced penalties of two to six months imprisonment and a fine.[128] This does not seem to deter would-be migrants, and in June 2020 it was reported that authorities had arrested 1,433 people trying to depart illegally from Algeria.[129] This was not entirely new. In fact, multiple October 2017 reports revealed that Algerian migrants were crossing the Mediterranean from the port city of Annaba in eastern Algeria to the Italian island of Sardinia, a distance of 280 kilometers.[130] About 1,200 had already arrived that year and this was a marked increase from earlier estimates of around 1,000 arrivals per year.[131] The report noted that "unlike refugees arriving from Syria and other war zones, migrants from Algeria cannot seek asylum in Italy and must leave within seven days of receiving an expulsion notice from Italian authorities."[132] While many were rounded up, some would exploit the window of opportunity and board a ferry to mainland Italy with the intention to travel elsewhere in Europe.[133]

Another point of arrival for Algerians was the Balearic Islands, including Majorca, Minorca, Ibiza, and Formentera, all of which are part of Spain.[134] With 480 migrants arriving in 2018, 199 in 2019, and more than 1,400 in 2020, officials acknowledged that the migrant route had become permanent.[135] This was confirmed in 2021, with "a record number of arrivals on the islands—164 boats with a total of 2,402 migrants."[136] In 2022 there was a further increase as 2,637 people arrived aboard 176 boats—although fifty "captains" of migrant boats were arrested.[137] The journey of 270 nautical miles usually takes around twenty-four hours, while the price "depends on the number of people travelling, the type of boat and the origin. The average cost of the trip is usually 1,000 euros if they are Algerian and 1,500 if they are sub-Saharan."[138] Although this trip is far less dangerous than the voyage to the Canary Islands, it is not without peril. In November 2022, for example, two boats set off from Boumerdès, Algeria, for Cabrera in the Balearic Islands. One had twenty-six Algerian men on board while the other had twelve Algerians and nine sub-Saharan Africans. Neither boat arrived at its destination, and it is likely that all the passengers drowned.[139]

Mainland Spain was also a destination, and on October 6 and 7, 2020, "228 Algerians, on 18 different boats, were intercepted by the Spanish coast guard off Murcia."[140] Indeed, Algerians accounted for almost 40 percent of irregular migrants arriving in Spain during January–October 2020.[141] The trend continued in 2021 when "authorities registered 10,000 irregular entries from Algeria, a 20% increase from 2020."[142] In 2022, Spain remained a major destination for Algerian migrants, with numbers increasing while irregular migration from Morocco to Spain was declining. According to news reports, between September 9 and 11, 2022, 907 irregular Algerian migrants reached Spain with 371 to the Balearic Islands, 294 to Almeria, 209 to Murcia, 35 to Alicante, and 18 arriving in Granada.[143]

The trend of migrants crossing the Mediterranean to Spain from Algeria has involved two forms of increased diversity: migrants from a wider variety of countries, and a composition of Algerian irregular migrants that includes more older people and women trying to make the voyage. Among the push factors is the failure of the Hirak to bring about fundamental political change. This has created a sense of profound disappointment for Algerians. When combined with a bleak economic and financial outlook, increased repression and lack of hope for the future act as compelling push factors for many Algerians seeking to migrate to Europe.

Although it remains difficult to identify reliable data about embarkation points in Algeria, one NGO has noted that departures would often go from the coasts of Oran and Mostaganem to the Spanish mainland or the Balearics. Annaba was the main starting point for the journey to Sardinia in Italy.[144] There was also increased diversification of routes, with ten provinces providing departure points.[145] The Algerian coast guard intercept many of the boats, and in September, the Algerian defense minister declared that between September 15 and 25, 2020, members of the coast guard intercepted 1,200 Algerian nationals.[146] Most of these were likely arrested given Algerian laws on leaving the country illegally.

The smugglers who arrange the dangerous crossing across the Mediterranean from Algeria can vary from fishermen who now use their boats to smuggle people to criminals who are willing to transport people as well as drugs. In a seminal article, Alberto Aziani has argued very persuasively that not all human smugglers are the same.[147] Indeed, he has highlighted the heterogeneity of migrant smugglers and their activities along six different dimensions: target/victim, purpose, geopolitical scope, intensity, operational scale, and organization.[148] He also noted that contrary "to the public conception of human smugglers, they are often motivated by empathy, are active for short periods, and coordinate themselves through loose local networks."[149] At the other end of the spectrum are "profit-oriented groups stably conducting large-scale operations that may end in the victimization of the migrants."[150] From this, Aziani developed two ideal types—the migrant facilitators and the professional smugglers—while recognizing the diversity in between.[151] Significantly, interviews with 373 smugglers in West Africa and North Africa resulted in a division between those—largely in North Africa—who themselves were generally migrants and were interested in helping those "in need of passage" and those—primarily in West Africa—who saw human smuggling as a way of earning more money than would otherwise be feasible.[152] The facilitators tended to see themselves as transporters and connectors. There were also end-to-end coordinators who took care of the whole trip and local facilitators who provided a modular system in which migrants were passed on to the next stage. Both professional smugglers and facilitators were sometimes guilty of physical or sexual abuse of migrants, fraud, abandonment, or robbery. As Aziani argues, however, a key distinction "is the willingness of professional smugglers to victimize migrants to increase their profits."[153] This is perhaps most evident in maritime smuggling operations where there is frequently a tendency to overload the boat or use vessels that are barely seaworthy. Unfortunately, this reflects the reality that quality control is impossible to ensure in illicit markets that operate outside the law and do not comply with regulatory norms.

This concern about the quality of the services provided by professional smugglers could well explain the growing phenomenon in Algeria—as well as Tunisia and Morocco—of emergent behavior and what has been described as "self-smuggling."[154] This can take various forms, but it typically involves families, friends, and communities pooling "their resources and collective knowledge" and "relying on the skill and knowledge of others in the group."[155] There are two advantages to this. First, it is perhaps less likely that the boat will be overcrowded. Second, it is also less likely that the group will be discovered or intercepted.[156] This is not to suggest that all voyages are self-organized, and although this does seem to be a growing trend among North Africans, it seems likely that migrants from sub-Saharan Africa and elsewhere will still depend on brokers and human smugglers for their Mediterranean crossing. While the addition of self-organizing voyages is an important corrective and valuable addition to the body of knowledge about irregular migration across the Mediterranean, it does not mean that human smugglers and the profits earned can be relegated to the margins.

Human Trafficking

One of the most dangerous aspects of irregular migration is that migrants inevitably and perhaps even routinely find themselves in harm's way. As discussed earlier, some smugglers are essentially informal travel agents and transportation providers, while others are more ruthless in exploiting those they are supposedly assisting. Not surprisingly, therefore, a key component of human trafficking in Algeria involves exploitation of irregular migrants. "Some smugglers operating along the Mali–Algeria border in particular have a reputation for exploiting migrants' vulnerability, forcing them into labor or sexual servitude, or for extortion under threat of violence."[157] One aspect of this is that "Tamanrasset has become a destination for the trafficking of women and children from Niger, particularly from the region of Zinder, to beg for money in the streets."[158] The forced begging phenomenon has also been evident in Algiers. In November 2018, ninety-three children from various African countries, including sixty from Niger were rescued by authorities in two separate law enforcement operations.[159] The first involved thirty-nine children and the second freed fifty-four children, twenty-eight of whom seemed to be organized and controlled by two men from Niger.[160] This seems to have been merely the tip of a large iceberg as in 2020 "a civil society organization estimated criminal begging networks exploit more than 6,000 unaccompanied migrant children in Algeria."[161]

Several years earlier another report had suggested that children, "primarily unaccompanied sub-Saharan migrants," were being "subjected to commercial sexual exploitation, including by being trafficked into prostitution in bars and informal brothels."[162] Girls are compelled to do domestic work, while boys are made to work in the construction industry.[163] It was also reported not only that human traffickers based in northern Mali and southern Algeria were forcing refugee children "to draw water from wells," but also that "those children are often beaten and robbed of their possessions, including their identification documents."[164]

Exploitation is not limited to children. In one instance, a group of fifty-five Bangladeshi men who paid a recruiting agency—the Singapore Skills Training Center (subsequently renamed the Asian Skills Training Center)—"for jobs in Algeria and the promise of illegal passage into Spain" found themselves doing "indentured labor under subhuman living conditions."[165] Their working conditions were long and harsh, and the men also had to live in the building they were constructing—which had neither doors nor windows and was full of construction supplies.[166] There was no attempt to move them to Spain, and when they tried to withdraw from their contracts they were told they had been "bought" and owed money to the company.[167] As a Bangladeshi newspaper stated, "it was nothing but modern-day slavery in the guise of construction jobs."[168]

Although the Algerian government has taken formal measures to deal with the human trafficking problem, these moves have been both too little and too late. In contrast to its commitment to forced repatriation of sub-Saharan migrants, the government seems to have neither the will nor the capability to make serious inroads against human trafficking. The June 2021 Trafficking in Persons (TIP) report by the US Department of State was emphatic, if diplomatically so, that Algeria was failing to meet fully the "the minimum standards for the elimination of trafficking and is not making significant efforts to do so, even considering the impact of the Covid-19 pandemic on its anti-trafficking capacity."[169] Consequently, Algeria retained its Tier 3 status, which was the lowest possible category and one that is given only reluctantly. Algerian officials have vehemently criticized the low rankings, but with little basis for their comments. The Algerian government is almost willfully ignorant of the trafficking problem. Yet, within the government's worldview, this is understandable, even if that worldview is blinkered, overly nationalistic, and lacking subtlety or nuance. Traditional concerns over interference by the former imperial powers in Europe and concerns about national sovereignty were intensified by the collapse of the Gaddafi regime in 2011, the instability in Mali the following year, and the In Amenas terrorist attack in 2013. The result was to restrict Algeria's single focus to national security. Containing foreign threats at its southern borders and ensuring that instability in the Sahel did not spill over into Algeria itself required a strong response to migrants, terrorists, drug traffickers, and criminal organizations alike—all of whom seemingly coalesced in Algeria's threat assessment. It was not surprising, therefore that Algeria adopted "a uniform strategy of deportation towards all irregular migrants—whether women, children, or adults, and regardless of nationality—without screening for victims or perpetrators of trafficking" even though it is highly likely that they were—and are—there.[170] The concomitant of this was denial and deflection about the possible prevalence of human trafficking in Algeria either of sub-Saharan migrants or Algerian women. And within the trafficking realm, the almost singular focus has been on migrant children forced to beg, not least because the coercive element of this crime is readily provable in court. Beyond this, the government has devoted little attention to combating human trafficking within the country.

Despite this, there were a few promising signs. Algeria has increasingly cooperated with the International Organization for Migration and the UNODC to build capacity to counter human trafficking. It has had training programs to familiarize members of the judiciary and law enforcement with trafficking indicators and more generally to increase their awareness of the problem. Moreover, successive TIP reports have acknowledged that Algeria has a rolling national action plan, a generally appropriate legal framework in place, and penalties for trafficking—but it also has had loopholes. One of these loopholes was partially closed when the parliament in April 2023 passed a law that removed the requirement of proving force, fraud, or coercion for the prosecution of child trafficking—albeit with the proviso that "proof of force, fraud, or coercion" was required "when the exploitative purpose" had not been achieved. This law was insufficient to meet international standards whereby sex trafficking of children is automatically a crime.[171] An additional problem is that, despite the training, few law enforcement or judicial figures have much experience or expertise in these areas.[172] As a result, prosecutions are rare, with convictions even less frequent. Moreover, the trend seems to be going in the wrong direction:

- In 2017, Algerian authorities conducted twenty-six trafficking investigations, prosecuted twenty-two, and convicted fourteen individuals for "child labor offenses."[173]
- In 2018, the government prosecuted sixteen people for trafficking—two were convicted.[174]
- In 2019, thirteen people were prosecuted and five were convicted. Two were Algerian and the other three were from Niger.[175]

- In 2019, Algerian authorities reportedly prosecuted three cases involving thirteen alleged traffickers.[176] Of these three cases, "two involved sexual exploitation and one involved both sexual exploitation and forced labor."[177] None of those accused was convicted.

Although the number of prosecutions was already minuscule, in 2020—perhaps in part because of Covid-19—the government did not prosecute a single forced labor or sex trafficking case. In 2021 it initiated six new investigations.[178] The following year the government reported that it investigated two new cases (one labor trafficking and one sex trafficking) while continuing another investigation initiated earlier. It did, however, begin twenty-two new prosecutions, with five involving sex trafficking, one forced labor case, and sixteen for "unspecified forms of trafficking."[179] Over a two-year period, five traffickers were convicted, with two of them sentenced to three years in prison and a fine of 500,000 Algerian dinar (US$3,660).[180] This trend of modest efforts and even more limited results was reflected in the ranking for Algeria. Between 2012 and 2016, Algeria was a fixture on Tier 3 of the TIP reports. From 2017 to 2019, its increased efforts placed it on the Tier 2 Watch List. In the 2020 and 2021 reports, it was relegated to Tier 3 once again, before moving back up to the Tier 2 Watch List in 2022 and falling to Tier 3 in the 2023 report.

Although Algeria protested its ranking, there was little to support this. The prosecution rate for human trafficking in Algeria is low by any standard, while the conviction rate is abysmal. These factors, taken together, create a culture of impunity—a concept that is discussed with far less frequency or intensity in North Africa than it is in Central America or even the whole of Latin America. The prevention side is equally limited and, beyond broad aspirations, there is no effective strategic plan. The government spent 12 million euros "to take in child and women victims of trafficking networks," but such schemes are not characterized by sufficient transparency.[181] Consequently, it is uncertain if resources are targeted strategically and with clear measures of effectiveness or metrics in mind.

Against this background, it is very likely that the problem was temporarily exacerbated by Covid-19 in several distinct ways. Border closures and other restrictions likely resulted in migrants taking more risks, exposing them to abuse, exploitation, and human trafficking.[182] Moreover, some of the routes became "more clandestine, sometimes overlapping with those of drug traffickers and arms dealers, in turn creating greater dangers for migrants" who suddenly found themselves entangled with "more dangerous entities and trafficking groups."[183] Yet if continued movement is dangerous, things can be even worse when migrants are compelled to stay in one place. As one commentary noted, "the closing of borders in North Africa and the Sahel has especially deprived unaccompanied sub-Saharan females of ways to collect money and send remittances to their families."[184] Unable to move toward their destination or return home, women have found themselves in a situation where they are "extremely susceptible to human trafficking."[185] And all this, of course, does not consider the pandemic itself and the possibility of migrants catching the disease. Given that migrants were already marginalized and that health facilities in Algeria left much to be desired, the likelihood of serious illness and death was high.

One final point to consider with human smuggling and trafficking is the extent of involvement by jihadist groups in human trafficking. In a judicious and careful study, Djallil Lounnas concluded that there is little evidence of any such involvement by AQIM or similar groups.[186] He argues that one reason is that human trafficking does not generate sufficient revenue for terrorists. Yet there is money to be made through human smuggling. The problem though from the perspective of jihadist groups is that such activities are complex and time-consuming. For a terrorist organization that has obtained significant quantities of funds through the much easier work of kidnapping for ransom, human smuggling requires a degree of effort and hassle that is not particularly appealing. A second and somewhat ironic observation is that "religiously and ethically" human trafficking is a "form of exploitation" they are against.[187] In some ways involvement in the business "would be a contradiction of the belief system that has motivated their engagement" in terrorist organizations.[188] Another factor that reinforces their reluctance is their sense of identity: they are fighters, not traders; warriors, not pimps. In the final analysis, the choice is about who they are and what they do—and neither includes human trafficking.

Arms Trafficking

Algeria has a long tradition of gun ownership. In 2010 there were reportedly 7.6 weapons per hundred people in the country.[189] Other assessments, however, suggest that this was a high estimate and that the number was 5.59 in 2005 and had fallen to 2.14 in 2017—although some of the decline clearly reflected an increase in population of approximately 8 million.[190] The official interpretation is that Algeria did not officially produce weapons, only ammunition, and that it purchased all of its weapons from other countries, especially Russia. In fact, it does produce some of its own weapons. These include an outdated assault rifle developed by China known as the Type 56. One commentary noted that this was "baffling" given Algeria's "exorbitant purchases of sophisticated air defenses and fighter jets" but suggested that it was "a matter of convenience."[191] "The price of a locally made Type 56 is negligible and is easier to supply in large quantities," whereas importing one from China could cost up to $700. The Mechanical Construction Establishment of Khenchela has been mass-producing Type 56 and Type 56-1 assault rifles since the 1990s. In June 2023, however, it was also announced that Algeria would be producing heavier and more complex weapons, some under license from China.[192]

None of this is particularly problematic, and it was only after the collapse of Libya that arms trafficking became seen as a major national security threat. For Algeria, having Libya as a neighbor has posed serious challenges over the last decade, ranging from concerns of spillover violence to the widespread diffusion of weapons. As a result of the collapse of the Gaddafi regime, Libya was transformed into a vast arms bazaar. One British newspaper described it as "the Tesco of the world's illegal arms trade," while Mokhtar Belmokhtar, an infamous jihadist leader, kidnapper, cigarette smuggler, and arms trafficker, acknowledged that his organization had been "one of the main beneficiaries of the revolutions in the Arab world. . . . As for our acquisition of Libyan armaments that is an absolutely natural thing."[193] Certainly, it was a major boost to terrorist organizations in North Africa and the Sahel, especially but not exclusively AQIM. Belmokhtar subsequently played a key role in the attack on the Tiguentourine Gas Plant near In Amenas in January 2013. At least thirty-seven foreign hostages and an Algerian worker were killed along with twenty-nine terrorists.[194] Algeria claimed in the aftermath of the attack that Libyan weapons were used.[195] Such claims were plausible to say the least.

Estimates of Gaddafi's armory ranged from 400,000 to 1 million firearms (especially Kalashnikovs), in addition to a variety of other weapons that entered the country during the 2011 civil war.[196] Inevitably, the loss of control over weapons stockpiles spilled over to Libya's neighbors, with particularly significant consequences for Mali and Niger. As the UN Security Council (UNSC) Panel of Experts on Libya noted: "The western borders of Libya, from Tunisia in the north to Niger in the south, were the focus points for illicit trafficking from Libya quite early on in the uprising, with Algeria reporting its first seizure of weapons coming from Libya in April 2011."[197] One study argued very persuasively that "the availability and circulation of weapons in the black market in North Africa was substantially changed by the Libyan revolution and the subsequent conflicts in that country. Weapons dynamics since then can be regarded as a driver of regional instability."[198] By 2015 there was even an acknowledgement by Europol that weapons from the conflicts in Libya, Syria, and Mali were available for purchase on the European black market.[199]

Closer to the source, however, it was reported (by the UNSC panel) that between April 2011 and March 2012, Algeria had seized "103 Kalashnikovs, 63 machineguns, 17 other firearms, 510 rockets, and 3 rocket propelled grenades," all originating from Libya.[200] Algerian authorities also acknowledged that weapons trafficking was conducted by a range of entities from petty criminals at one end of the spectrum to "organized terrorist and criminal networks" at the other.[201] Seizures continued over the next several years, with most of them on Algeria's borders with Niger, Mali, and Libya. These included the following:

- In April 2013, Algerian security forces seized an arms shipment that was in transit from Libya to northern Mali, killing five terrorists in the process.[202] The terrorists "reportedly belonged to al-Qaeda splinter group, Movement for Tawhid and Jihad in West Africa (MUJAO) and were in charge of protecting the arms shipment."[203]
- In April 2016, in a progress report on the year up to that point, it was announced that Algeria's armed forces had killed thirty-one terrorists and captured thirty-three more.[204] In addition, they had seized "more than 300 weapons of war, including Kalashnikovs."[205]
- In May 2016, it was announced that youth violence had increased.[206] It was also reported that "in Batna, a network of gun traffickers was stopped by the national gendarmerie and two shotguns, one revolver, 227 cartridges and 960 capsules were seized."[207]
- In the same month, it was also reported that an arms trafficking group had been dismantled, noting that "police arrested two people and seized 22 American pump-action shotguns, three Turkish shotguns, one handgun and ammunition, all from Libya."[208]
- In November 2016, Algerian customs seized a cache of weapons on the borders with Tunisia and Libya. The weapons were described as "very sophisticated" and "equipped with new technologies."[209] It was alleged that "they belong to trafficking networks and terrorists from Libya, where there are 20,000 illegal firearms in circulation."[210]

Table 3.1, drawn from an informative article by Nicholas Marsh, provides a summary of reported seized arms caches in Algeria during the period 2011 to 2016.[211]

A more complete picture of weapons seized in Algeria in 2016 was provided by the UNSC Panel of Experts and is reproduced as Table 3.2.[212] According to one source, during the "1st semester, 2016," weapons seized in Algeria included 6 mortars, 39 machine guns, 46 hunting rifles, and 167 Kalashnikovs.[213]

Although these reports highlight "the what," they offer little detail on "the where." Two other sources, however, provide some of the missing detail. Francesco Strazzari and Francesca Zampagni note that although some seizures are reported on the northern coast (i.e., at Ain Defla, Tipaza, and Bouira), most of them are in southern Algeria: "Tamanrasset, on the border with Niger; Bordj Badji Mokhtar, bordering Mali; and In Amenas, on the border with Libya."[214] It is striking that some of these are towns—especially Tamanrasset and In Amenas—also loom large in the analysis of human smuggling. The importance of Tamanrasset is highlighted by Querine Hanlon and Matthew Herbert in a 2015 publication. They noted that "residents in . . . Tamanrasset indicated that over the last two to three years, the rate of weapons smuggling

Table 3.1. Seized Arms in Algeria 2011 to 2016

Location	Caches	Items Included	Amount
Identified as from Libya	16	Ammunition	>49,104
		Antiaircraft gun	1
		Antiaircraft missiles	≥43
		Firearms	175
		Mortars	—
		RPG launchers	—
Suspected to have come from Libya	3	Explosive belts	2
		Guns	20
		"Heavy arms"	52
		Shoulder-fired missiles	—
		Surface-to-air missiles	6
		RPG launchers	3
Near the border with Libya	6	Ammunition	—
		Explosives	—
		Firearms	—
		Landmines	—
		Mortars	—
		Rocket launchers	—

Table 3.2. Seizures of Weapons in Algeria, 2016

Firearms	
Katashnikov automatic rifles	668
FMPK machine guns	48
Mortars	37
Hunting rifles	82
Semiautomatic rifles with telescopic sight	35
Shotguns	26
Simonov semiautomatic rifles	64
RPG-7 rocket propelled grenades	18
Machine guns (12.7 mm)	13
Machine guns (14.5 mm)	7
Repeating rifles	36
PKT machine guns	9
PSH machine guns	2
Dictariov machine guns	5
M-16 machine gun	1
MAT-44 machine guns	4
3-cannons rocket launchers	1
Strela rocket launchers	1
RPG-5 rocket propelled grenades	5
RPG-2 rocket launchers	2
Anti-aircraft missiles	6
Artisanal hand-crafted rifles	56
Automatic pistols of various types	35
RPD machine guns	1
MAT-49 machine guns	1
MAS-36 rifles	3
Grenades	792

Source: UNSC Panel of Expets (2017, annex 47).

through the area has increased dramatically. At least some of the weapons smuggled through southeastern Algeria are intended for distribution in Mali and other nations in sub-Saharan Africa."[215] They also confirm that some weapons are moved to the northern areas within Algeria where AQIM remains active. In 2018 Algerian authorities noted that the trafficking route from Mali to Algeria was "the third most common route for firearms trafficking in the region."[216] Sometimes too the weapons are smuggled across underpopulated areas of southern Tunisia and then to Algeria's Kabylie region. Several arms trafficking networks transporting Libyan weapons have been disrupted in the *wilayas (provinces)* of Tabessa and Annaba, suggesting that weapons are also being trafficked along the Tunisian-Algerian border.[217] In terms of Algeria's border with Morocco, they see little evidence of arms trafficking, while acknowledging that drug traffickers seem to be better armed than in the past.[218]

It is also worth noting that in 2017 Algeria seized firearms that were produced in France.[219] Moreover, in Bordj Badji Mokhtar in August 2017, units of the People's National Army found a cache of weapons containing one RPG-2 type rocket launcher, one PK type machine gun, one RPK machine gun, seven Kalashnikovs, two semiautomatic rifles of the Simonov type, and a large quantity of ammunition. Also, 162 kilograms of treated hashish was confiscated.[220] Such seizures have continued to be a regular occurrence. Although the sense of crisis associated with the diffusion of Libyan weaponry has clearly declined, Algeria has remained alert to the danger. Indeed, at a meeting in New York in June 2022 on the Program of Action to combat the illicit trade in small arms and light weapons, Algeria emphasized the importance of the issue and "stressed that any transfer of SALW [small arms and light weapons] to a group, entity or person without prior permission from the receiving State should be considered illegal."[221] The official statement at the end of the meeting, though, was far weaker than this, simply acknowledging that diversion was a "global challenge."[222] Nevertheless, Algeria's statement at the meeting emphasized that it was taking concrete steps to combat arms trafficking and had launched in cooperation with Mauritania, Mali, and Niger the Joint Operational Staff Committee based in Tamanrasset that was dedicated to combating terrorism, transnational crime, and the trafficking of small arms and light weapons. The statement noted that this collaborative mechanism was supported by a Fusion and Liaison Unit, which facilitated "intelligence and information sharing among seven countries of the region."[223]

Despite its commitment to combat arms trafficking, Algeria has an additional problem of illicit production. In its 2020 Global Study on Firearms Trafficking, the UNODC noted that the illicit manufacture of firearms "as legal grounds for seizure was most marked—even if still very small in relative terms—in Africa, driven mainly by Algeria, which reported 265 arms seized in 2016–17 on these grounds (18 per cent of the total arms seized in these two years)."[224] Indeed, even as early as 2014 Algeria was expressing concerns over artisanal firearms, including hunting weapons.[225] In February 2014, in Biskra province, Algerian police seized what was clearly a family-run artisanal workshop arresting a man and his son and confiscating "five guns, shooting rifles, 10 knives, five kilograms of gunpowder, 400 ready-to-use bullets and arms making equipment."[226] In the final analysis, however, such production efforts are small-scale and would only become significant in the event that Algeria descends again into instability or civil war resulting from its economic fractures and increasing resentment of the military's role in politics and governance.

Cigarette Smuggling

Algerian cigarette smuggling is best understood in terms of its French connection.[227] Yet it is also deeply embedded in the cigarette smuggling system across North Africa. In addition, Algeria is a producer of licit cigarettes including the Rym brand, which is smuggled into neighboring countries. It is also a major consumption country and a pivotal transshipment country to Europe. The difficulty in assessing the extent of cigarette smuggling is that different studies use different categories and, almost invariably, come up with different results in terms of numbers. Some studies, for example conflate *counterfeit* cigarettes (which use name brands even though the cigarettes have not been produced by the brand company) and *contraband* cigarettes (which are clandestinely exported and imported to avoid taxation but do not purport to be anything other than what they are). Allowing for these difficulties, however, it is possible to obtain some sense of the trends in the illicit market.

As with illicit cigarettes in other North African countries, the flow to Algeria starts with production in the United Arab Emirates and other states in the Middle East.[228] The cigarettes are then moved by ship to Mauritania, entering through the ports of Nouakchott and Nouadhibou, the latter of which is also a free trade zone.[229] An estimated 300 million cigarettes are moved through Mauritania to Algeria, while another 80 million go through the Western Sahara.[230] Some of the cigarettes enter Algeria from its eastern border with Libya; some come in through the southern borders with Mauritania, Mali, and Niger; and some come in through Morocco, especially Tan-Tan.[231] Although the border between Morocco and Algeria is formally closed and Morocco has taken steps to strengthen its border with Algeria to counter cigarette (and human) smuggling, these efforts have not been completely effective.[232]

Cigarette smuggling through Algeria, Libya, and Mali benefits Tuareg tribes, which operate along what Transcrime describes as the Niger corridor between Mali, Libya, and Algeria.[233] Terrorist organizations, especially AQIM and the spinoff group al Mourabitoun led by the elusive Belmokhtar, provide protection for the tribes in return for payment.[234] Whether this is really cooperation between smuggling organizations and terrorist groups or is simply an extortion scheme and an "offer the smugglers cannot refuse" is a moot point. Whether voluntary or imposed, the arrangement is one that ultimately benefits both parties, albeit not equally. It remains debatable whether the arrangement constitutes a crime-terror nexus.

Perhaps most significant, "Algeria is the principal outflow country in the region towards Europe, mainly France and Spain, where the price of cigarettes is considerably higher. Almost half of the illicit cigarettes consumed in France in 2017 originated from Algeria (about 3.4 billion illicit cigarettes)."[235] These included 1.4 billion from the United Arab Emirates, 0.9 billion from Mauritania, and 0.7 billion from South Korea.[236] The key point of entry in France is the port of Marseilles, which was also the conduit for heroin smuggling in the heyday of the French connection.[237] As Louise Shelley noted in her congressional testimony in 2017, "Marseille is the French hotspot for illicit cigarette sales—approximately 40% of all sales are of illegal imports."[238] Unlike the response to heroin trafficking, however, "police allocate few resources against the petty cigarette traders. . . . This inattention is not a result of corruption, as the sellers lack the funds and the contacts to corrupt French officials."[239] Nevertheless, "France is the contraband cigarette capital of Western Europe."[240] Moreover, Marseille is the key node or hub in the network, with illicit cigarettes proving pervasive. As one news report noted, "cigarette smuggling is taking place everywhere: on the flea market under video surveillance cameras, in the port, and even in the vicinity of the city's police stations."[241] Another report added that one smuggling technique was wrapping the cigarettes and concealing them in the gasoline tank of vehicles.[242] Some consumers complained though that the cigarettes smelled of gasoline.[243]

If all this largely reflects a form of disorganized crime at the street level in Marseilles, Shelley persuasively argues that the supply chain to France is far more organized.[244] As she notes, "the Algerian-origin cigarettes are produced for a legal market in Algeria. For millions of cigarettes to arrive in France illegally, there need to be factory workers, shippers and vendors in Algeria capable of diverting this product en masse to France. There are also high-level Algerian officials implicated in this trade. This quantity of product requires containers arriving from Algeria, revealing corruption in the French port."[245] In addition, Shelley described how truck drivers "move large quantities of illicit cigarettes overland from Spain to France," with Facebook being used "to advise truck drivers and distributors where to pick up these illicit shipments."[246]

Although customs and law enforcement failed to do much about the Algerian connection, the Covid-19 pandemic seems to have been far more consequential in the short term. According to a news report, quoting KPMG, "flows from Algeria to France decreased by 78% to reach 0.4 billion cigarettes during 2020."[247] The KPMG report attributed this major decline in smuggling to border closings and the massive decrease of both shipping freight and airline travel between North Africa and France.[248] By 2022, however, counterfeit and contraband flows (including illicit whites) from Algeria had bounced back. Indeed, they had increased by 0.7 billion and stood at 1.06 billion cigarettes—the highest level seen in the reporting period of the study, which covered 2018 to 2022.[249] This was not surprising—the price of cigarettes quadrupled from Algeria to France, and those involved were skillfully engaged in arbitrage that exploited the price asymmetries between the two countries.

Natural Resource Exploitation and Wildlife Trafficking

Although a large part of Algeria is desert, the country is not only rich in hydrocarbons, but also has substantial gold deposits in the south, coastal beaches, and a rich wildlife. Moreover, the waters off the Algerian coast have some of the most abundant reefs of red coral in the world.

Algeria's single most important resource is its oil industry. Unlike Libya, however, where there has been large-scale smuggling of oil by criminal networks that include militia leaders, businessmen, and organized crime figures, there is a two-level problem in Algeria. At the top level is the corruption that is endemic globally in an industry that is not only highly opaque but also full of middlemen and fixers. At the lower level, fuel becomes a form of contraband that is smuggled across Algeria's borders with at least some of its neighbors—largely in response to the arbitrage opportunities stemming from the low prices of Algerian oil and gasoline. These two dimensions are both discussed more fully elsewhere in this chapter. The high-level corruption in the Algerian oil industry has precipitated a series of scandals implicating major political and business figures that are discussed more fully in the section on corruption, illicit financial flows, and money laundering. The low-level problem is discussed as part of the contraband smuggling that is endemic in North Africa and is carried out by organized and disorganized crime. Separating these two levels is not to dismiss the problem, as smuggling is believed to cost the Algerian state close to a billion dollars a year. It bears emphasis, however, that smuggled fuel in Algeria's neighbors typically sells for less than the normal price of gasoline in those countries. Indeed, cross-border fuel smuggling could be understood as an unintended form of subsidies for those in border regions. Although fuel smuggling could be exploited by transnational criminal and terrorist networks, it is perhaps more important to recognize that such activities benefit poor communities and might even be a force for regional stability.

Oil is not the only natural resource that is exploited in Algeria. The prevalence of illegal gold mining in southern Algeria provides another example of increasing criminality, although one on which there is limited information. The Global Initiative Against Transnational Organized Crime in 2023 noted that foreign criminal groups dominated illicit gold mining in the south of Algeria and that few locals were involved. Reportedly, airline employees had recently become involved in smuggling gold bars abroad, which added another dimension to a problem that seemed to emerge around 2015 and created increasing consternation for the government.[250] Much of the mining is in the Hassi Tiririne region near the border with Niger. January 2019 witnessed the beginnings of a clampdown as authorities arrested smugglers and confiscated weapons from an illegal gold mining group. In June 2019 police arrested thirty-nine illegal gold miners,[251] with another twenty-three arrested in Tamanrasset and Djanet in August.[252] In 2020 the efforts to investigate and disrupt illegal gold mining were intensified. What seemed to be a coordinated operation between the army and the judicial police arrested 4,755 prospector and smugglers and seized 2,376 pressure hammers, 3,460 generators and 186 metal detectors.[253] Moreover, an investigation by the judicial police "revealed the existence of international cells operating in 12 special cities of the south of the country, specialized in selling American-made exploration equipment."[254] A second policy strand was also developing, however, with the announcement by the minister of mines in August 2020 that young people were "allowed to form cooperatives to explore and exploit gold mines in the south."[255] Some weeks later, the minister described artisanal gold mining as an "an added value" to the development and diversification of the national economy.[256] New licenses for gold mining were issued. What remains uncertain, however, is whether this is a real effort to diversify or simply an attempt to restore and maintain a government monopoly over the process.

Illegal sand mining in Algeria typically receives far less attention. Yet even though such activities are less blatant and less extensive than in Morocco, they remain highly damaging to the environment. Episodic reports over the last ten to fifteen years suggest that the problem is serious, enduring, and occurs at different locations. The reasons for this are more complex than might be thought. According to Coastal Care (coastalcare.org), sand has diverse properties that make it attractive for different reasons. "Mineral sands are rich in heavy minerals, such as ilmenite and zircon, and are primarily extracted for use in metal production and other industrial applications."[257] Aggregate sands, which are angular and contain a mix of granules of various sizes, are primarily used in construction; desert sand, unlike beach sands, lacks this angular property and is too smooth for construction.[258] Unfortunately, "the current rate of coastal sand extraction outstrips the natural replenishment rate of quality sand suitable for standard uses, which makes it unsustainable."[259] About 85 percent of sand extracted is used for construction and about 10 percent for mineral extraction, with some sand used for beach replenishment.[260] Construction in Algeria—especially in the north—has increased with urbanization. This has resulted in beach sand depletion in various locales along Algeria's coastline. In 2014 Coastal Care reported that illegal beach sand mining activities were increasing in western Algeria, most notably in Oran, and even when there was a police presence, what the organization termed the "sand mafia" was not deterred.[261] There were similar reports about illegal sand mining along "the coastal region of El Taref and Skikda" and near the border with Tunisia.[262] In 2018, eighteen cases of illegal sand mining were recorded, but only about three-quarters of them were investigated.[263] In 2019, however, all thirty-two cases were investigated, and twelve persons were arrested.[264] Moreover, police "seized 34 trucks, 3 vehicles, 1 tractor, 2 donkeys and 12 motorcycles; they also recovered the equivalent of 75 truckloads of sand worth about 470,000 US dollars."[265] It seems unlikely though that these law enforcement successes have solved the problem.

If sand depletion is one rather surprising problem, illegal harvesting of red coral is another. While it has traditionally been a form of jewelry, red coral is now used in the manufacture of plane and rocket screws because it is "resistant to high atmospheric pressures."[266] Unfortunately, the coral—which can sell for as much as 5,000 euros per kilogram—is in danger of extinction.[267] In 2001 Algeria imposed a twenty-year moratorium on the harvesting of red coral. The result was typical for prohibition regimes with price increases encouraging illegal harvesting and smuggling. During the moratorium Algeria's coastal security services seized over 15 tonnes of red coral that had been illegally harvested.[268] Specific cases include one in November 2017, when 165 kilograms of red coral worth an estimated 74,000 euros were interdicted near the Tunisian border.[269] In October 2019, 59 kilograms were intercepted in the Algerian province of Tizi Ouzou.[270] More significantly, a few months earlier, in May 2019, Tunisian security forces arrested seven Tunisians, two Spaniards, and an Algerian trying to smuggle nearly 700 kilograms of red coral worth almost 2 million euros from Algeria to Tunisia.[271] Estimates suggest that about 3 tonnes of red coral are "trafficked annually from Algeria to Torre del Greco near Naples which is the global center of red coral processing"[272] More generally, an estimated 80 percent of Algeria's coral "is illegally exported to Europe."[273] At the end of the moratorium, limits were placed on how much could be collected and at which specific locations. A limit of 3,000 kilograms per year was imposed in certain areas, and those who acquired the coral were required to sell 70 percent of their product to the state company AGENOR.[274] Critics contended that the end of the moratorium created new opportunities "to sell excess coral in the illicit markets."[275] They were also concerned that poaching might "be replaced by state-approved looting."[276] The problem was exacerbated by the failure of efforts by the United States and the European Union to protect red coral through its inclusion in the Convention on International Trade in Endangered Species (CITES).

Fauna and flora are also at risk in Algeria. The illegal logging of cedar and fir trees in the Atlas Mountains has destroyed established forests and is "endangering species such as the Tassili cypress, Numidian fir, and black pine."[277] Moreover, Covid-19 exacerbated the problem. With law enforcement authorities preoccupied elsewhere, new opportunities for illegal timber trafficking emerged, while it also became a source of sustenance in straitened economic circumstances. These problems are not confined to flora, with "several fauna species in Algeria . . . in danger of extinction. . . . The illegal hunting of the endangered gazelle and bearded mouflon is particularly concerning and is often underreported."[278] There is also an illegal trade in birds—especially goldfinch and African Grey parrots—both online and in open-air markets. In one three-month study in late 2018 and early 2019, investigators identified "5400 live animals belonging to 19 species for sale" on the Algerian online selling platform Oued Kniss.[279] A 2017 study found seven barbary macaques for sale on the same platform.[280] Although there are numerous CITES violations, it seems that most of the species were for local sale. In effect, this is a small and disorganized market. The one qualification to this, however, is that individuals from the Gulf are reportedly involved in poaching. One study even suggested that this was facilitated by high-level politicians. In the 2020 trial of a former prime minister, he acknowledged that he had received sixty gold bars worth $2.6 million from "emirs of the Persian Gulf countries who regularly came to hunt antelopes, Houbara bustards," and "other animals in the Algerian desert" even though these species were protected by Algerian law.[281]

Contraband Smuggling

On Algeria's eastern border with Tunisia, contraband smuggling is rife. Indeed, the population suffers from poverty, high levels of unemployment, and marginalization. As Dalia Ghanem noted, "In Algeria, spatial disparity and economic inequality are intertwined. Many of the provinces situated in the extreme northeast of the country, on the border with Tunisia, suffer from profound socio-economic marginalization. This situation is unlikely to change."[282] She also argues, similar to Gallien and Herbert, that smugglers and border officials have developed symbiotic rather than adversarial relationships—for good reason.[283] As she noted, the "rationale for lax enforcement of the law is that smuggling goods into Tunisia serves as the engine of the local economy in an underdeveloped and marginalized region. Concomitantly, it mitigates resentment of the central government in Algiers."[284] Local officials have developed a high degree of discretion if not complete autonomy, partly because, although the state is not absent, it is certainly not present in a meaningful way. As Ghanem noted, a region that was supposed to have one public official for every 341 inhabitants has one per 1,794 inhabitants.[285] In other words, "the borderlands are a place where the authority of the Algerian state is more than nominal yet less than total."[286] As a smuggler wryly observed, "Where you live matters. Here we've been penalized by geography."[287]

The smuggling economy provides a livelihood and coping mechanism. Ghanem's findings include a diversity of products being smuggled from Algeria into Tunisia, to include " "gasoline, livestock (especially sheep), auto parts, copper, electronics manufactured by the Algerian brand Condor, perfume, cosmetics, yogurt, powdered milk, and potatoes. Traffic is not one-way, however. Products smuggled into Algeria from Tunisia are similarly varied and include pasta, cooking oil, canned tomatoes, halva, flavored tobacco for water pipes, and bananas."[288] Gasoline is critical: it costs a third in Algeria of its cost in Tunisia and reportedly accounts for 75 percent of the economic activity in the region.[289] From the state perspective there is a principal-agent gap. From the perspective of those on the ground, the principal is in Algiers and distance allows discretion. At the same time, there is tacit agreement that information about terrorists and serious drug traffickers will be passed on to the authorities.[290]

Algeria's southern borders with Mali and Niger have already been discussed in relation to arms trafficking and human smuggling. Measures taken to contain these security challenges have made commodity smuggling over these borders more difficult, but far from impossible. Part of the reason smuggling remains prevalent is that although borders demarcate geographical space, they do not cut enduring economic, social, and kinship ties. It is not entirely surprising, therefore, that, as one study has observed, "the Kidal region of Mali has been practically integrated into Algeria's economy. . . . The Algerian and Malian Tuareg population is effectively allowed free movement across the border, with many obtaining dual citizenship and conducting business in both countries. The two provinces of Mali that border Algeria, Kidal and Timbuktu, are almost entirely supplied with contraband fuel from Algeria."[291] Moreover, one of the paradoxes of borders is that they accentuate price differentials, thereby offering major arbitrage opportunities. These are exploited by both low-level or "ant" traffickers who are authorized fuel dealers and professional smugglers who move much larger amounts of fuel.[292] Twice a month the border is opened by local authorities, allowing the registered fuel dealers to take excess fuel of 150 to 200 liters—or almost one drum—into Mali; the professional smugglers in contrast carry five to six drums per vehicle.[293] They typically pick up the fuel in Tamanrassett and Adrar and stow it in warehouses along the border before transporting it across difficult terrain to avoid formal checkpoints.

Algeria's border with Morocco is likely the hardest border in North Africa to cross with contraband largely because of the fractious relationship between the two states rather than security concerns—although the cannabis trade from Morocco to and through Algeria has given some legitimacy to the Algerian government's much more restrictive approach. The transformation of the border trade between Algeria and Morocco has been delineated brilliantly by Matthew Herbert. As he noted, "along the frontier, the contraband trade was historically dominated by consumer commodities, such as petrol, food, medicines, and electronics. Ready availability of the goods in either Algeria or Morocco led to low barriers to entry for prospective smugglers, leading to a smuggling ecosystem comprising numerous small smuggling networks. State authorities in both Morocco and Algeria easily dominated the networks, profiting off them via joint-extractive systems and largely halting the emergence of smuggling-linked violence."[294] This system was not inhibited by the poor relationship between the two countries. Even when the border was closed, as one Moroccan security expert remarked, it was "only closed for legal things."[295] In large part, the cross-border smuggling was facilitated by family, kinship, and social links that transcended the formal border.[296] Moreover, entry barriers to the smuggling business were low and this led to many networks that mostly remained small.[297] Arbitrage strategies that exploit price differentials in different countries were also at work. In the 2000s, gasoline prices increased in Morocco, whereas the continued subsidies in Algeria kept prices much lower there. Consequently, gasoline became the dominant commodity smuggled between the two countries.[298] This system changed drastically, largely because of changes in the price of oil and gasoline. Indeed, "the boom time for smugglers along the Algeria-Morocco border ended in 2014, when the global price of oil dropped sharply. This lowered the price of licit petrol in Morocco, constricting smugglers' profits. It also significantly limited Algeria's earnings from exporting oil, which spurred the government to crack down on illicit petrol trade."[299] The concomitant of this is that although the smuggling of cannabis has increased, it now requires much more elaborate efforts to move without interdiction.[300] Because it is so specialized it is also far less diffuse than contraband smuggling with much higher entry costs.[301] It is also associated with some increases in violence.[302] The overall result though is that the coping strategies of many people who earned a living from smuggling contraband have been seriously undermined. As a result, the drastic change in smuggling between Morocco and Algeria contrasts very starkly with the continuity of smuggling commodities across the Algeria-Tunisia border. In some respects, there is an interesting parallel here with the preceding discussion of human smuggling. The difficulties that migrants have faced in Maghnia resemble those that contraband smugglers have also faced.[303] In effect, contraband smuggling has been seriously undermined, with significant damage to communities on both sides of the Algeria Morocco border. Some contraband smugglers have become cannabis smugglers; most of them, however, have lost their livelihood and simply become unemployed.

In this connection, it is difficult not to take issue with a 2018 OCP Policy Center brief in which Alexander Babuta and Cathy Haenlein emphasize that commodity smuggling in the Maghreb is "a silent threat" insufficiently appreciated.[304] "Far from being an 'innocent' phenomenon, it can form a critical part of much broader, larger-scale illicit networks, with significant negative impacts on national and regional security."[305] Part of the authors' logic seems to be that commodity smuggling can act as a gateway, and that those involved all too easily graduate from smuggling innocuous commodities to trafficking arms, drugs, and people. The authors are also critical of "dual smuggling" whereby "those involved in commodity smuggling . . . supplement their profits by offering transportation to illegal migrants—and vice versa."[306] Even though the authors recognize that some small-scale smuggling is linked to "survival strategies," this seems far less important to them than the impact of state revenue losses and the challenge to security.[307] This approach not only belies the realities on the ground but also is based on a national security paradigm that ignores human security, human needs, and human dignity. Yet even from a national security perspective, it is wrongheaded. Commodity smuggling is both a safety net for marginalized and unemployed youth and a safety valve for states that are failing to provide adequate employment opportunities. By choking off these lifelines the prospects for violent resistance against the state are likely to increase, while the recruitment opportunities for terrorist organizations will also expand. Even if commodity smuggling is not completely innocent, therefore, further interference with it by the authorities is likely to be counterproductive.

Corruption, Illicit Financial Flows, and Money Laundering

Corruption is an abiding problem in Algeria, albeit one that is also used as a political weapon by competing elites. It has been used by the Tebboune regime in part to distance itself from the Bouteflika presidency and consolidate the idea of a new Algeria. Yet this strategy has not been entirely successful. Transparency International (TI) in 2022 gave Algeria a grade of 33 out of 100 and ranked it as 116 out of 180 countries, placing it close to the bottom third of all those included in the TI index.

While Algeria is not among the worst offenders in North Africa when it comes to corruption, it does languish in the lower half of the league table well behind Tunisia, which has a score of 40 and is ranked number 85, and Morocco, which scores 38 and is ranked 94.[308] Algeria, however, is well above Egypt, which scores 30 and is ranked at 130, and Libya, which scores 17 and ranks close to the bottom at 171 out of 180.[309] Nevertheless, the relatively poor ranking is not really surprising, as Algeria readily meets the preconditions for extensive corruption. Robert Klitgaard's well-known and compelling framework argues that corruption arises when there is "monopoly plus discretion minus accountability."[310] Algeria has long exhibited these characteristics with a military authority that had very little accountability to the politicians or the public, political elites that exhibit the worst kinds of cronyism and have little sense of respect for the demarcation between public and private interests, and an oil industry that for decades provided sufficient revenues to remove any impetus for political or economic reform.

Although the global hydrocarbons industry is permeated by corruption, the scandals in the oil and gas sector of the Algerian economy are in part a function of the deeply interwoven relationships between the state apparatus and Algeria's state-owned oil and gas company, Sonatrach, which dominates industry in the country. Although there have been pressures for reform and even the privatization of Sonatrach, this has not happened largely because the governing elites "rely upon Sonatrach for revenue from which they gain power, patronage, and privileges."[311] Indeed, patronage networks and competition among the political and military elites for economic rents are central to the Algerian state and are both facilitated and perpetuated by the opaque nature of political power in the country, the role of the military, and the reliance on rents from the oil and gas industries.

The first major Sonatrach scandal began in 2009 when the Department of Intelligence and Security began to investigate allegations of corruption. The following year the Sonatrach chief executive officer (CEO) Mohamed Meziane was forced to resign for allowing preferential contracts in return for bribes and kickbacks.[312] From there the probe extended to include Chakib Khelil, who had been appointed minister of energy and mines in 1999 and acted as CEO of Sonatrach from March 2001 to 2003. Khelil had been a promoter of reform in the energy sector and was close to President Bouteflika but was dismissed from his ministerial position in May 2010. In 2013 he left Algeria and became the target of an international arrest warrant. By then Meziane had received a two-year prison sentence but still proclaimed his innocence. In 2015, he along with his two sons and sixteen other defendants were charged with "granting privileges to third parties, hiking prices of contracts with a state company, embezzlement, money laundering and corruption."[313] Meziane and his sons appeared in court, but the trial was then postponed.

In another case, Italian prosecutors requested that the Italian oil company Eni and its subsidiary Saipem be prosecuted for paying bribes to win contracts in Algeria. An Algerian businessman and official Farid Bedjaoui, who had worked in Khelil's office, seemed to be at the heart of this scheme. Operating from the Bulgari Hotel in Milan (at a cost of $100,000 over five years) he acted as an intermediary between Algerian government officials and Saipem executives, effectively implementing a massive $200 million to $275 million bribery scheme that enabled Saipem to win "more than $10 billion in contracts to build oil and gas pipelines from the North African desert to the shores of the Mediterranean."[314] Bedjaoui, who was known as "Mr. 3%," used the opacity of offshore companies to move and hide the money.[315] He registered seventeen shell companies, twelve of which were created by Mossack Fonseca—which, of course, claimed that it was simply facilitating a process essential to the global economy and was not responsible for how these companies were used.[316] Italian investigators characterized one of these companies, Minkle Consultants S.A., as a "crossroads of illicit financial flows" linked to the bribes.[317] It seems likely that others were used in the same way to hide shady deals, obfuscate culpability, and make it difficult to follow and seize the money. For its part, Saipem declared the bribes as "intermediary fees placed with the Hong Kong–based Pearl Partners Limited company controlled by Farid Bedjaoui."[318] A Canadian company, SNC-Lavalin also had contracts with Sonatrach and between 2003 and 2013 made $6 billion from its business in Algeria.[319] With the release of the Panama Papers, it emerged that SNC-Lavalin had also paid millions in bribes "to a clandestine company, Cadber Investments SA" set up by Mossack Fonseca in 1999 and registered in the British Virgin Islands.[320] Although SNC-Lavalin had six contracts with Cadber from 2000 to 2004, it had no idea who it was really dealing with.[321] It had all the hallmarks, however, of the kind of illegal scheme carried out by Bedjaoui.

Algerian authorities have also continued to target Khelil, although he left Algeria in 2013. Khelil returned in 2016 after the charges against him had been dropped, only to leave again after Bouteflika was compelled to step down. He was charged in 2022 and was sentenced, in absentia, to twenty years' imprisonment. In a separate case in January 2023, he was also sentenced to twenty years and subjected to an international arrest warrant.[322] This was part of a broader effort to target corrupt officials in the energy sector.

In November 2022 Abdelmoumen Ould Kaddour, CEO of Sonatrach from March 2017 to early April 2019, was sentenced to fifteen years in prison for corruption, while Ahmed Mazighi, his former assistant, received a sentence of seven years. This case revolved around Sonatrech's 2018 purchase of the Augusta refinery and other infrastructure in southern Italy from Esso Italy—a subsidiary of American ExxonMobil. Although those involved claimed it was a cost-effective purchase, many of the details suggested the refinery was antiquated and that the purchase was illogical. Even if the criticisms were exaggerated, the price of $2.1 billion was considered excessive—leading to charges of "squandering public funds, abuse of office and conflict of interest."[323] The sentences were slightly lower than prosecutors had requested even though this was not the first time that Ould Kaddour had been involved in corruption. He had led the oil engineering company Brown and Root

Condor—a subsidiary of Sonatrach that was dissolved in 2007 because of suspicions of corruption in contracting.[324]

In December 2022, the US Securities and Exchange Commission announced that Honeywell had accepted responsibility for acts of bribery in both Brazil and Algeria and agreed to pay more than $81 million to settle the charges. Although the main issue was Brazil, where over $4 million was paid in bribes, "in 2011, employees and agents of Honeywell's Belgian subsidiary paid more than $75,000 in bribes to an Algerian government official to obtain and retain business" with Sonatrach.[325]

Another recent scandal implicating Sonatrach involved the sale of fuel oil to Lebanon. The deal was announced with some fanfare in 2005 and was implemented from 2006 onward. The agreement was for Algeria to deliver 1.1 million tonnes of fuel and 1 million tonnes of gas per year for the next three years to Lebanon's national electric company, Electricite du Liban. Initially the arrangement seemed to work well, and the contract was successively renewed at three-year intervals. In early 2020, however, Sonatrach delivered a load of "non-compliant fuel oil, intended for . . . Lebanese power plants. The fuel on board the ship Aspo, chartered by Sonatrach, was found to be defective after tests conducted by Lebanese laboratories, according to the local news channel."[326] This led quickly to an investigation resulting in arrest warrants for "several people, including Sonatrach's representative in Lebanon, Tarek Faoual" and claims of bribery and payoffs.[327] One hypothesis advanced in the Lebanese press was that the low-quality fuel was from "an old Sicilian refinery, bought at an exorbitant price by Sonatrach almost two years ago, and which produces, with the complicity of the Italian mafia, a very poor quality fuel oil."[328] It also appears that Sonatrach had subcontracted the implementation of the supply process to ZR Energy. In this connection, one source contended that "ZR Energy loaded the tainted fuel via ship-to-ship transfer off Malta, where the fuel oil was possibly blended with a cheap additive. When it came to Lebanon (with a Malta inspection certificate), the cargo was discharged into a storage tank. But the sediment now prevents it from being pumped out—resulting in damage and impaired storage capacity."[329] Significantly, the US Treasury imposed sanctions on the two bothers Raymond Zina Rahme and Teddy Zina Rahme, who owned ZR Energy, on the grounds that they had engaged in corrupt practices.[330]

Yet there are a few positive signs. In September 2023, for example, Sonatrach announced that it had created a digital platform where "employees, partners, customers and other stakeholders" could report acts of corruption or bribery.[331] In November 2023, eight vice presidents were dismissed as Sonatrach seemed to be developing a new focus on opportunities in Libya. Given Sonatrach's record, however, this could prove to be a high-risk activity that rapidly devolves into another round of corruption.

Not all the corruption scandals have revolved around the oil and gas sector. One of the first corruption scandals of the Bouteflika era occurred in 2002. Frequently described as the "scandal of the century," it centered on Rafik Khalifa and the El Khalifa Group, a massive conglomerate that included "a bank an airline and television stations."[332] Khalifa, who was "the son of a former intelligence chief and minister" was close to political and military elites.[333] About 1.3 billion euros of public money, including pension funds, were deposited in the Khalifa Bank. Moreover, the bank "provided a more covert path for the transfer of irregular funds abroad—estimated at €689 million between 1999 and 2003—allowing figures in the regime to export and launder embezzled funds from the country, principally to France."[334] These transfers were not supervised by Algeria's Central Bank. Nevertheless, the Central Bank intervened in November 2002 to prevent further transfers abroad, "thus belatedly arresting what had become a major capital flight operation costing the state treasury an estimated $1.5 billion."[335] Khalifa fled to Britain but was eventually extradited to Algeria and subsequently sentenced to eighteen years in prison in 2015 for embezzlement. No government officials were formally implicated despite their likely involvement in capital flight.

The other notable corruption case centered around the East-West Highway, which was an infrastructure project that cost almost three times as much as its initial estimate of $6 billion. With multiple foreign firms involved in the project, opportunities for bribes and kickback were rife—and were fully exploited. It was estimated that at least $5 billion of the cost stemmed from corruption.[336] In 2015 a court sentenced fourteen people to prison for money laundering and embezzlement of public funds and fined seven foreign firms.[337]

The quasi-demise of the auto industry in Algeria stemmed from a combination of corruption and mismanagement. The project began very promisingly in 2012 with Renault working with the Algerian government to create a major assembly plant in Oran. It expanded with similar projects involving Hyundai and Volkswagen but then became mired in controversy as accusations were made that Hyundai was bringing in "semi knocked-down" units that were quickly and easily reassembled in Algeria. Critics alleged that these were "disguised imports" rather than cars being produced in Algeria.[338] The resulting crisis of confidence became entangled with another corruption scandal as it emerged that

Bouteflika's cronies had been given preferential treatment in the fledgling auto industry, benefiting from "state incentives and tax exemptions."[339] Two former prime ministers were convicted for "misappropriation of public funds, abuse of power and granting undue privileges."[340] More seriously, lots of employees in the automobile sector lost jobs that had once seemed promising. In 2023, there were glimmers of a recovery, however, as a leading global automaker, Stellantis, began to produce several kinds of Fiat cars in Algeria.

Some of these corruption cases involved money flowing out of Algeria. One such case resulted from the Panama Papers disclosures and compelled Algeria to initiate a money laundering investigation.[341] "This highlighted the abuse of a government-run milk powder subsidy program" run by Algerian entrepreneur Zoubir Bererhi, the brother of a former government minister, and his son.[342] As an Algerian journalist noted, "their offshore company, which they claimed not to own, bought the milk powder at the global market price and sold it to their own dairy company sometimes for as much as twice the price."[343] Much of the proceeds were placed in Swiss bank accounts, highlighting once again the nexus between fraud and embezzlement on the one side and money laundering on the other.

Algeria's record in combating money laundering has been far from stellar. Although Algeria is not a major money laundering country, its Anti-Money Laundering system has gaps and deficiencies.[344] Algeria's mutual evaluation by the Financial Action Task Force (FATF) in 2020 identified serious deficiencies in the country's efforts to combat money laundering and terrorist financing.[345] Indeed, for several years, Algeria had been on what was called the gray list of countries that required monitoring because of their compliance deficiencies. It was only removed from the list in February 2016.[346] Yet much remains to be done. This was reflected in the US Department of State's 2021 INCSR. The report noted that money laundering through Algeria's formal financial system was minimal due to stringent regulations. "However, a large informal, cash-based economy, estimated at 40 percent of GDP, is vulnerable to abuse by criminals. The real estate market is particularly vulnerable to money laundering"[347]

This was hardly a glowing endorsement, and the INCSR further noted that "customs fraud, the use of offshore tax havens" and trade-based money laundering "increasingly concern Algerian authorities. Algeria's extensive informal economy and nearly exclusive use of cash heighten the risk of financial crimes."[348] At the same time, the report observed that Algeria's Financial Intelligence Processing Unit (CTRF), had some success. In 2019, the CTRF initiated fifty-nine money laundering investigations and thirty-nine terrorist financing cases, resulting in 105 convictions.[349] In 2020, however, momentum seemed to have been lost as the CTRF referred only fourteen cases to the Ministry of Justice.[350] Nine concerned corruption, and none of the cases of suspected money laundering related to trafficking of narcotics.[351] The weaknesses in Algeria's Anti-Money Laundering Program were underlined by the MENA Financial Action Task Force Mutual Evaluation in May 2023, which concluded that although some progress had been made, major deficiencies remained, including weaknesses in identifying and managing risks. After the 2023 FATF Plenary in October 2023, Algeria was added to the B list part ii accompanied by countries such as Burundi, Côte d'Ivoire, Cuba, Egypt, Lebanon, Niger, Pakistan, Suriname, Tajikistan, Ukraine, and Venezuela.

In terms of illicit financial flows—which result from corruption and bribery, tax evasion, criminal proceeds, corporate profit shifting, and currency regulation evasion—the situation appears to be even more serious.[352] In a 2018 study covering the period from 1970 to 2015, it was determined that Algeria had lost $141.5 billion in constant 2015 US dollars.[353] In some respects, this underlined a 2015 study that noted that Algeria accounted for over 20 percent of all illicit financial flows from Africa in the oil sector.[354] These findings were not surprising given the endemic corruption surrounding Sonatrach.

Conclusion

Algeria, until the resurgence of its oil and gas prices, was suffering from dual crises—one political and one economic—that were intersecting in complex and unpredictable ways. The economic crisis, although tempered in the short term, has exacerbated the structural problems in Algeria regarding a growing cohort of fifteen- to twenty-four-year-old citizens who are unable to find adequate employment opportunities, despite projections of a decrease of the youth labor force (fifteen to twenty-four year olds) by 0.9 percent by 2030 compared to 2015.[355] At the same time, the military remains the most powerful political actor in the country, albeit with a growing sense that it can no longer hide behind the smokescreen of civilian control. Should there be a resurgence of the Hirak, the military leadership will have to decide either to relinquish some of its power or to become more blatant and obvious in its wielding of that power. Moreover, military power has already become more overt in the fight against criminality and illicit markets in Algeria. The focus on hardening and militarizing borders and the harsh treatment of migrants and refugees—something that has consistently been denied by the Algerian authorities—has had a perverse impact and unintentionally encouraged a shift away from relatively innocuous commodity smuggling based on arbitrage opportunities to a greater emphasis on various forms of trafficking.[356] Unless Algeria can deal with its corruption problems and make fundamental rather than cosmetic shifts toward democracy, therefore, governance will remain problematic and stability could be eroded. Oil price rises in 2022 and 2023 provided a breathing space, but if these high prices come to an end, so too could the era of stability that has prevailed since the end of Algeria's civil war.

Notes

1. Viorst, "Algeria's Long Night."
2. Mundy, *Imaginative Geographies of Algerian Violence,* p. 7.
3. Volpi, "Algeria Versus the Arab Spring."
4. Daoud, "The Algerian Exception."
5. Davis, "Democracy or Dependence?"
6. Kilavuz and Grewal, "Algerians Have Been Protesting."
7. Bertelsmann Transformation Index (BTI), *Algeria Country Report 2022.*
8. Bryant, "As Algeria Prepares."
9. Al Jazeera, "Algeria's FLN Wins."
10. Leggewie and Ouaissa, "Algeria's Gramscian Situation."
11. International Crisis Group, "Breaking Algeria's Economic Paralysis"; Laoubi and Yamao, "Challenge of Agriculture in Algeria."
12. Davis, "Democracy or Dependence?"
13. Ghanem and Benderra, "A Looming Crisis"; Reuters, "Algeria's Foreign Exchange Reserves."
14. Ratcliffe, Karam, and El Wardany, "Algeria's Oil and Gas Exports."
15. Ibid.; Saadi, "Algeria's 2020 Hydrocarbons Production."
16. Leggewie and Ouaissa, "Algeria's Gramscian Situation."
17. Hamaizia and Zoubir, "Algeria's Perfect Storm."
18. Francesco Serrano, "Higher Oil Prices."
19. Ratcliffe, Karam, and El Wardany, "An Oil Country No More?"
20. Soufan Center, "Algeria Positioned to Help Europe."
21. Serrano, "Higher Oil Prices."
22. ENACT, *Organized Crime Index 2019—Algeria.*
23. Ibid., pp. 1–2.
24. Global Organized Crime Index, *Algeria 2023,* p. 1.
25. Ibid., pp. 1, 4.
26. ENACT, *Organized Crime Index 2019—Algeria.*
27. Global Organized Crime Index, *Algeria 2023.*
28. US Department of State, *International Narcotics Control Strategy Report,* Volume 2. (March 2021), p. 39.

29. Global Organized Crime Index, *Algeria 2023*, p. 5.
30. Herbert and Gallien, *A Rising Tide*, pp. 27, 29–33, 40.
31. Ibid., p. 28.
32. Ibid., p. 30.
33. Herbert and Gallien, *A Rising Tide*.
34. Ibid., p. 14.
35. Ibid.
36. Ibid.
37. Ibid., pp. 14–15.
38. Ibid., p. 15.
39. Ibid.
40. Ibid., pp. 15–16.
41. Ibid., p. 14.
42. Ibid.
43. Ibid.
44. Ibid.
45. Ibid.
46. Ibid.
47. Ibid., p. 13.
48. MoroccoLatestNews.com, "Algeria, a Hub for Hard Drugs."
49. Algeria Press Service, "Over 25 Tonnes of Cannabis."
50. Algeria Press Service, "Nine Drug Traffickers Arrested."
51. Herbert and Gallien, *A Rising Tide*, pp. 13, 17.
52. Yahia and Farrah, "Algerian Cocaine Bust."
53. Ibid.
54. Yahia and Farrah, "Algerian Cocaine Bust"; Herbert and Gallien, *A Rising Tide*, p. 18.
55. Yahia and Farrah, "Algerian Cocaine Bust"; Herbert and Gallien, *A Rising Tide*, p. 18.
56. Herbert and Gallien, *A Rising Tide*, p. 18.
57. Rahim and Halasz, "Half a Ton of Cocaine"; *Guardian*, "Coastguard Seizes Half a Tonne"; MoroccoLatestNews.com, "Algeria, a Hub for Hard Drugs."
58. *Guardian*, "Coastguard Seizes Half a Tonne."
59. Yahia and Farrah, "Algerian Cocaine Bust."
60. CSO Alliance, "Has Algeria Joined?"
61. *Algiers Herald*, "Cocaine Trafficker."
62. Ibid.
63. Soto, "Record Cocaine Busts"; Gaye, "Connections Between Jihadist Groups," pp. 10, 15; Caulderwood, "Drugs and Money in the Sahara."; Lewis and Diarra, "In the Land of 'Gangster-Jihadists'"; Lounnas, "Links Between Jihadi Organizations," p. 7.
64. McDermott et al., *Cocaine Pipeline to Europe*; Yahia, "Is Cocaine the New Cannabis?"
65. UNODC, *Global Report on Cocaine 2023*, p. 115.
66. Global Organized Crime Index, *Algeria 2023*, p. 4.
67. Ibid.
68. UNODC, *Global Report on Cocaine 2023*, p. 112.
69. For a brilliant analysis related to this point, see Levi, "Money for Crime and Money," pp. 275–297.
70. EMCDDA, *Overview of Drug Markets*, p. 25.
71. Herbert and Gallien, *A Rising Tide*, p. 21.

72. Ibid., p. 22.
73. Ibid.
74. Ibid., pp. 22–23.
75. Ibid., p. 23.
76. Pope, "Spain's National Police."
77. Global Organized Crime Index, *Algeria 2023*, p. 4.
78. EMCDDA, *Overview of Drug Markets*, p. 35.
79. Ibid., p. 32.
80. Ibid.
81. Tinasti, "View from the Ground"; Kasraoui, "Morocco Arrests Moroccan, Algerian."
82. *Morocco Latest News*, "Algeria, a Hub for Hard Drugs."
83. Ibid.
84. Global Organized Crime Index, *Algeria 2023*, p. 3.
85. Farrah, *Algeria's Migration Dilemma*, p. 9.
86. Ibid., p. 9.
87. Ibid., p. 1.
88. Ibid.
89. Ibid., pp. 1–2, 19–22, 26–30.
90. Ibid., p. 1.
91. Ibid., p. 20.
92. Ibid., p. 22.
93. Ibid., p. 26.
94. Ibid., p. 30.
95. Ibid., pp. 30–31.
96. Ibid., p. 11.
97. Ibid., p. 28.
98. Ibid., p. 10.
99. Ibid., pp. 8, 29–30.
100. Interpol and ENACT, *Overview of Serious and Organized Crime*.
101. Ibid.
102. Farrah, *Algeria's Migration Dilemma*, p. 43.
103. Ibid., p. 13.
104. Ibid., pp. 13–15.
105. Ibid., p. 15.
106. Ibid., p. 17.
107. Lensari and Bellal, "Illegal Migration from the Sahel."
108. Gnes, *Maghnia: Crossing the Uncrossable Border*, p. 2.
109. Ibid., p. 2.
110. Ibid., p. 13.
111. Ibid.
112. Ibid., p. 18.
113. Ibid., p. 16.
114. Ibid., p. 19.
115. Ibid.
116. Ibid.
117. Ibid., p. 23.
118. Tognini, "A New Migrant Gateway."
119. Malakooti and Fall, *Migration Trends Across the Mediterranean*, p. 39.
120. Ibid., p. 40.
121. Ibid.

122. Farrah, *Algeria's Migration Dilemma*, p. 1.
123. Hinnant, Delay, and Jansenn, "Algeria Forces 13,000 Migrants."
124. Ibid.
125. Human Rights Watch, "Algeria: Migrants, Asylum Seekers."
126. Naceur, "Ruthless, Illegal, and Dangerous."
127. Zardo and Loschi, "EU-Algeria (Non)Cooperation on Migration."
128. Immigration and Refugee Board of Canada, "Treatment of Failed Refugee Claimants."
129. *Arab Weekly*, "Growing Number of Algerians Tempted."
130. Worldcrunch, "Algeria to Sardinia"; Herbert, "*La Mal Vie*," For an earlier report on the Annaba-Sardinia route, see *Echorouk El Yawmi*, "Annaba-Sardinia."
131. Worldcrunch, "Algeria to Sardinia."
132. Ibid.
133. Ibid.
134. InfoMigrants, "More Than 190 Migrants in 13 Boats"; Alarm Phone, "Shocking Number of Deaths."; Herbert, "*La Mal Vie*," pp. 8, 13.
135. *Majorca Daily Bulletin*, "Migrant Route from Algeria."
136. Carter, "33 Illegal Immigrants Intercepted."
137. Ede, "Illegal Migration to Mallorca."
138. Ibid.
139. Caminando Fronteras, "Missing: 47 Men."
140. EuroMed Rights, "Migrants and Refugees in Algeria."
141. Alarm Phone, "Shocking Number of Deaths."
142. Gheboiuli, "Algerians' Clandestine Exodus."
143. Benazizi, "Spain Reports Increase."
144. Alarm Phone, "Shocking Number of Deaths."
145. Ibid.
146. Ibid.
147. Aziani, "Heterogeneity of Human Smugglers."
148. Ibid., p. 80.
149. Ibid., p. 82.
150. Ibid., p. 80.
151. Ibid., p. 82.
152. Bonfiglio et al., "Smuggling Networks ."
153. Aziani, "Heterogeneity of Human Smugglers," p. 82.
154. Schaer and Guizani, "To Get to Europe"; "Report Overview" in Triandafyllidou and McAuliffe, *Migrant Smuggling Data and Research*, p. 5; Malakooti and Fall, "Migration Trends Across the Mediterranean," pp. 45, 48; Herbert, "*La Mal Vie*," p. 11.
155. Sanchez et al., *Beyond Networks, Militias and Tribes*, p. 82.
156. Micallef et al., *Conflict, Coping and Covid*, p. 55.
157. Farrah, *Algeria's Migration Dilemma*, p. 24.
158. Micallef et al., *After the Storm*, p. 49.
159. China Global Television Network Africa, "93 African Children Freed."
160. Ibid.
161. US Department of State, "2021 Trafficking in Persons Report: Algeria."
162. US Department of Labor, *2015 Findings on the Worst Forms of Child Labor*, p. 79.
163. Ibid.; US Department of State, "2021 Trafficking in Persons Report: Algeria."
164. US Department of Labor, *2015 Findings on the Worst Forms of Child Labor*, p. 79.

165. Islam, "Workers Tricked, Trafficked."
166. Ibid.
167. Ibid.
168. Ibid.
169. US Department of State, "2021 Trafficking in Persons Report: Algeria."
170. Adenwala, Benlakehal, and Chiang, *Determinants of Anti-Trafficking Efforts*, p. 6.
171. US Department of State, "2021 Trafficking in Persons Report: Algeria."
172. Ibid.
173. US Department of State, "2018 Trafficking in Persons Report: Algeria."
174. US Department of State, "2019 Trafficking in Persons Report: Algeria."
175. US Department of State, "2021 Trafficking in Persons Report: Algeria."
176. US Department of State, "2020 Trafficking in Persons Report: Algeria."
177. Ibid.
178. US Department of State, "2022 Trafficking in Persons Report: Algeria."
179. US Department of State, "2023 Trafficking in Persons Report: Algeria."
180. Ibid.
181. Farrah, *Algeria's Migration Dilemma*, p. 25.
182. Bajec, "Cashing in on Misery."
183. Bajec, "Cashing in on Misery." Comments by Jonathan Tossell.
184. Bajec, "Cashing in on Misery."
185. Bajec, "Cashing in on Misery." Comments by Raouf Farrah.
186. Lounnas, "Links Between Jihadi Organizations," p. 4.
187. Ibid.
188. Ibid.
189. Strazzari and Zampagni, "Illicit Firearms Circulation," p. 437.
190. Gun Policy, "Algeria—Gun Facts, Figures."
191. Monitoring the 21st Century Asian Arms Race, "Cheap Chinese Assault Rifles."
192. Military Africa, "Algeria Embarks on Manufacturing."
193. Marsh, "Brothers Came Back with Weapons."
194. BBC News, "Algeria Siege: 37 Foreigners Died"; BBC News, "Mokhtar Belmokhtar Charged."
195. Harchaoui, "Too Close for Comfort," p. 13.
196. Marsh, "Brothers Came Back with Weapons."
197. UN Security Council, *Final Report of the Panel of Experts Established Pursuant to Resolution 1973*, p. 25.
198. Strazzari and Zampagni, "Illicit Firearms Circulation," p. 435.
199. Ibid., p. 436.
200. Marsh, "Brothers Came Back With Weapons," citing information from UN Security Council, *Final Report of the Panel of Experts Established Pursuant to Resolution 1973*, p. 28.
201. Marsh, "Brothers Came Back With Weapons," citing information from UN Security Council, *Final Report of the Panel of Experts Established Pursuant to Resolution 1973*, p. 30.
202. Ramzi, "Algeria Thwarts Mali Arms Smuggling."
203. Ibid.
204. *El Watan*, "More Than 300 Guns Seized."
205. Ibid.
206. *Le Matin d'Algérie*, "Gun Trafficking Gangs Arrested."
207. Ibid.
208. *El Watan*, "Libya-Linked Gun Trafficking Ring."

209. *Réalités*, "Algeria Seizes Many Guns."
210. Ibid.
211. Marsh, "Brothers Came Back With Weapons."
212. Strazzari and Zampagni, "Illicit Firearms Circulation," p. 447.
213. Ibid., p. 448.
214. Ibid., p. 446.
215. Hanlon and Herbert, *Border Security Challenges*, p. 27.
216. UNODC, *Firearms Trafficking in the Sahel*, p. 15.
217. Hanlon and Herbert, *Border Security Challenges*.
218. Ibid., pp. 26–27.
219. UNODC, *Illicit Trafficking in Firearms*.
220. DZ Breaking, "Algeria: A Cache Of Weapons."
221. Dansseart, "States Gather."
222. Ibid.
223. Statement of Nazim Khaldi, First Secretary, Permanent Mission of Algeria to the United Nations, at the Eighth Biennial Meeting of States to Consider the Implementation of the Programme of Action to Prevent, Combat and Eradicate the Illicit Trade in Small Arms and Light Weapons in All Its Aspects, 2022, https://docs-library.unoda.org/Programme_of_Action_on_Small_Arms_and_Light_Weapons_-EightBiennial_Meeting_of_States_(2022)/ALGERIA-STATEMENT-BMS8-AGENDA-ITEM-8.pdf.
224. UNODC, *Global Study on Firearms Trafficking 2020*, p. 34.
225. Ibid., pp. 34, 39; Herbert and Gallien, *Divided They Fall*, Institute for Security Studies, North Africa Report 6, December 2020, p. 12.
226. Kuwait News Agency, "Algerian Police Seize Arms."
227. Terrorism, Transnational Crime and Corruption Center, *Research Findings: Illicit Hubs*, pp. 2, 16.
228. Meneghini and Milani, "Mapping Cigarette Trafficking Along the Maghreb," pp. 10–12.
229. Ibid., p. 12.
230. Ibid.
231. Ibid., p. 23.
232. Ibid., pp. 15, 23.
233. Ibid., pp. 17, 23.
234. Ibid., pp. 18, 23.
235. Ibid., p. 14.
236. Ibid.
237. Michalopolous, "Tobacco Smuggling"; Collins and Lapierre, "The French Connection—In Real Life"; Meneghini and Milani, "Mapping Cigarette Trafficking Along the Maghreb," p. 14.
238. Testimony of Louise Shelley, United States Commission on Security and Cooperation in Europe, "A Hazy Crisis: Illicit Cigarette Smuggling in the OSCE Region," July 19, 2017, pp. 3–4. https://www.csce.gov/sites/helsinkicommission.house.gov/files/Shelley%27s%20Testimony.pdf.
239. Ibid.
240. Ibid., p. 4.
241. Fortuna and Michalopoulos, "OLAF: Up to France."
242. Michalopolous, "Tobacco Smuggling."
243. Ibid.
244. Testimony of Louise Shelley, United States Commission on Security and Cooperation in Europe.
245. Ibid., p. 6.

246. Ibid., pp. 6–7.
247. Alioua, "Flow of Cigarettes from Algeria."
248. Ibid.
249. KPMG, *Illicit Cigarette Consumption*, pp. 16, 75.
250. Global Organized Crime Index *Algeria 2023*, p. 3.
251. Algeria Press Service, "Army Arrests Three."
252. Algeria Press Service, "23 Illegal Gold Miners."
253. *Echorouk El Yawmi*, "Mafia of Illegal Exploration."
254. Ibid.
255. Algeria Press Service, "South: Young People."
256. Algeria Press Service, "Illizi: Artisanal Gold Mining."
257. Rangel-Buitrago and Neal, "Unsustainable Harvest of Coastal Sands," p. 3. Excerpted in Coastal Care.
258. Ibid., p. 4.
259. Ibid.
260. Ibid.
261. Coastal Care, "Environmental Concern: Sand Mining."
262. Coastal Care, "Beach Sand Mining."
263. Coastal Care, "470,000 US Dollars Worth."
264. Ibid.
265. Ibid
266. Abderrahmane, "Plunder of Algeria's Red Gold."
267. Ibid.
268. Ibid.
269. Ibid.
270. Ibid.
271. Ibid.
272. Ibid.
273. Ibid.
274. Ibid.
275. Ibid.
276. Ibid.
277. Global Organized Crime Index, *Algeria 2023*, p. 3.
278. Ibid.
279. Atoussi et al., "Illegal Wildlife Trade in Algeria."
280. Bergin, Atoussi, and Waters, "Online Trade of Barbary Macaques."
281. Atoussi et al., "Corruption and Poaching in Algeria."
282. Ghanem, *Algeria's Borderlands*, p. 3.
283. Ibid., pp. 1–3, 9–13.
284. Ibid., p. 3.
285. Ibid., p. 4.
286. Ibid., p. 9.
287. Ibid., p. 5.
288. Ibid., p. 6.
289. Ibid.
290. Ibid., p. 10.
291. UNODC, *Fuel Trafficking in the Sahel*, p. 17.
292. Ibid.
293. Ibid.
294. Herbert, "From Contraband to Conflict," pp. 235–236.
295. Ibid., p. 240.

296. Ibid., pp. 240–241.
297. Ibid., pp. 236, 241, 264.
298. Ibid., pp. 245–246.
299. Ibid., p. 249.
300. Ibid., pp. 254–258.
301. Ibid., pp. 254–255.
302. Ibid., pp. 251, 262–264.
303. Gnes, *Maghnia: Crossing the Uncrossable Border*, p. 2. See also Tognini, "Border Row Is Bad News"; Malakooti and Fall, *Migration Trends Across the Mediterranean*, p. 39.
304. Babuta and Haenlein, "Commodity Smuggling in the Maghreb," pp. 1–8.
305. Ibid., p. 1.
306. Ibid., p. 5. Article cites researchers Peter Tinti and Tom Westcott in context of this point.
307. Ibid., pp. 6–7.
308. Transparency International, "Corruption Perceptions Index: Algeria."
309. Transparency International, "Corruption Perceptions Index: Egypt."
310. Klitgaard, "Three Levels of Fighting Corruption."
311. John Entelis, quoted in Ouali and Schemm, "Algeria Reels from Tales."
312. Chama, *Anti-Corruption Tabloid Journalism*, pp. 57, 68–69.
313. Chikhi, "Algerian Ex Oil Executives."
314. African Network of Centers for Investigative Reporting, "Algerian Gas Deals."
315. Ibid.
316. Ibid.
317. Ibid.
318. Chama, *Anti-Corruption Tabloid Journalism*, p. 70.
319. Yeager, Shelden, and Holden, "Political Economy of Corporate Bribery."
320. Ibid.
321. Ibid.
322. Ahram Online, "Algeria Sentences Ex-Energy Minister."
323. Agence France-Presse, "Algeria Jails Former Energy Boss."
324. See Nacer, "From Rags to Riches to Rags," pp. 13–14.
325. US Securities & Exchange Commission, "SEC Charges Honeywell."
326. Khoury, "On the Algerian Involvement."
327. Ibid.
328. Ibid.
329. Fairbanks, "Lebanon's Fuel Oil Scandal."
330. US Department of Treasury, "Two Politically Connected Brothers."
331. Middle East Monitor, "Algeria's Energy-Giant Sonatrach."
332. Chama, *Anti-Corruption Tabloid Journalism*, p. 59.
333. Ibid.
334. Willis, *Algeria*, p. 147.
335. Ibid., p. 148.
336. Chama, *Anti-Corruption Tabloid Journalism*, p. 66.
337. Ibid., pp. 65–66.
338. *Arab News*, "Cronies, Corruption."
339. Ibid.
340. Ibid.
341. Fitzgibbon, "Algeria Launches Money Laundering Probe." The author quotes Lyas Hallas, an Algerian journalist who did much of the investigation.

342. Ibid.
343. Lyas Hallas, quoted in ibid.
344. US Department of State, *International Narcotics Control Strategy Report*, Volume 2 (March 2021), pp. 39–41.
345. MENAFATF, *Mutual Evaluation Report of the People's Democratic Republic of Algeria*. See also, US Department of the Treasury, "Guidance to Financial Institutions."
346. Rubenfeld, "Algeria, Angola, Panama Removed." See also, MENAFATF, *7th Follow-Up Report for Algeria*.
347. US Department of State, *International Narcotics Control Strategy Report*, Volume 2 (March 2021), p. 39.
348. Ibid., p. 40.
349. Ibid., p. 41.
350. US Department of State, *International Narcotics Control Strategy Report*, Volume 1 (March 2022), p. 38.
351. Ibid., p. 41.
352. Price, "Illicit Financial Flows in North Africa," p. 4.
353. Ndikumana and Boyce, "Capital Flight from Africa," pp. 6–7; Price, "Illicit Financial Flows in North Africa," p. 2.
354. UNECA, *Illicit Financial Flows: Report*, p. 97; Price, "Illicit Financial Flows in North Africa," p. 7.
355. Abouzzohour and Mimoune, "Algeria Must Prioritize "; European Training Foundation, "Algeria: Education, Training and Employment," pp. 9, 13; Ahmed, "Algeria Blighted by Youth Unemployment"; Statista.com, "Algeria: Youth Unemployment Rate"; UNICEF, "Algeria—MENA Generation 2030 Country Fact Sheet," p. 2.
356. Boukhars, "Barriers Versus Smugglers"; Herbert and Gallien, *A Rising Tide*.

4

Tunisia: Oasis or Mirage of Stability?

WITHIN NORTH AFRICA, TUNISIA HAS BOTH THE BLESSING AND THE CURSE of being, by far, the smallest country. In some respects, its small size is an advantage; in others, it is a significant weakness. As a small country Tunisia perhaps has smaller, if not necessarily fewer, problems than its larger neighbors. Yet it is also highly vulnerable to spillover effects from its neighbors, especially Libya, with whom it shares a 461-kilometer border. The Arab Spring started in Tunisia with the self-immolation of a shopkeeper, Mohammed Bouazizi, who was the victim of "incessant harassment from corrupt authorities."[1] His death sparked massive protests that overthrew the Ben Ali regime, which had become infamous for its extensive corruption and self-aggrandizement. As one scholar wrote, "Ben Ali and his one-time hairdresser wife, Leila Trabelsi, and her clan crossed the line with their overt corruption and abuses of power and . . . inability and unwillingness to meet the basic needs of an increasingly discontented population."[2] Reportedly the Trabelsi family "operated like a mafia, extorting money from shop owners, demanding a stake in businesses large and small and divvying up plum concessions among themselves. Their control over the North African country's economy was vast."[3] While the regime prospered though this system of "institutionalized theft,"[4] Tunisia "suffered terribly from high unemployment, a corresponding youth bulge, high rates of university graduates who faced joblessness and economic stagnation, gross corruption that penetrated all levels of society, and deficiencies in the rule of law."[5] This set the scene for the so-called Jasmine revolution: the regime was so unpopular even within government and law enforcement that it crumbled quickly. Since then, as Hayat Alvi noted, "Tunisia has mostly maintained stability throughout its post-revolution transitions, notwithstanding some serious obstacles and tribulations. Tunisia is the anomaly in the region."[6] It developed and implemented anticorruption measures, allowed civil society groups to flourish, consolidated the rights of women, and held free and fair elections. Indeed, for a while it appeared to have made almost a full democratic transition that rendered it unique in the MENA region. This was to be reversed however, after Kais Saied, an academic who ran as an independent candidate, won the presidency in 2019. His victory was overwhelming. As Britannica noted, "for many Tunisians, it was a major victory for the people, but the ease with which Saied won foreshadowed just how commanding his presidency would be."[7]

Indeed, Saied's rule was turbulent almost from the outset. The first nominee for prime minister was rejected by the legislature. Eventually, Elyes Fakhfakh, former finance minister, became prime minister in late February 2020—but resigned within five months because of corruption allegations. Hichem Mechichi, who became prime minister in September, clashed with Saied, and the government seemed to be paralyzed. In early 2021, the stalemate, economic stagnation, and botched rollout of the Covid-19 vaccine provoked widespread protests. In July 2021, Saied fired Mechichi, "dismissed the government and froze the parliament, concentrating executive powers in his hands and ruling by decree."[8] Subsequently "senior officials, governors, and even mayors were purged and restrictions on civil society organizations were implemented."[9] In early 2022 "Saied dissolved the Supreme Judicial Council," and in June he released "a draft constitution that would transform Tunisia's government into a presidential system with few parliamentary or judicial checks on presidential power."[10] The July referendum on the constitution supposedly had a 96 percent approval—although it was likely that critics and opponents had simply not voted. Nevertheless, Saied retained popular support, much of it generated by his commitment to combating illegal migration and human smuggling.[11] While this was reminiscent of populist leaders in Europe and the United States, it reversed what had appeared to be an impressive "democratic evolution" since the Arab Spring.[12]

Tunisia also suffers from major economic challenges. The pandemic hit the economy hard with a significant contraction in 2020. Subsequently, Vladimir Putin's war in Ukraine slowed economic growth, while inflation created considerable hardship. Food security became a concern for the poor and even for some middle-class families.[13] In addition, a severe drought in the first half of 2023 exacerbated Tunisia's economic woes. The *African Research Bulletin* in November 2023 described Tunisia as going through "an unprecedented economic and financial crisis. Inflation reached 9.3% in August and growth in the second quarter did not exceed 0.6%, according to official figures."[14]

In addition, Tunisia has major structural problems, including the continued struggle between the secular parties and the Islamist parties, a massive wealth gap between the coastal areas and the interior, high levels of youth unemployment, fiscal deficits, and a trade deficit. Tunisia has "a debt equivalent to around 80% of its GDP" and is "engaged in long negotiations with the International Monetary Fund" to obtain a new US$2 billion loan to cover its budget deficit.[15]

Beyond the drought, agriculture remains a problem, with small farmers facing pressure from large producers while also receiving fewer exemptions from water and irrigation taxes.[16] In addition, corruption has not disappeared, becoming less concentrated but far more diffused. Tunisian security has also been periodically undermined by "the flow of terrorists, traffickers, weapons and migrants" from Libya.[17] Terrorist attacks on the Bardo Museum and the Sousse resort, both in 2015, damaged tourism as did the pandemic. An attack in May 2023 targeting a synagogue in Djerba further added to security concerns.[18] Given this turbulent context, the informal economy seems very likely to expand significantly during the next few years. This could also increase organized crime in Tunisia, which currently seems to be increasing but, overall, remains rather modest.

Tunisia did well in 2019 on the Organized Crime Index run by ENACT. In Africa, Tunisia was "the second best performing country in the Index in terms of low levels of criminality, ranking 53rd overall, and with the lowest overall criminality score in North Africa. Unlike the majority of African countries, Tunisia's criminal markets' score was higher than its criminal actors' score."[19] The cannabis trade was thriving, and while the human smuggling score was "above the continental average, the majority of criminal markets" were "far less pervasive in Tunisia than elsewhere in Africa."[20] In terms of criminal actors, there were few mafia-style groups, while criminal networks were confined largely to cross-border smuggling with Libya and Algeria. The most serious criminal actors were within the state, and in large part this reflected the diffusion of corruption discussed above and the willingness of law enforcement and other officials to accept bribes.[21] In terms of resilience to organized crime, Tunisia was twelfth in Africa, and second to Morocco in North Africa. "The country receives notably high scores on various indicators, such as political leadership and governance and non-state actors, both of which score 7. The government has launched a national campaign against corruption and contraband networks."[22] There is a strong and robust legal framework to counter organized crime domestically—although not at the transnational level—while civil society is also highly dynamic and involved in the fight against corruption.[23] Nevertheless, serious deficiencies remain, particularly in the areas of crime prevention and the judicial system, where there is little discretion and a highly punitive approach with limited discretion.[24] In addition, law enforcement suffers from corruption as well as bureaucratic rivalry between the National Guard and the National Police, while the prison system—as elsewhere—has become "a breeding ground for organized crime, and criminal control of networks on the outside from within prison is common."[25] In the 2021 Global Organized Crime Index, Tunisia continued to do well. Its overall criminality score was 3.79, ranking it forty-ninth of fifty-four African countries and the lowest in North Africa. Its 4.83 resilience score was the highest in North Africa, fourteenth in Africa, and ninety-sixth globally.[26] It stemmed in large part from "a very robust legal framework pertaining to organized crime, including strong legislation related to drug trafficking, terrorism, money laundering and human trafficking legislation."[27] Weaknesses included a lack of "national crime prevention, anti-crime policy, or national crime prosecution."[28] In the 2023 index the score for criminality had moved up to 4.45, and Tunisia's resilience score had dropped to 4.50.[29] Although the organized crime threat remained moderate rather than high, the decline in the ability to respond to it was not reassuring. Two areas of criminality stood out as remarkably high, with both assessed at 8.0—human smuggling (which was 7.0 in 2021) and financial crimes, which was a new addition in the 2023 index.[30] Although Tunisia is still doing comparatively well on both the indices, there are some warning signs. The return to authoritarianism, the likely expansion of the informal economy, and the continued challenge of high levels of unemployment among educated youths and young people are not a good combination, to say the least. This last issue, which was a key factor in the downfall of the Ben Ali regime, remains a major challenge for the government and potentially a flash point for future protest. One observer noted that for many young people in North Africa faced with frustration at the limited opportunities for social and economic advancement, there is an unpalatable choice between extremism and emigration.[31] In fact, there is a third option where organized crime becomes the only ladder of economic mobility. This suggests that criminality could become far more pervasive, with frustrated potential entrepreneurs moving into the illicit economy and using their education and skills in ways that were not intended. If this occurs, the current assessment might be overly optimistic.

Drug Trafficking

During the past several years, there has been growing alarm about drugs in Tunisia. It has even become embedded in rap songs about the *harga*, the journey migrants make to Europe, with the theme of addiction being added to deprivation and marginalization.[32] Yet there needs to be some perspective on this. In 2013, the Institute for War and Peace Reporting published an article written by Samir Nefzi entitled "Drugs to Suit All Tastes in Tunisia," which noted that a survey by the Tunisian Ministry of Health of 2,453 people between the ages of fifteen and twenty-four had found 10 percent had used drugs, 3.5 percent had injected, and 3.3 percent had become habitual users.[33] A member of the Tunisian police drug squad noted that the drugs came into Tunisia in a variety of ways, saying that "drugs come from Morocco through Tunisia's western border with Algeria, and also from several African countries via our southern border with Libya."[34] The officer also noted that "in recent years, our maritime borders have also seen smuggling by the European mafia bringing in large quantities of cocaine and heroin. . . . Consignments are delivered directly under cover of darkness, or dumped in the sea to be picked up and distributed by their Tunisian partners."[35] The most popular drug was cannabis resin from Morocco, followed by heroin, with cocaine a long way behind.[36] The author also highlighted the growing popularity of pharmaceuticals.[37] This was an early assessment of a problem that has subsequently intensified, but one that succinctly captured all the key trends. Indeed, subsequent reports noted that between 2013 and 2017 cannabis consumption more than doubled among students, while the consumption of ecstasy (MDMA) pills increased sevenfold.[38] A report published in 2021 was based on a three-year study ending in December 2018 of drug users in the north of Tunisia that identified through toxicology screening the drugs they used. "On a total of 11,170 urine samples screened, 5,409 (48.4%) were positives for illicit drugs. The prevalence of positive samples was 55.4% in 2016; 50.45% in 2017 and 40.8% in 2018. Cannabis was the most widely consumed drug (95%), followed by Benzodiazepines (1.2%), Buprenorphine (1%), cocaine (0.95%), MDMA (0.24%) and opiates (0.13%). Polydrug abuse was observed in 79 specimens (1.5%)."[39]

More details have also emerged about drug trafficking routes involving Tunisia, which is a (relatively modest) destination or market country but is also used as a transshipment country.

Several cannabis resin routes emanating from Morocco involve Tunisia:

- The route between Morocco and Egypt is a mix of maritime and overland smuggling. It is likely to include Tunisian ports or some land crossing Tunisian territory. As one study noted, "a significant quantity is moved across the Tunisian border in Jendouba, Kef or Kasserine either overland or, near Tabarka, across the maritime border" between Algeria and Tunisia.[40]
- According to Herbert and Gallien, a second route from the Morocco-Algeria border goes through the center of Algeria and into Tunisia through the border governorates of Kasserine, Gafsa, and Tozeur.[41] "Large shipments on this route also move from El Oued into the far southern reaches of Tunisia, both near the official crossing point at El Borma and via points further south."[42] A lot of this is done at night using the terrain as cover and avoiding border patrols.[43] The cannabis resin is passed from Algerian to Tunisian networks.[44]
- Once in Tunisia, some of the shipments are moved to Tunis and the coastal areas for local consumption and for transshipment to Europe. "A significant volume of cannabis resin heads east towards Libya, however. Coming from the areas around Tabarka, Kasserine, and Tozeur, in Tunisia, these shipments follow secondary roads from the main north–south highway, before passing through the city of Gabets and heading towards the Libyan border. At the Libyan border, some smuggling takes place through the Ras Ajadir and Dehiba–Wazin ports of entry."[45] These border crossings involve either a mix of concealment and deception or facilitation through bribery.
- Cannabis resin is also trafficked across the border between Tunisia and Libya, avoiding the official border crossing. The military zone in the south of Tunisia is also used, but this is heavily patrolled, and the transporters use dry riverbeds and the like to avoid detection.[46]
- There is also a Morocco-Libya maritime route through the Mediterranean. This is done using a mix of yachts and fishing boats at one end and cargo ships, often registered in Syria, at the other.[47]

During the 2000s, largely in response to the success of Spanish maritime interdiction efforts, Colombian and Venezuelan drug trafficking organizations began to move cocaine to Europe via West Africa, from which it was transported overland and by air to Europe. While this route is still used, more direct connections with North Africa, especially Morocco, have been established. Most of the cocaine entering North Africa is transshipped to Europe, yet there is also a small, but growing market in the Maghreb. Unlike Algeria, Tunisia has had only a few relatively small seizures of cocaine. In 2017, 30 kilograms was found in a yacht near Cape Bon with a similar seizure on the island of Kuriat, leading to speculation that a Tunisia-Italy pipeline was being established.[48] According to Interpol, "links with Sicily-based Italian criminal organizations can be assumed in both cases, given the geographical proximity between the two locations and Sicily, in addition to statements from Tunisian coast guards reporting new forms of trafficking with Italy."[49] Here once again we see the importance of Italy as a criminal hub. In addition, cocaine shipments have been intercepted on the border of Tunisia and Algeria, some of which were found in cars, while in Tunisia itself, drug trafficking networks in Gafsa, Tunis, and Bizerte have been dismantled.[50] Perhaps the most significant cocaine seizure in recent years, however, occurred in Ecuador in January 2022. Authorities seized 656.7 kilos of cocaine "concealed in a shipping container carrying bananas headed for Tunisia. According to the police, the drugs were dispersed among ten jute bags in the form of 660 brick-type packages, with an estimated value of $42 million."[51] It was also reported that "the criminal affairs branch of the National Guard in Ben Arous city" would be heading the investigation and working "in cooperation with the Ecuadorian police through Interpol."[52] Given the size of the load, however, it seems more likely that Tunisia was a transshipment country rather than the final destination.

Heroin is less prevalent than cocaine in Tunisia, although in September 2020 a Tunisian passenger from Istanbul was arrested at Tunis-Carthage International Airport with over a kilogram of heroin.[53] Herbert and Gallien, however, suggest that heroin use might be more widespread than generally thought.[54] Even so, it seems less common than synthetics and pharmaceuticals. The most common drug is ecstasy, often brought in by passengers on ferries from Italy and France.[55] Moreover, "both Algerian and Tunisian authorities routinely arrest couriers coming from France carrying buprenorphine (sold under the brand name Subutex) or tramadol and intercept packages containing drugs such as lorazepam."[56] Tunisia appears to be a distribution point for pharmaceutical smuggling to both Algeria and Libya. Herbert and Gallien cite one seizure in central-western Tunisia involving 115,000 pills while acknowledging that smaller scale smuggling involving several hundred or several thousand pills, remains prevalent.[57] In the final analysis, the widespread sense of disillusionment in Tunisia over the lack of economic opportunities helps to create a sense of apathy and despair that is increasingly likely to fuel the growth of drug consumption.

Human Smuggling

Tunisia maintains a comparative advantage when it comes to human smuggling across the Mediterranean—the proximity of Sicily as well as the Pelagie Islands, which form the administrative unit of Lampedusa. Moreover, there are incentives and pressures for Tunisians to get involved in the smuggling business both as customers and service providers. On the customer side, demand has increased during the past several years as the number of would-be irregular migrants from Tunisia has once again ticked up. There are several reasons for this. The first is that although Tunisia, until July 2021, made considerable progress in terms of democratization, it has not been able to deal with its structural problems, most especially the burgeoning youth population and the continued constriction of economic opportunities. Closely related to this, multiple polls and studies have revealed widespread disillusionment with politics in the country and resentment at the inability of the government to make fundamental improvements in the opportunities available for well-educated young people.[58] The structural problems that existed during the Ben Ali regime have proved enduring, with high levels of resilience. Freedoms in the country are obviously greater than they were—with the freedom to protest being one of them. The difficulty is that the protests seem to have little impact. Moreover, by June 2021, the rate of inflation was 5.7 percent.[59] In 2020 and 2021, there was an increase of 300,000 people living in poverty compared to the previous two years, with the Covid-19 pandemic likely influencing these figures.[60] As one Tunisian official explained, "when you stop being able to afford to live, you would want to leave."[61]

Consequently, the desire to emigrate and find opportunities in Europe remains powerful. As one observer noted, "the trip, a search for greener pastures to the north, is known as the *harga*. *Harga* is an exit strategy of those experiencing intense marginalization at home. They seek out alienation in foreign countries; it may be less painful than socio-economic and political exclusion at home. The government in Tunis, meanwhile, has failed to address the deeper problems of exacerbating inequalities underlying the *harga*."[62] Indeed, the *harga* has taken on almost a mythical status in Tunisia: it has become deeply embedded in the culture and is even the theme of many rap songs.[63] The origin of the word, which translates as "burning," is found in Tunisians going to Europe on tourist visas and staying there after they had expired, and the practice by illegal immigrants in Europe of burning their travel documents to forestall identification and deportation back.[64] According to one scholar, "in recent years, *harga* has been used to refer to the clandestine migration to Europe in makeshift boats."[65] The songs legitimize and perhaps even encourage irregular migration. They also "document a missing chain in Tunisia's history. It is the history of thousands of Tunisians who have left the country in death boats or those still planning or dreaming of joining them soon. These songs represent acts of protest against the persistent and systematic marginalization and alienation of a large section of the Tunisian society."[66] In a fascinating study in the port city of Zarzis, Valentina Zagaria discovered that there was considerable moral ambivalence about the *harga*, particularly among some of the older generation.[67] Mothers were sometimes blamed for encouraging their sons to migrate, especially when they drowned at sea.[68] It was also felt that young men who wanted to go to Italy and France had been seduced by what they saw as a glamorous lifestyle. Yet many of the men themselves felt "socially dead" already and "reasoned that risking actual death at sea was worth it for a second chance at being reborn into a new life of possibilities."[69] Ironically, Zarzis was the main embarkation point for irregular migration in the immediate aftermath of the collapse of the Ben Ali regime.

Another factor, but one that has been given less attention, concerns the problem that many fishing communities are having to confront. "Years of declining yields have strained the financial viability of the fishing industry . . . all along the Tunisian coast. . . . Fish are smaller, less abundant, and further away from the coast now than they were in the past—a trend that has accelerated over the past decade. This is consistent with an overall decline in the population of fisheries in the Mediterranean since the 1990s."[70] A UN report in 2018 described the Mediterranean as the most overfished sea in the world, with 62 percent of fish stocks at serious risk of depletion.[71] Small fishing communities have been hit the hardest and direct part of the blame to illegal trawling in shallow waters.[72] The lack of controls and enforcement efforts against illegal fishing methods was succinctly summarized by the head of a local fisherman's association, who stated "there are many boats and there is no control."[73] An additional problem for Tunisian fishermen has been the arrival of the blue crab, a highly invasive species that "destroys fishing nets and crowds out local species."[74] The fishermen have nicknamed the crabs "Daesh," the name of the Islamic State, because of the destruction they cause.[75] The result is that fishing has become far less rewarding, with smaller catches and smaller profits. In addition, Tunisian fishermen also faced the disruptions caused by the Covid-19 pandemic.[76]

Against this background, the migration business looks increasingly attractive. Many of the fishermen have the knowledge and skills to take boats to Sicily or Lampedusa and see this as their only lifeline. Furthermore, other members of the community also get involved, with some acting as lookouts against the authorities and others providing food for migrants prior to their departure.[77] While some fishermen want nothing to do with the irregular migration business, they have sold their boats as they can no longer make a living through fishing. Moreover, the younger generation of fishermen seem more willing to incur the risks involved. They face economic pressures and incentives, have the skills and resources, and take advantage of the increasing opportunities that are available. As one commentary noted, "Young men with some knowledge of the sea . . . have come to play an important role in the recent exodus. They pilot small boats, which are usually destined for fishing, on a one-way journey to Italy, unlike the boats in previous years that would return to Tunisia after delivering larger groups of up to 100 passengers."[78] Unfortunately, they do not have the same level of wisdom as the older fishermen and are also more likely to take risks, which might help to account for some of the tragedies that have occurred.

Yet it is important to acknowledge that, the rhetoric of the European press and politicians notwithstanding, those who organize and man the boats across the Mediterranean are not human traffickers. Many of them are not even criminals and are simply providing irregular transportation services for irregular migrants. In this connection, a Sicilian prosecutor noted that in relation to migrant smuggling across the Mediterranean, Tunisia is very different from Libya, where "the trafficking of migrants is managed by solid and structured criminal organizations."[79] In contrast, "in Tunisia the smuggling racket is often run by groups of fishermen," who will "move 70 to 80 people and when they arrive within a few miles of the island, they put the passengers in small boats to complete the journey on their own. Then they return to the Tunisian coasts and carry on with their fishing activities."[80] Thus, in Zarzis, irregular migration "remains very much an artisan affair" and one where fishermen "occasionally make their boats available to pilots, who will then steer the tiny craft to Italy, undisturbed by international radars. Given the huge scale of the sprawling port, passage is not hard to find."[81] This is also consistent with the prosecutor's view that smuggling has become "an additional source of income for some Tunisian fishermen as their earnings have also decreased" because of Covid-19.[82] As noted, above, however, the challenges facing the fishermen preceded Covid-19 and have endured since the end of the pandemic.

Historically, most of the migrants seeking to cross the Mediterranean from Tunisia were Tunisian citizens. As one scholar noted, "few foreign migrants leverage Tunisia to get to Europe. Of the 4,678 irregular migrants apprehended by Tunisian authorities in 2018, only 401 were non-Tunisian" with most of them coming from sub-Saharan Africa.[83] By spring 2021, however, this seemed to have changed, and it was reported that "for the first time the majority on the boats trying to cross the sea is not Tunisian."[84] In part, this reflects the relatively permissive visa policy Tunisia had adopted for Middle Eastern and sub-Saharan countries.[85] Many migrants from countries such as Côte D'Ivoire enter Tunisia by air. Many get stuck there, however, with menial jobs and low pay. An estimated 20,000 migrants from sub-Saharan Africa, most of them Ivorian, live in Tunisia.[86] Unfortunately, as the head of a Tunisian NGO noted, "neither the legal framework nor the cultural framework favors integration."[87] In addition, to those from sub-Saharan Africa, there is a contingent of migrants from Bangladesh who have been encouraged to believe that Tunisia and Libya offer an easy entry to Europe. To compound the problem, Covid-19 put many migrants as well as many Tunisians out of work. On May 3, 2020, the International Organization for Migration (IOM) reported that since March 22 when the government imposed a quarantine on Tunisia, the employment rate for migrants in Tunisia dropped precipitously from 64 percent to 11 percent.[88] As a result, many migrants stranded in Tunisia concluded that the only alternatives were "Europe or death."[89]

Boats carrying irregular migrants to Italy embark from multiple locations along Tunisia's coast. In 2017, there were twenty-nine separate and distinct points of departure. These are identified in Figure 4.1.[90]

In some respects, the diagram can be interpreted as one very large and important hub, several smaller and less important hubs, and a long tail. By far the most popular embarkation points were on the Kerkennah islands. A long way behind in numbers of departures were Kelibia and

Figure 4.1 Tunisian Boat Departures by City of Departure, 2017

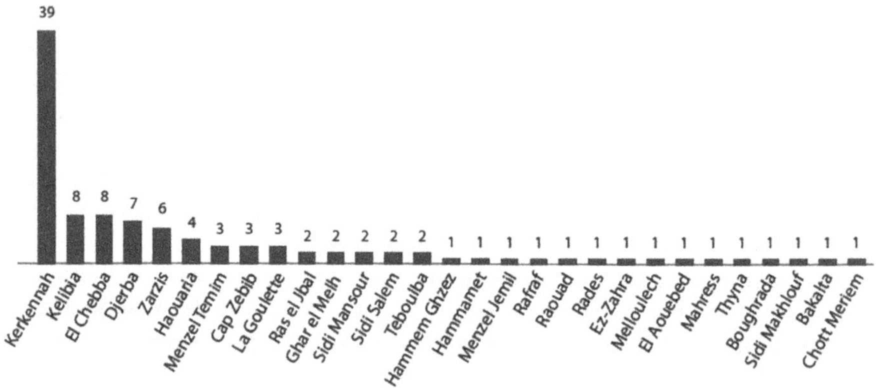

Source: Tunisian Forum for Social and Economic Rights (Forum Tunsien pour les Droits Economiques et Sociaux).

El Chebba followed by Djerba and Zarzis. The twenty-nine points of departure and over 100 separate sailings show just how pervasive irregular migration from Tunisia had become even in 2017—and how difficult it was to stop. It is also plausible that this was an underestimation of the number of migrant boats leaving the Tunisian coast. Whatever the case, since then the exodus has increased significantly. In the first eight months of 2020, about "8,000 Tunisians crossed the Mediterranean to Italy."[91] Moreover, fishermen in Zarzis claimed that during the summer months in 2020 an average of two migrant boats departed every night from the port.[92] Given that this was all done covertly so that there were no formal records of departures or in many cases of arrivals, and that some boats likely sank without trace, both the extent of the irregular migration and the cost in lives lost might be much larger than many assessments suggest. Various problems can arise with migrant smugglers: there is no guaranteed level or quality of service; some smugglers become greedy and carry far more people than is safe; and those in charge of boats do not always have the level of maritime expertise that is needed. Impatience, desperation, and greed all too often combine to create the perfect storm. The involvement of experienced Tunisian fishermen, therefore, is to be applauded. Indeed, there are numerous incidents where the fishermen have alerted the authorities to boats in distress and played a central role in the rescues.[93]

Despite the dangers, there has been another significant upsurge in human smuggling during the past several years. According to Herbert the wave began in 2020 "with Italian and Tunisian authorities intercepting a total of 26,488 individuals."[94] It was "triggered by deteriorating socio-economic conditions" and exacerbated by the pandemic.[95] Irregular migration from Tunisia to Europe in 2021 surpassed levels recorded in 2020, reaching the highest point since the months immediately after the 2011 revolution.[96] In 2021 at least 23,328 irregular migrants were intercepted by Tunisian authorities, almost double the 11,789 caught in 2020.[97] Italian authorities registered a similar rise in interceptions of migrants leaving from Tunisia totaling 20,218 in 2021, compared to 14,685 in 2020.[98] About two-thirds of the migrants intercepted by Tunisian authorities were Tunisian, compared to three-quarters of those apprehended by Italian authorities.[99] Ironically, in June 2021, Italy reached an agreement with Tunisia in which the Italian government is offering significant money to induce its Tunisian counterpart to become the first and most important line of defense against migration from Tunisia to Italy. The Tunisian government effectively agreed to be the bouncer in a nightclub which is so large and sprawling that people can come in and out at will, and the capacity of the bodyguard to engage in more than token enforcement is seriously limited.

This became increasingly evident as the migration trend intensified in 2022 driven by continued push factors in the Tunisian economy. These included a massive rise in the poverty level, with 960,000 families in need—more than triple the number in 2010.[100] Over the same period, 1.6 million middle-class people sank into poverty.[101] With nearly 6 million poor people in Tunisia and little sense that economic conditions would improve any time soon, it was hardly surprising that irregular migration expanded significantly. Yet low salaries and unemployment had a dual impact—increasing incentives to leave while reducing the wherewithal to do so.[102] Even so, 32,371 Tunisian and foreign migrants arrived in Italy, surpassing the approximately 28,000 in 2011.[103] Interceptions by the Tunisian authorities rose to 38,713, although this included preemptive apprehensions "in the country's littoral areas."[104] The pattern also changed with more women, children, and entire families seeking to reach Europe across the Mediterranean.[105] The change also included a massive increase in foreign migrants, with 27,495 apprehended by Tunisian authorities after departing Tunisia.[106] Foreigners accounted for 71 percent of all apprehensions, up 40 percent from the previous year, with those from Guinea and Côte d'Ivoire looming large.[107] Moroccan irregular migrants were also embarking from Tunisia.[108]

In terms of smuggling dynamics, smuggling networks remain small but widely distributed along Tunisia's coast.[109] The networks that move foreign migrants, in contrast, are mostly concentrated in Sfax and Zarzis.[110] In summer 2022, prices in Sfax were 1,333 to 1,479 euros for Tunisians and up to 1,777 euros for foreign migrants; when demand dropped in the winter so did prices, which are reduced to 592 euros.[111]

Partly because of a lack of trust in the smugglers, there has also been a growth of self-smuggling, including by migrant communities. This, in turn, has ignited the growth of "an illicit business around boats" and the emergence of "agents in departure hubs who trade in stolen, old, burnt or damaged boats and motors. The agent illegally buys boats from fishermen, individuals owning leisure boats or those trading in stolen boats."[112] The other key dynamic in 2022 was increased enforcement—directed against both the irregular migrants and the smugglers. "1,023 smugglers and middlemen were reportedly arrested during the year, along with the seizure of 978 boats and 106 cars used for transporting migrants to departure points."[113] In addition, multiple arrests were made as would-be migrants were preparing to leave. Authorities also restricted access to the Kerkennah Islands, a major point of departure for Lampedusa. Although this was sometimes circumvented, the most obvious result was to increase embarkations directly from Sfax.[114]

As Tasnim Abderrahim persuasively observes, however, there was another form of displacement or adaptation in 2021 and 2022 with "the growing popularity of the Western Balkans route among Tunisians. While migrating through the Balkans route tends to be more expensive and complicated than maritime options for Tunisian migrants, the journey is perceived to be safer and surer."[115] While only "1,339 Tunisians were intercepted on the route between January 2009 and December 2021 . . . in 2022, 6,782 Tunisians were apprehended . . . underscoring a substantial shift in the itinerary for Tunisian irregular migration."[116] Indeed, there is speculation that as many as 15,000 migrants from Tataouine might have arrived in Europe via the Balkan route between January and August 2022.[117] Some fly directly to Belgrade, while others go via Istanbul. The key is to move from Serbia into Hungary, and this typically requires the assistance of smugglers who can be contacted in Belgrade through WhatsApp.[118] The deluxe "package" offered by the smugglers is to cross into Hungary and then a car to Vienna; the cost is, between 2,500 and 4,000 euros.[119] A cheaper and riskier alternative is simply to be moved into Hungary, after which the migrants are on their own.[120]

This permissive route likely suited the Tunisian government—given the growing importance of remittances for many families—as well as Serbia, which was able to highlight its importance to the European Union in either facilitating or impeding the flow of migrants to Europe.[121] Although the Balkans route provided an alternative to the dangerous Mediterranean crossing, Serbia might have overplayed its hand. Under pressure from the European Union, the Serbian government, starting November 20, 2022, imposed visa requirements on all travelers from Tunisia.[122] As a result, according to Abderrahim, the route has become far less attractive.[123]

In 2022 things were difficult for Tunisians seeking to emigrate and for migrants from sub-Saharan Africa in Tunisia. The difficulties compounded in 2023, especially for the latter. The roots of this can be found among Tunisian nationalists who seized on the "Great Replacement" concept articulated by white nationalists in Europe and the United States.[124] After this was briefed to the president's office, it was enthusiastically embraced by Saied, who then announced in a national security meeting—subsequently summarized and released on Facebook—that "uncontrolled immigrants from sub-Saharan Africa" were not only a security threat but part of a "criminal plan" to change Tunisia's demographics.[125] As one observer noted, "It started as this completely crazy conspiracy theory that Sub-Saharans were trying to colonize Tunisia, to make Tunisia black again. Then the president—who loves conspiracy theories—backed it. And it became a disaster."[126] Indeed, the populist rhetoric sparked a massive backlash against migrants in Tunisia, who have been "assaulted, robbed, spit on, raped, stabbed, and dragged through the streets."[127] The European Union—whose "Fortress Europe" stance is less blatant but not fundamentally different—has tacitly condoned this approach. On July 16, 2023, the European Union and Tunisia signed a memorandum of understanding to increase funding to Tunisian security forces to help stem migrant boats across the Mediterranean. The same month, security forces, in a move that mimicked—if on a smaller scale—Algerian expulsions of migrants, moved 1,300 people to the border with Libya where twenty-seven people died.[128] Subsequent reports suggest that sub-Saharan Africans who are intercepted at sea have also been sent to the border and ordered to go to Algeria. Such measures do little to halt the exodus. Between January and the end of October 2023, 96,175 people had arrived in Italy from Tunisia—12 percent were Tunisians, 12 percent were from Guinea, and 11 were from Côte d'Ivoire.[129]

Human Trafficking

One of the problems with human smuggling is that although those who want to be smuggled are acting voluntarily in what is a crime against a state or states, they put themselves in jeopardy. It is all too easy to go from being someone who has agency and autonomy to being coerced or deceived into becoming a victim of trafficking—which is a crime against the person. While Tunisia is far from being the worst offender in this regard, the presence of a significant transit migrant community in the country as well as a high level of poverty are both factors that increase individual vulnerability.

Little attention was given to human trafficking under the Ben Ali regime. In 2013, however, Tunisia, with the help of US funding, conducted a baseline assessment designed not only to identify the scale and scope of human trafficking in Tunisia but also to identify and establish countermeasures. The results of the assessment were sobering. Tunisia was identified as "a source, destination, and potentially transit country."[130] The traffickers' victims, according to the IOM assessment, were mostly children, women, and the disabled. Further, the IOM assessment explained that victims often ended up being forced into various criminal enterprises linked to begging, sexual exploitation, forced labor, and domestic servitude. Specifically, Tunisian women were, according to IOM, exploited in Gulf countries, Lebanon, and Western Africa, while Tunisian men were often trafficked to Europe where they ended up in forced labor situations.[131]

One key factor emphasized by the report was the country's high level of unemployment; another was that 42 percent of employment was in the informal sector.[132] Together, these factors increased the risk of exploitation, especially for women and children. Young girls working as domestic servants with payments being made to their fathers was identified as a serious but not fully understood problem.[133] Some children were also being forced into begging.[134] In addition, authorities identified 125 child victims of sexual exploitation in 2012.[135] The report also found cases of clandestine prostitution with the involvement of pimps.[136] With a careful reading of the report, however, it appears that, at least domestically, the sex trade was largely a case of disorganized crime rather than a business run by well-established criminal enterprises. Internationally, it appears that Tunisian women, especially from the Kef region in northwest Tunisia, are recruited and trafficked into sexual exploitation in Lebanon, the Gulf states, and even West Africa.[137] Concerns were also noted about Tunisian men forced into agricultural labor in

Italy and prostitution in France.[138] The transit migrant population in Tunisia was also deemed to be at risk.[139]

Since this study was completed, the development of laws, policies, and institutions to combat trafficking has been slow but steady. In 2012, Tunisia had arrested and convicted eighty women who had been forced into prostitution in Lebanon and were clearly victims of trafficking.[140] In 2016, Tunisia passed laws that included protection for victims of trafficking as well as ten-year imprisonment for human trafficking and fifteen years for cases involving children.[141] An anti-trafficking website was created in 2020, and Tunisia also operates a hotline for reporting of possible trafficking.[142] These measures represented a step forward. Although progress has continued since then, however, it remains incremental, with governmental efforts characterized by gaps and deficiencies.[143]

During the last several years, the number of victims of trafficking has increased to 285 in 2018, and 780 in 2019.[144] Moreover, between April 2019 and February 2020, national authorities identified 1,313 victims of trafficking.[145] In the period April 2020 to March 2021, the figure was 907.[146] "More than half of the identified victims were women and children, and 366 were foreign victims from Algeria, Burkina Faso, Cameroon, Cote d'Ivoire, Guinea, Madagascar, Mali, Uganda, Senegal, Sierra Leone, Togo, Japan, and Philippines. . . . traffickers subjected 62 percent of identified victims to forced labor and 32 percent to sex trafficking."[147] Most disturbing, the percentage of identified child victims subjected to sex trafficking jumped from 59.2 percent in 2019 to 75 percent in 2020.[148]

Victimization was pronounced within the transit migrant community. Indeed, in its June 2021 report on human trafficking, the US State Department highlighted the plight of migrants from Côte D'Ivoire in Tunisia. It observed that in Sfax and Grand Tunis smuggling "intermediaries confiscate migrants' identity documents until they can pay for the next leg of their journey, creating vulnerabilities to trafficking. During the previous reporting period, the Tunisian government, NGOs, and international organizations had identified an estimated 1,470 Ivoirian potential trafficking victims in Tunisia, approximately 80 percent of the total trafficking victims."[149] Moreover, it reported that "Ivoirian migrant smuggling networks based in Tunisia" were increasingly becoming "involved in trafficking as European governments blocked migration inflows and that these networks also coerced Ivoirians to engage in criminal acts, including drug smuggling."[150]

The difficulty in interpreting this apparent expansion of the problem is that there is now far greater attention devoted to the issue, and this inevitably brings with it discovery of victims who in the past would simply have been overlooked or ignored. It seems likely though that both elements are involved: trafficking is increasing and is being detected more frequently as more resources are being devoted to its combat. The effectiveness of the countermeasures, however, remained problematic. As the June 2021 US State Department Trafficking in Persons (TIP) Report noted, Tunisia remained in Tier 2 because it did "not fully meet the minimum standards for the elimination of trafficking."[151] On the positive side, the report noted that Tunisia was making serious efforts to meet these standards. "The government demonstrated overall increasing efforts compared to the previous reporting period, considering the impact of the Covid-19 pandemic on its anti-trafficking capacity."[152] Among the biggest areas of deficiency were prosecutions and convictions. The TIP 2021 assessment noted that "poor understanding of trafficking among judicial and law enforcement officials inhibited authorities from effectively using the 2016 anti-trafficking law to prosecute and convict traffickers."[153] For the second year running there were no convictions for trafficking.[154] This represented both a failure of deterrence and a culture of impunity. This is entirely consistent with the assessment discussed in the introduction to this chapter, which emphasized the weaknesses of the judiciary and the corruption of law enforcement in Tunisia.

Both the 2022 and 2023 TIP reports echoed these themes while noting some improvements. The 2022 reported acknowledged that in 2021 the Ministry of Interior, which had only initiated 181 investigations in 2020, had opened 332 investigations in 2021. These "included 27 cases of sex trafficking, 122 cases of forced labor, 135 cases of child 'economic exploitation' (forced labor), 12 cases of child forced criminality, and 36 unspecified forms of trafficking."[155] Yet the results were not commensurate with the effort. In 2021 courts concluded fifty-six trafficking cases but obtained only eight convictions—one for sex trafficking, three for child forced labor, three for forced begging, and one for forced criminality in drug trafficking.[156] These were the first trafficking convictions since 2018.[157] Sentences remained modest, with five years' imprisonment being the highest—although five traffickers received prison terms greater than one year.[158] The year 2022 witnessed a significant increase in convictions, with fifty-nine perpetrators incarcerated, fifty-five for sex trafficking and four for forced labor trafficking—although no information was provided regarding the severity of the sentences.[159]

If there were at least some indications that traffickers could no longer operate with impunity, many deficiencies remained in the Tunisian government's response to human trafficking. The 2023 TIP Report identified the need for better victim identification, adequate protection and care services, better staff training, and enhanced intergovernmental cooperation.[160] Perhaps most pointedly, the recommendations emphasized the need to "reduce the vulnerability of sub-Saharan migrants to trafficking by ceasing rhetoric from government officials that increases incidents of violence against this population and discourages cooperation with authorities on trafficking."[161] It perhaps would have been even more salutary to place Tunisia on the Tier 2 Watch List.

Arms Trafficking

According to a 2014 article, "estimated civilian gun possession rates in North Africa ranged from Africa's lowest in Tunisia (0.1 firearms per 100 people) to one of Africa's highest in Libya (15.5)."[162] It is hardly surprising then that "despite targeted political assassinations and armed clashes between violent extremists and security forces, the use of firearms has remained relatively low even after the revolution of 2011."[163] In relative terms, therefore, arms trafficking in Tunisia is less of a problem than elsewhere in North Africa and the Sahel. In absolute terms, however, it is far from insignificant and continues to reflect the inevitable and enduring spillover from the continued conflict in Libya.

Given the condition of Libya, it is hardly surprising that Tunisia during the last decade has witnessed an increase in arms trafficking. As Hanlon and Herbert noted, "the Libyan revolution fundamentally changed arms smuggling patterns in North Africa. . . . Libya's revolution led to the private appropriation of the nation's weaponry, fueling chaos within the country and flooding the region with arms."[164] According to a Small Arms Survey report, in the aftermath of the collapse of Gaddafi's regime, many of those loyal to him crossed into Tunisia, where they sold their weapons.[165] This marked the beginning of what was virtually an open arms bazaar in the region that continues to operate, if less blatantly than in the past.[166] For a few commodity smugglers, weapons are simply one more commodity, although others might try to avoid them because of the risks, including long prison sentences.

At the same time, the weapons themselves changed the nature of smuggling, not only making it more violent but leading, as Shaw and Mangan noted, to an economy of protection on Tunisia's borders. "The pervasive presence of weapons has combined with the absence of state control to ensure the growth of the protection market for legitimate trade as well as for illicit activities."[167] Smuggling across Tunisia's borders with Libya and Algeria had been a relatively structured, predictable, and largely nonviolent activity.[168] Since the Arab Spring, however, violent clashes have occurred among competing tribes as well as with customs and border agents.[169] A Tunisian police officer noted that historically the only problem "was fists," but now "everyone has a Kalashnikov."[170] In a similar vein, an Algerian customs officer acknowledged that "smugglers on the Tunisian border are aggressive, and there are a lot of incidents. Their mentality is tribal; if you arrest one smuggler, the tribe will attack you."[171] This happened at the Tunisian border post in Bouchebka after a tribal member was arrested.[172]

Firearms trafficking to and within Tunisia remains a problem whether animated by profit, politics, or extremism. Although there were some tendencies in the immediate aftermath of the revolution to dismiss this as an "ant trade," some substantial arms caches were discovered.[173] An early example occurred in Medenine in 2013, which suggested that jihadist groups were smuggling small but substantial loads of weapons and explosives into Tunisia.[174] In March 2016, Tunisian security forces seized a substantial number of weapons and, in the follow up search, discovered six arms caches in the Ben Gardane area.[175] Two months later in Ben Gardane, they apprehended a cache of 130 machine guns and 29 AK-type assault rifles.[176] In November 2016, five caches of arms and explosives were found that included 50 guns, including 27 Kalashnikov assault rifles and dozens of missiles.[177] While these weapons likely crossed Tunisia's eastern border with Libya, other weapons come into Tunisia via Algeria through the Chaambi mountains, where between 2012 and 2015 al-Qaeda in the Islamic Maghreb (AQIM) maintained a strong presence. Even though it is legitimate to claim that, in relative terms, "Tunisia is a peripheral market for small arms and light weapons," the weapon flows along with a series of jihadist attacks created a deep sense of insecurity.[178] After the June 2015 attack on the Tunisian resort at Port El Kantaoui, 10 kilometers north of Sousse, the government took additional steps to secure the border, building a 200-kilometer-barrier consisting of earth walls and trenches supported by electronic surveillance systems.[179] The extent to which this has been effective, however, remains uncertain.

Some weaponry is also smuggled into Tunisia from other sources, including Europe. In June 2014, three arms seizures at the port of Tunis included one with thirty different caliber weapons. These weapons were reportedly en route to the town of Kasserine on a car ferry from Marseilles.[180] While the source of these weapons remains unclear, at least in the public domain, they seem to be something of an anomaly. Even more unusual, in January 2020, Tunisian security forces seized weapons and cash from a car in Medenine and made five arrests.[181] The weapons emanated from Turkey and were intended for the Government of National Accord of Libya, which is supported by Ankara. Their seizure led to the Tunisian government rejecting "any foreign interference in Libya, including the Turkish intervention."[182]

In sum, arms trafficking in Tunisia is a serious problem that cannot be ignored but seems to have been dealt with effectively, if somewhat slowly, by the Tunisian government. This was reflected in the 2023 Global Organized Crime Index, which noted that "while arms trafficking remains an issue in Tunisia it is not as widespread as other forms of illicit trafficking. Some networks that smuggle firearms into the country store them in deserted places. While some smuggled weapons have allegedly been used in terrorist attacks, most have been sold on to hunters or residents of rural areas."[183]

Cigarette Smuggling

Tunisia has become a major transshipment country for a significant portion of the more than 10 billion illicit cigarettes "trafficked along the Maghreb Route. The United Arab Emirates is the main origin of illicit cigarettes entering the Maghreb countries. Libya is a key transit country for illicit cigarettes from the United Arab Emirates to Algeria and Tunisia. Illicit cigarettes intended for the EU mainly transit through Algeria, Tunisia, and Morocco. France is the main destination for illicit cigarettes outflowing from the Maghreb region."[184] A comprehensive study carried out by Transcrime highlighted both the drivers and the facilitators for cigarette smuggling throughout North Africa. Noting that about 45 percent of the illicit cigarettes consumed in the Maghreb area are illicit whites—especially Business Royals, Gold Seal, Pine, and American Legend—the report identified Berber (Tuareg) and Saharan Bedouin (Tebu) as being involved in cigarette trafficking.[185] The Transcrime study also observed that terrorist groups such as AQIM cooperated with the tribes to finance their campaigns of violence.[186] Given this local involvement, the highly permeable borders, and the ease of moving cigarettes through the Mediterranean to Europe, it was not surprising that "the total volume of illicit cigarettes smuggled along the Maghreb Route increased by more than 10% between 2008–2012 and 2017. Outflows towards Europe tripled from 2008–2012 to 2017."[187]

The source of many of these cigarettes is the Jebel Ali Free Trade Zone in the United Arab Emirates, which has ten factories with a capacity to produce as many as 63 billion cigarettes a year.[188] Several routes from the United Arab Emirates to North Africa have been well documented. Whatever the precise route, however, the key hub is Libya. "In 2017, Libya was a transit point for 2.1 billion illicit cigarettes flowing to Tunisia," which is an important consumer country with illicit cigarettes—44 percent of which are illicit whites—making up 43 percent of the total consumption.[189] Perhaps even more important, Tunisia has become a major transshipment country for cigarette smuggling to both France and Italy. According to Transcrime, "in Tunisia, total inflows increased by 44% over the period 2008–2017. In particular, flows from Algeria and Libya to Tunisia registered a strong expansion, increasing by 26% and 73% respectively. Outflows from Tunisia towards Europe—especially France—almost tripled."[190] In March 2021, authorities in Marseille arrested three flight attendants from a Tunisair flight on charges of smuggling 3,000 packs of cigarettes into France.[191]

Although France is clearly a primary destination for cigarettes being transshipped through Tunisia, the role of Italy as an important market should not be ignored. In 2016 and 2017, as part of a law enforcement operation called Doge Vesuviano, Italian authorities intercepted a container that was supposedly carrying glass wool but in fact had approximately a million euros worth of illicit cigarettes.[192] The shipment had come from Tunisia and was en route to the southern region of Campania. The criminal operation was carried out by a relatively small group of Italians (from Livorno and Campania) and Tunisians.[193] With Campania as the destination, it is possible that Camorra families were involved in the smuggling. Whether or not that was the case, the pattern of Italian-Tunisian collaboration in cigarette smuggling goes well beyond this example. Indeed, there are several instances in which relatively small Tunisian and Italian networks have collaborated in smuggling both cigarettes and migrants to Sicily.

- On June 6, 2017, Italian authorities announced the results of an operation called Scorpionfish that had placed a group of Tunisians and Italians under surveillance for six months. The group had made at least five trips from Tunisia to Sicily, one of which included fourteen migrants and 100 kilos of illicit cigarettes.[194] As well as the arrest of twelve suspects, a car and several speedboats were seized.[195] Migrants paid 2,000 to 3,000 euros, and the group made about 40,000 euros per trip.[196]

- In April 2018, a criminal gang smuggling migrants and cigarettes between Nabeul in Tunisia and Trapani in Sicily was dismantled by Italian police.[197] The thirteen individuals arrested included Italians, Tunisians, and Moroccans.[198] The group was charging as much as 5,000 euros per person and taking as many as fifteen migrants per trip.[199] According to the authorities, the gang completed two trips per week, and each trip, with the cigarettes included, yielded about 70,000 euros.[200] It was also suggested that members of the gang had jihadist affinities and that an associate was planning a suicide attack in France.[201]
- In January 2019, Italy's Finance Police (Guardia di Finanza) announced the dismantling of a "criminal association dedicated to the exploitation of illegal immigration (and) tobacco smuggling."[202] The authorities made fourteen arrests and seized assets worth over 3 million euros.[203] Composed of Italians and Tunisians, the group was led by a Tunisian who "organized multiple transports by sea over the past two years, reinvesting large sums of illicitly gained money in the purchase of a farm, a shipyard and a luxury waterfront restaurant" in Sicily.[204] The boats transported ten to fifteen migrants—each paying 3,000 euros—from Tunisia to Sicily each trip.[205] The leader had been arrested in 2012 for drug and arms trafficking and had provided some of the migrants with fake work contracts. During seven trips, the group had also smuggled several tons of illicit cigarettes.[206]
- On November 30, 2021, the Guardia di Finanza in Palermo arrested twelve suspects and seized one speedboat, seven vehicles, and 16,000 euros in cash.[207] The suspects had been moving counterfeit cigarettes from Tunisia to Sicily with a clear division of labor that suggested there were two distinct criminal organizations collaborating closely with one another. The Tunisian group acquired the cigarettes and arranged shipments from the coast to the maritime border with Italy.[208] The Italian organization, seemingly based in Palermo, "purchased large amounts of the goods illegally imported and transported them by car to sell on the retail market in Sicily."[209] It was reported by the prosecutor's office that "the smuggled cigarettes had a market value of €3.5 million and caused damages of more than €6 million to the national and EU budget."[210] On December 22, 2022, a judge announced ten convictions in the case, with a combined total of fifty years of imprisonment. Those convicted were also ordered to pay a fine of 70 million euros.[211]

What remains uncertain, of course, is the extent to which this is simply part of a much larger phenomenon, that in many other cases has simply gone undetected. Were those involved just unlucky to be caught or was it simply that this mode of smuggling is particularly vulnerable to interdiction? The answer seems to be primarily bad luck: an interview with Tunisian coast guard members in April 2017 highlighted the difficulties of catching the speedboats and noted that in late 2016 and early 2017 the coast guard had spotted five Italian speedboats but was unable to capture any of them.[212] It seems likely, therefore, that the arrests were simply a small segment of the crossings that took place. The 2021 European Prosecutor's report, however, also noted that in the past two years the Guardia di Finanza had "already intercepted numerous illegal shipments, arrested 36 smugglers in flagrant offence and seized 23 tonnes of counterfeit cigarettes, 10 boats (4 fishing boats and 6 speed boats)" valued at a half million euros.[213] Given the likely scale of the smuggling and the comments by Tunisian coast guard members, it seems likely that the seizures—literally and metaphorically—were little more than a drop in the ocean.

Natural Resource Exploitation and Environmental Crime

Unlike its larger neighbors, Algeria and Libya, Tunisia has relatively limited natural resources that can be exploited or pillaged. Nevertheless, the oil and gas industry—as elsewhere—has attracted, its share of corruption, while both the phosphate industry and unscrupulous criminals have caused serious environmental harm.

According to the 2023 Global Organized Crime Index, illegal logging in Tunisia appears to be expanding. In the country's northwest, especially the near the mountain town of Ain Draham, Algerian oak trees have reportedly been cut down. In April 2020, taking advantage of the Covid-19 lockdown, illegal loggers "cut down 400 endangered Algerian oak trees, some more than 300 years old, to make charcoal."[214] Some people who had lost jobs in the legal economy turned to illegal logging, where they could reportedly earn "up to $690 per month, more than double the country's average salary."[215] Nor was this the only location where this occurred. As the Organized Crime Index reported, the "clearing of eucalyptus trees for the Bouhartma Dam in Jendouba, overseen by a contractor operating illegally in the area, has contributed to the destruction of old-growth forests."[216] Wildfires have further exacerbated the problem and are often "attributed to human recklessness and intentional criminal activity."[217] It is also possible that climate change is at work as well. A heat wave in Tunisia in summer 2023 "ignited wildfires in its picturesque hinterland, devastated harvests of drought-stricken farmers," and made it extremely uncomfortable for outside workers.[218]

Illegal trade in wild animals is also a problem in Tunisia, especially in the southern desert. As in other countries in North Africa, the problem is rich Arabs from the Gulf who engage in indiscriminate hunting. "The animals are smuggled illegally through regulated export chains and sold at high prices in international markets."[219] In addition, irregular, unreported and unregulated fishing in Tunisian waters is both endemic and highly problematic. The Gulf of Gabès is home to the last remaining seagrass meadows in the Mediterranean but is threatened by the waste from phosphate plants as well as by industrial-scale sea-bottom trawling.[220] What has been called a culture of tolerance for the trawling developed in the aftermath of the Arab Spring, not least because much of the catch was exported to Europe—something that was critical to the livelihoods of the 45,000 fishermen in Tunisia.[221] As many as 576 *kys* (an artisanal vessel) boats trawl the sea bottom illegally in the shallow waters of the Gulf facing the artisanal fishermen.[222] Moreover, "artisanal fishers find themselves in a difficult dilemma: whether to join the destructive *kys* trawlers or keep practicing artisanal fishing, knowing that stocks are declining and they can't compete with the *kys* vessels' efficiency."[223]

In relation to natural and nonrenewable resources, Tunisia is at a major disadvantage when compared to its neighbors. Its phosphate industry has declined significantly, although only after causing major environmental damage in the country, while its oil and gas industry has been marred by corruption, poor management, and a lack of vision. The size of the bribes has been reduced since the Ben Ali era—when a $2 billion bribe was reportedly paid by a British company to a Ben Ali son-in-law to ensure award of a contract—but officials still demand bribes for contracts. Tunisia also has problems regarding water security, partly because of its inadequate dam and water storage system, government investment choices that led to depletion of water resources, and a poorly managed potable water and irrigation system. Of the 2,500 water associations that manage water distribution outside the cities, only 400 are "exemplary" and not characterized by corruption, favoritism, and poor management.[224] With climate change this could become a real problem; the water associations could all too easily be infiltrated by criminal groups seeking the profits that can be obtained from scarcity markets and commodities. A similar dynamic is evident with the "theft of copper wire from public infrastructure," which disrupts "public lighting, telephones and internet services."[225] All this also highlights some of the challenges faced daily by ordinary Tunisians. It also helps to explain why so many of them are involved in contraband smuggling.

Contraband Smuggling

Border regions in North Africa—as throughout much of the world—generally develop cross-border smuggling economies that provide an entire range of benefits, from individual and family coping mechanisms at a low level, to significant concentrations of wealth at the top range. Although borders appear to be fixed and immutable, conditions across borders are not static. On the contrary, they are highly dynamic and continuously morphing, developing a form of liquidity that transcends fixed locations. The border mores are also constantly shifting and are sometimes contested, but often consensual. As Matthew Herbert has noted, "in the decades after independence, Tunisian and Algerian government officials developed joint-extractive systems to profit and control the smuggling networks. This approach offered petty smugglers protection from arrest and prosecution in exchange for the routine payment of bribes and the provision of information on terrorists or traffickers in narcotics and arms."[226] Under the Ben Ali regime, high-level smuggling was largely controlled by the Trabelsi family, with subsistence smugglers picking up the scraps.

With the collapse of the regime, however, and the overthrow of Gaddafi in Libya, smuggling networks exploited new opportunities and Tunisia became something of a smuggling nirvana. This golden era of smuggling lasted for a few years. As a result of jihadist attacks in Tunisia, growing nervousness about the deterioration of security and stability in Libya and concern that jihadist activities and smuggling were somehow connected, both Tunisia and Algeria took steps to reestablish control over the borders.[227] During this period smuggling was portrayed as a threat to national security. This made things more difficult for smugglers and seriously harmed the marginalized border communities in Tunisia that depended on smuggling for subsistence. In response to community protests, municipality involvement in negotiating with Libyan power brokers, as well as learning and adaptation by those involved, smuggling across Tunisia's borders appears to have moved into its third phase since the 2011 revolution. It is a phase characterized by coexistence between the state and the smugglers, but also one in which concerns about security in Libya make cross-border smuggling more dangerous and more difficult. Indeed, smuggling has become less predictable, more volatile, and, for many smugglers, less profitable.

One problem is that not all smuggling is the same. In fact, this has been tacitly acknowledged by some of the governments in North Africa, including at various times by the Tunisian authorities. As one study noted, "hundreds of thousands, even millions of people, have no option but to participate in this system to survive, often working with the state agents who are supposed to stop it. To a certain extent, these fraudulent practices act as a safety valve that defuses social violence, slows down the rural exodus, reduces unemployment and offers sources of income to people living in rebellious regions that are deprived of almost any public investment."[228] Much of the smuggling comes from the arbitrage opportunities that have arisen because of subsidies and the resulting price differentials between countries. These differentials are prime examples of Passas's notion of criminogenic asymmetries elucidated in Chapter 1. The drivers of commodity smuggling, therefore, are widespread poverty and exclusion combined with asymmetries and arbitrage opportunities. These increased significantly after the Jasmine revolution. "The Algerian government, concerned by the Tunisian revolution, sought to limit social unrest by increasing subsidies on food, including wheat, milk, sugar, and cooking oil. While this helped to limit protests, it further exacerbated the price imbalance for basic goods between Algeria and Tunisia. This in turn fueled cross-border smuggling."[229]

Commodity smuggling on the Algerian-Tunisian frontier "is concentrated in the northern section, encompassing the Algerian wilayas of Tabessa, Souk Ahras, and El Taref and the Tunisian governorates of Gafsa, Kasserine, Kef, and Jendouba. . . . Smuggling nodes . . . include the Algerian cities of Tabessa and Annaba and the Tunisian cities of Jendouba, El Kef, Kasserine, and Gafsa. Smuggling is also carried out at south of Gafsa, though it is less frequent and easier for security forces to interdict."[230] The facilitators are partly geographical and partly cultural. "The porosity of the border between Tunisia and Algeria is due both to its flat, steppe-like terrain, especially to the south of Kasserine, which facilitates traffic across it, and to the way the region is settled by a population that sees its vital economic and social space as being divided by the line of the border. In fact, many tribal groups, such as the Ouled Sidi Abid, the Ouled Sidi Tlil and the Frechiches, were divided by the border as a result of the vagaries of history and the colonial demarcation of national boundaries."[231] These communities transcend imposed borders that were a product of colonialism, providing bonding mechanisms and levels of trust that facilitate cross-border smuggling.

Alyssa Marie Miller, an anthropologist who researched contraband smuggling in the Tunisian province of Kasserine on the western border with Algeria, highlighted the importance of smuggling as a coping strategy and, for many, a basic source of subsistence. In Miller's view, Tunisia's provinces in the borderlands with Algeria and Libya can be understood as "shadow zones" in which public investment is severely limited.[232] She also noted that Kasserine, which had become known during the revolution as the region of martyrs, expected but did not receive a "development dividend."[233] After some jihadist groups infiltrated the region, it even became stigmatized as a security threat. In fact, however, most of the smuggling remained benign and even positive in character. As she noted, "for unemployed youth living in the shadow of underdevelopment, smuggling offers a rare avenue of insertion into productive life, where the border serves as a natural resource for generating value through arbitrage."[234] Buying commodities in Algeria where they are cheaper and then selling them in Tunisia provides a livelihood when little else is available. Indeed, "households rely on smuggling to provide everyday consumer products at prices that they can afford."[235] Perhaps the best description is that the smuggling economy in the region is an "economy of necessity."[236]

That economy—like most illicit economies—is populated by a variety of participants. At the lowest level are the simple commodity smugglers. One study, on a basis of interviews with those involved, offered a provisional categorization of the low-level smugglers:

- The grafters are young people seeking to survive. "Rather than being a simple transitory phase while waiting to return to what would be seen as a normal career path, the grafters (many of whom are unemployed graduates) enter a humiliating spiral of debt and dependence."[237]
- The disconnected are families who engage in smuggling "to ensure funds are raised and debts are paid."[238]
- The climbers are often school dropouts for whom smuggling provides a sense of identity and helps them to support their families.[239]
- The temps find occasional employment as porters and lookouts.[240]
- Women in the "suitcase trade" buy "clothing, cosmetics and domestic goods in Algeria and return to Tunisia, hiding their purchases or passing them off as items for personal use to avoid paying taxes."[241]

In those few instances where they are interviewed, smugglers emphasize that smuggling is better than being unemployed and offers them ways of supporting their families. It is seen as an important lifeline in communities that are struggling. Yet, there is also a sense of danger that is welcomed by some of the participants who "share their feats online, glorifying this risky and illegal business on TikTok."[242]

This low-level smuggling is accompanied by large-scale smuggling by what are typically, albeit inappropriately, described as cartel operations. "These powerful businesses are governed by wholesale bosses who employ a network of drivers and lookouts," include alcohol among the smuggled commodities, and appear to be connected to powerful figures at various levels of government.[243]

One particularly important part of the smuggling economy between Tunisia and Algeria is gasoline, with extremely low prices in Algeria providing the impetus. In some respects, this is a few steps up the smuggling ladder—more volatile than foodstuffs and retail goods, but not as pernicious as drugs and weapons. Its importance was underlined by a 2013 World Bank study, which concluded that "60% of the 3,000 vehicles operating on the border between Tunisia and Algeria are used for fuel smuggling. The study also found that these routes accounted for the importing of 25% of the fuel consumed in Tunisia."[244] Fuel smugglers favor certain vehicles, including Peugeot 504 and 505, the Toyota Hilux, the Isuzu D-Max, and the Kairouan Isuzu (*el karwiyya*).[245]

Yet even with vehicles the smugglers find themselves squeezed. Many of them cannot afford to buy the required vehicles outright and lease them instead—at high interest rates. This can entrap them in a vicious spiral. As one study noted, "smuggling is turning into a fatal trap that swallows up economic resources, as many smugglers resign themselves to selling plots of land, if they own any, or some livestock, in order to pay their leasing instalments, support their families, or meet healthcare costs or other welfare obligations."[246] In addition, the costs of smuggling—the bribes they are required to pay—are increasing and becoming more frequent as patrols and checkpoints increase in number. Not only is smuggling becoming less profitable, it is also more difficult.[247] The Tunisian side of the border is less strictly enforced than the Algerian side, with a minimal presence in Kasserine of two border posts and ten outposts.[248] According to some reports, the strengthening of barriers on the Algerian border, however, resulted in a significant decline in smuggling—perhaps as much 70 percent.[249] Yet, it also comported with Herbert's thesis and placed the focus more on the formal crossing points. This meant a shift in the smugglers' toolkit from circumvention of controls to facilitation through bribery. Herbert described this is as a joint-extractive system.[250]

Although there are many similarities between Tunisia's border with Algeria and its border with Libya, especially in terms of the marginalized population and the arbitrage opportunities, there are also some key differences. Most of the smuggling on the Algerian border is based on circumvention and avoidance of border posts—which account for only 2 percent of the informal trade between the two countries[251]—while the smuggling with Libya goes primarily through the border crossing at Ras Jedir,[252] with the southeastern city of Ben Gardane acting as a hub. As a Clingendael study noted, "the border between Tunisia and Libya has always been characterized by constant, intense and tolerated cross-movements of people and goods. Communities on both sides (especially in towns like Ben Gardane in Tunisia or Zuwara in Libya) have built long-standing relations and trading activities based on an informal economy in order to fill the lack of public services and provide for their own security."[253]

Indeed, much of the smuggling was and is innocuous and came from the Tunisian side, with some of the commodities coming back as cheaper subsidized goods. In 2013, the *Economist* reported that smuggling of eggs from Tunisia to Libya was such a lucrative sector that "some Tunisians fear they will run out at home."[254] Milk was another commodity that was in great demand.[255] Historically though most of the flows have come from Libya. "Textiles, white electronics and similar consumer goods are shipped to the port of Tripoli, loaded on fleets of smaller cars, and brought into Tunisia, where they are sold on markets throughout the country."[256] As these goods move through Ras Jedir, they are "completely undeclared, mis-declared or under-declared, with the avoidance of the full legal import tariff making up a significant section of the profit margins of local traders."[257] Flows moving in the other direction, are "largely of food staples and agricultural goods" and on a "small scale."[258] Given the prominence of the Ras Jedir border crossing, "the most widespread activity is carried out by people who transport goods on a small scale and bribe customs officials to accept false declarations and false papers in order to avoid paying taxes and fines."[259]

Economic relations across the Libyan border were historically organized by tribal affiliation, through cooperation between the Tunisian Touazine tribe and their Libyan counterparts, the Nouayel.[260] The tacit quid pro quo from the state was that smuggling was allowed so long as weapons and drugs were not included and that the authorities were informed about suspicious anomalies.[261] Different tribes took on different functions, with the Touazines involved in finance, the Nouayels and Zouaris focused on the wholesale trade, and the Ouerghemma (or Ouderna) running illicit convoys.[262] With all the turbulence, it is likely that tribal influence has declined somewhat. Yet this does not mean that the smuggling is entirely unstructured or unpredictable.

Indeed, Max Gallien has offered a novel and compelling interpretation of the smuggling that not only extends the idea of a quid pro quo but also challenges notions of smuggling across the Tunisia-Libya border being an uncontrolled or out-of-control activity. He notes that officials specify "the quantity and types of goods that could be smuggled, and their costs" and that this has been tacitly and possibly even explicitly agreed through negotiations with smugglers and civil society actors.[263] In his view, smuggling is negotiated, regulated, and governed at the official border crossing.[264] Yet, not all smuggling goes through this channel. Circumvention of the formal border crossing was also an option and was used for "tobacco, gold, foreign currency, large quantities of consumer products, and subsidized gasoline from Libya to Tunisia, as well as alcohol and pharmaceutical products from Tunisia to Libya."[265] This required more elaborate bribery and protection schemes and was both riskier and more lucrative. It also required vehicles that could handle the rough terrain and outrun interdiction efforts.[266]

Whichever way goods from Libya were brought into the country, they were quickly and easily absorbed into the economy through small markets that were created in Medenine and elsewhere and widely known as "Souk Libya" (Libyan bazaar).[267] The irony is that although all the goods are smuggled, each market has a small police station to ensure that business is conducted normally and efficiently.[268] For all the social, economic, and political acceptance of smuggling as a fact of life in Tunisia, however, it has become more difficult. It is also expensive to move smuggled gasoline from the border inland because of the increased prevalence of patrols and ad hoc checkpoints. The payments for "free" passage increase the farther away from the Libyan border one gets, although it is the number of these that are regarded by smugglers as particularly irksome. The increase of checkpoints is a problem for smugglers beyond oil. One analyst, for example, noted that in February 2017, a trader of couscous to Libya who was returning with carpets, had to pass "4 checkpoints between Ben Gardane and Ras Jedir, set up by the Tunisian National Guard, Police, Military, and Customs Officers, and another 5 checkpoints between Ras Jedir and Zelten in Libya, set up by a variety of local authorities and armed groups."[269] In other words, smuggling is less smooth and is costlier than it once was.

According to some observers, circumvention has also become more difficult, not least because of increased fortifications on the border. The employment of "sand banks and water-filled trenches" on the Libyan border between Dhiba and Ras Jedir has made circumvention more challenging, albeit far from impossible.[270] It is likely that circumvention, although more difficult, has also become more prevalent because of the Tunisian government's closure of Ras Jedir. From February to June 2016 the border crossing was closed in response to increased instability in Libya.[271] Problems also arose because of a change in control of the crossing on the Libyan side.

Continued difficulties with the crossing and the lack of an agreement on how the cross-border trade could be expanded provoked strikes and protests in Ben Gardane during 2018. These ended with a new municipal council coming to an agreement with the Zuwara city authorities who had claimed control of Ras Jedir on the Libyan side. In 2020, however, in response to the Covid-19 pandemic, Tunisia ordered a national lockdown and the sealing of the borders. This included the shutting down once again of Ras Jedir—with a serious impact on Ben Gardane. It was reopened for travelers in November 2020 and for the transportation of goods in June 2021.[272]

As the International Crisis Group pointed out in a 2013 report, the Tunisian government faced an inescapable dilemma in its desire to enhance border security without disrupting the "informal cross-border trade" that "acts as a safety valve, helping to maintain social peace in regions that are neglected by the authorities."[273] The choice was between national security, as traditionally defined, and human security in terms of the well-being of the citizens in the borderlands and their ability to meet their basic needs. The government, for all the promise of the Jasmine revolution, seemed to give priority to national security—a tendency exacerbated by continued Libyan instability and the pandemic.

A large part of the reason was the conflation of smuggling and smugglers on the one side and terrorism and terrorists on the other. The most extreme version of this was the notion of "Islamo-gangsterism," first used by the International Crisis Group (ICG) in 2013, which suggested a merger of criminals and extremists.[274] Although such a label is facile, there is some evidence of cooperation between hashish traffickers and militant organizations. According to Herbert, who offers brilliant insights into smuggling in Tunisia, some traffickers developed connections with AQIM and Islamic State militants offering "protection against interdiction by the Tunisian government in exchange for payments."[275] Such arrangements might have even gone beyond simple protection to include diversions, such as attacks on security posts or patrols to facilitate the smuggling of cannabis resin. It is worth keeping in mind, however, that protection is often a euphemism for extortion and that cooperation is sometimes enforced rather than voluntary.

Another version of the conflation thesis was encapsulated in a comment by an Algerian border official who claimed that the border challenge could be summed up "quite simply as a problem of tomatoes and terrorists."[276] The implication, of course, was that it was as easy for terrorists (or weapons or drugs) to cross borders as it was for innocuous commodities. It was also linked to the suspicion that jihadists could become part of the smuggling economy or at the very least could benefit from it. In this connection, Hanlon and Herbert noted, "indications are scant that terrorist groups in the region are active participants in the smuggling economy, but they do benefit from it. A culture of low-level corruption engendered by generations of smugglers makes it easy for terrorist groups to move people and supplies throughout the region."[277] In this connection, considerable concern has been expressed about the National Guard forces on the western border. As the ICG wrote in a 2015 report, "the corruption of some officers of the National Guard is a serious security concern: in certain circumstances a bribe is enough for a vehicle to be allowed to pass a checkpoint without being searched. The value of the bribe increases in direct proportion to the level of suspicion that the vehicle or truck provokes."[278]

Such fears on the part of the government, therefore, were certainly not groundless. The issue, however, is one of balance, and it appears that the obvious, overt, and immediate threat of terrorist attack is attracting attention and policy initiatives, while the more insidious and long-term consequence of further marginalization in terms of provoking instability—as well as in terms of facilitating radicalization and swelling the ranks of terrorist organizations—is largely being ignored. As one study observed, "the counter-terrorism agenda has now led to a situation where subsistence smuggling is conflated with criminality and the demands from young people in the region for social justice and inclusion are delegitimized."[279] The danger with overprioritizing the security challenge and ignoring social and economic marginalization is that this will "worsen the pre-existing fault lines in the border regions and weaken Tunisia's resilience, namely the ability of the state and society to manage external crises and to implement much-needed reforms to address the long list of social grievances, economic alienation, and political disillusionment in the periphery."[280]

Corruption and Illicit Financial Flows

Until 2011, corruption was highly concentrated in the families of Ben Ali and his wife, Leila Trabelsi; it has since become much more diffuse in Tunisia, with far more petty corruption accompanied by occasional hints of corruption on a larger scale. Although there were 8,000 mentions of Tunisia in the Panama Papers, the impact was fleeting. A part of the reason for the limited response was that the reports by Inkyfada, an investigative website working with the International Consortium of Investigative Journalists, immediately became a matter of internecine squabbling among political rivals. The first report on April 4 revealed that Mohsen Marzouk, a prominent politician and campaign manager for Beji Caid Essebsi, had contacted Mossack Fonseca about opening an offshore account.[281] "The report provoked quick and forceful reactions. The Inkyfada website was hacked the following night and a fake article appeared falsely alleging that Moncef Marzouki—Tunisia's former president and Essebsi's rival in the 2014 presidential run-off election—had appeared in the Panama Papers."[282] Inkyfada shut down its own website and clarified that Marzouki was not mentioned in the Panama Papers. Nevertheless, "the false claim was republished in other media outlets."[283] Several other reports by Inkyfada identified other politicians, and there were some modest moves toward investigating corruption. The difficulty, as Sarah Mersch astutely noted, is that corruption in Tunisia is treated as "a matter of party politics rather than a public policy challenge."[284] This has been accentuated during Saied's tenure as political opponents who challenge his autocratic rule have been accused of corruption and even terrorism. Even allowing for what can only be called the politicization of corruption allegations, however, corruption in Tunisia remains a serious challenge. According to Transparency International in 2022, Tunisia received a score of 40 out of 100 and was ranked 85 out of 180 countries.[285] Moreover, 67 percent of people thought corruption had increased in the previous twelve months, while 35 percent acknowledged paying a bribe.[286]

In 2020 and 2021, however, there were two corruption scandals. The first involved Italy and in some respects was anomalous, even while being part of a larger pattern in which toxic waste from the Global North is moved to the Global South. The anomaly was that most of the illicit flows from Tunisia are either north toward Europe and especially Italy or across the Maghreb in an easterly or westerly direction. Yet, there is also a north to south flow that is longstanding but in 2020 became a cause célèbre in Tunisia. Toxic waste disposal in and from Italy is one of the most corrupt sectors of the economy, often involving deals with mafia clans and companies that offer much lower costs than legitimate firms.[287] In this case, however, the issue was not only some likely organized crime involvement, but also corrupt Tunisian officials accepting forms of waste imports that were prohibited by law from entry into the country.

"Between May and July 2020, Italian company Sviluppo Risorse Ambientali (SRA) based in Polla, Italy, shipped 282 containers of mixed municipal waste (including household waste) across the Mediterranean to Soreplast, a Tunisian company" via the Tunisian port of Sousse.[288] "The first 70 containers reached the importer, while Tunisian customs seized the remaining 212 containers in July after an inspection revealed that they contained municipal waste."[289] The waste had been certified as "post-industrial plastic waste destined for recycling."[290] The issue was publicized by Tunisian TV channel Elhiwar Ettounsi in November 2020, and the following month the minister of the environment was dismissed and arrested.[291] Other arrests targeted customs agents, officials from the Tunisian National Waste Management Agency, and a diplomat at the Tunisian consulate in Naples.[292] It appears that rebranding the waste was a means of avoiding costs associated with household waste disposal.

As one investigation reported, by recategorizing the waste as industrial plastic for recycling, SRA avoided Italian waste disposal fees of 100 euros per ton for mixed municipal waste, instead paying low disposal fees of 5.60 euros per ton in Tunisia.[293] For its part, Soreplast received 48 euros per ton for recycling and final disposing of what could not be recycled even though it had no real sorting and recycling capacity and no incinerator.[294] It is highly probable that Soreplast intended to dispose of the waste in a local landfill.[295] The case sparked protest and demands that Italy repatriate its waste.[296] The head of Soreplast, Moncef Noureddine, reportedly left for Europe ten days before his arrest warrant was issued.[297] According to one source, his family is "well-established in the Port El-Kantaoui neighborhood of Sousse," was "linked to Ben Ali's inner circles," and is "very influential in the region. It is very easy for him to get in touch with a minister or an influential person."[298] For many Tunisians already disillusioned with the resilience of corruption since the Jasmine revolution, Noureddine's involvement in an environmental scandal of this magnitude was an unwelcome confirmation of their fears. With NGOs pressuring the Tunisian government, however, it was finally agreed that the waste should be repatriated to Italy, and in February 2022, 213 containers were loaded on a Turkish ship and departed Tunisia for Italy.[299] It was discovered that sixty-nine containers had been destroyed in a fire, which led to speculation that the Italian mafia had been involved in the business. Although there was no proof of such involvement, the possibility took on greater credence when it was revealed that Soreplast had initially signed the deal with a Calabrian company with Bulgarian ties called Eco Management S.P.A. and that Eco Management S.P.A. had then passed the task on to SRA.[300] An Italian friend of Noureddine had reportedly acted as an intermediary between Soreplast and Eco Management S.P.A.[301] A spate of arrests made in December 2020 included the environment minister.

Another supposed corruption scandal emerged in Tunisia in 2021—although it has become mired in political accusations and what appear to be legitimate rebuttals. The scandal revolves around Rached Ghannouchi, speaker of Parliament and head of the Ennahda Movement. It began, somewhat bizarrely, with information provided by Qatar to the Egyptian government that was the basis for an investigative article in the Tunisian newspaper *Al-Anwar* in March 2021 under the heading "Al-Anwar Opens Ghannouchi's Wealth File."[302] The article included allegations that, if verified, would undermine Ghannouchi's public stance as a moderate Islamist. Noting that he had a fortune of around $1 billion, or 2.7 billion dinars, the newspaper claimed that most of the money was in Swiss bank accounts and in companies outside Tunisia, including three French companies.[303] More serious were the allegations about the source of the money. It was claimed that Ghannouchi's role in facilitating the smuggling of weapons to Libya had resulted in $30 million in commissions.[304] He had supposedly benefited far more from a passport trade scheme run by the former secretary of state for immigration that reportedly provided him with $220 million as well as from other smuggling ventures run by a leader of the Ennahda Movement and parliamentary deputy, Said Ferjani.[305] According to another commentary, "those who were buying these passports were the families of jihadis who wanted to go to fight in Syria with armed groups. The smuggling of jihadis enabled Ghannouchi and his family to make large amounts of money from this trade and exert his influence both through money and international politics."[306]

These supposed revelations were firmly rejected by Ghannouchi. Significantly, they had echoes of earlier attacks against him, claiming that his moderate stance was a veneer, that he supported terrorism, and that he had received funds from Qatar, which was thereby interfering in Tunisian politics. These claims, made in an article published on July 5, 2019, by Middle East Online Limited and its editor, Haitham El Zobaidi—both based in London—led Ghannouchi to sue for libel damages in the UK. He won the case and received 45,000 pounds sterling. According to Middle East Eye, a correspondent in Qatar, Ahmed Yusuf, claimed that media backed by Saudi Arabia, the United Arab Emirates, and Egypt had launched a "systematic campaign" against Ghannouchi, publishing "simultaneous deceitful news" and claiming he had "gained huge financial wealth since his return to Tunisia" in 2011.[307] The analysis by Middle East Eye also suggested that Ghannouchi had revealed his assets, which were relatively modest.[308] Against this background, the 2021 claims about his wealth, his support for terrorism, and his corruption simply seem more of the same. This did not prevent him being called before a judge to defend himself against claims of money laundering. Significantly, though, Ghannouchi has consistently stood up against President Saied and is among prominent opposition figures who have been imprisoned under an authoritarian leader who seems to be reverting to a manner of ruling reminiscent of Ben Ali.

The Ghannouchi case notwithstanding, both corruption and smuggling are widespread in Tunisia. Much of the smuggling is about subsistence and survival. Many reports, however, suggest that there is a hierarchy of smugglers and that there are some big players who make substantial profits from the trade. In terms of money laundering, however, it is not clear that the Tunisian banking and financial system is primed for detection or that law enforcement agencies and the judiciary are equipped for effective investigation and prosecution. The 2016 Financial Action Task Force (FATF) report identified major deficiencies in dealing with money laundering while also noting that the main threat came from terrorist financing, including financial support for terrorists to travel to conflict zones and for their families in the event of their deaths.[309] For its part, the United States in its 2016 International Narcotics Control Strategy Report (INCSR) reported concerns about smuggling, hawalas, and trade-based money laundering but also acknowledged that "Tunisia has strict currency exchange controls, which . . . mitigate the risk of international money laundering"[310] Since then Tunisia seems to have been largely neglected by the United States, and there is not a single mention of Tunisia in the 2022 INCSR Volume 2 on money laundering. The FATF, however, in 2017 identified strategic deficiencies in Tunisia's anti-money laundering and counterterrorist finance regime and subjected it to enhanced monitoring. By June 2019, Tunisia had improved its compliance to a level where it was no longer subject to the FATF's monitoring process.[311]

Despite this, Tunisia has had—and continues to have—a major problem in terms of illicit financial flows. In one recent analysis, Abdelkader Abderrahmane observed that "Tunisia loses about US$1.2

billion annually to illicit financial flows (IFFs)—around 3% of the country's gross domestic product."[312] He also identified three sources of these flows: "commercial activities (such as tax evasion), criminal activities (such as trafficking in drugs, arms and people, and fraud and money laundering), and corruption" while noting that "the primary source of IFFs in Tunisia is government corruption at the highest levels."[313] The criminal activities such as cross-border smuggling are part of the problem but are also a means of subsistence for those in marginalized borderlands. Occasionally, though, there are prominent criminal cases that differ from this. A good example is that of a Franco-Tunisian rapper known as Swagg Man who made a fortune through extortion and fraud and moved much of it to Switzerland. After he was convicted in 2021 of money laundering, Swiss authorities repatriated $5.6 million to Tunisia, where it was used for charitable purposes.[314] More significant, however, are both corruption and tax evasion. Yet there is some light at the end of the tunnel that goes well beyond compliance with the FATF. In 2021 the Tunisian Central Bank's Financial Analysis Committee rolled out a blockchain platform called Hannibal. Blockchain is a distributed ledger that records transactions and provides transparency and easy access to reliability checks. In the Tunisian case, it also seems to have facilitated trust and cooperation between the public and private sectors. The platform also provides information on currency transactions and enables customs and other investigators to investigate irregularities and anomalies.[315] Hannibal is not a panacea, and it remains to be seen whether adequate human resources will be deployed in ways that maximize use of the technology.

Conclusion

Looking closely at Tunisia, what stands out most prominently is the sharp contrast between the "successful transition to democracy" narrative that seems to have been embraced enthusiastically and uncritically by the international donor community, and the realities on the ground. Indeed, comments by young Tunisian men, supplemented by those who have done ethnographic research in Tunisia, highlight a pervasive sense of profound disappointment and despair that the Jasmine revolution has ultimately changed so little, especially when it comes to the availability of jobs and economic opportunities in the formal sector. This is reinforced by the fact that irregular migration is paralleled by an exodus of professionals who leave the country through legal means. As researcher

Mohamed Chamekh noted, "50 per cent of newly graduated doctors left the country between 2016 and 2019. Similarly, in 2018, 72 per cent of highly qualified Tunisian graduates" left the country in search of better employment opportunities and conditions.[316]

Irregular migration from Tunisia and continued extremism within the country are both symptoms of a large and insidious structural problem in which opportunities are constricted and most of the country away from the coast is disenfranchised, marginalized, and largely ignored. This is also a fertile breeding ground for the growth of organized crime. Closely related to this, some elements of the Tunisian diaspora in Europe almost certainly have close links with members of Italian mafia clans. Indeed, some of the smuggling of migrants and cigarettes seems to have been organized as a joint venture between Italians and Tunisians. It is not far-fetched, therefore, to anticipate that criminal linkages will deepen and strengthen as Tunisian criminal organizations and networks emerge from what has become, in essence, a failed revolution. To answer the question in the title of this chapter, the Tunisian democratic success story is little more than a mirage, and it is increasingly apparent that Tunisia is once again a bastion of authoritarianism rather than an oasis of stability. As one Spanish scholar succinctly noted, it might even be "the sick man of North Africa."[317]

Notes

1. Alvi, *Political Economy and Islam*, p. 35.
2. Ibid., p. 42.
3. Al Jazeera, "The Family' Tunisians Hate Most."
4. Partridge, "Book Review: *The Force of Obedience*."
5. Alvi, *Political Economy and Islam*, p. 10.
6. Ibid., p. 3.
7. Zeidan, "Kais Saied, President of Tunisia."
8. Resta, *Tunisia and Egypt After the Arab Spring*.
9. Ibid.
10. Zeidan, "Kais Saied, President of Tunisia."
11. Bongarra, "Tunisia Reiterates Commitment."
12. Phrase adopted from Alvi, *Political Economy and Islam*, p. 81.
13. Herbert, *Losing Hope*, p. 20.
14. AfricaNews, "Tunisia: President Saied."
15. Ibid.
16. Alvi, *Political Economy and Islam*, p. 138.
17. Ibid., p. 136. See also, Wehrey, *Tunisia's Wake-Up Call*.
18. Kourdi and Alam, "At Least Five Killed."
19. ENACT, *Organized Crime Index 2019—Tunisia*, p. 1.
20. Ibid.

21. See, for example, Aliriza, "Tunisia's Crooked Cops Are Undermining."
22. ENACT, *Organized Crime Index 2019—Tunisia*, p. 4.
23. Gall, "Corruption Crackdown Intensifies in Tunisia."
24. See also, Dhaouadi, "Crime and Excessive Punishment in Tunisia."
25. ENACT, *Organized Crime Index 2019—Tunisia*, p. 4.
26. Ibid., p. 1.
27. Ibid., p. 4.
28. Ibid.
29. Global Organized Crime Index, *Tunisia 2023*, p. 1.
30. Ibid.
31. Miller, "Shadow Zones," p. 77.
32. Chamekh, "Illegal Migration in Tunisian Rap," pp. 45–58.
33. Nefzi, "Drugs to Suit All Tastes."
34. Ibid.
35. Ibid.
36. Ibid.
37. Ibid.
38. Herbert and Gallien, *A Rising Tide*, pp. 29, 31.
39. Chaouali et al., "Illicit Substances Identified in the Urine."
40. Herbert and Gallien, *A Rising Tide*, p. 14.
41. Ibid., p. 15.
42. Ibid.
43. Ibid.
44. Ibid.
45. Ibid.
46. Ibid.
47. Ibid., p. 16.
48. Ibid., p. 19.
49. Interpol and ENACT, *Overview of Serious and Organized Crime in North Africa*, p. 11.
50. Herbert and Gallien, *A Rising Tide*, p. 19.
51. Middle East Monitor, "Ecuador Seizes Over Half a Ton."
52. Ibid.
53. AllAfrica, "Attempt to Smuggle 1049g of Heroin."
54. Herbert and Gallien, *A Rising Tide*, p. 33.
55. Ibid., p. 23.
56. Ibid.
57. Ibid., p. 25.
58. See, for example, Center for Insights in Survey Research, *Survey: Residents of Tunisia*.
59. AllAfrica, "Tunisia: Inflation Rate Up."
60. Saleh, "Population Below the Poverty Line."
61. Herbert, "Just Across the Sea," p. 100.
62. Sadiki, "Tunisia's Migration to the North."
63. See also Luck, "'Break the Silence.'"
64. *Arab Weekly*, "Tunisian TV Series."
65. Chamekh, "Illegal Migration in Tunisian Rap," p. 45.
66. Ibid., p. 55.
67. Zagaria, "Morally Fraught *Harga*," pp. 57–73.
68. Ibid., pp. 67–70.
69. Ibid., p. 66.

70. Foroudi, "'The Sea Is Dead.'"
71. Cuddy, "World's Most Overfished Sea."
72. FishAct, "Investigating Illegal Bottom Trawling."
73. Foroudi, "'The Sea Is Dead.'"
74. Ibid.
75. Ibid.
76. Jlassi, Mahjoub, and Crespi, "Preliminary Analysis of the Impact of COVID-19."
77. Foroudi, "'The Sea Is Dead.'"
78. Ibid.
79. Cordall and Tondo, "'Entire Families Are Arriving.'"
80. Ibid.
81. Ibid.
82. Ibid.
83. Herbert, "Just Across the Sea," p. 94.
84. *Arab Weekly*, "Arab Migrants in Tunisia."
85. Herbert, "Just Across the Sea," p. 94.
86. France 24, "'Europe or Death.'"
87. Ibid.
88. InfoMigrants, "53% of Migrants Lost Jobs."
89. France 24, "'Europe or Death.'"
90. Malakooti and Fall, *Migration Trends Across the Mediterranean*, p. 86.
91. Parker, "Economic Fallout from Coronavirus."
92. Ibid.
93. Agence France-Presse, "Tunisia Fishermen Become Lifesavers "; Bertoluzzi, "Tunisian Fishermen on the Frontline."
94. Herbert, *Tunisia: Growing Irregular Migration*, p. 2.
95. Ibid.
96. Ibid.
97. Ibid.
98. Ibid.
99. Ibid.
100. Abderrahim, *Tunisia: Increased Fragility*, p. 6.
101. Ibid., p. 6.
102. Ibid., p. 7.
103. Ibid., p. 2.
104. Ibid., p. 13.
105. Ibid., p. 15.
106. Ibid., p. 3.
107. Ibid., p. 15.
108. Ibid.
109. Ibid., p. 18.
110. Ibid.
111. Ibid., p. 19.
112. Ibid.
113. Ibid., p. 23.
114. Ibid.
115. Ibid., p. 24.
116. Ibid.
117. Ibid. For further details on this see Meddeb, *Leveraging Lives*.
118. Ibid., p. 24.
119. Ibid.

120. Ibid.
121. Meddeb, *Leveraging Lives*, pp. 8–10.
122. Ibid., p. 10.
123. Abderrahim, *Tunisia: Increased Fragility*, p. 26.
124. Faiola, "Racist Roots of the Rise in Migration."
125. Ibid.
126. Ibid.
127. Ibid.
128. Human Rights Watch, "Tunisia: African Migrants Intercepted."
129. UNHCR, "Italy Weekly Snapshot."
130. International Organization for Migration, "Baseline Study on Trafficking," p. 8.
131. Ibid.
132. Ibid., p. 31.
133. Ibid., pp. 52–53.
134. Ibid., pp. 35, 42, 51, 55–57, 70, 75.
135. Ibid., p. 58.
136. Ibid., p. 43.
137. Ibid., p. 61.
138. Ibid., p. 64.
139. Ibid., pp. 38–39.
140. Dhaouadi, "New Hope."
141. US Department of State, "2021 Trafficking in Persons Report: Tunisia."
142. Ibid.
143. Dhaouadi, "Put Human Trafficking Laws to Work."
144. US Department of State, "2021 Trafficking in Persons Report: Tunisia."
145. US Department of State, "2020 Trafficking in Persons Report: Tunisia," p. 496.
146. US Department of State, "2021 Trafficking in Persons Report: Tunisia."
147. Ibid.
148. Ibid.
149. US Department of State, "2021 Trafficking in Persons Report: Cote d'Ivoire."
150. Ibid.
151. US Department of State, "2021 Trafficking in Persons Report: Tunisia."
152. Ibid.
153. Ibid.
154. Ibid.
155. US Department of State, "2022 Trafficking in Persons Report: Tunisia."
156. Ibid.
157. Ibid.
158. Ibid.
159. US Department of State, "2023 Trafficking in Persons Report: Tunisia."
160. Ibid.
161. Ibid
162. Alpers and Wilson, *Guns in North Africa.*
163. Strazzari and Zampagni, "Illicit Firearms Circulation," p. 438.
164. Hanlon and Herbert, *Border Security Challenges*, p. 26.
165. Kartas, "On the Edge?"
166. See also Marsh, "Brothers Came Back with Weapons."
167. Shaw and Mangan, *Illicit Trafficking and Libya's Transition*, p. 19.
168. See also Meddeb, *Volatile Tunisia-Libya Border.*

169. See also Boukhars, "Potential Jihadi Windfall."
170. Hanlon and Herbert, *Border Security Challenges*, p. 15.
171. Ibid., p. 18.
172. Ibid.
173. Strazzari and Zampagni, "Illicit Firearms Circulation," p. 444.
174. Ibid.
175. Letter dated 1 June 2017 from the Panel of Experts on Libya Established Pursuant to Resolution 1973 (2011) addressed to the President of the Security Council, United Nations Security Council, June 1, 2017, p. 49, https://undocs.org/pdf?symbol=en/S/2017/466.
176. Strazzari and Zampagni, "Illicit Firearms Circulation," p. 445.
177. Yahoo News, "Tunisia Finds Arms Caches."
178. Strazzari and Zampagni, "Illicit Firearms Circulation," p. 444.
179. Amara, "Tunisia Finishes Libya Border Fence"; Bobin, "Troubling New Wall Arises."
180. Hanlon and Herbert, *Border Security Challenges*, p. 41.
181. Saidani, "Tunisia: Interior Ministry."
182. *North Africa Post*, "Tunisia: Security Forces."
183. Global Organized Crime Index, *Tunisia 2023*.
184. Meneghini and Milani, "Maghreb," p. 10.
185. Ibid.
186. Ibid.
187. Ibid., p. 11.
188. Moiseienko, Reid, and Chase, *Improving Governance and Tackling Crime*, p. 10.
189. Meneghini and Milani, "Maghreb Route," pp. 14, 16.
190. Ibid., p. 25.
191. *North Africa Post*, "French Court Frees Flight Attendant."
192. Interpol and ENACT, *Illicit Goods Trafficking*, p. 34. Drawn from C. Spada and F. Marone, *The Impact of Illicit Trafficking and Jihadist Infiltrations Inside Italian Seaports: Looking Towards a Way Forward* (Turtle Group Consulting, 2018).
193. Ibid.
194. The Local, "Italian Police Bust Migrant."
195. Balay, "Italy Cracks Migrants."
196. The Local, "Italian Police Bust Migrant."
197. BBC News, "Italy Smashes Speedboat Trafficking Gang."
198. Ibid.
199. Ibid.
200. Ibid.
201. Ibid.
202. Xinhua, "Italy Busts 14-Member."
203. Ibid.
204. Ibid.
205. Ibid.
206. Ibid.
207. European Public Prosecutor's Office, "Counterfeit Cigarette Trafficking Scheme."
208. Ibid.
209. Ibid.
210. Ibid.
211. European Public Prosecutor's Office, "First Verdict in EPPO Case."

212. *Saudi Gazette*, "Tunisian Coastguard Tackles High-Speed Smugglers," April 28, 2017.
213. European Public Prosecutor's Office, "Counterfeit Cigarette Trafficking Scheme."
214. *Yale Environment 360*, "Amid Coronavirus Lockdown."
215. Ibid.
216. Ibid.
217. Global Organized Crime Index, *Tunisia 2023*, p. 3.
218. Quillen, "Forest Fires, Wilting Crops."
219. Global Organized Crime Index, *Tunisia 2023*, p. 3.
220. Manisera, Mancini, and Poletti, "Trawling Ravages Tunisian Seagrass."
221. Ibid.
222. Ibid.
223. Ibid.
224. Abdelmoula, "Natural Resources in Tunisia."
225. Global Organized Crime Index, *Tunisia 2023*, p. 3.
226. Herbert, "From Contraband to Conflict," p. 192.
227. See also Ghanem, "Specter of Jihadism."
228. International Crisis Group, *Tunisia's Borders: Jihadism and Contraband*, p. 8.
229. Herbert, "From Contraband to Conflict," p. 220.
230. Hanlon and Herbert, *Border Security Challenges*, p. 15.
231. Meddeb, *Young People and Smuggling*, p. 9.
232. Miller, "Shadow Zones," pp. 16–22.
233. Ibid., p. 21.
234. Ibid., p. iv.
235. Ibid., p. 49.
236. Meddeb, *Young People and Smuggling*, p. 9.
237. Ibid., p. 5.
238. Ibid.
239. Ibid.
240. Ibid.
241. Ibid.
242. Hamad, "Daredevil Drivers Smuggling Fuel."
243. Miller, "Shadow Zones," pp. 67–71.
244. Meddeb, *Young People and Smuggling*, p. 11.
245. Ibid., p. 21.
246. Ibid., p. 19.
247. Ibid., p. 20.
248. Ibid., p. 10.
249. Ibid., p. 11.
250. Herbert, "From Contraband to Conflict," p. 16.
251. Ayadi et al., "Attempt to Estimating Informal Trade."
252. International Crisis Group, *Tunisia's Borders: Jihadism and Contraband*, p. 12.
253. Chauzal and Zavagli, *Post-revolutionary Discontent and F(r)actionalisation*, p. 18.
254. *Economist*, "Trafficking in North Africa."
255. Reuters, "Tunisia Closes Libya Border Post After Smugglers Kill Soldier," March 11, 2013.
256. Gallien, "Smugglers and States," p. 75.
257. Ibid., p. 100.
258. Ibid., p. 75.

259. International Crisis Group, *Tunisia's Borders: Jihadism and Contraband*, p. 9.
260. Ibid., p. 11, footnote 50; Chauzal and Zavagli, *Post-revolutionary Discontent and F(r)actionalisation*, p. 21.
261. Santini, *Limited Statehood in Post-revolutionary Tunisia*, p. 72. International Crisis Group, *Tunisia's Borders: Jihadism and Contraband*, p. 23; Miller, "Shadow Zones," p. 58.
262. Chauzal and Zavagli, *Post-revolutionary Discontent and F(r)actionalisation*, p. 21.
263. Gallien, "Smugglers and States," pp. 15–16.
264. Ibid.
265. *North Africa Post*, "Tunisian Forces Kill One Citizen."
266. Gallien, "Informal Institutions and Regulation of Smuggling," p. 500.
267. Gallien, "Smugglers and States," p. 128.
268. Ibid.
269. Ibid., pp. 105–106.
270. Al Jazeera, "Tunisia Completes Barrier Along Libya Border."
271. Meddeb, *Volatile Tunisia-Libya Border*.
272. ReliefWeb,"UNHCR Tunisia Operational Update—30 November 2020," Situation Report, December 15, 2020, https://reliefweb.int/report/tunisia/unhcr-tunisia-operational-update-30-november-2020; AllAfrica, "Tunisia: Medenine."
273. International Crisis Group, *Tunisia's Borders: Jihadism and Contraband*, p. 2.
274. Ibid., pp. 27–32.
275. Herbert, "From Contraband to Conflict," p. 231.
276. Hanlon and Herbert, *Border Security Challenges*, p. 8.
277. Ibid., p. 6.
278. International Crisis Group, *Reform and Security Strategy in Tunisia*, p. 16.
279. Meddeb, *Young People and Smuggling*, p. 4.
280. Meddeb, *Precarious Resilience*, p. 2.
281. Mersch, "Panama Papers Arrive in Tunis," pp. 1–2.
282. Ibid., p. 2.
283. Ibid.
284. Ibid.
285. See Transparency International, "Our Work in Tunisia," 2022, https://www.transparency.org/en/countries/tunisia.
286. Ibid.
287. Winfield, "Italy Confirms Higher Cancer."
288. Global Alliance for Incinerator Alternatives, *Illegal Shipments*, p. 1.
289. Ibid.
290. Ibid., p. 2.
291. Ibid., p. 1.
292. *Taipei Times*, "Tunisia Detains Ex-official."
293. *Packaging Insights*, "Activists Call for Justice."
294. Ibid.
295. Global Alliance for Incinerator Alternatives, *Illegal Shipments*, p. 2.
296. See also Delpuech, "Italian Waste. Part 2: New Protagonists."
297. Delpeuch and IrpiMedia, "Italian Waste: Vast Corruption Network."
298. Ibid.
299. Gorman, "Tunisian NGOs Triumph ."
300. Delpuech, "Italian Waste. Part 2: New Protagonists."
301. Ibid.
302. *Arab Observer*, "Newspaper Reveals Huge Fortune."

303. Ibid.
304. Al Marsad, "Ghannouchi Receives US$30."
305. Ibid.
306. Ibid.
307. Middle East Eye, "Tunisia's Rached Ghannouchi Wins."
308. Ibid.
309. MENAFATF, *Anti-Money Laundering: Tunisia*, pp. 4–17.
310. US Department of State, "Money Laundering and Financial Crimes Country Database," pp. 457–459.
311. For a good overview see "Tunisia: Know Your Country," October 2019, https://www.knowyourcountry.com/tunisia.
312. Abderrahmane, "Tunisia's Crippling Illicit Financial Flows."
313. Ibid.
314. Ibid.
315. Talan, "Hannibal: 1st Regtech."
316. Chamekh, "Illegal Migration in Tunisian Rap," p. 51.
317. Ghilès, "Tunisia Is the Sick Man."

5

Libya: Chaos, Conflict, and Crime

ALTHOUGH THEY TYPICALLY ESCAPE NOTICE, THE PARALLELS BETWEEN IRAQ and Libya, while far from comprehensive, are in some respects very striking.[1] In both cases, ruthless and charismatic strongmen ruled what can be termed highly repressive and even "fierce states."[2] Both countries were also subject to biting international sanctions, which, as Peter Andreas astutely observed, have significant and long-term criminalizing consequences by creating new illicit markets that did not previously exist.[3] One response to sanctions common to both countries was that their authoritarian leaders permitted and encouraged illegal activities, almost as a pressure release valve. Not only did this offset some of the consequences of sanctions, but it also allowed the dictator and his cronies among the political elite to profit both directly and indirectly from these activities. In effect, both Saddam Hussein and Muammar Gaddafi acted as mafia godfathers at the top of large criminal enterprises functioning under the auspices of the state. In Libya, Gaddafi even promoted black markets as "people's markets," co-opting a negative experience brought on by his own misrule and attempting to harness it as a part of Libya's revolutionary zeal.[4] In practice, though, direct access to criminal networks was limited. The state's ability to provide for the population was negatively impacted by a bevy of factors, including sanctions, a drop in oil prices, and a dysfunctional economy. In turn, black markets and illicit smuggling filled the void. Still, a combination of tribes, families, and communities close to Gaddafi were the primary beneficiaries, helping him construct a vast and mostly loyal patronage network.[5] Such restrictions notwithstanding, the result was that "systemic and structural preconditions for a massive expansion of organized crime and the illicit economy were present and needed only the collapse of the regime as a catalyst."[6] This comment was made specifically about Iraq, but applied equally well to Libya. Once Gaddafi was killed, the resulting power vacuum enabled and facilitated both the democratization and diffusion of both organized crime and illicit markets—as it had done in Iraq after the toppling of Hussein's regime.

At this point, however, the trajectories of the two countries diverged, with the United States and its allies occupying Iraq, creating the Coalition Provisional Authority, and subsequently transferring power to a new Iraqi government. In the case of Libya, the North Atlantic Treaty Organization's (NATO's) military actions, which were an ambiguous mix of humanitarian intervention and regime change, resulted in deposing Gaddafi without putting an effective successor regime in place. The Gaddafi regime was decapitated and destroyed, but NATO then walked away, in effect disowning the problem. Without a successor regime, a vacuum of power and authority resulted in chaotic forms of conflict. Competition among rival militias deteriorated into a full-scale civil war, during which organized crime and illicit markets expanded and flourished. Conflict zones are massive opportunity spaces for some illicit entrepreneurs.[7] Armed actors, especially those with smuggling expertise and knowledge about the local terrain (urban, coastal, or desert), comprehensively exploit the opportunities, becoming even more formidable in the process. In effect, illicit economies, smuggling, and trafficking all fuel and perpetuate conflict, which further erodes governance structures and empowers a range of nonstate actors, including criminal networks. Moreover, conflict and criminality are mutually reinforcing, preventing the emergence of a single legitimate authority with a monopoly of coercive power. Once external actors get involved, they can provide even more opportunities for illicit activity, as states fund proxy forces and warlords emerge in control of various fiefdoms. In some parts of Libya, the situation is beginning to resemble state capture, wherein mafia-like groups essentially control all formal and informal activities.

Libya, perhaps more than any other North African country—apart from Morocco—was also influenced by the Mediterranean context described in Chapter 1. Libya's proximity to the criminal hub in Italy and to the island of Malta became particularly important in oil smuggling, while Turkey subsequently played an important role in supplying arms to Libya despite the UN arms embargo. With several states looking at Libya as a proxy conflict, there has been more external involvement and meddling by countries including, but not limited to, Turkey, Russia, and the United Arab Emirates (UAE). Moreover, as noted in Chapter 1, illicit flows in North Africa move in all directions: north to south, south to north, west to east, and east to west, as well as along diagonal lines. Keeping this in mind, Libya's location and geography are enormously important. "Libya sits at the center of long-established trans-Saharan trade routes, a nexus for trade crossing the Sahel to reach the Mediterranean and from the Maghreb into the Mashriq. It is home to desert, land, and sea routes in all directions that Gadhafi used and exploited, ultimately normalizing smuggling in Libyan society."[8] Consequently, illicit flows are both well-established and multidirectional, while methods of conveyance vary significantly depending on several factors, including direction and terrain. The goods and products are also fungible and ebb and flow in value, depending on exogenous factors like scarcity and ease of transport.

It is hardly surprising, therefore, that in the Organized Crime Index created by ENACT and the Global Initiative Against Transnational Organized Crime, Libya has consistently scored high in criminality and low in resilience.[9] This assessment has continued through the 2019, 2021, and 2023 indices. Libya has had one of the highest criminality scores in Africa, while it has also had by far the highest score in North Africa. As the 2019 report noted, mafia-style militia groups control many areas across the country and are heavily involved in many criminal markets, including drug trafficking, human smuggling, human trafficking, and illicit oil smuggling.[10] Libya essentially has two competing governments, both with close links to militia groups and criminal actors. "In some cases, they feed off one another, making the political process indirectly dependent on the proceeds of organized crime."[11] This is a corrosive and vicious cycle that is serving to further undermine the trappings of a functioning state—which Libya has not been for some time—by ceding entire regions to militia groups able to marshal enough weapons and ammunition to dominate these areas. Consequently, it was little surprise that in the 2021 index, Libya's resilience score of 1.54 placed it 193rd of the 193 countries assessed, 54th of 54 African countries, and last in North Africa.[12] Although its placings were marginally better in 2023, the level of criminality seemed to increase rather than abate, going from 6.55 in 2021 to 6.93 in 2023. Moreover, Libya suffered from high scores in both the categories of criminal markets and criminal actors. Several criminal markets were added to the index in 2023, and Libya scored a 9.50 for financial crimes to accompany its 9.50 for both human smuggling and resource crimes, its 9.0 for extortion and protection racketeering and arms trafficking, as well as a slightly generous 8.50 for human trafficking.[13] As for criminal actors, mafia-style groups scored 9.0 only to be surpassed by state-embedded actors with 9.50.[14] One result of the multiplicity of illicit markets in the country is that income streams become highly fungible: if one market is constrained or reduced, readily available alternatives can be exploited, often efficiently. The product might change, but the criminal actors simply adapt by changing the commodity and expanding alternative illicit revenue streams. In an interview conducted as part of this research, Nick Snaith of Rose Partners explained how a smuggling network can "use a truck to smuggle migrants one day but the next day could pivot if necessary to use the same truck to move drugs."[15] As discussed more fully below, for several years the most dynamic illicit economic sector was people smuggling. It was not coincidence, however, that as this dried up, variants on the theme of human trafficking increased in importance while drug trafficking also expanded.

It is also crucial to track how the situation in Libya has evolved over time, particularly as the country is still mired in civil war and essentially divided between two major fiefdoms. The ENACT Global Organized Crime Index suggested in its 2021 report on Libya that the country suffered from "little to no political leadership" and from governance deficits, which significantly plagued its efforts to make any meaningful headway on organized crime issues.[16] Although major military operations ended in late 2020, the situation failed to stabilize, as detailed by the Bertelsmann Transformation Index (BTI), which assessed in its country reports that Libya ranked number 127 out of 137 countries analyzed in terms of how poorly it fared on governance indicators.[17]

Drug Trafficking to Libya, in Libya, and from Libya

"Illicit drug trafficking in Libya is not new. Nor is the recreational consumption of drugs. Both, though, have been reshaped in the wake of the country's 2011 uprising, meriting analysis of how they relate to the ongoing conflict, both feeding from it and fueling it."[18] In this connection, Mark Micallef has identified what he described as "two concurrent and conflicting developments in drug trafficking."[19] First, Micallef explains that militias serve as enablers for organized crime by facilitating large-scale import, storage, and re-exportation of drugs in Libya, particularly along the coast of Tripolitania. Second, in what is a conflicting development according to Micallef, militias have competed against drug traffickers, particularly at local markets. Despite this challenge, since the 2011 uprising, state and local law enforcement agencies have strengthened and are better positioned to operate against criminal elements in Libya.[20]

More vigorous law enforcement efforts, notwithstanding, drug trafficking has become what Fiona Mangan has described as "a top-tier element of Libya's criminal economy."[21] This reflects the fact that there are now domestic markets for psychotropic drugs as well as for pharmaceuticals. Libya has gone from being primarily a relatively modest transshipment location to being a more significant transshipment country as well as a serious consumer of narcotics and pharmaceuticals—especially tramadol.[22] This perspective was echoed by Samuel Juett, a diplomatic official based in the US embassy in Tunis but responsible for the counter-drug account for US interests in Libya. Juett explained in a February 24, 2021, interview that the illicit trade of tramadol had significantly expanded in Libya and that "ubiquitous scooters" were moving the product at low risk but with high rewards.[23] Juett further explained that many low-level peddlers are engaged in the illicit trade to "take care of their family."[24] Mangan, however, sees a large part of this in terms of "the frenzied competition that required ever greater amounts of capital, 'graduating' revolutionary brigades from political violence to resource predation."[25] She also noted that the revolutionary brigades that fought against Gaddafi included "members of drug dealing and trafficking gangs active in the local market" as well as former prisoners who had escaped when the prisons were opened during the uprising.[26] While not on a scale similar to Hussein's release of prisoners in 2003—which complicated US efforts at governance in Iraq—the escapes did introduce professional criminals into the mix and provided enormous opportunities for the expansion of criminal activities. "With access to weapons, and many gaining legitimacy by becoming quasi-state security actors, they were able to expand their criminal enterprises relatively unhindered."[27]

Both Mangan and Micallef have provided enormously useful details on these developments, although Mangan has focused on the different segments of the drug market. Micallef adopted a more regional approach—looking at the varying dynamics in Tripolitania in the northwest part of the country, Cyrenaica in the northeast, and Fezzan in the southwest, the three main regions of Libya. These two approaches are complementary, and the analysis here combines both.

If the militias have facilitated the expansion of the drug business in Libya, the fighting has also created temporary disruptions, leading relatively quickly to rapid and effective adaptations. During and after the revolution, militia groups captured Tripoli International Airport and protected the movement of drug shipments. When the civil war broke out in July 2014, however, the fighting destroyed airport infrastructure as well as "an entire fleet of aircraft that previously connected Tripoli directly to several African and European cities, through which drugs and other illicit goods were procured."[28] Although this subsequently meant that most of the drug trafficking involved overland or maritime routes, the use of an air bridge for arms trafficking to Libya has become a major problem and will be discussed more fully later in this chapter.

Cannabis

Much of the cannabis resin from Morocco that does not go through Spain ends up elsewhere in North Africa. Libya is both an in important trans-shipment country, especially for cannabis going to Egypt, and a destination. "Blocks of cannabis resin from Morocco, transiting Libya to Egypt and onward to Europe through the Balkans, are Libya's most steady traffic. Shipments tend to flow through southern Algeria, sometimes dipping into northern Niger, and enter the country through the so-called Salvador Pass, where the borders of Libya, Algeria, and Niger converge in an ungoverned stretch of desert."[29] Most major shipments transit through or around the southern cities of Sebha, Ubari, and Murzuq, which act as "storage hubs and logistics centers for illicit flows of all kinds."[30] In southwestern Libya, there are cannabis markets in Sebha and other cities, while other shipments move north through Bani Walid to western coastal cities and towns.[31] Some of the shipments also go from Bani Walid to Benghazi or to Tobruk.[32] In an interesting twist in 2021, Lionfish III, a massive counter-narcotics operation coordinated by Interpol, seized 17 tonnes of cannabis resin, valued at 31 million euros in Niamey, Niger, and "destined for Libya."[33] The shipment had been sent from Lebanon to the Togolese port of Lomé and then transported to Niger by lorry.[34]

Mangan notes that cannabis is moved into Egypt across established overland routes.[35] Some of the traffic crosses "north of Kufra in south-eastern Libya through transit hubs such as Tazirbu and Rebiana and onward into Egypt through a variety of crossing points. Transit is managed by smugglers from the Tebu or Tuareg tribes who guide and manage logistics for convoys of 4x4 vehicles through the desert terrain."[36] She also notes the seasonal element, with the "largest consignments . . . usually between the end of winter and beginning of spring when conditions for movement through the desert are optimal."[37]

In addition to the land routes, a considerable amount of cannabis comes in via the Mediterranean coast. Some of this involves multiple movement along the coast. Larger shipments, however, are transported via "a well-organized system of large cargo vessels moving directly from the Moroccan coast towards ports in Libya, such as Zuwara, Misrata and Tobruk. Between 2013 and 2016, 20 large vessels were apprehended and 280 tonnes of resin seized."[38] One Moroccan trafficker, Ben Ziane Berhili, is estimated to move 400 tonnes per year.[39] Many Syrian-registered ships have been used but increasingly have been intercepted and the cannabis shipments seized.[40] As a result, some drug traffickers are moving the cannabis on yachts and fishing boats.[41] Tobruk has emerged as a hub while Misrata and al-Khoms have also been used.[42] From these locations, blocks of cannabis are moved to Egypt either via the main checkpoint at Salloum or through the village and oasis of Jaghbub.[43] Within Libya itself prices vary: a kilo of cannabis in Bani Walid is worth 1,500 dinar (just over $1,000) but doubles in value in Tripoli.[44] At this point Libyan dealers delegate labor-intensive tasks to migrants before passing the cannabis to Libyan retailers for final distribution.[45]

The more important destination, however, is Europe. According to Micallef, much of the cannabis heading to Europe is "typically loaded off Casablanca, in the Atlantic, or between Nador in Morocco and Oran in Algeria and is transported on board fishing vessels or commercial vessels to points off the Libyan coast. Similarly, the transfer in Libya is done either at sea or directly on land in container ports."[46] Not surprisingly, many of the cannabis shipments then move to and through Malta or Hurd's Bank, "a free shallow-water harbor" that is just outside Malta's territorial waters.[47] Because it lies in what is essentially a jurisdictional void, it is a perfect place for transferring illicit cargo, including cannabis. On other occasions the cannabis is "shipped directly to disembarkation points in southern Italy or the western Balkans."[48]

Cocaine

The development of the West African route for cocaine changed in the 2000s, and this resulted in adjustments to trafficking routes, with land transportation through the Sahel and into Libya becoming more popular. As the Sahel became more unstable and dangerous, however, the pattern of shipments changed once more with transportation directly to North Africa. Morocco has been one destination, while there have been substantial cocaine shipments discovered off the Algerian coast and in containers destined for Libya:

- In 2016, in scenes reminiscent of cocaine discoveries in Algerian waters, fishermen found 70 kilograms in the sea near Tobruk.[49]

- In July 2018, Colombian National Police discovered a shipment of 43 kilograms of cocaine at the port of Buenaventura, "hidden within the structure of a container" destined for Benghazi.[50]
- In December 2020, "authorities at the port of Guayaquil in Ecuador seized 582 kilograms of cocaine hidden in 19 pieces of teak wood bound for Libya and Syria."[51] Three days later, customs officers in Malta "seized 612 kilograms of cocaine concealed in a cargo of cooking oil that had been shipped from Ecuador and moved through Colombia before it arrived in the Malta Freeport prior to being moved to its destination of Libya.[52]
- In February 2023, Libyan customs authorities announced the seizure of 269 kilograms of cocaine at the port of al-Khoms. The cocaine was discovered in a 40-foot container with frozen chicken from Brazil.[53]

While Libya does not have a large cocaine consumer base, Latin American drug trafficking organizations might well have noticed the oil and migrant trafficking from Libya to Europe, especially Italy. It seems a reasonable business strategy to add cocaine to the mix. What makes this even more attractive—and this has been alluded to in relation to other illicit markets—are the anecdotal, but still compelling, reports about links between Italian mafia organizations and various armed groups in Libya. Given the importance of the Mediterranean's illicit economy that increasingly seems to encompass Libya, Malta, and Italy, as well as the well-established cocaine trafficking links between the 'Ndrangheta and Colombian organizations, exploiting the new criminal opportunities that have emerged in Libya appears to be a natural diversification strategy. In this connection it is worth noting that in October 2018 authorities seized 17 kilos of cocaine in the Gioia Tauro container port; it was apparently destined for Benghazi.[54] What is slightly puzzling, however, is that Gioia Tauro is widely believed to be under the control of the 'Ndrangheta. It is possible, therefore, that this was a sacrificial lamb to allow law enforcement a modest but symbolic success.

Pharmaceuticals

When first approved in 1995, tramadol was not considered an opiate (like morphine or oxycodone) even though it acted in similar ways. However, because there were cases of abuse and addiction with its use, the thinking and warnings changed.[55] By 2012, tramadol began to appear in Libya, including in areas that had not traditionally seen widespread drug abuse. Its use grew enormously after the civil war broke out in 2014. This expansion is understandable in terms of the attributes of the drugs as well as the context in which it took place. There are four advantages to tramadol and other pharmaceutical drugs: (1) they are a comparatively cheap option, especially when compared to more traditional psychotropic drugs; (2) they can be diverted from the licit stocks held by pharmacies; (3) they do not provoke the same level of opprobrium as traditional hard drugs; and (4) they help users deal with stress during a period when intense stress is a daily occurrence.[56] In terms of context, "the increasing supply of tramadol is in part a result of the criminalization of migrant smuggling in Niger in 2015, which rendered the transport of prescription drugs a low-risk alternative to migrant smuggling."[57] The supply was not confined to the southwest. Although northern Nigeria was—and has remained—an important source of tramadol coming in through Libya's southern borders, it also flows in through Libya's Mediterranean ports.[58] Indeed, "it is a growing problem across Libya, a country that to this day lacks adequate substance use prevention programs or infrastructures."[59] The extent of Libya's tramadol problem is illustrated by some spectacular seizures made over the past few years.

- In February 2016 in the port of Tobruk, three abandoned shipping containers from India held 45 million tramadol tablets.[60]
- "In May 2017, 37 million tramadol tablets (with an approximate street value of some EUR 60 million, at EUR 2 per tablet), were seized in three containers at the port of Genoa. The containers—labelled as containing blankets and shampoo—had come from India and were on their way to Misrata and Tobruk."[61]
- In November 2017, Italian authorities confiscated 24 million tablets in the port of Gioia Tauro that had come from India and were destined for Libya. One report suggested the cargo had a value of 40 million euros.[62]
- "In September 2018, port authorities in Colombo, Sri Lanka, stopped a cargo of 15 million tramadol tablets enroute to Libya from southern India."[63]

Equally, if not more, disturbing, in September 2021, Libya's Anti-Narcotics General Authority seized a tramadol tablet-making plant at Tripoli port. The machinery was supposedly a sweet-making plant but had a capacity to make 10,000 tramadol tablets per day. It had come from Lebanon via Italy in a container. According to Herbert, however, the tramadol problem has diminished slightly since 2020.[64] Nevertheless, it is unlikely to disappear anytime soon. Moreover, if it were effectively regulated, this could conceivably open the door for increased heroin imports and use—although the higher prices of heroin could decrease the chances of this. A more immediate threat is the increased trafficking of pregabalin, a medicine prescribed for pain, epilepsy, and anxiety.[65] "Pregabalin smuggling has mainly been concentrated in western Libya, with interviewees indicating that maritime shipments of the drug arrive from Turkey and Montenegro. There is reportedly also some overland smuggling from Tunisia."[66] Profits from the drug are very high, but it is also subject to taxation by various armed factions.

Drug trafficking overlaps and intersects with almost all other flows in Libya's complex illicit economy. The profits from the drug business sustain some groups and communities, but creeping use and abuse tends to harm others. Ultimately, drug trafficking and drug use both fuel and feed off violence. The business has become more violent and contributes to pervasive instability throughout Libya. Moreover, as one astute observer has commented, "the state has come to be defined by seemingly contradictory tensions: illicit drug trafficking simultaneously undercuts the ability of the state to rebuild even as its networks are among the few things that knit the fractured state together."[67] The kinds of tensions that drug trafficking creates are especially evident in Zawiyah, which appears to be a hub for several criminal networks. It is also "home to a notorious illicit narcotics market named 'Sifaw' for the sale of hashish and Bafra rolling papers."[68] What makes it especially problematic is that the "the head of the Anti-Drug Unit of the Ministry of the Interior in Zawiyah, Mohamed Sifaw, is openly associated with this location" and "Ministry vehicles are trading in illicit narcotics under a bridge at this location."[69] In this instance, the gamekeeper has become the poacher. Yet this is indicative of the corrosive nature of drug trafficking on both law and governance. Libya, of course, has little of both. The key point, though, is that drug trafficking will make it much more difficult to establish good governance, even if there is, at some point, an end to the factional violence.

Human Smuggling

The line between human smuggling and human trafficking is clear in theory, but in practice it can become somewhat hazy with migrants who are voluntarily being smuggled finding themselves in situations where they no longer have choices and have become victims of trafficking or other heinous crimes. This is particularly the case in Libya where the absence of a legitimate and accepted government and competition for political influence among various groups has created a predatory, free-for-all characterized by ruthless opportunism and a total lack of honor among thieves and militias alike. Yet it is critical to recognize that human smuggling through Libya did not begin with the collapse of the Gaddafi regime. Well before then, Libya was described as "the main receiving country" in North Africa for migrants, whether long-term or seasonal.[70] In 2005, government estimates suggested that 1.0 million to 1.2 million irregular migrants lived in Libya, although others claimed that the number could be as high as 2 million.[71] Reportedly, between 2003 and 2005, 145,000 irregular migrants were expelled from Libya. At this time, the main flow from Agadez, Niger, to Sebha in Libya was believed to involve tens of thousands of migrants each year.[72] Fifty percent of sub-Saharan migrants entering Libya were from Nigeria, and 20 percent from Ghana.[73] It was also noted that "the so-called Libyan route" was "still the cheapest way to reach Europe from East Africa."[74] The main hub for irregular migrants from Chad and Sudan was the city of Kufra in the province of the same name located on the border with Egypt.[75] As in other parts of North Africa, the results from Kufra are somewhat counterintuitive and present a dilemma for policymakers—much of the revenue generated by smuggling helped with economic development and overall stability in the city and its surrounding environs.[76] Most of the coastal departures were from Zuwara, where five separate networks or clans with links with police were deeply involved in the human smuggling business.[77] Reportedly, the groups had different backgrounds. Some were former police or intelligence officials, some were small businessmen, and some were criminals, traffickers, or terrorists.[78] Many were the "owners of estates and villas with . . . spaces (garages, stables, apartments, farmhouses or sheds) in which migrants could be hidden" prior to departure.[79] Still, based on some research the argument has been made that the link between terrorism and migrant smuggling and trafficking remains localized and benefits individuals rather than terrorist groups or organizations as a whole.[80]

In 2008, President Silvio Berlusconi of Italy and Gaddafi signed a Treaty of Friendship that included an agreement by Libya to restrict irregular migration to Italy—an agreement that human rights groups and nongovernmental organizations (NGOs) denounced but that almost a decade later would be replicated by a different Italian government.[81] Although money was provided in exchange for preventing migrant boats from leaving Libya, Gaddafi almost certainly allowed some boats to leave simply to underline his leverage. He was even more explicit with his extortion attempt on a 2010 visit to Italy when he made clear that the European Union should pay Libya at least 5 billion euros a year "to stop illegal African immigration" and prevent Europe from turning into Africa.[82] After the fall of Gaddafi, however, Libya became the primary route for human smuggling from sub-Saharan Africa to Europe. It also became a market with low entry barriers and lucrative profits—as well as one that experienced a massive, if temporary, surge with the war in Syria and the exodus of refugees.[83] By 2016, most Syrians were no longer using the Libyan route, opting instead for the route through the eastern Mediterranean.[84]

As with most other illicit markets, the human smuggling sector in Libya encompassed a wide variety of distinct actors, ranging from large to small organizations, and from the highly professional to opportunistic amateurs. For the most part, however, it can best be understood as a series of overlapping and intersecting networks, some of which were limited in geographic range, while others were much more extensive. For the smaller organizations and more localized networks, there is a modular approach with different transportation groups covering different parts of the migrants' journey. In some cases, the handoff from one group to another is direct and smooth; in other instances, the smugglers are simply hired to get to a specific destination, and it is the migrants' responsibility to find another smuggler organization for the next part of the journey.

At the other end of the spectrum, some organizations offer end-to-end service from point of departure to final arrival. One of these seems to be run, or at least was at one point, by an Ethiopian called Ermias Ghermay.[85] Considerable insight was developed into this network of networks by anti-Mafia prosecutor Calogero Ferrara, who began to investigate the networks as a result of the Lampedusa sinking in October 2013.[86] Beginning with the survivors and using telephone toll analysis and tapped calls, Ferrara built up a picture of what have been described as "several new multinational organized crime syndicates together worth around $7 billion a year."[87] Ghermay was a key figure, and his network offered "a complete service to migrants, running from the center of Africa to Libya to Italy to another country from there. It includes all accommodation, transport, and food."[88] Ferrara, described it as "a criminal operation like no other. No name, no fixed base, a fluid membership, and, most remarkably, "'totally without risk' since, unlike drugs, payment is made in advance."[89] Moreover, drowned migrants do little to stifle demand, highlighting the willingness of migrants to incur the enormous risks of crossing the Mediterranean because staying where they are is so intolerable.

Ghermay at that time reportedly ran twenty to thirty boats a year—many of which he regarded as dispensable.[90] He made phone calls to contacts he called "colonels," who in turn acted as facilitators, agents, and advisers to the migrants, often through text messages.[91] These calls

> reveal . . . a sprawling network of such sophistication and flexibility as to dampen any expectations of a quick fix. To ensure a steady supply of migrants, he works with those in Sudan, Somalia, Nigeria, or Eritrea who run trucks across the Sahara. Simultaneously, he continually establishes fresh relationships with people traffickers further down the line: those in Sicily, operating in migrant centers, or in Rome, Milan and, at times, even further afield in Berlin, Paris, Stockholm or London.[92]

In a wiretapped conversation between Ghermay and an associate, the two men seemed to agree that US and Canadian accounts were better than UAE accounts because "there they don't ask you where the money comes from."[93] Although Ghermay is a significant player, he has remained elusive. Moreover, an attempt to arrest and try one of his associates and another major player in the smuggling business, Medhanie Yehdego Mered, went badly wrong. The man extradited to Italy was the wrong man—with considerable embarrassment for the prosecutors.[94]

It is also worth noting that even removing some of the major players does not always have the expected impact. The supply side of the market is both crowded and competitive. One reason for this is the extensive use of social media. As one commentary noted, "in a smartphone era, many of the smuggling services are available on Arabic-language Facebook and other social media sites. Migrants also communicate with one another along the journey using messaging tools such as WhatsApp to warn about where police coverage is heaviest."[95] A former smuggler from the Libyan coastal town of Zuwara spoke to the BBC in May 2015 and claimed that between ten and twenty migrants contacted him via Facebook per day.[96] The ex-smuggler who started using social media in 2012 acknowledged that by 2015 it accounted for 30 percent to 40 percent of his business.[97] One way of thinking about human smuggling, therefore, is as a market eco-system. Another approach is to think about it in terms of logistics and geography.

According to a valuable study in 2017, migrants coming from or through Niger enter Libya at the border town of Tummo where the border crossing is guarded by Tebu fighters.[98] Others come to Libya from Mali via Algeria and the smuggling hub of Tamanrasset and "cross into either Ghat or Ghadames on the Libyan side of the border. They subsequently continue onto Sebha or directly north to smuggling hubs like Tripoli and Zuwara."[99] Typically, they travel with human smugglers who use Toyota pickup trucks and travel in convoys.[100] The key locations in these flows are reflected in Figure 5.1.

Tebu smugglers drive migrants north. Reportedly, they "have monopolized the smuggling industry in south Libya up to around 20 kilometers from the desert town of Sebha" the capital of the Fezzan region and "the undisputed heart of the human smuggling industry in southern Libya."[101] Sebha itself is controlled by the Awlad Suleiman tribe, which also owns most of the gasoline stations in the region.[102] Sebha has also appropriately been described as "a place of transaction" for migrants.[103] As Floor El Kamouni-Jansenn noted, "migrants are held by Tebu smugglers in private residences after which they are sold to other smuggling groups or handed over to Libyan security officials who are most often associated with a certain militia. . . . Many migrants are held captive and exploited for weeks in Sebha."[104] In some cases, they are only released when their families have provided money.[105] In other instances, "male migrants are bought by local businessmen and then forced into slave labor, while women often end up in prostitution to secure their release."[106] After the migrants are freed, the Awlad Suleiman tribe along with the Magarha tribe and one or two other tribes move them from Sebha to the coast.[107] Those who come in from Algeria are moved to Ghadames, which is controlled by the Zintani brigades, who then move migrants to the coast.[108] Although there is less detail about this route, it seems likely that these migrants are also highly vulnerable to exploitation as they are moved through Libya.

Many migrants from East Africa and the Horn travel though Sudan to Libya. One of the most important groups taking this route have been Eritreans. "In 2014, the number of Eritreans arriving in Italy via the Central Mediterranean Route increased sharply to 33,559, up from 10,398 in 2013 and 1,889 in 2012."[109] This trend continued in 2015. As one report noted, "in 2015, an estimated 154,000 migrants entered Europe via the Central Mediterranean Route—an increase of nearly 400% over the previous year, and more than 1,000% over 2012—most of them from the Horn of Africa. By far, the largest contingent of migrants—nearly 39,000 in 2015—is from the sub-region's second smallest country: Eritrea."[110] They face enormous hazards going through Sudan and then face further risks of abuse, kidnapping, and detention as

Figure 5.1 Key Locations for Migrant Flows Through Libya

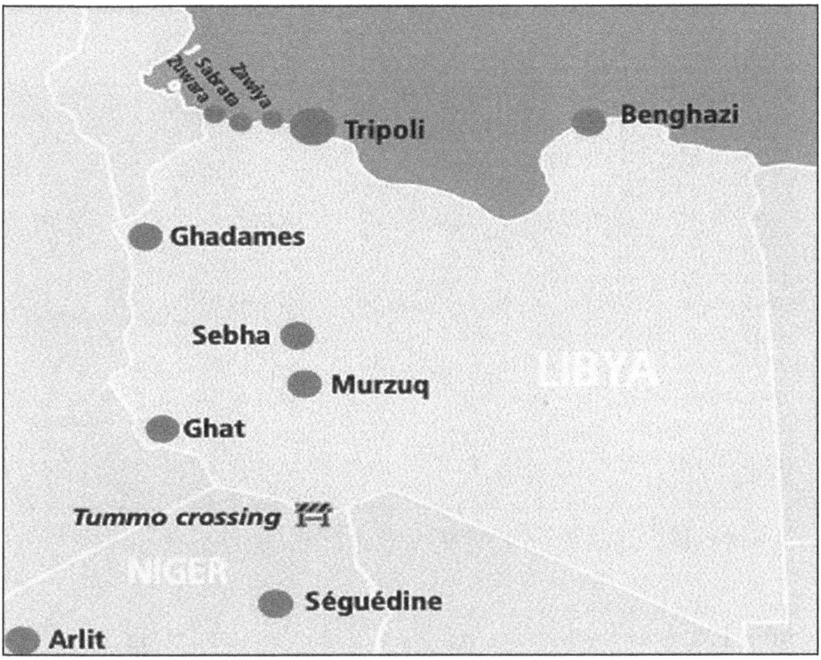

Source: Floor El Kamouni-Janssen, *Only God Can Stop the Smugglers* (Clingendael, February 2017), p. 3.

they are moved through Libya.[111] One of the key transit points in Libya is Kufra, though fighting in the town has made this route particularly dangerous, and some smugglers find an alternative that goes around it.[112] The eastern routes are highlighted in Figure 5.2. The western and eastern routes converge at Bani Walid, and migrants are moved from there to various points of departure along the coast.[113] In 2017, Altai Consulting published a comprehensive report on the key embarkation points from Libya across the Mediterranean to Italy. These points can be seen on the map in Figure 5.3. The conditions in detention facilities are so deplorable that the UN Human Rights Council found that the exploitation of migrants in Libya entailed not just violations of international human rights law and international humanitarian law, but also the commission of crimes against humanity.[114]

Perhaps the most important themes concerned the constant change in the municipalities of departure. This reflected the continued conflict

Figure 5.2 Eastern Migrant Routes Through and to Libya

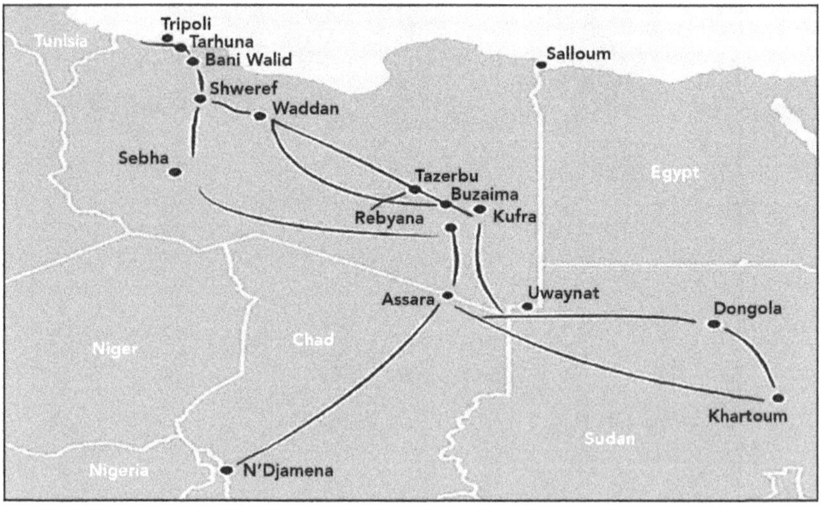

Source: UNHCR, *Mixed Migration Trends in Libya* (2017), p. 91.

within Libya as well as the reaction of the community in Zuwara—which had long been regarded as the most important human smuggling hub—against the smugglers after several major catastrophes.[115] In other key locations along the coast, clan and militia rivalries were rife, with the result that things remained fluid. Sometimes armed groups taxed the smugglers; at other times they entered the smuggling business themselves. Then the agreement with Italy was implemented, and in a variant of the poachers becoming gamekeepers, smugglers and the militias who taxed and protected them became the coast guard.

Zuwara, a town of about 55,000 people, had a long history of smuggling that included sanctions evasion during the Gaddafi years.[116] It was also closer to Lampedusa than other Libyan towns, which provided it with a comparative advantage.[117] Although migrant smuggling had become a part of the community and an estimated 500 to 1,000 smugglers were operating in the town in 2015, a series of shipwrecks with massive losses of life provoked hostility toward the business.[118] A counter crime unit known as "the masked brigade" had been created in 2013 and was entrusted with the clampdown.[119] This succeeded in displacing the human smuggling networks and organizations from the town—at least temporarily. Much of the smuggling was displaced to Sabratha, but after that collapsed in 2017, some of the smugglers

Figure 5.3 Points of Embarkation Across the Mediterranean

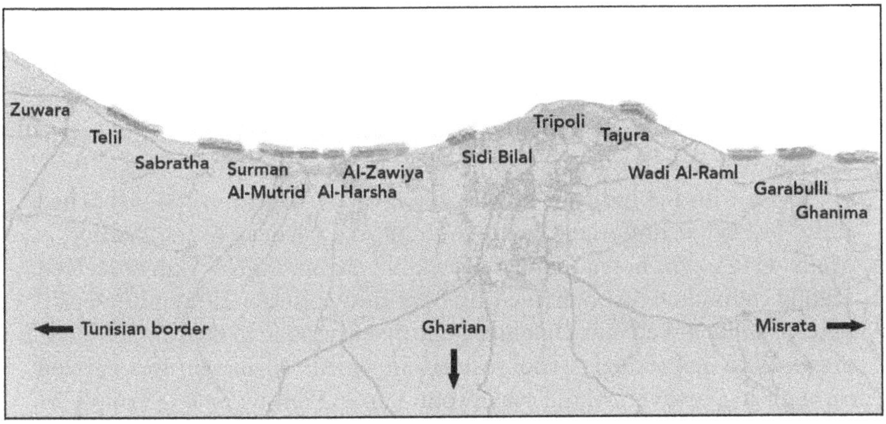

Source: Altai Consulting, *Leaving Libya: Rapid Assessment of Municipalities of Departures of Migrants in Libya* (June 2017), p. 6.

returned to Zuwara.[120] This was facilitated by the fact that the masked men had arrested a major fuel smuggler and had subsequently been redeployed away from Zuwara.[121]

With the crackdown in Zuwara, Sabratha replaced it as the largest hub for smuggling on the entire coast.[122] Many of the smuggling organizations there were highly professional and linked to networks in southern Libya.[123] Some were also reported to be "working closely with networks in certain countries of origin and even Europe."[124] One major local smuggler, Musab Abu Grein, reportedly had "contacts to the Italian mafia" and was also working with the Ethiopian smuggler Ghermay.[125] Sabratha was far less peaceful than Zuwara, with rival clans and militias competing for influence.[126] There were also clashes between local smuggling gangs and some who had moved from Zuwara.[127] The presence of some Islamic state fighters further complicated the situation.[128] Nevertheless, Ahmed Al-Dabbashi, nicknamed "the uncle," was widely regarded as "Libya's most powerful migrant smuggler."[129] He ran his own militia, the Anas Al-Dabbashi Martyrs Brigade, and his organization acted as both "a local security provider and a criminal enterprise."[130] In July 2017, he agreed to cease smuggling migrants. Soon after, he and his forces were ejected from Sabratha by rival militias.[131] Nevertheless, with the agreement followed by his expulsion, migrant smuggling declined dramatically.[132] "Over 2018 there was a shift of smuggling activity to the east of Tripoli, reflecting the pressure on the former smuggling hubs in the west and the attractiveness of the coastal towns of Garabulli and al-Khoms as historic hubs with established and experienced smugglers. Garabulli had already played a key role as a smuggling hub prior to 2016. In 2017, there was a gradual resumption of business, which accelerated notably after the collapse of departures from Sabratha."[133] This uptick was reversed, however, when another militia following the law enforcement agenda took over the town.[134]

Even with the reduced flow, some migrant boats have still reached Italy. The other important destination largely because of its location is Malta. One report noted that between 2002 and mid-2014 Malta received 19,000 individuals who arrived by boat from Libya—although over 70 percent of them had subsequently gone elsewhere.[135] In the project interviews with individuals who resided in North Africa or had moved through it, however, Malta was prominent. Given the small sample of interviewees, however, too much should not be read into this. Nevertheless, there is some suggestion that Malta was the easiest destination to reach because of proximity. One irregular migrant who made this point also described his experience:

> I managed to travel illegally after receiving assistance from smugglers in Zuwara, a coastal Mediterranean city located near the Tunisian border. I paid the smugglers 1,800 euros to help me reach Malta and had to wait around 3 days until they had 15 people. We were then sent by boat to Maltese territorial waters, where the smuggler provided us with a phone and left. After issuing a distress call, the Maltese navy approached our boat and escorted us to the Maltese ports where we were interrogated and sent to shelters until it was time for our release. We were then given the status of humanitarian asylum seekers and issued Maltese cards identifying us as protected persons until such time as the matter of granting us Maltese citizenship has been decided.[136]

Another irregular migrant from Morocco heading for Europe paid 400 euros to be smuggled into Algeria, then another 200 euros to cross the border into Tunisia.[137] After ten days there he traveled overland to Zuwara, where he met some well-known smugglers and paid 2,000 euros for a transfer to the embarkation point and the voyage across the Mediterranean.[138] He and forty-four others—mainly Egyptians and Pakistanis—were put on a rubber boat intended for thirty passengers and set sail.[139] In his words, "the boat started to take on water due to the heavy load and rising sea level and was spotted by an Italian Coast Guard craft that was patrolling territorial waters. The Italians told the refugees that they were in Maltese territorial waters before informing their Maltese counterparts who ended up dispatching a large rescue boat."[140] Those on the overcrowded boat were rescued.[141] In yet a third account, a migrant was on a boat when the engine broke down. The passengers were stranded for three days. A commercial ship provided food and water and made a distress call to authorities in Malta, who sent a rescue boat that arrived the following day and took the passengers to a refugee center in Malta.[142]

These stories are typical of so many more accounts by irregular migrants traveling from Libya on the Central Mediterranean route. Yet this route, which had provoked enormous anxiety about what was called Europe's migrant crisis, reached a peak in 2016 and then declined significantly in 2017 and precipitously in 2018. This reduction stemmed from two main factors. One was the change in the law in Niger and the criminalization of migrant smuggling—which led to substantial reductions in northward migration.[143] Even more important was the Memorandum of Understanding signed between Italy and Libya in February 2017 and the subsequent transformation of some militias and human smuggling organizations into a coast guard.[144]

In many respects, this is a large-scale example of the old story about the poacher turned gatekeeper or the fox guarding the hen house. It was also a replay of the 2009 agreement between Berlusconi and Gaddafi—and was equally controversial. It was renewed on February 2, 2020, leading to an outcry from NGOs such as Human Rights Watch.[145] The outcry is justified, not least because the agreement has already had unintentional consequences, helping to transform the dynamics in Libya from human smuggling to human trafficking and encouraging forms of brutality that, even if they fail to meet each specific criterion for human trafficking, certainly represent its functional equivalence. Moreover, because this has gone hand in hand with the proliferation of detention centers, it became institutionalized in Libya.

Even so, the decline in migrant smuggling from Libya was little more than a hiatus. The "era of suppressed smuggling networks and vastly reduced departure levels . . . lasted from 2018 to the end of 2020."[146] It was "bolstered by disruption and hindrance to mobility caused by the war for Tripoli of 2019–2020 and the COVID-19 pandemic."[147]According to the Global Organized Crime Index, however, between 2021 and 2023, human smuggling once again increased significantly, with tens of thousands of individuals taking advantage of the relative stability in western Libya to set sail for Europe, enabled by sophisticated logistical networks developed by smugglers.[148] Indeed, smuggling networks that had been modest in their activities were resurgent in 2021 once again expanding the illegal trade in humans departing Libya for Europe. Over 60,000 irregular migrants left Libya in 2021.[149] This number increased to over 80,600 in 2022, an increase that "was primarily driven by a form of hybrid migration whereby Egyptians, Bangladeshis and, to a lesser extent, Syrians travelled to Libya and from there attempted a sea crossing using a mixture of regular and irregular means."[150] In other words, these migrants arrived and stayed in Libya legally; the only illegal aspect came with their departure for Europe on the boats.[151] Surprisingly, Egyptians, Bangladeshis, and Syrians accounted for 48,600 departures from Libya in 2022, more than doubling the figure for 2021.[152] "Pakistanis also began to leave from Tobruk in 2022, a trend that dramatically intensified in 2023."[153] The corollary was that human smuggling of migrants from the Sahel and sub-Saharan Africa continued but made up "only a fraction of total departures."[154] In 2023, the pattern seemed very similar, although observers also noted that the conflict in Sudan could once again increase the flow of refugees and irregular migrants into Libya.[155] The ups and downs in the numbers of illegal migrants leaving Libya for Europe is summarized in Table 5.1.

Not only did the composition of irregular migrants departing Libya change, but so did points of embarkation. In early 2022, maritime departures from Tobruk in the east increased significantly, and by mid-2023, this area had "roughly as many embarkations as coastal Tripolitania."[156] Departures from the east to Italy are longer and more fraught with danger but also typically use larger and more seaworthy vessels. The cost of a voyage ranged quite widely from a low of 600 euros to a high of around 3,000 euros.[157] None of this is intended to suggest that embarkations from western Libya diminished. Indeed, in 2021 Zuwara—which was then experiencing a temporarily lull in enforcement—reemerged as Libya's premier location for maritime human smuggling.[158] The masked men, however, once again revitalized enforcement and began to make

Table 5.1 Number of Irregular Migrant Departures from Libya

	2016	2017	2018	2019	2020	2021	2022	2023
Number of migrants	183,284	126,620	39,006	19,539	27,086	60,252	79,800	71,500

Sources: Global Initiative Against Transnational Organized Crime monitoring and Istituto per gli Studi di Politica Internazionale for 2016 to 2021. The sources for 2022 and 2023 are the *Joint Annual Overviews of IOM and UNHCR: Migrant and refugee movements through the Central Mediterranean sea*. In 2022, 31 percent of the migrants were intercepted or rescued and disembarked in Libya, while in 2023 that fell to 24 percent.

inroads against the smuggling organizations. In response, some Zuwaran smugglers moved to Sabratha, where they not only worked with the locals but also brought their expertise and contacts.[159] "In return for this capital and know how, the Zuwaran smugglers gained access to an area of coast that was far easier to operate in due to the absence of effective anti-smuggling efforts."[160] While some migrant boats were stopped at sea, and some tragically sunk, there were increasing signs that the flows could reach a level that would once again become a crisis for the European Union.

Human Trafficking

The problem in Libya is not that there are large, sophisticated, and dedicated human trafficking organizations but that the smugglers can easily transform into traffickers, captors, and even torturers. To be sure, the line between human smuggling and human trafficking becomes blurred and virtually nonexistent at times. Irregular migrants are highly vulnerable and, at one point or another, almost invariably find themselves in a situation where they are being coerced and brutally mistreated, placed in positions of forced labor and sexual servitude, or held captive until they or their families can pay enough to secure their release. Cases of torture and sexual abuse are reported regularly to NGOs.[161]

This differs in some ways from the traditional notion of human trafficking where, for example, women from the former Soviet Union traveled to Europe voluntarily in the expectation of normal work only to find themselves forced into prostitution. Most such cases involved deception at the place of origin and coercion at the destination. In Libya, in contrast, the migrants are being exploited en route rather than at the end of their journey. That is one key difference.

A second difference is that this is all taking place within a conflict zone in which there is no accepted rule of law, apart from local tribal laws—which is why the US Department of State has treated Libya as a special case for at least eight years. Nor are there established authorities such as law enforcement agencies that can rescue the migrants. On the contrary, those who are formally recognized as being the "government" are part of the problem, not the solution, and contribute significantly to the detention of migrants—which is often the pathway to them becoming victims of predatory behavior, whether sexual or financial. It is hard therefore to disagree with Katie Kuschminder and Anna Triandafyllidou that the spaces of migrant transit in Libya are also "transit spaces of exception" in which "there is no government or state authority that claims jurisdiction and to whom one could address a claim and expect to find protection."[162]

A third key difference is the element of kidnapping for ransom that has been introduced into the situation. Yet even this is ambiguous since, as Julien Brachet and Judith Scheele discuss, it can simply be about debt collection, which they explain as follows:

> As migrants generally prefer to travel without cash or valuables, given the current insecurity of trans-Saharan roads, they must find ways of raising money as soon as they get to their destination. They might call home for a cash transfer, ask a friend locally to pay for them, or look for work. In all these cases, it will take some time before they can pay up. Meanwhile, the drivers, who are generally from the southern Sahara or the Sahel, cannot or do not want to wait, given the volatile security situation in Libya. Their best option is to sell their passengers' debts to residents, who undertake, for a cut, to get the money from the migrant in due course. This they do through any means available to them, including hiring them out as forced labor, selling on their debt, forcing migrants to ring home to ask for ransom payments, and violence and torture—sometimes filmed to put pressure on relatives back home.[163]

There are critical differences in these options, however, that are glossed over. Violence and torture can never be justified, even if the debt is large. Issues about equity also arise. When has a migrant actually paid off his or her debt? In conventional human trafficking, one of the ways in which women are kept in a position of sexual servitude is that new charges or "expenses" are frequently imposed on them, making it difficult for them ever to pay off their debts and buy freedom. Given the degree of lawlessness that prevails in Libya, it would be foolish indeed to believe that similar practices are not at work.

Competing militias cause an additional problem. Indeed, "militias in Libya not only profit from government contracts, letter of credit fraud, the arms trade, and smuggling, but they also generate income though engaging in human trafficking," a trade and source of revenue they are reluctant to relinquish.[164] Migrants can find themselves released by one group only to be detained or kidnapped by another, and a ransom payment is demanded once again. Although it is impossible to obtain any adequate estimates of this phenomenon, it is likely that repeat victimization of this kind is common. As far as migrants are concerned, the problem is not simply targeted criminality but that much of this criminality is both chaotic and competitive. Moreover, the absence of any penalties for the mistreatment, exploitation, or even torture and killing of migrants means that a climate of complete impunity has been established. The Milad case exemplified this. Coast guard commander Abd al-Rahman Milad, known as Bija and widely recognized as one of the most ruthless figures in Libya in terms of exploiting migrants and sinking migrant boats, was arrested in October 2020. In April 2021, however, he was released on the grounds of a "lack of evidence," a decision that could only strengthen the culture of impunity.[165] Having introduced these caveats, it is hard to disagree with the argument by Brachet and Scheele that a "political economy of human containment" has developed in Libya.[166]

Whereas human smuggling in Libya was in some ways sufficiently structured to be understood as organized crime, human trafficking and migrant exploitation are much more opportunistic. Yet they also became systemic. Largely because of the pressure from European states, especially Italy, and their success in effectively moving their southern border to North Africa, there was a transition away from moving migrants along a smuggling chain toward Europe and toward exploiting them in place. In a chilling study that, in some respects, parallels that of Brachet and Scheele, Arezo Malakooti dissected "the political economy of migrant detention in Libya."[167] One result of Italy's agreement with the Libyan coast guard to intercept migrant ships and to engage in search and rescue efforts was a significant increase in the number of migrants held in detention centers. Although the Directorate for Combating Illegal Migration formally controls the official centers, armed groups in Libya are so pervasive that they retain significant influence in many of these facilities.[168] Moreover, there are other unofficial detention centers.[169] "The business models vary slightly, but also overlap in official and non-official detention centers. In the unofficial centers these models consist of extortion, enforced labor, prostitution, selling migrants to Libyans who require laborers, selling migrants between centers, selling migrants to smugglers and armed groups using migrants in their own security or smuggling work."[170] Women migrants are systematically forced into prostitution. Trafficking usually denotes movement or mobility, but this is an activity that can best be described as stationary trafficking or trafficking in place. Consequently, as militias faced declining revenue from migrant smuggling, "trafficking inside migrant detention centers increased, as an alternative source of income, and the number of centers in the country increased."[171] Despite the resurgence of migrant smuggling across the Mediterranean, many of these detention centers remain in the business of what might be termed stationary human trafficking.

Much of this was already evident in the US State Department's 2021 Trafficking in Persons Report, which not only treated Libya as a special case but also noted that in Libya forced labor has not yet been criminalized and that both the Government of National Accord and its militia allies recruited and used child soldiers.[172] In addition, detention centers had become profit centers in the worst way. The report also identified the almost complete lack of concern with this problem and the absence of any effort to combat it, concluding that "the government did not have any policy structures, institutional capacity, widespread political will, or resources to proactively identify and protect trafficking victims among vulnerable groups."[173] As mobility and migration from Libya have both increased since 2020, the detention centers and warehouses for migrants have become less blatant and less visible, but not less harsh and inhumane. Indeed, the most depressing thing about the 2023 *Trafficking in Persons Report: Libya* is the continuity of misery that it describes. It noted, for example, that in January 2023, an international organization had estimated that between 8,500 and 11,500 migrants and refugees were held in fourteen official Department to Combat Illegal Migration (DCIM) centers as well as various unofficial detention centers.[174] It also observed that various factions and forces in Libya were recruiting Syrian child soldiers.[175] In a similar vein, the 2023 Global Organized Crime Index observed that minors and adults were "being lured into mercenary work," a process often facilitated by government officials.[176] Libya has had a modicum of stability since 2020, but exploitation and impunity as well as degradation and despair remain pervasive. The UN Security Council (UNSC) Panel of Experts (POE) Report on Libya in 2023, for example, described how the isolation of detainees along with the lack of protection "turned the Mitiga detention facility into a tool of systemic mistreatment."[177] It also identified "nine incidents of . . . torture, cruel, inhuman and degrading treatment of civilians in two unofficial detention facilities under the control of the TBZ [Tariq Ben Zeyad] brigade."[178] One of these was in a military base in Sidi Faraj, Benghazi, while the other was the Gernada detention facility in Al Bayda.[179] According to the POE Report, thirty detention centers were holding about 6,570 migrants.[180] What the POE termed the expanded Zawiyah network set up smuggling boats that were then deliberately intercepted at sea, with the migrants moved to detention centers until they or their relatives paid for their release.[181] The 55 Brigade, which controlled the Al Maya detention center, made about half a million US dollars "from the release payments of around 130 detainees over the period of six months."[182]

Arms Trafficking

Libya in 2011 devolved quickly from stability to chaos. A society in which weapons had been plentiful—with 15.3 weapons per hundred people the highest in North Africa—but carefully controlled and monitored seemed to transform into an arms bazaar overnight.[183] It was deemed by a British tabloid to be the Tesco of weapons, a description that probably displeased both weapons dealers and corporate managers at the UK grocery chain.[184] There were indeed lots of weapon caches, largely because Gaddafi had prepared for popular resistance in the event of a foreign invasion. Estimates typically put the regime's stockpile at somewhere between 400,000 and 1 million weapons.[185]

The countrywide political instability that has engulfed Libya for the past decade has led to "the emergence of a vast regional black market in firearms."[186] And while a thriving black market trade in weapons existed prior to 2011, Gaddafi's regime was capable of controlling the illegal arms trafficking that did take place.[187] With the regime no longer available as a bulwark, new opportunities emerged for criminal networks, especially as warring militias were in dire need of weapons and ammunition.[188] Following the overthrow of Gaddafi in Libya in 2011 and unfolding over the course of the Arab Spring, vast quantities of man-portable air-defense systems (MANPADS) were looted from Libyan military depots and warehouses. The diversion of national stockpiles, including what occurred in Libya after Gaddafi's fall, has contributed drastically to the proliferation of illicit civilian-held arms in the region. Smuggling and trafficking to nonstate armed groups has included terrorist organizations.[189] It should also be noted that "readily convertible alarm weapons" have flowed from the Middle East to North Africa, including Libya, "where both merchants and end users, including armed groups, are converting them."[190] For the past decade, Libya has served as a regional hub for illicit arms flows.[191] Moreover, arms trafficking not only is a destabilizing factor in Libya, but it also has direct implications for its neighbours.[192]

An estimated 5,000 missiles have been located and destroyed, but there could be as many as 15,000 MANPADS still unaccounted for.[193] While most of them are believed to have fallen into the hands of Libyan rebel groups, there is the possibility that dozens—possibly more, possibly fewer—made their way to groups including al-Qaeda in the Islamic Maghreb (AQIM), Ansar al-Sharia, or the Islamic State in Iraq and Syria's (ISIS's) affiliate in Libya.[194] MANPADS have turned up across North Africa and the Middle East, in Algeria, Egypt, and

Gaza. MANPADS are thought to be in the possession of today's most capable terrorist groups—including al-Qaeda and ISIS. Given current trends, al-Qaeda and ISIS (and their affiliates) seem the most likely candidates to attempt an attack using MANPADS, but there are a host of other terrorist groups throughout the globe that have the capability to conduct such an attack. One key concern is that the shifting nature of the conflicts in places like Libya could bring terrorist groups into contact with one another, leading to cooperation that ultimately involves the exchange of either MANPADs themselves, or the tacit knowledge necessary to use these weapons effectively.

In September 2016, Rukmini Callimachi and Lorenzo Tondo reported in the *New York Times* on a new drug trafficking route discovered by the Italian Navy stretching from Sicily to Libya.[195] The new route is thought to be a response to increased surveillance along the Spanish coastline and the opportunity provided by the implosion of Libya, where drugs can now transit en route to Egypt and the Middle East before entering Europe through the Balkans.[196] An investigation by Italy, which also included other European countries and the US Drug Enforcement Administration, revealed that, at least for a time, drugs were transiting through territory in Libya controlled by ISIS. This drug trafficking was likely taxed by the group, which conducted similar procedures in Iraq and Syria. Other reports have detailed a transactional relationship between ISIS militants in Libya and the Calabrian 'Ndrangheta, which is working with the Neapolitan Camorra.[197] The drug trade would not be possible without small arms and light weapons (SALW), which provide the traffickers with the coercive threat necessary for any criminal transaction. Indeed, arms and ammunition, antiquities and artefacts, counterfeit pharmaceuticals, and other contraband all transit smuggling routes between Europe and North Africa.

There were, in fact, several distinct, if at times overlapping, phases in arms trafficking involving Libya. The first phase was the outflow of Libyan weapons and ammunition, and this occurred primarily between 2011 and 2013, but with some lingering flows thereafter. Some of these flows came from the arms depot in Barak Shari, near Sebha.[198] Conflict Armament Research has documented some of the flows and their destinations. These include the following:

- Russian-manufactured SA-7b MANPADS were documented in southern Libya, Lebanon, and Mali, while North Korean–manufactured 40-millimeter F7-type rockets were found in both the Central African Republic and Lebanon.[199]

- M79 90-millimeter HEAT rockets were identified not only in Tripoli, which was to be expected, but also in Syria.[200]
- Polish assault weapons from the Libyan stockpile were found in the Central African Republic, Côte d'Ivoire, Libya, and Mali.[201]

The smuggling route to northern Mali has usually been through the Salvador Pass area, along the Algerian and Nigerien border.[202] Other routes have gone southeast to Sudan and southwest to Chad, although it bears emphasis that, more recently, Chad has been providing both weapons and fighters to Libya.[203] Even if some of the flows have been reversed, however, their impact should not be underestimated. The destabilizing effects were felt not only in North Africa and the Sahel but also in the Middle East. "Proliferation of arms from Libya . . . had an important effect upon conflicts in Mali and Sinai, significant quantities were sent to Gaza and Syria, and arms have proliferated into the hands of nonstate groups in North Africa and beyond."[204] Egypt also faced a challenge as weapons were brought across the border and then smuggled to Sinai.

While many of the weapons were diffused across Libya's long and porous borders, those that stayed in the country fed into what was already a highly competitive environment among armed groups. With the rise of the militias and the beginning of the civil war, weapons went from being a commodity for export to being a source of survival in what has become a chaotic and anarchic environment. This is not to suggest that weapons have ceased to be trafficked, nor is it to claim that weapons caches are no longer being looted or individual guns have ceased to be stolen. It is also likely that weapons are treated as spoils of war and acquired by those groups that prevail in large or small firefights. It is somewhat ironic though that one consequence of the Libyan civil war was that the initial outflow of arms was staunched not because of any regulatory measures but simply because small arms and light weapons were now in greater demand in Libya itself. This certainly seemed to be the case in Chad, where the flow diminished "from the second half of 2012 onwards."[205] Conflicts in Libya "generated internal demand that appears to have outweighed the importance of external demand for intermediaries and traffickers, despite the fact that trading routes connecting Chad and Libya are now more easily passable" than under Gaddafi.[206]

Within Libya itself the arms not only fed into conflict among armed groups but also meant that groups that traditionally had a limited capacity for violence suddenly found themselves both needing arms and having ample opportunity to acquire them. In effect, therefore, the sudden injection of arms into a situation where there was a continuing struggle for political control contributed significantly to the outbreak of civil war in 2014. Indeed, by then, not only had outflows declined to a trickle, but inflows had expanded. Prior to August 2014, Libya was the recipient of "60,000 handguns, 65,000 assault rifles, 15,000 submachine guns, and 4,000 machine guns of various calibers, as well as more than 60 million rounds of ammunition for small arms and machine guns."[207] These were lawfully supplied by states and reported to the UN as such.

The arms trade within Libya also began to develop a logic and structure, even though some of the sales and flows remain difficult to discern. The development of local arms markets in Tripoli and elsewhere was a sign of this while also reflecting the prevailing insecurity and the desire of those who were not part of organized militias to be capable of at least some form of self-defense. The fish market Souk el Out on Rashid Street in Tripoli as well as more general street markets in the Old City became popular arms outlets.[208] They often included guns that had been manufactured for firing blanks but had been (or could be) modified to become lethal weapons.[209] Other markets were subsequently established elsewhere. The UNSC Panel of Experts in 2017 noted that it had "received reports of active arms trading at markets in Zintan, Misratah, Ajdabiya and Waw. The materiel offered includes heavier and more sophisticated systems. A functioning Milan anti-tank system including four missiles, for example, is available for $9,000. In some cases, fighters and arms are offered together."[210]

Cyberspace, especially social media platforms, also developed into a major source for light weapons purchase—much as they did for looted antiquities. A 2017 study done by the Small Arms Survey of the online arms market examined 1,346 instances in which weapons were offered for sale. These "unique attempted trades," as the study termed them, all occurred between mid-November 2014 and mid-November 2015.[211] Among the findings, the study noted the following:

- Small arms and light weapons manufactured in twenty-six states "were offered for sale or trade on the illicit online market in Libya."[212] Most of them were pre-embargo imports by the Gaddafi regime.
- "Small arms and light weapons produced from 1992 to the present day and documented as circulating in the illicit sphere in Libya consist of materiel manufactured in 12 states: Austria, Belgium, Bulgaria, China, France, Germany, Italy, the Russian Federation, Serbia, South Africa, Turkey, and the United Arab Emirates."[213]

- Handguns were "disproportionately represented in the dataset compared to the estimated percentage of the total small arms holdings in Libya that they comprise. This is primarily due to the high demand for concealable firearms in Libyan cities."[214]
- "Substantial numbers of blank-firing handguns—primarily produced in Turkey—were documented in Libya."[215] As with the physical markets, some are converted into lethal firearms by the seller or the customer.
- "Legacy firearms—both obsolete and obsolescent types—remain in circulation in the Libyan black market. Many of these weapons, especially handguns, remain highly sought after."[216]
- Most purchases are for sport, hobby, or self-defense, but some of those involved in the transactions were linked to militias.[217]
- There were both small-scale commercial traders, usually individuals, and large-scale commercial traders who also sold from shops and stalls.[218]

Perhaps even more important has been a growing trend toward trafficking weapons into Libya. This has evolved through two phases, the first of which involved individual and small networks that appeared to be rather amateurish in their approach. Two cases became public. The first seems to have been potentially the more substantial of the two and resulted in a six-year prison sentence for Abdurraouf Eshati, a Libyan who had been living in Wrexham, Wales.[219]

Eshati was arrested in Dover on his way to France with others in the back of a truck but does not seem to have been specifically targeted for arrest.[220] Although police found serious and incriminating evidence on his phone, it appears that Eshati's role was relatively minor—he was acting primarily as a translator of the documents "for a friend and senior Libyan Army officer, Ibrahim El-Tumi, who was believed to have brokered the deal."[221] The two documents on his telephone, however, provided some details of the scheme, which reportedly involved approximately £18.4 million to be paid for what would have been a "huge consignment of ammunition" of 1,100 tonnes to Tobruk, "via a contact in Italy."[222] As well as the invoice from the arms supplier, Eshati reportedly had a document about "chartering a cargo jet for £163,000 for use in Libya."[223] The money for this, however, disappeared, and the deal supposedly fell through. According to the Crown Prosecution Service, "such was the scale of his activity . . . his arrest and the finding of these documents has led to Italian authorities discovering large scale illegal arms supplies being imported from eastern Europe to conflict zones in Libya and other places."[224]

According to one report, Eshati was part of "a complex network that included Egyptians and Italians and whose main agent was a seventy-year-old Italian arms dealer already implicated in the trafficking of weapons to the Balkans in the 1990s."[225] The UNSC POE identified the man as "Franco Giorgi, who received a first installment from his Libyan clients for the transfers. The money was, however, apparently stolen from him in Italy, and he travelled to Libya in March 2015, probably to discuss the issue with his clients."[226] He was detained there "for accepting a monetary advance on a shipment of weapons that failed to materialize," was held for four years, and was extradited to Italy in March 2019.[227] Although the Italian investigation had clearly paid dividends, the fortuitous discovery of the scheme raises questions about how much more is being missed.

The other case occurred in 2017 and had some bizarre aspects. In 2017, the Shura Council in Benghazi "used a wide range of connections to purchase weapons."[228] An Italian luxury yacht salesman and fraudster who was selling the same yachts to multiple people somehow became involved.[229] Giulio Lolli, who played a central role in an elaborate fraud scheme called Rimini Yacht, had fled to North Africa in 2010 to escape justice. He had become involved in a jihadist organization in Libya and had used his two remaining yachts to provide weapons for the Shura Council in Benghazi. His boat *Leon*, renamed *Buka El Areibi*, had been used for one shipment of arms.[230] His other boat, initially moored in Rimini and registered in Italy under the name of *Mephisto* before being renamed *El Mukhtar*, was intercepted in 2017 while carrying a shipment of mines and rocket launchers.[231] He was arrested in Libya in 2017 and extradited to Italy in 2019, where he was imprisoned.[232]

As one report noted, "Libya has provided an expanding weapons market to a transnational class of dealers and middlemen based in southern Europe and the eastern Mediterranean."[233] The arms broker trafficking networks, however, were increasingly overshadowed by weapons inflows from states trying to influence the outcome in Libya. Some countries had been pouring in arms almost from the outset. As Peter Kirechu noted, in 2011 and 2013 Libyan and Armenian aircraft "transferred hundreds of thousands of ammunition rounds into Benghazi, reportedly on behalf of the United Arab Emirates."[234] This trend toward external supplies intensified in response to changing conditions on the ground with the crystallization of a more structured struggle for control of Libya between the Government of National Accord and General Khalifa Haftar who led the Libyan National Army, which subsequently became known as the Libyan Arab Armed Forces.

The UAE, Egypt, and Saudi Arabia all backed Haftar, as did Russia, which provided not only weapons but also mercenaries in the form of the Wagner Group in addition to aerial support. Turkey and Qatar supported the Government of National Accord. In June 2016, the UNSC passed Resolution 2292, which focused on maritime supplies to the belligerents and ignored shipments of weapons sent to Libya by air. Although this still allowed air supplies to be shipped and, at one level, penalized Turkey, which was moving arms to Libya by sea, Turkey was not deterred and continued to act cavalierly, even establishing a weapons supply air bridge of its own. Against the background of these developments, the POE lamented that "the arms embargo remains totally ineffective. For those Member States directly supporting the parties to the conflict, the violations are extensive, blatant, and with complete disregard for the sanctions. Their control of the entire supply chain complicates detection, disruption, and interdiction. These two factors make any implementation of the arms embargo more difficult."[235] This became increasingly evident with the influx into Libya of armored vehicles. According to the POE Report on Libya in 2023, the UAE supplied multi-role armored vehicles as well as armored personnel carriers.[236] In addition, some of Haftar's forces had access to thermobaric fuel air grenades, while a variety of groups also had various kinds of sniper rifles.[237] In many cases, it was impossible to trace the source of weapons and ammunition. On the rare occasions this succeeded, the communications from the POE were simply ignored. In other words, not only was it relatively easy to violate the arms embargo, it could also be done at low risk and with a high level of impunity.

It is not surprising then that weapons in Libya have simultaneously become a commodity for sale, a source of profits for militias, a source of survival in what has become an unpredictable environment, and the spoils of war for those groups that prevail in large or small firefights. Increasingly, weapons supplies have also become an instrument of geopolitical influence as competing states seek to determine the outcome of the conflict in Libya through arms flows that violate the UN Embargo and underline the ineffectiveness of efforts to bring hostilities to a close.

Oil Smuggling

The introduction to this chapter noted the parallels between Iraq after 2013 and Libya after the fall of Gaddafi. In both cases, one of the big components of the conflict economy was oil. Moreover, in both Iraq and

Libya, oil smuggling was multifaceted, involving both land and maritime dimensions. Oil smuggling overland to Tunisia was far from new but assumed new contours with the conflict and chaos in Libya. There has also been considerable oil smuggling from Libya to various European countries including Spain, Italy, France, and Germany often via Malta, which emerged as a critical criminal hub in relation to oil smuggling. Interestingly, there have also been major problems with gasoline distribution in Libya itself.

The background to all this, as one investigation noted, is that Libya "has the largest oil reserves in Africa, with current production levels at over a million barrels per day, down from 1.7 million barrels" under the Gaddafi regime.[238] The National Oil Corporation (NOC), Libya's national oil company, is still the only body authorized to sign export contracts for Libyan crude oil and to import and export petroleum products.[239] It has been challenged by the "eastern" NOC in Benghazi, where 80 percent of Libya's oil fields are located, which exports crude oil without authorization from Tripoli to fund weapons for Haftar.[240] As a result of the conflict, Libya's refining capacity has declined precipitously. In a very similar predicament to Iraq after 2003, Libya has had to import fuel every year. Between 2013 and 2017, Libya spent US$23.5 billion on imported petroleum products, which the central bank then subsidized to the tune of US$30 billion between 2012 and 2017.[241] An estimated 30 to 40 percent of fuel imported or refined in Libya every year is diverted, stolen, and smuggled to neighboring and European countries.[242] According to the head of the NOC, Libya loses about US$750 million.[243]

Although there is a great deal of information available about Libyan oil smuggling provided by the UNSC POE, one of the fullest and clearest cases of oil smuggling is the Maltese case, which has been investigated thoroughly by Trial International and Public Eye. The Swiss company Kolmar, based in Zug, allegedly received smuggled oil from Libya that it then resold at sea and on the European market.[244] The cast of characters is fascinating and includes a militia leader and known human trafficker in Libya, a former soccer player from Malta who owned a highly regarded seafood restaurant, and a Maltese businessman with a passion for different color Ferraris. All played a crucial role in the process. The Maltese businessman and the seafood restaurant owner shared the same surname but were not related. There is also a phased component of the smuggling process, with Kolmar seeming to drop out of the business but the other members of the network carrying on.

The role of Malta itself is pivotal. In recent years the reputation of the island has been tarnished by corruption scandals and by the assassination in October 2017 of Daphne Caruana Galizia, an investigative journalist who was exploring fuel smuggling from Libya to and through Malta, along with other illicit activities, when she was killed.[245] Although it is not certain the investigation into fuel smuggling led to her killing, the smuggling was certainly a lucrative business and one to protect. Moreover, Malta itself—as noted in Chapter 1—had become a haven for various forms of illicit activity. One analyst has identified "four different domains of extra-legal economies to which Malta provides a hub: the citizenship-by-investment scheme; the gaming industry; the smuggling of fuel from Libya; and international money laundering."[246] The most important of these, at least for several years, was the illicit fuel business. As such, the importance of the Malta connection in the oil smuggling business from Libya is hard to overestimate. In July 2013 the crew of the oil tanker Santa Maria was arrested after another ship, the MV *Alice*, began to leak 80,000 liters intended for transfer to the Santa Maria.[247] Since then, Malta has become a logistical hub where fuel smuggling groups operate with relative impunity to access the larger and more profitable European market.[248]

Luca Raineri attributes this to what he describes as "an environment of criminal-political-family collusion prevailing in Malta."[249] Yet this only reinforced what was already a highly permissive environment for oil smuggling. As the Organized Crime and Corruption Reporting Project noted, "Maltese authorities have said they could do nothing to prevent the fuel smuggling because it happened outside the 12-mile limit of their territorial waters. However, according to international law, Malta is within its rights to police a 24-mile area—its 'contiguous waters'—to prevent 'infringement of its customs, fiscal, immigration or sanitary laws and regulations within its territory or territorial sea.'"[250]

In many respects the Maltese case is a classic example of the use of several components of the smugglers' toolkit described in Chapter 1. It involved covert actions by ships, false documentation, and possible corruption. It also involved an ostensibly legitimate company ignoring red flags about oil smuggling from a conflict zone in pursuit of profit.[251] For convenience, the smuggling process is divided into various stages. In some ways these can be understood as narrative criminal scripts that identify the flow of a crime.[252] In this case, although it is slightly arbitrary, there are seven readily identifiable stages of the process.

Stage 1

The first stage is the theft and diversion of oil from the refinery of the Azzawiya Oil Refining Company in Zawiya, 45 kilometers west of Tripoli. The real power broker in this area is Mohammed Koshlaf, the leader of the Shuhada al Nasr brigade and head of the Petrol Refinery Guard.[253] Koshlaf appears to be a patron and protector of Fahmi Ben Khalifa, who has been allowed to divert and smuggle oil from the refinery so long as the Guard also gets a share.[254] Once the fuel is diverted, it is moved in tanker trucks to Zuwara and Abu Kammash, where Ben Khalifa has a rudimentary oil terminal.[255] Zawiya is a microcosm of other parts of Libya and indeed of the region itself—home to "an unruly and competitive security sector that has mushroomed in size . . . public services and infrastructure have declined, and its licit economy has stagnated while its illicit economy has grown uncontrollably due to human smuggling and trafficking."[256]

Stage 2

The next stage of the process resembles oil bunkering in Nigeria and indeed anywhere else in the world. Small fishing boats move the fuel from shore to sea and unload their shipments onto oil tankers that are owned or leased by Darren and Gordon Debono. These ships sail toward Tunisia and Libya coast and typically turn off their Automatic Identification System (AIS) when they are 40 to 60 nautical miles off the coast so that they are much harder to track.[257] Once all the fuel is loaded, the ships travel to Malta.

Stage 3

At this stage the recipient of the fuel, Kolmar, the Swiss oil trader, provided the Maltese customs authorities with documentation that included the certificates of origin produced by Tiuboda Oil Refining Company that belong to Ben Khalifa.[258] Subsequent investigation revealed that these certificates of origin were not only fraudulent but also that they had been created using the scanner of a Maltese company.[259]

Stage 4

Allegedly, Kolmar had already leased eight fuel tanks at the Ras Hanzir fuel wharf and five more at the Has Saptan underground storage facility near Malta Airport.[260] The Libyan fuel was moved from the ships to these oil storage facilities. The process was then repeated. Indeed, between May 27, 2014, and July 18, 2015, three ships—the *Ruta*, the *Amazigh F*, and the *Selay*—"offloaded marine gasoil 22 times at the dolphins of Ras Hanzir (19 times) and Has Saptan (3 times) at a time when Kolmar was leasing these storage units."[261] On each of these occasions, almost 51,000 tonnes of gas oil was offloaded.[262]

Stage 5

The next stage in the process was what could be called commodity laundering, or in this case blending gas oil to hide its Libyan origins.[263] In many ways this was similar to money laundering as it was designed to obscure the fact that the oil was from a conflict zone and make it appear that it came from a licit and noncontroversial source.

Stage 6

Kolmar made payment via bank transfer to the supplier, Oceano Blu Trading Ltd., which had appeared in the Panama Papers.[264] As the investigation noted, the overlap between the dates was striking. "From 15 June to 17 July 2015, the Amazigh F and the Selay moored at the Ras Hanzir and Has Saptan dolphins nine times. On nearly the same dates, i.e., from 18 June to 22 July 2015, the Zug-based company transferred over USD 11 million to Darren Debono's company."[265] It should be noted that by then Oceano Blu Trading Ltd. was being administered by Nicola Orazio Romeo, who was Darren Debono's partner in the company.[266]

Stage 7

Once the blending process was complete and the oil had been "cleaned," Kolmar was able to move and sell the laundered fuel. Based on AIS data, the investigation suggested that the oil "was partly sold on the local bunkering market, where Kolmar supplied barges that came to fill up their tanks. The smuggled fuel was also sold in Europe."[267] According to Trial International and Public Eye, there might have been some corruption and collusion at this stage too: "the customs authorities and the Libyan-Maltese chamber of commerce gave the green light to the re-export of the gasoil, either because they were incompetent or because they were also involved in the fraud."[268]

It appears though that, for whatever reason, in mid-2015 Kolmar ceased its involvement. In response, the ships running between Libya and Malta offloaded the fuel to another ship called the *Solia*, owned by Michael and Eddie Zammit, proprietors of "several small tankers and petrol stations on Malta."[269] *Solia* acted as a "floating fuel station in

Malta's territorial waters."[270] As the smuggling network continued to grow, the cast of characters grew even more varied.

Much of the initial business seems to have been the work of Darren Debono communicating directly with Ben Khalifa. When Gordon Debono was brought in, he had expertise in the oil industry and owned a company, Petroplus, that gave him access to more tankers and allowed the smugglers to "forge certificates of origin stating that the fuel they were transporting was really from Saudi Arabia."[271] Moreover, Gordon Debono's business connections in Turkey gave him access to "ships of the Selay Group to transport diesel. . . . The large Istanbul-based oil trader and shipyard owner is run by the Çolak family, which also owns companies in Malta."[272] Rodrick Grech, another Maltese fuel broker, also joined the group.[273] He had connections with Turks, Russians, and Libyans and access to two tankers owned by Manchester Shipping based in Ukraine.[274] An Egyptian-Maltese citizen, Ahmed Ibrahim Hassan Arafa, was instrumental in forging fuel certificates, while a Maltese national, Terence Micallef, used a shell company to sell the smuggled fuel in Europe.[275]

For his part, Darren Debono had also partnered with Nicola Orazio Romeo. "From their headquarters in Malta, Debono and Romeo illegally purchased smuggled fuel from Libya, and redistributed it to southern Italy and across the rest of Europe, generating an alleged income that according to Italian prosecutors exceeded 30 million euros."[276] According to another commentary, Darren Debono moved the smuggled and laundered fuel to "Italy (either via Sardinia, Venice, or Civitavecchia), through Marseille to France or to Spain."[277] The network also provided a large part of an 82,000-tonne shipment to Maxcom Bunkers SA, a company based in Augusta, Sicily.[278] In 2016, however, tensions developed between key individuals in the network and several of their ships were seized. More important, Italian police had also initiated an investigation called Dirty Oil and had put together a detailed assessment of the network, its key assets such as ships, and its operating methods. In October 2017, the Guardia di Finanza investigators from Catania arrested the Debonos and Romeo.[279] With Ben Khalifa already detained in Libya, it appeared that a large dent had been made in at least one major network that was smuggling fuel from Libya to Europe. Subsequently, in February 2018, the US Department of the Treasury sanctioned parts of the network, including six individuals, twenty-four entities, and seven vessels.[280]

Although the network organized by Ben Khalifa and Darren Debono was removed from the picture, there remained multiple players involved in maritime smuggling of oil and gasoline from Libya. The UNSC POE identified ships that were turning off their AIS close to Libya as well as ships docked in close proximity to one another that were likely transferring oil. In effect, they had developed a set of red flags regarding behavior and activities linked to oil smuggling from Libya by sea. In May 2016, for example, a ship named *Yamuna* was detected near Zuwara: it was linked to another Maltese company called Patron Group Limited.[281] For Malta, it was simply business as usual. Based on information from Italian law enforcement, it was reported in May 2018: "Maltese authorities have not taken steps to prevent ship-to-ship transfers that have taken place about 12 miles (19km) off the Maltese coast, in the country's contiguous waters. The Guardia di Finanza, Italy's financial police, have spotted at least 12 acts of ship-to-ship smuggling operations in Malta's contiguous waters over the past six months, the same area where the practice occurred in 2016."[282] An Italian prosecutor also claimed that false Saudi certificates were still being used to legitimize the shipments—a classic example of the deception component in the smugglers' toolkit.[283] Italian requests for information from Malta remained unanswered.[284]

Yet not all cases involve Malta. In one instance when a flagless ship was stopped, it then ran up a Russian flag.[285] Nor was maritime smuggling the only concern; as described in Chapter 4, there were also problems within Libya and with oil and gasoline going from Libya to Tunisia. One issue was that "illicit exports of refined petroleum products are made possible through the persistence of networks exploiting the subsidized importation of fuel and its distribution in the country."[286] One of these was Brega Petroleum Marketing Company, a subsidiary of the National Oil Corporation, responsible for storage and distribution.[287] The wholesale distribution goes to four companies that supply petrol stations. As the POE noted, however, Brega failed to implement stronger control mechanisms over the distribution companies.[288] The panel also succinctly explained the challenge: although since 2011 over 480 new petrol stations have been established, "most of them only exist on paper, allowing fuel smugglers to receive fuel."[289] This allowed for the re-export of subsidized imported gasoline, which could be resold outside Libya for a much higher price. Once again, the parallels with Iraq are striking.

In its 2019 report, the POE noted that some serious steps were being taken with the licensing of trusted petrol stations and new regulatory standards.[290] Moreover, in February 2019 the attorney general "issued arrest warrants for more than 100 individuals and owners of petrol stations involved in smuggling, and ordered the Central Bank of

Libya to freeze the accounts of the respective businesses."[291] While this had some impact, the Covid-19 pandemic likely had even more. The POE in 2021 observed, "the illicit exports of refined petroleum products have decreased substantially compared with previous years. Local dynamics, in conjunction with the impact of the coronavirus outbreak on the global economy, have brought fuel smuggling by sea to a temporary halt."[292] The price of oil and refined products declined significantly, and this helped. The caveat though was that "the infrastructure of the smuggling networks from Zuwarah and Abu Kammash remains intact and their readiness to conduct illicit exports is undiminished. A resumption of their illicit activities, once global demand for bunker fuel recovers, is to be expected."[293]

The POE also noted that "fuel diversion overland persisted and even increased in some regions, although it continued to be a relatively low-scale activity."[294] Particularly important in this context are diversions from the Zawiyah oil refinery and their movement "via Jawsh and Nalut" to the border with Tunisia.[295] The trade here is long-standing and reflects arbitrage opportunities in communities where smuggling is both a way of life and a means of survival. Far more serious in terms of security is the Islamic State's involvement in smuggling oil (and drugs) across the borders with Chad, Niger, and Sudan and its retention of a haven in Bani Walid.[296]

The bottom line on oil smuggling in Libya is that although it was disrupted by both law enforcement and the pandemic, the underlying dynamics remained strong. Overland fuel smuggling, within the country as well as across its southern and western borders, increased.[297] The 2023 POE Report also noted that fuel supplies to the Sabha distribution point had doubled to 1.2 million liters per day since August 2022, which was inconsistent with market demand but revealed "the scale of cross-border fuel smuggling."[298] As restrictions eased, it was also anticipated that maritime smuggling of oil would see a strong and sustained resurgence. In the event, this has happened but not to the extent expected. Matt Herbert, Rupert Horsely, and Emadeddin Badi noted that by mid-2023 there was only "a minor rebound, with relatively small quantities of fuel being moved offshore by diffuse networks, mainly using fishing trawlers."[299] They also observed that "coastal fuel smugglers are selling off their equipment . . . to human smuggling networks in eastern Libya."[300] The implication is that a resurgence of maritime smuggling to the levels it reached from 2013 to 2018 has not occurred. The UN POE on Libya, however, noted suspicious behavior of several ships that turned off their identification systems as they neared Libya. In addition, it found that a new focal point for some of the smuggling was the old harbor of Benghazi, which had traditionally been used for scrap metal but had been modified for illegal oil exports.[301] Indeed, twenty-four small and extra-small oil vessels, many registered in Cameroon, visited the port—some more than once—on thirty-six occasions between March 2022 and the first half of 2023.[302] The fuel came from the Brega Company's Benghazi depot and was moved to the vessels by tanker-trucks. If the eastern Libya oil connection was new, the western Libya area around Zuwara also made something of a comeback. Several vessels reportedly used the Sidi Ali pumping station in Abu Kammash, which had been reactivated in response to the increase in oil prices.[303] There were also reports of suspicious activities involving ships berthing at the anchorage at Hurd's Bank, which is supposedly beyond Malta's jurisdiction.[304] Moreover, as the network involving Darren Debono and Gordon Debono revealed, it does not take much temptation or effort for legitimate businessmen to cross the line into illicit activities.

Cigarette Smuggling

Cigarette smuggling is rife throughout North Africa. The Libyan case is an example of cigarette smuggling on steroids. "In 2016, the highest number of illegal cigarettes in the Maghreb region were consumed in Libya—6.44 billion, or 93 percent of all cigarettes smoked in the country."[305] The transformation into a lawless zone where the writ of the state was absent also made Libya a particularly attractive transshipment country for illicit cigarettes being smuggled to Europe. As with other North African countries, the major source is the UAE.[306] The cigarettes produced there enter the Maghreb either via Turkey, Southern Europe (mainly Greece), and then into Libya or through Egypt, either after transiting through the Arabian Peninsula or directly from the Red Sea.[307] The cigarettes are then moved from Libya to Tunisia and Algeria and then into Europe.[308] As the Nexus report noted, "in 2017, Libya was a transit point for 2.1 billion illicit cigarettes flowing to Tunisia and for 1.3 billion illicit cigarettes moving to Algeria."[309] Although the UAE source is the most important, the UAE does not have anything approaching a monopoly. In 2017 "cigarettes produced in about 100 different countries" passed "through Libya before reaching 47 different final destinations."[310]

Historically, Libya played a very modest role in the production of illicit cigarettes, but with the civil war, cigarettes were seen as another source of funding for militias. The result, as several sources have noted, is that Libya began to import tobacco, and the militias "and even local communities began purchasing tobacco and producing counterfeit cigarettes."[311] These are primarily sold to meet local demand, but some are moved across North Africa and to a minor extent beyond. "In 2017, about 0.3 billion illicit cigarettes originating from Libya were smoked in the Egyptian market. In the same year, smaller volumes of illicit Libyan cigarettes were consumed also in Ukraine, France, the United Kingdom, and Malta."[312]

Many groups in Libya benefit from cigarette smuggling. Most obviously, the sale of the counterfeit cigarettes provides another important income stream for the militias, allowing them to continue their military campaigns and, in effect, perpetuate the conflict. Tribes also benefit and play crucial, if localized, roles in the borderlands. As one report noted, "the Tuareg took control of the south-western borders; the Tebu are involved in trades in south-eastern Cyrenaica; the Qadhadfa tribe controlled the smuggling route in Sirte (north of Libya); and Awlad 'Ali tribes are involved in smuggling activities across the Egyptian-Libyan border."[313] The tribes both engage in smuggling themselves and tax other smugglers whether they are bringing cigarettes or other goods into Libya. In addition, terrorist organizations in Libya also benefit. AQIM has a long pedigree in cigarette smuggling, and it is indicative that the infamous jihadist leader and smuggler Mokhtar Belmokhtar was known as "Mr. Marlboro."[314] Jihadist organizations also seem to be involved in the cigarette smuggling business, and there have been credible claims that they have been working with Italian mafia organizations operating in southern Italy and Malta.[315] This is not surprising, but its importance should not be exaggerated. In the upperworld, transactions of this kind are called commerce; yet when they occur in the underworld, they are given sinister connotations with undue claims that they exemplify a nexus between organized crime networks and terrorist groups.

The links between Italian mafia organizations and terrorists, militias, and smugglers in Libya also highlight the importance of the Mediterranean and the lure of criminal hubs such as Italy for smugglers of various kinds operating out of North Africa. The Mediterranean provides so much access for criminals that a small island state like Malta can play a critical facilitation role in some illicit activities and markets. At the same time, it is important not to overlook the porous land borders that Libya has, especially with Egypt, Niger, and Tunisia. Nor should we ignore the connections between the Balkan countries and North Africa, with cigarettes from the Jebel Ali Free Trade Zone sometimes moving directly to North Africa and on other occasions being smuggled through Greece and the Balkans and then to Libya.[316] Reportedly, contraband cigarettes move through Southern Europe and the Balkans and are then "transported by ship from a seaport, such as Bar in Montenegro, to Libya using fictitious paperwork."[317] An alternative is to do an exchange between ships either at an assigned meeting point in the open sea or at an anchorage such as Hurd's Bank.[318] Another wrinkle is that the China Tobacco International Europe Company set up a factory in Romania in 2007 and regards Libya as both a useful transshipment hub and a lucrative market.[319]

There is also an interesting case study on cigarette smuggling involving an Italian naval ship, the *Caprera*, which in 2018 spent three and a half months near Tripoli assisting the Libyan coast guard with both intercepting migrant boats and carrying out search and rescue missions.[320] When the ship was inspected after its arrival back in Italy, about 700,000 contraband cigarettes were discovered.[321] In 2020, a *New York Times* headline described the *Caprera* as "the ship that stopped 7,000 migrants and smuggled 700,000 cigarettes."[322] The occasion for the article was the trial in Brindisi of five sailors from the Caprera.[323] The *Times* report noted, however, that the investigation had widened. The authors also claimed to have seen invoices showing "that the Caprera's sailors purchased the cigarettes in Libya using a method apparently developed by crew members of a second Italian ship, the Capri, moored in Tripoli in January 2018. A third warship involved in the mission was raided in Naples in May on suspicion of smuggling, according to other court documents."[324] The chief Italian investigator was reportedly expecting to see further developments in the case.[325]

Antiquities Theft and Smuggling

The illicit market for antiquities in Libya is very different from antiquities theft and smuggling in both Iraq and Syria, where looting occurred on a large scale, involved experienced and knowledgeable brokers, and was exploited by insurgent and terrorist groups, which often taxed the looters and smugglers. The market in Libya is smaller, less professional and organized, seems to involve individuals more than organizations, and appears to be largely opportunistic rather than systemic. Somewhat surprisingly, there is not extensive involvement by the militias. The main reason for militia abstention is not any concern about Libyan cultural heritage, but rather the simple fact that this illicit market is far less lucrative than those for oil, people, and drugs.

None of this is intended to downplay the challenge or the damage that is being done. Nor is it to underestimate the international dimension of the trade. As the major study of antiquities looting and smuggling noted "the geographical extent of this trade clearly extends well beyond Libya. Following smuggling routes, it reaches intermediates in neighboring countries such as Tunisia and Egypt, and eventually connects with international art auction houses and networks of private collectors throughout the Middle East, the Gulf, Europe, and the United States."[326]

Looting antiquities in Libya is neither novel nor unprecedented. In fact, "Libya is home to an abundance of archaeological and historical sites spanning millennia, civilizations, and a vast expanse of territory."[327] During the colonial era, however, little or no respect was shown for cultural property that was simply something that could be appropriated or traded. During and after World War II, major artifacts were stolen, with some ending up in Europe and the United States. During the Gaddafi era a strong legal framework designed to protect Libyan antiquities was established. Since then, "the steady erosion of rule-of-law following the 2011 Revolution, and political fragmentation since 2014, has meant that in practice, these laws have been difficult to enforce."[328] At the same time, the incentives for looting and smuggling antiquities have increased. Economic dislocation has obviously been important; so too has been the attitude that artifacts are the vestiges of colonialism. More surprising is the impact of construction projects. Antiquities are now typically looted "from archaeological sites many of them uncovered through the process of clearing land for development. The large-scale clearing and subdivision of formerly public lands to build new housing and vacation properties has been concentrated in areas previously protected by the state, including along the coast and on the flat plateaus of the Jabal al Akhdar. These regions have been attractive places to build for millennia, and they are therefore densely filled with archaeological sites."[329] Clearing the land almost invariably leads to discoveries that are then appropriated for profit.

The market within Libya has also been facilitated by social media, especially Facebook, which in 2020 accounted for more than two-thirds of social media usage.[330] Archaeological items are frequently posted on Facebook. In some instances, they are overtly and openly for sale; in others, only the picture is posted but with the implication that the item is likely for sale. The initial destinations for the transnational smuggling of artifacts from Libya are its neighbors, Egypt and Tunisia.[331] Cyrenaican funerary items—sculptures of funerary divinities and funerary portraits—are particularly important as they were "uniquely produced in the ancient Cyrenaica."[332] In November 2015, the search of a container routed to Bangkok from Damietta, Egypt, led to the seizure of more than a thousand artifacts including Cyrenaican funerary sculptures.[333] Authorities strongly suspect that a Dubai smuggling network was involved.[334] While this was an example of interdiction, many other funerary sculptures have been smuggled successfully and surfaced in the United States, Britain, France, and Israel—and even in Thailand.[335] In Spain, one gallery owner selling ten Libya funerary statues was arrested.[336] The more refined funerary artifacts can sell for between $100,000 and upward of a million dollars.[337] Meanwhile, Tunisia is an important transshipment point for Jewish artifacts, including Hebrew manuscripts, which also end up on international markets.[338]

Most of the perpetrators are males aged between fifteen and forty-five, working "alone or in small groups. They appear to be acting opportunistically and independently, seeking to monetize their finds in a casual, relatively open manner."[339] In two cases, however, there were apparent connections to armed groups.[340] Although these connections were disturbing, the positive trends are that thefts from museums, by and large, have ceased, while members of the public are also returning artifacts.[341] Nevertheless, the antiquities market could become more dynamic if more lucrative and expansive illicit markets in Libya are somehow choked off. Even if this does not occur, the threat to cultural heritage will remain. Indeed, in 2022, Ahmed Issa Faraj, head of the scientific committee at the Federation of Libyan World Heritage Municipalities, told a news outlet that "the drain of archaeological heritage in Libya will continue, and perhaps in an upward manner, in light of uncontrolled looting and smuggling and the lack of any punishment for those who destroyed archaeological sites in recent years."[342] There are some glimmers of hope. In November 2022, Spanish authorities returned to the Libyan embassy in Spain twelve antiquities that had been stolen from Libya and smuggled to Spain.[343] Moreover, in both 2022 and 2023 the United States also returned antiquities that had been recovered. Unfortunately, these were more than offset by the continued threats to cultural heritage in Libya.

Commodities Smuggling

Commodities smuggling is important across Libya's borders with Tunisia and Egypt. Much of the smuggling between Libya and Tunisia, however, is covered in Chapter 4 of this book. Consequently, the discussion here focuses on Libya's border with Egypt. The commentary draws on a brilliant analysis by Thomas Husken, who describes smuggling as "a transgressive economic practice that is embedded in the wider social, political, and cultural connectivity. This connectivity transgresses state borders, colliding with state sovereignty and territorial integrity."[344] He makes a compelling case, however, that smuggling across the borderlands of Egypt and Libya can best be understood not as "a criminal exception to normal conduct per se, but as a type of economic, political and cultural action that is connected to and embedded in a wider setting of practices."[345] Husken argues that smuggling is simply the economic dimension of what he terms "shared sovereignty between (trans-) local populations and states."[346] He also notes—in a similar vein to Max Gallien, whose work is discussed elsewhere in this book—that "smugglers, soldiers, customs officers, police officers and ordinary citizens are closely intertwined actors for whom smuggling is a field of economic cooperation, social relationships and political strategies."[347] The incentives for smuggling are very similar to those found in borderlands throughout North Africa. The legal economy is sclerotic rather than dynamic; unemployment is high, desert agriculture is limited, and tourism is run from the Nile valley.[348] In such an environment smuggling becomes a means to survive and, for the more successful, perhaps even prosper.

Husken also observes that "smuggling is socially embedded in and regulated by kinship associations of the borderland" and that the Awlad 'Ali tribes play a critical role in the borderlands of Libya and Egypt.[349] About 15,000 of the Awlad 'Ali reside in Libya, many in Tobruk, while most of them live in the Matrou governorate in Egypt and have somewhere between half a million and a million members.[350] The enduring "kinship alliance between the 'Ilat al-Bayda, a lineage of the Quinishat in Egypt, and the 'Ilat al-Khadra of the Qutu'an in Tobruk" has also facilitated cross-border cooperation.[351] Significantly, Husken notes that none of the smugglers or kinship associations he knows has ever become involved with militants: "pragmatism, profit orientation and self-interest, rather than ideology and politicized Islam, are the typical markers of the smugglers."[352] At the same time, the police and military forces in the borderlands are not well trained, while customs officials are either acquiescent or collusive.[353]

Most of the commodity smuggling—as elsewhere in North Africa—is based on price asymmetries and arbitrage opportunities. As one commentator noted, "the price gaps are huge among tax-free or low-tax products, from gasoline to products coming from Morocco and Tunisia, such as perfumes, medicinal herbs, handicrafts, leather goods, clothing, electrical appliances, cosmetics and Chinese computers, as Egypt imposes high taxes on imports."[354] Indeed, "one of the most important economic incentives for smuggling between Libya and Egypt were the free trade ports across Libya," which crystallized the arbitrage opportunities.[355] Many goods smuggled across the border are transported to the Libyan market in Marsa Matrouh, where they are purchased by tourists motivated by the relatively low prices.[356] Some of the products are even moved to Alexandria and Cairo and sold there.[357] Accordingly, "with the exception of the Libyan revolution . . . when arms and equipment were smuggled into the country from Egypt, and the current smuggling of people, almost all smuggling activity between the two countries is Egypt-bound."[358] It is also facilitated by mobile phones.[359]

Younger men between the ages of seventeen and forty do most of the smuggling, although they also have other jobs and are not full-time smugglers.[360] Moreover, the cross-border activity is regarded as a form of self-help and as acceptable trade (*tigara*) not smuggling (*tahrib*), with the latter term reserved largely for harmful products such as arms and drugs.[361] Particularly striking is that groups involved in *tahrib* "are considered illegal in the sense of the codified state law but also unjust and unacceptable in the sense of Awlad 'Ali morality and juridical understanding."[362] Following on from this, Husken identifies four different kinds of smuggling:

- Trading by bag (*tigarat-al-shanta*) is a common and widely accepted form of petty trade, and members of the Awlad 'Ali come to Libya, load up on goods, and return, often bribing customs officers in the process.[363]
- Night smuggling (*tahrib/tigara bil-leyl*) involves circumventing the border checkpoints and carrying goods across desert tracks. The smugglers who are aged between seventeen and twenty-five receive the goods from pickup trucks, carry them across the border, and hand them off to another transporter.[364]
- Smuggling by sea using fishing boats enables the movement of larger consignments of goods but is also dangerous because it too is done at night.[365]
- Desert smuggling (*tahrib sahari*) involves "transporting goods through the deep desert by pickup. In the borderland, this form of smuggling is almost solely in the hands of international networks based in Libya, Egypt, Chad, Sudan and other countries and regions."[366] This form of smuggling involves drugs, cigarettes,

> arms, and people.[367] The Awlad ‘Ali is involved in some of these smuggling networks but does not dominate the market the way it does in smuggling the more innocuous products.[368]

In the final analysis, these various forms of smuggling all reflect the paradoxes of borders: they are both the ultimate statement of sovereignty and the greatest challenge to sovereignty. Libya’s borders certainly offer arbitrage opportunities that can be lifesaving for the destitute, enriching for criminal networks and militia groups, and frustrating for authorities seeking to restore some semblance of order to the war-torn country.

Corruption and Illicit Financial Flows

Identifying and assessing illicit financial flows in Libya is much harder than elsewhere in North Africa because of the chaos and anarchy. Yet this environment has also included intensive resource exploitation and various forms of trafficking that have proven highly lucrative. Some of this money is often spent locally; it has been used to purchase arms, thereby perpetuating the armed conflict, but also to “benefit local communities,” especially in “areas where few alternative livelihood opportunities exist.”[369] In a study of Libya’s war economy, Eaton observed that in “almost every case, actors with significant interests in the war economy also have significant financial interests outside the country.”[370] Not surprisingly, much of this connectivity occurs through the hawala or informal value transfer system, which appears to have been particularly important in relation to migrant smuggling—partly for the migrants themselves and partly for those who profit from them. “Money and gold traders operating from the old city in Tripoli and a more formal financial transaction system with bank accounts and companies” comprise other elements in the overall picture.[371] Criminals and militia leaders involved in different forms of smuggling and trafficking are also linked “with companies and businessmen with interests in legitimate trade in Libya, Malta, Italy, Spain, Greece, Cyprus, Albania, Montenegro, Turkey, Syria, Lebanon, Egypt and the United Arab Emirates (Dubai), among other places.”[372] Letters of credit also play an important part in linking Libya with the global economy, and even though they have to be authorized by the Central Bank, they help to create and maintain liquidity in black markets.[373] All of this helps explain both the inflows and outflows of money.

There are also varying degrees of corruption in Libya, as elsewhere in North Africa. In Derna, Libya, years of corruption, waste, and abuse led to badly designed and poorly designed infrastructure projects, including the two dams that burst in September 2023 and led to devastating floods that killed at least 4,000 people.[374] The Panama Papers shed even further light on widespread corruption in Libya, revealing that a Gaddafi-era procurement official stole millions of dollars from his country's own government and hid the money within a complex web of offshore companies and bank accounts.[375] Once again this is facilitated by a lack of regulation and oversight and by pervasive corruption. Yet none of this is new. Gaddafi systematically misappropriated "public assets," used "opaque privatization processes," and embezzled huge amounts, moving the proceeds to the United States (US$37 billion), United Kingdom (US$15 billion), the Netherlands (US$2.1 billion), Austria (US$1.8 billion), Sweden (US$1.6 billion), and Switzerland (US$416 million).[376] Looting of the national treasury has continued since Gaddafi, and Libya has few barriers to help protect against this. Its anti-money-laundering efforts are deficient, its capacity for asset recovery is weak to nonexistent, and its high levels of corruption and lack of institutional coordination simply exacerbate these weaknesses.

There is also evidence that corruption in the country is getting worse, with one study describing much of what is going on in Libya as a "kleptocratic boom."[377] Meanwhile, according to the UN, "24% of women and 30% of children in Libya required targeted humanitarian assistance."[378] The study also highlighted Libya's dismal standing in Transparency International's corruption perceptions index as well as "the frailty, opacity, and excessive personalization of state institutions" that provided "Libya's political entrepreneurs, armed group leaders, and organized crime bosses with numerous ways to steal or misuse public resources."[379] Moreover, far from heading to a new equilibrium or new order of some kind, Libya is in danger of destroying its "most essential institutions, including the National Oil Corporation (NOC), which is responsible for almost all of the nation's income."[380] The analysis also noted that the Central Bank not only regulates the banking sector but also owns much of it.[381] Meanwhile, powerful financial figures have aligned with armed groups as a matter of both preservation and self-interest, a process encouraging the "militarization of Libyan politics."[382] With an absence of consensus and the inability of any group or individual to project a sense of legitimacy or articulate a compelling notion of the public good, almost everything in the country is up for grabs. In these circumstances, lines between the licit economy and the black market or illicit economy range from the indistinct to the nonexistent.

Conclusion

Libya in the decade or more since Gaddafi was overthrown has descended into a Hobbesian state of nature. It represents a Greek tragedy on a mythic scale and one in which it is hard to find any silver lining. In the words of Nick Snaith, "Libya has 200,000 police on the books, 15 police officers to every Libyan, but they don't show up for work."[383] Inevitably, this contributes to the vibrancy and resilience of Libya's illicit economies, which despite their predatory excesses represent a "success story" that is all the more striking amid the chaos, despair, death, and disorder. Unfortunately, the high degree of criminality and its proceeds will perpetuate the conflict and chaos. War profiteering is lucrative, and so long as these impressive and fungible revenue streams are being generated, there is no incentive to compromise and every incentive to keep at least low-level conflict going and the money coming. In this connection, Herbert, Horsely, and Badi have argued very persuasively that "efforts to prevent criminal penetration of the Libyan state have failed. Actors linked to illicit economies have increasingly become embedded within the security forces, while others seek opportunities for high-level positions and political influence. This raises the risk that criminal interests, predation and corruption will be fused into the state. Equally problematically, it risks poisoning citizen trust in and possible acceptance of future governance and security structures involving compromised actors."[384] It also means that if Libya does move to reconstitute state structures, then the power of state-embedded criminal actors will not only reach new and unprecedented heights but also give new meaning to the concept of the captured state.

Notes

1. For more on illicit markets in Iraq, see Williams, *Criminals, Militias, and Insurgents*.
2. See Ayubi, *Overstating the Arab State*.
3. Andreas, "Criminalizing Consequences of Sanctions."
4. Fiona Mangan, *Illicit Drug Trafficking and Use*, p. 4.
5. Ibid.
6. Williams, *Criminals, Militias, and Insurgents*, p. 36.
7. Ibid. See also Eaton, *Libya's War Economy*.

8. Mangan, *Illicit Drug Trafficking and Use*, p. 5.
9. ENACT, *Organized Crime Index 2019—Libya*, p. 37.
10. Ibid., p. 37.
11. Ibid., p. 37.
12. Global Organized Crime Index, *Libya 2021*, p. 1.
13. Global Organized Crime Index, *Libya 2023*, p. 1.
14. Ibid.
15. Jason Blazakis, senior advisor at the Soufan Group, interview of Nick Snaith of Rose Partners via Zoom conducted on March 15, 2021. Rose Partners is a strategic risk consultancy contracted by the UK government to examine a range of challenges related to crime in Libya. Rose Partners has deployed regional experts and former law enforcement personnel to engage in capacity-building activities in Libya.
16. Global Organized Crime Index, *Libya 2021*, p. 4.
17. Bertelsmann Transformation Index (BTI), *Libya Country Report 2022*, p. 1.
18. Mangan, *Illicit Drug Trafficking and Use*, p. 3.
19. Micallef, *Shifting Sands*, p. 4.
20. Ibid., p. 4.
21. Mangan, p. 3.
22. Micallef, p. 4.
23. Jason Blazakis, Senior Advisor at The Soufan Group, interview conducted via Zoom with Samuel Juett on February 24, 2021.
24. Ibid.
25. Mangan, *Illicit Drug Trafficking and Use*, p. 6.
26. Ibid.
27. Ibid.
28. Micallef, *Shifting Sands*, p. 8.
29. Mangan, *Illicit Drug Trafficking and Use*, pp. 7–8.
30. Ibid., p. 8.
31. Ibid.
32. Ibid.
33. Interpol, "Massive Drug Seizures."
34. Ibid.
35. Mangan, *Illicit Drug Trafficking and Use*, p. 8.
36. Ibid.
37. Ibid.
38. Herbert and Gallien, *A Rising Tide*, pp. 27, 29–33, 40.
39. Ibid., p. 16.
40. Ibid.
41. Ibid.
42. Mangan, *Illicit Drug Trafficking and Use*, p. 8.
43. Herbert and Gallien, *A Rising Tide*, p. 16.
44. Mangan, *Illicit Drug Trafficking and Use*, p. 8.
45. Ibid., p. 10.
46. Micallef, *Illicit Drug Trafficking and Use*, p. 15.
47. Weekly Standard, "Whose Convenience? Hurd's Bank."
48. Herbert and Gallien, *A Rising Tide*, p. 16.
49. Ford, "Libya, North Africa Emerge."
50. Ibid.
51. Ibid.
52. Ibid.

53. “Libya Seizes Record Amount of Cocaine Coming from Brazil,” *Libya Review*, February 7, 2023.
54. Micallef, *Illicit Drug Trafficking and Use*, p. 19.
55. Harvard Health Blog, “Is Tramadol Risky?”
56. This draws on the work of Micallef, *Illicit Drug Trafficking and Use*, and Mangan, *Illicit Drug Trafficking and Use*.
57. Micallef, *Illicit Drug Trafficking and Use*, p. 4.
58. The point about Nigeria is drawn from ibid., p. 27.
59. Micallef, *Illicit Drug Trafficking and Use*, p. 4.
60. Ibid., p. 23.
61. Ibid.
62. Ibid.
63. Ibid.
64. Herbert, Horsely, and Badi, *Illicit Economies and Peace and Security*, p. 13.
65. Ibid., p. 14.
66. Ibid.
67. Mangan, *Illicit Drug Trafficking and Use*, p. 3.
68. Final report of the Panel of Experts established pursuant to resolution 1973 (2011) concerning Libya, S/2023/673, p. 6.
69. Ibid.
70. UNODC, *Smuggling of Migrants*, p. 6.
71. Ibid., p. 7.
72. UNODC, *Smuggling of Migrants*, p.14.
73. Ibid.
74. Ibid.
75. Ibid.
76. Chatham House, “Stability at What Cost?”
77. UNODC, *Smuggling of Migrants*, p. 23.
78. Ibid.
79. Ibid.
80. Rizk, “Exploring the Nexus.”
81. See for example, Human Rights Watch, “Italy-Libya Connection.”
82. BBC News, “Gaddafi Wants EU Cash.”
83. New Humanitarian, “Syrians Seeking Refuge in Libya.”
84. UNHCR, *Mixed Migration Trends in Libya*, p. 15.
85. See UN Security Council, “Ermias Ghermay.”
86. Perry and Agius, “Migrants and New Mediterranean Mafia.”
87. Ibid.
88. Ibid.
89. Ibid.
90. Perry and Agius, “Long Read: Evil Genius.”
91. Ibid.
92. Ibid.
93. Altai Consulting, *Leaving Libya: Rapid Assessment*, p. 34.
94. Toub, “Absurd Case of Mistaken Identity.”
95. Birnbaum, “Smuggling Refugees into Europe.”
96. Altai Consulting, *Leaving Libya: Rapid Assessment*, p. 27.
97. Ibid.
98. El Kamouni-Janssen, *Only God Can Stop the Smugglers*, p. 10.
99. Ibid., p. 11.
100. Ibid.

101. Ibid., p. 13.
102. Ibid., p. 14.
103. Ibid., p. 15.
104. Ibid., p. 16.
105. Ibid.
106. Ibid.
107. Ibid., p. 14.
108. Ibid.
109. Sahan Foundation and IGAD, *Human Trafficking and Smuggling*, p. 11.
110. Ibid., p. 5.
111. Global Detention Project, "Libya: Overview."
112. Ibid., p. 95.
113. Ibid., pp. 102–103.
114. ReliefWeb, "Independent Fact-Finding Mission on Libya."
115. Altai Consulting, *Leaving Libya: Rapid Assessment*, p. 6.
116. UNHCR, *Mixed Migration Trends in Libya*, pp. 63, 66.
117. Ibid., p. 66.
118. Ibid., pp. 66, 69.
119. Ibid., p. 64.
120. Micallef, Horsley, and Bish, *Human Conveyor Belt Broken*, p. 4.
121. Ibid., p. 2.
122. Altai Consulting, *Leaving Libya: Rapid Assessment*, p. 81.
123. Ibid., p. 82.
124. Ibid.
125. Ibid.
126. Ibid., p. 81.
127. Ibid., p. 83.
128. Ibid., p. 84.
129. Ibid., p. 82.
130. Ibid.
131. Micallef, Horsley, and Bish, *Human Conveyor Belt Broken*, p. 2.
132. Ibid.
133. Ibid., pp. 4–5.
134. Ibid., p. 5.
135. International Organization for Migration, *Migration in Malta: Country Profile 2015*, p. 9.
136. Interview conducted by authors.
137. PMI Interview.
138. PMI interview.
139. PMI Interview.
140. PMI Interview.
141. PMI Interview.
142. PMI Interview.
143. Micallef, Horsley, and Bish, p. 54.
144. Palm, "Italy-Libya Memorandum of Understanding."
145. Human Rights Watch, *Halt Abusive Migration Cooperation*.
146. Horsley, *Libya: Sophisticated Smugglers Thrive*.
147. Ibid., p. 3.
148. Global Organized Crime Index, *Libya 2023*, p. 3.
149. Horsley and Gerken, *Libya: Stability Fuels Rebound*, p. 2.
150. Horsley, *Libya: Sophisticated Smugglers Thrive*, p. 8.

151. See ibid., p. 11.
152. Ibid.
153. Ibid., p. 31.
154. Herbert, Horsely, and Badi, *Illicit Economies and Peace and Security*, p. 19.
155. Ibid.
156. Ibid.
157. Horsley, *Libya: Sophisticated Smugglers Thrive*, p. 29.
158. Ibid., p. 24.
159. Ibid., p. 25.
160. Ibid.
161. Boussel, "War Against Human Traffickers."
162. Kuschminder and Triandafyllidou, "Smuggling, Trafficking, and Extortion."
163. Brachet and Scheele, "Captives at Large," p. 5.
164. Al-Dayel, Anfinson, and Anfinson, "Captivity, Migration, and Power in Libya," p. 281.
165. Tondo, "Libya Releases Man."
166. Brachet and Scheele, "Captives at Large."
167. Malakooti, *Political Economy of Migrant Detention.*
168. Ibid., p. 11.
169. Ibid.
170. Ibid., p. 39.
171. Ibid., p. 19.
172. US Department of State, "2021 Trafficking in Persons Report: Libya," p. 613.
173. Ibid., p. 614.
174. US Department of State, "2023 Trafficking in Persons Report: Libya," p. 6.
175. Ibid., p. 8.
176. Global Organized Crime Index, *Libya 2023*, p. 3.
177. UN Security Council, S/2023/673, p. 16.
178. Ibid.
179. Ibid.
180. Ibid., p. 22.
181. Ibid., pp. 98–99.
182. Ibid., p. 100.
183. Libya ranked fortieth in the world in 2007 for gun ownership per hundred people. See Small Arms Survey, *Libya Ranked 40 in the World.*
184. Strazzari and Tholens, "'Tesco for Terrorists' Reconsidered."
185. Marsh, "Brothers Came Back with Weapons," p. 80.
186. According to some sources, more than a million tons of weapons were looted after Gaddafi fell. Strazzari and Zampagni, "Illicit Firearms Circulation," p. 113.
187. Dhaouadi, "Social Media and the Sale of Arms."
188. Demuynck, Mehra, and Bergema, *ICCT Situation Report.*
189. Bromley, Maletta, and Brockmann, *Arms Transfers and SALW Controls*, p. 3.
190. Small Arms Survey and African Union, *Weapons Compass*, p. 59.
191. Arieff, *Crisis in Mali.*
192. Marsh, "Brothers Came Back with Weapons."
193. Attkisson, "Thousands of Libyan Missiles."
194. Lebovich, "AQIM and Libya's Missing Weapons."
195. Callimachi and Tondo, "Scaling Up a Drug Trade."
196. Deknatel, "New Drug Routes."

197. Nadeau, "Italian Mob Trades Weapons."
198. Conflict Armament Research, *Investigating Cross-Border Weapons*, p. 16.
199. Ibid., p. 10.
200. Ibid.
201. Ibid.
202. Ibid., p. 18.
203. Ibid., p. 25.
204. Marsh, "Brothers Came Back with Weapons." p. 81.
205. Ibid., p. 22.
206. Ibid.
207. Ibid., p. 93.
208. Jenzen-Jones and McCollum, *Web Trafficking*, p. 25.
209. Ibid.
210. UN Security Council, S/2017/466, p. 64.
211. Jenzen-Jones and McCollum, *Web Trafficking*, p. 15.
212. Ibid.
213. Ibid.
214. Ibid.
215. Ibid.
216. Ibid.
217. Ibid.
218. Ibid., p. 28.
219. BBC News, "Activist Abdurraouf Eshati."
220. Dubuis and Pennink, "Muslim Preacher Jailed."
221. BBC News, "Activist Abdurraouf Eshati."
222. Ibid.
223. Ibid.
224. Cullinane, "Man Gets 6 Years."
225. Serra, "Beyond Migration."
226. UN Security Council, S/2016/209, p. 31.
227. Agenzia Nazionale Stampa Associata, "Arrest Warrant for Italian" and "Libya Extradites Italian."
228. Serra, "Beyond Migration."
229. Coppola, "Incredible Story of Giulio Lolli."
230. Ibid.
231. Ibid.
232. Ibid.
233. Serra, "Beyond Migration."
234. Kirechu, "Profiteers, Vultures, and Defeat."
235. UN Security Council, S/2013/99, p. 2.
236. UN Security Council, S/2023/673, annexes 37 and 38.
237. See ibid., annexes 39 and 41.
238. Public Eye and Trial International, *Libyan Fuel Smuggling*, p. 4.
239. Ibid.
240. Ibid.
241. Ibid.
242. Ibid., p. 6.
243. Ibid.
244. Ibid.
245. Rubino, Anesi, and Bagnoli, "Death in a Smugglers' Paradise."
246. Raineri, "Malta Connection," p. 4.

247. *Malta Independent*, "AFM Intercepts Vessel Spilling Oil."
248. Raineri, "Malta Connection," p. 8.
249. Ibid, p.10.
250. Rubino, Anesi, and Bagnoli, "Death in a Smugglers' Paradise."
251. Public Eye and Trial International, *Libyan Fuel Smuggling*, p. 17.
252. For a good explanation see Cornish, "Procedural Analysis of Offending."
253. See Government of Isle of Man, "Financial Sanctions: Libya."
254. Public Eye and Trial International, *Libyan Fuel Smuggling*, p. 9.
255. Ibid., p. 9.
256. Yousef and Eaton, "Dual Face of Migrant Smuggling."
257. UN Security Council, S/2016/209, p. 46.
258. Public Eye and Trial International, *Libyan Fuel Smuggling*, p. 13.
259. Ibid.
260. Ibid., p. 11.
261. Ibid.
262. Ibid.
263. Ibid., p. 10.
264. Ibid., p. 13. For the Panama Papers reference, see ICIJ, "Oceano Blu Trading Limited."
265. Public Eye and Trial International, *Libyan Fuel Smuggling*, p. 13.
266. Ibid., p. 9.
267. Ibid., p. 13.
268. Ibid.
269. Rubino, Anesi, and Bagnoli, "Death in a Smugglers' Paradise."
270. Ibid.
271. Ibid.
272. Ibid.
273. Ibid.
274. Ibid.
275. WorldECR, "OFAC Acts to Disrupt."
276. Raineri, "Malta Connection," p. 10.
277. Eurobsit, "Libyan Oil Fueled Crime."
278. Public Eye and Trial International, *Libyan Fuel Smuggling*, p. 8.
279. Vella, "Italians Arrest Ex-Malta Footballer."
280. US Department of Treasury, "Treasury Sanctions International."
281. UN Security Council, S/2017/466, p. 257.
282. Kirchgaessner, Tondo, and Daphne Project, "Malta 'Fueling Libya Instability.'"
283. Ibid.
284. Ibid.
285. UN Security Council, S/2017/466, p. 279.
286. UN Security Council, S/2018/812, p. 39.
287. Ibid., p. 39.
288. Ibid., p. 39.
289. Ibid., p. 40.
290. UN Security Council, S/2019/914, p. 47.
291. Ibid., pp. 46–47.
292. UN Security Council, S/2021/229, p. 36.
293. Ibid., p. 38.
294. Ibid., p. 36.
295. Ibid., p. 38.
296. Ibid., p. 6.

297. UN Security Council, S/2023/673, p. 38.
298. Ibid., p. 38.
299. Herbert, Horsely, and Badi, *Illicit Economies and Peace and Security*, p. 10.
300. Ibid., p. 11.
301. UN Security Council, S/2023/673, pp. 37–38.
302. Ibid., p. 242.
303. Ibid., p. 261.
304. Ibid.
305. Kasturi, "Libya's Future Is a Haze."
306. Meneghini and Milani, "Maghreb Route," p. 12.
307. Ibid.
308. Ibid., p. 14.
309. Ibid.
310. Ibid.
311. Kasturi, "Libya's Future Is a Haze."
312. Meneghini and Milani, "Maghreb Route," p. 14.
313. Ibid., p. 21.
314. BBC News, "Profile Mokhtar Belmokhtar."
315. Babuta and Haenlein, *Commodity Smuggling in the Maghreb*, p. 4.
316. Abderrahmane, "Trade and Counterfeit Goods."
317. Ibid.
318. Ibid.
319. Ibid.
320. Kingsley and Creta, "Ship That Stopped 7,000 Migrants."
321. Ibid.
322. Ibid.
323. Ibid.
324. Ibid.
325. Ibid.
326. American Society of Overseas Research, *State of Illicit Trade and Looting*, p. 2.
327. Ibid., p. 6.
328. Ibid., p. 22.
329. Ibid., pp. 29–30.
330. Ibid., p. 38.
331. Ibid., p. 60.
332. Ibid.
333. Ibid., p. 65.
334. Ibid.
335. Ibid., p. 69.
336. Ibid., p. 71.
337. Ibid.
338. Ibid., p. 67.
339. Ibid., p. 95.
340. Ibid.
341. Ibid., p. 97.
342. *All Arab News*, "Libyan Antiquities in Grave Danger."
343. LibyaMohammed, "12 Stolen Artifacts Smuggled."
344. Husken, "Practice and Culture of Smuggling," p. 897.
345. Ibid.
346. Ibid.

347. Ibid., p. 899.
348. Ibid., p. 906.
349. Ibid., p. 899.
350. Ibid., p. 900.
351. Ibid., p. 903.
352. Ibid., p. 912.
353. Ibid., p. 907.
354. El-Dine, "Eastern and Western Egyptian Borders."
355. Ibid.
356. Husken, "Practice and Culture of Smuggling," p. 908.
357. Ibid., p. 909.
358. Ibid., p. 902.
359. Ibid., p. 909.
360. Ibid., p. 905.
361. Ibid.
362. Ibid., p. 906.
363. Ibid., p. 908.
364. Ibid.
365. Ibid., p. 909.
366. Ibid.
367. Ibid.
368. Ibid.
369. Eaton, *Libya's War Economy*, p. 31.
370. Ibid., p. 33
371. Micallef, *Shifting Sands*, p. 14.
372. Ibid.
373. The Sentry, *Libya's Kleptocratic Boom*, p. 14.
374. Yee, "Years of Graft Doomed 2 Dams."
375. Farolfi and Orphandes, "Cyprus Records Shed Light."
376. UNICRI, *Illicit Financial Flows*, p. 21.
377. The Sentry, *Libya's Kleptocratic Boom.*
378. Ibid., p. 1.
379. Ibid.
380. Ibid.
381. Ibid., p. 3.
382. Ibid., p. 5.
383. Nick Snaith, interview by Jason Blazakis, senior advisor at the Soufan Group, conducted via Zoom on March 15, 2021.
384. Herbert, Horsely, and Badi, *Illicit Economies and Peace and Security*, p. 2.

6

Egypt: Antiquities, Arms, and Authoritarianism

EGYPT IS STRUGGLING. THIS ASSERTION HOLDS WHETHER THE FOCUS IS ON politics, economics, criminality, or illicit markets. The overthrow of President Hosni Mubarak in February 2011 was one of the most promising moments of the Arab Spring, yet it still ended in disappointment with the articulation, reestablishment, and perhaps even deepening of military control over Egyptian politics and society. The trajectory of the revolution was distorted, leading to a situation that was much closer to the status quo ante than almost anyone wanted or expected.

Political and Criminal Context

The government of Muslim Brotherhood leader Mohamed Morsi was democratically elected in June 2012 but proved inept, particularly at controlling crime, and was overthrown in a coup d'état by the military just over a year later. After polarizing the country, Morsi failed to deal with Egypt's underlying problems and presided over a turbulent and chaotic country unaccustomed to the freedoms that were now fully on display. The rule of the Muslim Brotherhood was regarded as highly ineffective, and the military "ended the experiment in July 2013."[1] The net result of this politically turbulent period was that it derailed the transition "in order to create a new regime" that was in some respects even more authoritarian than the Mubarak regime.[2] This is not entirely surprising: most revolutions create counterrevolutionary forces. In the case of Egypt, these forces proved dominant and were highly successful in "refashioning and reconstituting an authoritarian regime after revolutionary moments."[3]

Unfortunately, such regimes are typically far more concerned about regime survival than good governance. This was certainly underlined when "Abdel Fattah al-Sisi was reconfirmed as president in an unfair and unfree election in March 2018, and policymaking remained dominated by anti-democratic veto actors, with the military and intelligence agencies playing a particularly prominent role."[4] Egypt has gone from one dictator to another, while the economy has remained stifled and Cairo's place on the world stage, even within the region itself, continues to recede. So, from Mubarak to Morsi and now Sisi, Egypt is contending with multiple decades of poor governance. The capacity gaps and functional holes of the state have been compounded over time, leaving Egypt's government with an inability to respond to organized crime even if it had the political will to do so.

One result of this preoccupation with regime survival is that the Egyptian economy is not functioning well. Governance remains sclerotic and ineffective, with many of the elites in the government more concerned with profiting from the country's vast patronage networks rather than governing effectively. The military government has dealt with none of Egypt's structural problems, such as unemployment among the young and well-educated, or an economy that has not generated the dynamism needed to improve the lot of its people. And with no penalties for poor performance, the issues are swept aside and left for someone else to deal with down the road. In the past, this has contributed to extremism, with groups like Egyptian Islamic Jihad and al-Gam'a al-Islamiya serving as feeders to radical Salafi jihadist groups between the 1970s and 1990s. Guided by the International Monetary Fund (IMF), Egypt did make some reforms, such as imposing austerity measures and making external investment easier. At the same time, "the reforms and the government's policies aimed at generating growth proved a heavy burden on both fiscal and monetary stability, as well as the population."[5] The currency depreciated, inflation and debt increased, and budget deficits proved intractable. Moreover, the imposition of austerity measures increased poverty and perpetuated youth unemployment.[6] Formal markets were unpredictable, leading many Egyptians to consider alternative forms of earning money merely to survive. With ample smuggling and trafficking opportunities, organized criminal networks have been the beneficiaries of government ineptitude and indifference.

Nor is the record of dealing with organized crime and illicit markets any more impressive or effective than the other components of governance. According to the ENACT Organized Crime Index in 2019, "in terms of criminality, Egypt's Index score of 5.14 places it 22nd in

Africa and 2nd in North Africa."[7] In other words, its criminality score is higher than all other North African countries except Libya, and these scores remained roughly at the same level over the past several years. "The country's relatively high overall score is driven predominantly by its scores for criminal actors, characterized by moderately high scores for criminal networks, state-embedded actors, and foreign actors. Although certain criminal markets are not deemed to have a significant impact in Egypt, others have considerable negative impacts, most notably the synthetic drugs and cannabis trade and arms trafficking."[8] Egypt's Global Organized Crime Index score in 2023 was 5.05, ranking it again second in North Africa, with the report making explicit mention of the country's struggles with human trafficking. It is also worth noting that Egypt has both valuable and vulnerable antiquities and cultural heritage sites, many of which are being looted. The country also seems to have a problem with organ trafficking, which does not appear in the index but largely sets it apart from other North African countries. If Egypt has a criminality problem greater than average in Africa, "its resilience score is just above the continental average at 3.96, ranking it 24th in Africa and 4th in North Africa. This indicates a marginally higher resilience to organized crime than most African countries."[9]

Egypt also seems to have an organized crime problem, or perhaps more accurately, a disorganized crime problem. This certainly appeared to be the case during Morsi's tenure, with the weakness of the police, the rise of vigilante justice, and the proliferation of weapons among the citizenry. Guns became both an enabler of crime and a means of providing security when law enforcement had disappeared—the state had lost its monopoly of violence. "Distrustful of a police force known for being simultaneously abusive and incompetent, and wary of an increasingly politicized judicial system that rarely delivers justice, many Egyptians are administering law and order on their own terms."[10] The breakdown of law and order only further enables organized crime, as extortion and protection rackets emerge and calcify. Out of the chaos appeared to be a burgeoning criminal order. Criminal gangs are among the biggest beneficiaries of widespread lawlessness in Egypt, functioning as a stand-in for state security personnel in the dangerous slums of Cairo, allegedly with the tacit permission and apparent encouragement of the police. According to Haitham Tabei, an Egyptian journalist who reports on urban crime, the police have willingly abdicated control over entire neighborhoods of the city to criminal gangs. These predatory groups operate illicit fiefdoms with impunity—racketeering, trafficking, and prostitution—hiring thugs (and sometimes even children) to staff their private militias.[11] In the words of another Sinai-based Egyptian journalist, the government has "effectively legalized smuggling and trafficking."[12] This provides Cairo with a pressure release valve; incapable of providing for the needs of its population, the government turns a blind eye to illicit economic activity in a way that it would not to other criminal or illegal activity, such as terrorism. Although there has been some reimposition of law and order since the military reestablished control of the country, there is little to suggest that these underlying dynamics have changed much and indeed in some areas could soon grow worse as Egypt's economy struggles. According to a Bertelsmann Transformation Index (BTI) report in 2022, the Sisi government has failed to deal with many of the country's economic issues, including the Egyptian military's "economic empire and privileges," a heavy state hand in the economy, monopolies operated by prominent Egyptian elites close to the regime, and a large and growing informal sector, which includes criminal rackets.[13] Similar to countries like Turkey and Pakistan, Egypt's military feasts on the carcass of the state, savoring the spoils while leaving the vast majority of the population struggling to find ways to make ends meet. To be sure, one area where there has been a mix of amateur criminality and sophisticated transnational networks is the realm of antiquities looting and trafficking.

Drug Abuse and Drug Trafficking

In an interview undertaken for this research, an Egyptian respondent noted that "when it comes to drugs, the fact of the matter is that Egypt's geographic location overlooking the Mediterranean Sea from North Africa, its Suez Canal and its seaports offering access to Europe have all transformed the country into a key hub for trafficking drugs coming from Asian countries like Afghanistan bound for Europe using sea routes. In addition to that, locally grown weed (hashish) is smuggled to Europe using the same routes."[14] Interpol makes a similar observation, noting that Egypt is believed to be "an important transit hub of heroin bound for Europe or Turkey."[15] In the Interpol assessment, however, the entry points are airports rather than seaports.[16] Moreover, much of the heroin is destined for domestic consumption, "with heroin . . . often cited as the second or third drug most consumed by Egyptians" and one that is "on the rise."[17] Egypt also has a major problem with synthetic opioids and other prescription pharmaceuticals. The problem has expanded and diversified since the Arab Spring but was rife well before then.

Drug abuse and drug trafficking are far from new in Egypt. Hashish and opium smoking have been common in Egypt for decades. Moreover, reports in 1990 suggested that in 1989, 2 million people in Egypt had used illegal drugs, while in 1988, there were an estimated 250,000 heroin addicts.[18] It was also reported that in 1988, 300 kilos of heroin had been sold.[19] In addition, 3,500 people were convicted for drug trafficking, but most of them seem to have been low-level distributors who were sentenced to between six months and a year.[20] Although fifteen traffickers were given life sentences, the more usual sentence was less than five years of imprisonment.[21] If drug abuse and drug trafficking were widespread in the late 1980s, they have become even more pervasive since then. It was estimated in a 2007 report that "8.5 percent of Egyptians—or six million people" were drug addicts.[22] The problem was particularly serious among the fifteen to twenty-five age group.[23] Moreover, whereas the 1990 report had talked primarily about students and children of the wealthy using drugs, by the mid-2000s, drug abuse had spread into areas where poverty was also widespread. Indeed, "the slums of Cairo and Giza are hotbeds of addiction. These slums are among the largest in the world and are home to hundreds of thousands of street children. Some authorities estimate that the number of these children may reach one million. Population density reaches 60,000 people per square mile, far denser than Calcutta or Djakarta."[24]

The situation has deteriorated further in the decade and a half since the 2007 report. There are more drugs, a wider variety of drugs, more drug addicts, and almost certainly higher profits for drug traffickers and drug trafficking organizations. One of the most obvious changes is the massive expansion of tramadol use. Tramadol has become so widespread partly because it provides an unusual high for users, but primarily because it is so cheap.[25] A 2017 commentary noted that, at "roughly 30 to 40 Egyptians pounds ($3.8 to $5.1) for a strip of 12, or as little as two to three pounds per pill in very poor parts of Cairo," tramadol was "within reach for all but the most cash-strapped of the young."[26] An estimated 90 percent was produced in India and transported to Egypt in containers moving through "major harbor facilities in Alexandria, Port Said and Ain Sukhna."[27] Tramadol is popular among manual laborers and is used as both a pain killer and as something that enables them to work longer and harder.[28] Economic deprivation has fed into the equation. "With the cost of living in Egypt having drastically increased in the past few years due to the flotation of the Egyptian pound and the government's cutting of welfare for the poor, drugs like tramadol offer relief to people doing grueling work."[29] In the short term, tramadol can be a helpful coping mechanism; in the longer term, however, it creates dependencies and addiction while exacerbating rather than alleviating problems. By 2015, it had become the most abused drug in Egypt and accounted for nearly half of Egypt's 100,000 opioid users.[30]

At the same time, Egypt remained highly vulnerable to heroin. In this connection, the UN 2021 World Drug Report noted that 91 percent of the heroin and morphine seized in Africa in 2019 was confiscated in North Africa, and most of this in Egypt.[31] Rather astonishingly, Egypt accounted for 83 percent of all heroin and morphine seized in Africa in 2019.[32] Although the Covid-19 lockdown likely had some impact on flows into the region in 2020, Egypt still made one large heroin seizure and several small ones.[33]

More recently, two new synthetic drugs, Strox and Voodoo, have become popular. According to one commentary, "Voodoo is a combination of an aromatic plant, like marjoram or incense, which is infused with a synthetic cannabinoid that is up to 100 times as powerful as natural marijuana."[34] The drug is legal in Israel.[35] "Strox is also made with an aromatic plant like marjoram and incense, which is then sprayed with active medical substances used as pain relievers in case of cramps or stomach aches, like atropine, hyoscine, and hyoscyamine. These substances can have psychotropic effects when taken in large doses."[36] Both drugs are typically mixed with tobacco for smoking and can cause "hallucinations and paranoia."[37] Despite this, there is little sign that the use of synthetics is abating. On the contrary, the UN World Drug Report 2021 noted that "the quantities of Voodoo and Strox seized during the second half of 2020 were larger than in the past. Likewise, the Egyptian authorities reported an increase in the size of seizures of captagon and crystalline methamphetamine during the second half of the year after the easing of mobility restrictions. For example, 11 million captagon tablets were seized in the port of Damietta in November, accounting for the largest quantity of amphetamine seized in the country in 2020."[38]

In addition to heroin, tramadol, Strox, and Voodoo, Egypt is a hub for pharmaceuticals—some of which are diverted and some of which are counterfeit. Although it is impossible to ascertain a comprehensive picture of the scale of pharmaceutical smuggling or of those involved, the seizure cases suggest that pharmaceuticals are brought into Egypt by individuals and small groups of two or three people. In 2019, for example, 400 boxes of cancer medication were seized at Cairo International Airport after being discovered in a passenger's clothes on his arrival on a flight from Riyadh.[39] In another case, "7,408 units of pharmaceutical products for abortion, epilepsy and anti-viruses" were found in luggage at

Alexandria Airport.[40] Another significant seizure was made at Hurghada International Airport in 2019.[41] In this case, concealment failed and so did an attempt at facilitation of corruption. Foreign medication worth around US$60,000 was "smuggled by a Russian passenger of Syrian origin coming from Istanbul. An Egyptian national, suspected to be an accomplice of the smuggler, tried to bribe an airport custom official to facilitate the entry."[42] Although details are sparse, none of these smuggling ventures appeared to be especially sophisticated. It is possible, however, that larger shipments are made with more professional concealment or deception and are, therefore, more difficult to detect.

The Sisi government has taken measures to reassert control over Egypt's borders and to enhance the capacity for interdiction. Even so, drugs are smuggled into Egypt with remarkable regularity and probably a high rate of success. The choice of conduits is wide: seaports, airports, through formal checkpoints at land borders, and across land borders between the checkpoints. With its western border, Egypt has the misfortune of having Libya as its neighbor. This gives drug suppliers even more options, given the lack of governance and effective controls on the Libyan side of the border. Indeed, cannabis, "tramadol, and to a lesser extent, cocaine and heroin are also smuggled overland to the Egyptian border from the official border crossing at el-Salloum as well as from desert areas further south, between Jaghbub and Siwa."[43] The border between Libya and Egypt is discussed in Chapter 5, with considerable emphasis placed on commodity smuggling and the significance of the Awlad 'Ali tribal connections across the two countries. The licit trade and the tribal connections provide both the context and facilitators for the drugs being moved into Egypt. These include seaborne drugs that are then smuggled by land to Egypt via Ajdabiya.[44] While the route has reportedly diminished in importance, "Ajdabiya is also a transit point for drugs coming from the west, on their way to Egypt, mostly from south-west Libya after entering the country from Algeria and Niger."[45] Although overland routes from Libya into Egypt have been given a lot of attention—largely because of the pervasive lawlessness and the massive illicit economy in Libya—most of the more important seizures seem to happen elsewhere.

The Egyptian Navy, however, has enjoyed periodic successes with interdictions and significant seizures, while law enforcement has also had some notable arrests and seizures. These include the following:

- In December 2016, Egyptian Naval Forces intercepted *Abadan*, an Iranian vessel in Egyptian waters in the Red Sea, and confiscated

319 packages containing 171 kilos of heroin.[46] The authorities also seized nine mobile phones, "a satellite phone, and wads of cash in a number of different currencies" and arrested four Iranians, two Indians, and a Pakistani national.[47]

- In December 2017, the Egyptian Interior Ministry seized 200 kilos of heroin and 10 kilos of methamphetamine and arrested ten foreign smugglers at Safaga port in the Red Sea.[48]
- In July 2018, Egypt's Interior Ministry announced the seizure of a heroin factory and the arrest of five drug dealers in Obour City, Qaliubiya governorate.[49] The group was described as a "very dangerous gang" that "smuggled large shipments of heroin into Egypt" and then mixed, refined, and compressed the heroin in the factory.
- On October 1, 2018, a spokesman for the Egyptian armed forces announced that border guards had "foiled an attempt to smuggle 72 kilograms of heroin using a four wheeler across the southern border."[50] The only other detail was that the operation had been based on intelligence.
- In December 2018, a total of thirty-three suspects including four foreigners were arrested for prostitution and drug trafficking. The group reportedly pressured women into prostitution, where they were also expected to sell drugs to clients. "They smuggled heroin, tramadol, and other banned drugs from Turkey and India, getting them through airports and land crossings and then having prostitutes sell the drugs to customers."[51]
- In January 2019, authorities from Sharqiya Security Directorate arrested a drug dealer with 250 grams of heroin and an illegal firearm. The forty-one-year-old man who lived in Zagazig had previously faced charges related to "drugs, theft, and thuggery" and was likely a career criminal.[52] In April 2019, Egyptian naval forces in the Red Sea seized a ship with 2 tonnes of heroin and 99 kilos of methamphetamine. The ship had seven crew members, and it was not revealed whose flag it was flying.[53] Authorities also revealed the involvement of two Egyptian drug traffickers whom the police were looking for.[54] The narcotics were valued at "more than 2 billion Egyptian pounds" or US$115 million.[55]
- In July 2022, the Israel Defense Forces (IDF) seized approximately $2.5 million worth of cocaine and hashish (70 kilograms total) from Egyptian smugglers, who operate by throwing the drugs over the border to Israeli smugglers, who then sell the drugs in Israel.[56]
- In February 2023, a plan to smuggle $14 million from Egypt into Israel was foiled. Israel confiscated 92 kilograms of heroin and

> cocaine and an additional 28 kilograms of hashish. Throughout the Negev desert, Bedouin smugglers traffic marijuana and hashish grown in Egypt's Sinai Peninsula.[57]

The difficulty, as always, is knowing how representative these cases are when compared to the overall pattern. Nevertheless, the examples suggest that the concern over maritime entry is particularly well founded. Although there is ample material on drug abuse in Egypt and some decent interdiction cases, there is a paucity of knowledge about the drug traffickers themselves. There are claims that "Egyptian and Turkish syndicates are involved in heroin trafficking into Europe," and it seems likely that these groups are involved to some degree in trafficking heroin into Egypt itself.[58] On rare occasions, Egyptians with some political clout have been identified as being heavily involved in drug trafficking. Perhaps the most notorious example was the judge who chaired an Egyptian court while simultaneously forming a drug trafficking network that he linked to foreigners and businessmen in Iraq.[59] The case was publicly reported in February 2021. Even worse is that he is "the son of a senior judge who holds a post in the Court of Cassation, the highest judicial authority in Egypt."[60] He used the family palace as the base for the manufacturing and the distribution of drugs and exploited his "judicial immunity to protect the trafficking network by using heavy weapons and a fleet of cars to transport, smuggle and trade drugs within the Egyptian borders."[61] An Iraqi businessman and the Iraqi owners of an import-export company were among his accomplices.[62] In some ways, this could be a bellwether case with respect to impunity. A lenient sentence resulting from the judge's influential connections would signal a lack of accountability. In one case in 2017, another judge found in possession of 68 kilos of hashish worth less than US$100,000 was sentenced to life imprisonment (twenty-five years).[63] The 2021 criminal case seems much more structured, better organized, larger in scale, and more egregious, so anything less than an identical or even harsher sentence would reflect favoritism or high-level protection and immunity.

At the other end of the spectrum is the individual small-scale dealer who typically supplements a meager income from licit activities with limited retail-level drug distribution. In an interview, one dealer noted that he had always been law-abiding but had then been jailed for supporting one of the anti-Mubarak candidates in the 2005 election. After being released from prison, he began to deal cannabis from his cigarette kiosk. He only dealt to friends and those who had been sent to see him by his existing customers.[64]

Besides individuals, certain groups and state actors are heavily involved in drug trafficking. These include Egypt's Central Security Forces (CSF), which consist of an estimated 350,000 people.[65] The CSF was established in 1969 to ensure domestic security. Until the revolution, the CSF was disliked by the military, in part because it was "recruited from Egypt's large underclass of impoverished and illiterate youths."[66] Nevertheless, it has become a powerful exemplar of what the ENACT Organized Crime Index refers to as a state-embedded criminal actor.[67] Indeed, according to one observer, "the CSF is the source of tens of millions of dollars in off-the-record profits from the sale of drugs and guns, a percentage of which it shares with its allies in the more staid and respected Egyptian military."[68] It has been acknowledged that the CSF "controls the smuggling routes into and out of Sinai."[69] For those who study the CSF, this is hardly surprising: "this is their turf, it's where they operate. Smuggling is a big business for them."[70] A Pentagon official, speaking anonymously, even described the security service as "the largest criminal enterprise in Egypt."[71] The concomitant is that "Sinai troubles are fueled not only by disaffected 'Bedouin tribes' but also by 'Sinai CSF commanders' intent on guarding the drug and smuggling routes that they continue to control."[72] A separate report to European Union officials confirming the old adage that crime—like politics—makes strange bedfellows concluded that "the Sinai is flooded with contraband, with a lot of it hooked into the trade with Israeli mafia families. And a lot of that comes right out of CSF pipelines."[73]

The other major players in drug trafficking in the Sinai are the Bedouin tribes. One analysis of Egypt's borders noted that "Egyptian traffickers, mostly Bedouins, come to the 200-mile border fence with Israel and throw bags of smuggled material at their Bedouin counterparts in the occupied territories. These, in turn, collect goods in SUV vehicles and trucks, to later redistribute them. The Israeli media says that these smugglers are not affiliated with ISIS and the terrorists, but that they are armed and open fire indiscriminately if faced by Israeli forces."[74] On Egypt's border with Libya, members of the dominant tribe, the Awlad 'Ali, have primarily been involved in smuggling of illicit commodities. It seems very likely, however, that some elements have moved into the high-risk, high-reward trafficking of more dangerous commodities such as drugs and weapons.

In sum, Egypt has a major problem with a wide variety of narcotics, an addict population twice the size of the global average of national users, and a variety of routes through which drugs can enter. It also has powerful drug trafficking organizations, some of which are tribal-based and some of which are embedded deeply in the state. All these factors make the problem particularly intractable and difficult to address. As in many other countries, drug abuse and drug trafficking in Egypt readily fall into the category of "wicked problems," for which there is no easy or rapid solution.[75] Drugs are simultaneously a public health problem, a security threat, a market issue, a problem of crime and delinquency, a function of demographics, a dimension of globalization, and a challenge linked to poverty, alienation, and marginalization on the one side and surplus wealth on the other.

Human Smuggling and Human Trafficking

In other country studies, human smuggling and human trafficking have been treated separately. In Egypt, however, they intersect to such a degree that, at least analytically, it makes more sense to treat them together. Like most other countries in North Africa, Egypt is both a destination and a transit country, as well as a country of origin for irregular migrants. Given its location, it is a natural magnet for migrants from Sudan, Eritrea, South Sudan, Ethiopia, and Somalia—especially given the enduring conflicts and instability that continue to plague these countries. Over the course of the last two decades, Iraqis and then Syrians also began to seek refuge in Egypt. However, "in contrast to Syrians who have received priority resettlement outside Egypt, diaspora communities of Sudanese, Eritrean, and Ethiopian nationals who have been denied refugee status have settled in low-income neighborhoods, generally in the Greater Cairo region, for example, Faisal, Ard El-Lewa, Maadi, and Mohandeseen."[76] Moreover, "the classification of Sudanese migrants entering Egypt as 'asylum seekers' underpins a regime of strategic neglect, marked by legal barriers to citizenship that position migrants as a source of captive labor in the informal economy."[77] In essence, it condemns these individuals to the illicit market as a means of daily survival.

To revert to themes highlighted in Chapter 1, Egypt's southern neighbors play a critical role in both human smuggling and trafficking. In this connection, Sudan is particularly important. In 2015, Sudan was estimated to be hosting over half a million migrants, divided almost equally between males and females.[78] It is also a transit country for migrants from Somalia, Ethiopia, Eritrea, South Sudan, and Chad who are seeking to reach Egypt either as a destination or as a springboard for either a direct route across the Mediterranean to Europe or an indirect route from Egypt to Libya and then Europe.

One of the most important sources of migrants in both Sudan and Libya is Eritrea. Eritreans have been fleeing the country in droves. This is readily explicable. According to Human Rights Watch's World Report 2021, "Eritrea's government remains one of the world's most repressive, subjecting its population to widespread forced labor and conscription, imposing restrictions on freedom of expression, opinion, and faith, and restricting independent scrutiny by international monitors."[79] Politically, the country lacks check and balances and "remains a one-man dictatorship under President Isaias Afewerki," who has suppressed entrepreneurialism, fishing, and agriculture.[80] "Eritrea's economy is run without a budget, without a Central Bank and without a statistics bureau. Importing goods is illegal."[81] The ruling party, the People's Front for Democracy and Justice, controls the Red Sea Company and around thirty-four other companies, while the other component of the economy is a witches' brew of smuggling, trafficking, and political and military corruption.[82] The result for most people is a high level of reliance on the illicit economy and black-market activities. Some observers believe the regime is driving out people to ensure the retention of its power.[83] Yet leaving Eritrea is very difficult: it requires a permit that is rarely granted.[84] Consequently, desperate migrants require help from smugglers and the use of bribery and corruption.

Seen in this context, the key to understanding both human smuggling and human trafficking from Eritrea to Egypt—and especially the Sinai—is the role of state-embedded actors, particularly state officials in Eritrea. Without question, facilitating the mobility of people is a lucrative business. According to one assessment, 30,000 people from Eritrea were trafficked between 2009 and 2013 at an estimated value of over US$600 million.[85] The UN Security Council Monitoring Group concluded that such a business required the involvement of government officials.[86] This seems to have been pervasive, not only with people leaving Eritrea but also along the routes to Egypt. Given the continuing volatility in the Horn of Africa, there is reason to believe that citizens of Eritrea, Sudan, Somalia, and elsewhere will continue to cross borders in an effort to reach European shores, thus providing an endless revenue stream for human traffickers.

"Eritrean officials collaborate with ethnic Rashaida smugglers to move their human cargo through the Sudan into Egypt and beyond. This is in most respects the same network involved in smuggling weapons through to Sinai and into Gaza."[87] Some of the early human smuggling and human trafficking was closely linked to weapons trafficking from Eritrea to Sinai.[88] On several occasions, Israel attacked vehicles in

Sudan that were carrying weapons to Sinai, where an Islamic State affiliate once dominated. To inhibit such attacks, people being smuggled or trafficked were moved along with the weapons.[89] As described by one informant: "the weapons are taken in a big truck from Eritrea to Sudan. But when they are transported from Sudan to Sinai, they are covered with people so they are not exposed to the satellites. . . . The routes into Egypt come from all different directions but they all cross at exactly the same point on the Suez Canal. They carry the weapons in ships covered with cartons and bags so as not to be detected and people sit on them."[90] Even those who were smuggling people realized that it was far more lucrative to sell them to Rashaida, who would then sell them to Bedouins in Sinai.[91]

Most of the Sinai trafficking routes for Eritreans are through Sudan and Egypt, although some move first to Ethiopia and then Sudan. "Commonly, their journey begins as flight from Eritrea (often with the aid of smugglers) and can be transformed into trafficking at any point enroute. Some are abducted while in Eritrea, but many are abducted while crossing the border or residing in Sudan or Ethiopia."[92] Many Eritreans were simply hoping to get to refugee camps in Ethiopia or Sudan but found themselves "forced to pay for a journey through the Sinai to Israel that they had never wanted to take, in the hands of people with whom they had never made an agreement."[93] By 2013, abductions were even taking place in Eritrea itself, including from within Sawa Military Camp, where all Eritrean children attend their final year of school. Those who did get to refugee camps in Ethiopia or Sudan were also at risk of being abducted from the camps and subsequently trafficked, smuggled, or otherwise exploited.

Sudanese officials and police are also complicit in the business. "The long list of human traffickers and smugglers identified as operating in eastern Sudan and Khartoum . . . including the refugee camp of Shagarab, illustrate the point that this region is a crucial coordination point for the entire trafficking operation."[94] The Eritrean government also exerts considerable influence over the operations. From the holding areas in Sudan, migrants were taken to Egypt where they were handed over to Bedouin traffickers who arranged the further move to Sinai.[95] In the process they had to cross the Suez Canal. According to one informant, "there are three main routes across the Suez Canal: the Martyr Ahmed Hamdy Tunne, the Kobri (bridge) al-Salam and the canal itself, which they cross in small boats. . . . On the other side of the Suez Canal there are cars waiting to drive them to the Sinai. They then drive north to Arish, the capital of the Sinai. They enter Sheikh Zuweid, which is where the lawless part of the Sinai starts, and then move further to Almahdia. From Almahdia, they travel all the way to Raffa area, close to Gaza and the Israeli border" where the torture camps were located.[96] Reportedly, police and security officials colluded with traffickers in Egypt to facilitate the movements of the migrants.[97] Once in the camps, the migrants were compelled to provide telephone numbers of relatives. They were subsequently called, and the migrants were tortured during the calls so that their relatives could hear and thereby grow even more desperate to come up with the required hostage payment so the torture would stop. If the family could not or would not pay, the migrant was killed. In 2014, Egyptian forces moved into the Sinai to combat terrorist organizations linked to al-Qaeda and the Islamic State and largely eliminated the torture camps—although it is arguable that, at least in part, they simply relocated across the border to Libya.

Even though the worst abuses have been stopped or minimized, migrants in Egypt still face enormous difficulties. Israel's construction of a border wall has largely stopped the flow into Israel and, in effect, trapped migrants in Egypt. This left the sea route to Europe as the only real alternative. Yet this also resulted in some of the worst tragedies the Mediterranean has witnessed. In September 2014, almost 500 migrants lost their lives when a boat from Damietta was deliberately capsized by smugglers after those on board refused to move to a smaller vessel.[98] In September 2016, "a vessel carrying 600 migrants from Egypt to Italy overturned in the Mediterranean Sea. The boat was dangerously overloaded and sank 8 miles from the port city of Rosetta, in northern Egypt. The dead included Egyptian, Sudanese, Eritrean, and Somali nationals. The incident was reported to be 'the largest smuggling operation ever detected in Egypt.'"[99] But the data show that migrant crossings grow even more perilous each year. In 2021, the Mediterranean saw 123,540 arrivals with 3,231 dead and missing; in 2022, 160,070 arrivals with 3,017 dead and missing; and in 2023, 270,180 arrivals with 3,760 dead and missing, according to the UN High Commissioner for Refugees.[100]

This gave impetus to a legal framework that was already under consideration and a policy for combating irregular migration that was partially in place. Under Sisi, Egypt approached migration as, first and foremost, a national security issue. "The enactment of Egypt's Law 2016/82, 'On Combating Illegal Migration and Smuggling of Migrants' was embedded in this broader policy and legal shift."[101] Moreover, the law provided the basis for punishing those involved in migrant smuggling. Soon after its passage, fifty-six people were convicted of crimes, including manslaughter and murder, for involvement in the September

2016 disaster.[102] It was hoped the tough sentences would help to deter future smuggling.[103] And it seems to have made an impact.

Part of the new approach was designed to contain the dangers of spillover violence, arms trafficking, and terrorist infiltration from Libya. Egypt wanted to exert its territorial sovereignty and not only control its borders but also be seen controlling its borders in a very public way. It has further been suggested that Egypt wanted to control emigration to prevent the best and the brightest from leaving—in other words, to slow down the process of "brain drain."[104] Yet there was another important objective involved in efforts to stop migrants sailing from Egypt across the Mediterranean to Europe. As Lucia Bird's analysis suggested, the European Union–Turkey deal highlighted some of the benefits of adopting strong measures to limit migrant flows to Europe. Egypt, however, was less interested in aid and trade than it was in a tacit agreement whereby in response to Egypt preventing human smuggling across the Mediterranean, the EU would not criticize Egypt's human rights violations and its repression of civil society organizations.[105] However, the European Union also provided financial support and training for Egyptian security forces combating migration, thereby effectively endorsing Law 82 (On Combating Illegal Migration and Smuggling of Migrants), which the Egyptian parliament passed in November 2016.[106]

Prior to the new law, it was estimated that approximately 20,000 people per year migrated from Egypt.[107] They were "collected in small fishing boats from different embarkation points (e.g., Damietta, Mersa Matruh, and Rosetta) along the north Egyptian coast" and transferred onto a larger vessel with a fishing license that enabled it to go anywhere.[108] The more established and larger networks typically had collusive relationships with border officials that increased the prospects for success.[109] In some instances, the migrants were moved by sea to the Libyan coast, where a different set of smugglers took over, and from there, they were taken to Europe—albeit only after paying a second fare.[110] In some instances, however, migrants were taken out to sea and then brought back to a different part of Egypt and told that they had reached a Greek island and to wade ashore.[111] This highlights one of the major problems with illicit markets—there are no service standards, no forms of redress, and nothing to prevent fraud and extreme exploitation.

The other phenomenon—and this resembles developments in Tunisia—is that some fishermen began to sell their boats.[112] In some cases, this cut out the smugglers, relying instead on migrants with at least a rudimentary knowledge of navigation and seamanship. The extent of this form of migrant self-organization in Egypt is difficult to assess, but it does not seem to be nearly as extensive as in Morocco or Tunisia. In any event, Egypt appears to have had considerable success in clamping down on migrant boats to Europe and suppressing human smuggling across the Mediterranean. One military figure claimed human smuggling had been reduced by 90 percent, while a presidential spokesman announced that "not even one case" had "been recorded since September 2016."[113] This is almost definitely an exaggeration, but clearly outmigration has diminished significantly. In January 2020, the director of the International Organization for Migration, after a meeting with the Egyptian prime minister, applauded Egypt on a successful approach that had reduced illegal migration from Egypt to Europe to almost zero.[114]

Arrests have also likely increased on overland smuggling routes. Yet these continue to operate through the land border with Sudan, into Egypt from Syria by air, and in both directions across the Libya-Egypt border.[115] In February 2019, over seventy people were arrested for moving foreigners and Egyptians out of Egypt using false documents.[116] Another trend that emerged in 2019 involved "Egyptians flying into Niger from Cairo on work visas and then travelling northwards into Libya to find work. The speed at which this route developed suggests networks involved Cairo-based Egyptian groups. This movement was disrupted in September 2019 after intelligence reached the Egyptian embassy and Nigerien authorities, who conducted targeted raids and arrested over 80 Egyptian migrants in a convoy leaving Agadez."[117]

At one level, Egypt's approach to reducing migration to Europe has been remarkably successful. Yet the plight of many migrants remains absolutely dismal. Moreover, it seems likely that as human smuggling to Europe has declined, the number of victims of human trafficking to and within Egypt has likely increased. The gaps between national security and human security could hardly be more dramatic. According to the US Department of State, as of 2023, "Egypt does not fully meet the standards for the elimination of trafficking but is making significant efforts to do so."[118] Whether these efforts are in earnest or more cosmetic is yet to be determined.

Organ Trafficking

The illicit and informal trade in organs has been much discussed since the end of the Cold War. The problem, however, is that it has been largely sensationalized with claims that people are kidnapped for their organs. While some of the more lurid allegations occasionally have a basis in fact, the subject needed an analysis that was sober, detached, analytical, and scholarly. Sean Columb, in a book focused on organ trafficking in Egypt, has provided an examination of the subject that avoids sensationalism and describes a reality that links the trade to corruption, migrant smuggling, and the precarious lives of migrants from Sudan and Eritrea in Egypt.[119] He also traces the organ transplant business over time, showing how it has become increasingly criminalized.

In 2010, Egypt prohibited the sale or purchase of human organs, thereby putting it in line with most other countries. The problem, as Columb noted, is that "criminal measures do nothing to offset demand for illegal transplants. The prevailing law enforcement response does not capture or respond to the empirical reality. Conversely, crime and immigration controls have produced an anomic environment that fosters a subculture of organ sales among migrant populations."[120] Consequently, he argues, "the organ trade is better understood as an informal economic activity" than "a human trafficking offense. It is economic pressures and the demands of survival rather than traffickers that force people into exploitative arrangements (i.e., organ sale) that they would otherwise avoid."[121] He argues that the "dominant trafficking paradigm" should be replaced with what he terms an "exploitation paradigm."[122] The interviewees he met "were compelled to consider organ sale because of their socioeconomic status. Categorized as illegal and formally barred from legal employment, they were exploited for their kidneys."[123] Even though it was exploitative, however, for members of marginalized migrant communities, "the organ trade emerged as an informal economic activity"—even if typically selling a kidney was an "economic option of last resort."[124] The amounts the donors were paid varied from US$2,000 to US$14,000, although sometimes there were hidden costs or arbitrary decisions that reduced payments from the amounts initially promised.[125]

Columb also identified the networks that undergirded the illicit transplant market and allowed it to function effectively. They were transnational networks in the sense that they involved both Sudanese and Egyptians and "were composed of diverse individuals (e.g., organ brokers, sellers, buyers, physicians), each with a different role and function, operating across the illegal-legal divide. Analytic labs used for blood testing and tissue typing between prospective donors and recipients are the key nodal points of activity where intermediaries link up actors in both the formal and informal sectors of the economy."[126] He also noted that the diffusion of transplant capabilities to the Global

South facilitated "the emergence of organ trading as an economic activity. The organ trade is an illegal subsystem of the transplant industry, a market solution to the surplus demand for organs."[127] The supply side is provided by irregular migrants who are structurally vulnerable in that they lack the rights of normal citizens, are subject to arrest, and have no bargaining power with employers.[128]

The brokers are, in many respects, the key to the whole trade; they act as boundary spanners between supply and demand, between the licit and the illicit. They also act as fixers, providing the necessary certificates for the clinics that do the tissue typing as well as the hospitals that perform the transplants. The supply side is really a recruitment exercise, although it is not done in formal settings. In fact, the locations could hardly be less formal. "Intermediaries gather in coffee shops to broker organ transactions and solicit kidneys from migrants looking for a source of income and a route out of poverty. It is in these marginal spaces of the urban economy that Cairo's organ trade developed into an extralegal activity coordinated by a network of brokers."[129] Yet, as Sean Columb explains, the brokers and intermediaries also work

> on behalf of transplant physicians, acting as gatekeepers for patient-buyers and donor-sellers. Prohibition and the threat of criminal sanction changed the working conditions of the trade. What once was a self-regulating system . . . had become an extralegal activity loosely coordinated by a network of brokers with links to analytic labs and transplant centers in the Greater Cairo region. These brokers were responsible for soliciting and recruiting migrants for their kidney(s) and negotiating a price on behalf of profit-oriented transplant professionals. Their increased involvement in the coordination of organ trading has had a significant impact on the development of the trade from an informal economic activity into an organized crime.[130]

The brokers also put consistent, if subtle, pressure on those they had identified as potential donors to persuade them to sell their kidneys. Moreover, once they had agreed, it was very difficult for them to withdraw from the transaction. Once a suitable donor has been identified, the recruiter or another intermediary will handle the paperwork (passport, medical records, and consent form) to ensure that the transplant itself meets all legal guidelines. "In short, the illegal supply of organs is laundered by means of an arbitrary consent process, mediated by a segmented network of intermediaries. This process transforms what was an illegal transaction into a legitimate procedure. This process of 'organ laundering' disassociates the medical facility (transplant center or hospital) from criminal activity and negates any illegal activity on behalf of the recipient."[131] Columb also makes the point, however, that this is not a case of organized crime infiltrating licit business so much as hospitals and tissue labs outsourcing the supply side of the business—which was also the criminal side of the organ trade—to individuals operating in the informal economy.[132]

Criminal sentences relating to commercial sale of kidneys for transplant were increased in 2017 and, as Columb brilliantly articulates, this had a profound impact on the market dynamics, disadvantaging donors and making the market altogether more criminal. Increased risk demanded increased secrecy; it also increased transaction costs, with revised "payment arrangements... among brokers, buyers, sellers, and hospitals."[133] So-called "service fees between consulate staff, police, and members of the special committees responsible for approving transplants... have increased to accommodate the added risk of criminal sanction."[134] In addition, some transplant operations are now done in personal residences, including apartments outside Cairo, while more enforcers have been brought into intimidate sellers and compel them to secrecy.[135]

Columb's interview data from 2017 to 2020 revealed other changes in the organ market, with a much higher prevalence of physical violence and coercion as well as exploitation. Reports of cheating, which existed in the earlier period, had become more widespread and "damaged the social legitimacy of the trade as an economic activity."[136] The erosion of the trust that sellers had in brokers tilted recruitment toward greater reliance on coercion or force. Part of the problem was that the larger and more diverse the broker network, the less cohesive and less disciplined it became. Indeed, "as the network expanded and more transient brokers from diverse ethnic backgrounds (e.g., Egyptian, Sudanese, Eritrean, Ethiopian) began targeting incoming migrants with no support network to rely on . . . social controls began to break down. The objective was to solicit a kidney for the lowest price possible and sell it for the highest price available. Accordingly, there was a noticeable shift in people's perceptions and attitudes toward brokers between 2014 and 2019."[137] At the same time, "the market coalesced around more structured criminal groups composed of intermediaries with established partnerships developed over years of informal trading in the illicit economy. This shift in organizational structure brought about an escalation in violence and redefined the nature of organ trading in Egypt."[138] In effect, the process became much more criminalized, moving into the shadows where authorities, even if they wanted to, would have trouble monitoring it and responding accordingly. At least one "criminal group . . . recruited migrants from different nationalities (e.g., Sudanese, Eritrean, Ethiopian, Somali, Syrian) in Khartoum and brought them to Cairo for organ removal."[139] The migrants were taken to "apartments in Alexandria and the urban periphery of the Greater Cairo region" and were given no alternative to kidney removal.[140] The irony of all this is that by the end of his field work, Columb was seeing a phenomenon of organ trafficking that was not far removed from the model that, at the outset of his study, he had dismissed.

Arms Trafficking

Egypt has long had a weapons trafficking problem, some of it linked to Hamas and its on-again, off-again conflict with Israel, some to the Bedouin tribes that perpetuate a smuggling and trafficking culture that readily incorporates weapons into the broader trade, some to the Eritrean government's involvement in arms trafficking, and some to its border with Libya. As discussed elsewhere in this chapter, Eritrean human smuggling and trafficking was linked directly to arms trafficking—using migrants as both camouflage and a means to deter military strikes on convoys. It was the Libyan arms trafficking challenge, however, that caused greatest concern to Egyptian authorities as it exploded after the collapse of the Gaddafi regime. Weapons were moved into Libya using both land and sea routes. Some of the sea routes are reminiscent of the smuggling of cannabis, moving it eastward just off the North African coast. As one commentator noted, "boats make it to the shores of Marsa Matruh, and smugglers continue to other destinations in Egypt such as Sinai by land and Alexandria by sea using local Egyptian boats."[141] Land routes were also used. In 2011, "it became clear that Egypt's poorly secured western border had turned from an amateur 9-millimeter pistol market into a fully-fledged arms trafficking hub," and two border crossings that had previously been "known for drug smuggling operations across North Africa, became the floodgates of heavier weapons including high-caliber antiaircraft guns, rocket propelled grenades, and surface-to-air missiles."[142] While some of the weapons flows were destined for Gaza via Sinai, others were intended for terrorist and criminal organizations and tribes in Sinai. The result was what Marsh described as "a de facto remilitarization of the Sinai."[143] With the war between Israel and Hamas that broke out with intensity in early October 2023, many expect that the Sinai will be destabilized as a second-order effect, which could empower smuggling networks that have been dormant for the past several years.

In Gaza, the demand was coupled with a willingness to pay high prices.[144] According to a Bedouin arms trafficker "the majority of weapons coming from Libya were already paid for by Palestinians and were just cutting through Egypt to reach the Gaza strip."[145] Rafah, a town on the Egyptian side of the border with Gaza, emerged as a hub from 2011 to 2012 "where Libyan weapons were purchased by people from the Sinai and Gaza."[146] Although there were claims that Egyptian authorities were outgunned and overmatched, Egypt increased its efforts at interdiction and seizure and apparently succeeded in reducing some of the flows. In June 2012, for example, authorities seized a significant number of weapons from a car and truck near Marsa Matrouh after a chase and the killing of one of the smugglers. The shipment had come from Sirte, Gaddafi's hometown. The seizure—which was described as the biggest in the history of the Ministry of the Interior—included 138 Grad rockets and 7,000 rounds of ammunition.[147] Yet, such seizures were not enough to prevent other Grad rockets that had come from Libya being fired into Israel in 2012. Perhaps the most drastic and successful initiative taken by Egypt, however, was the flooding of the tunnels into Gaza that were used to circumvent border controls and smuggle weapons and other commodities.[148] Although at one level this was highly successful, it also inflicted extensive collateral damage and caused considerable economic hardship in Gaza. After the Hamas terrorist attacks of October 7, 2023, Hamas held more than 100 Israeli hostages in these same tunnels, which made flooding them a significant hazard for Israeli authorities who were exploring various options, including special operations forces raids, to recover the hostages that were not part of a hostage-for-prisoner swap that was engineered in late November 2023.

There was also a demand for weapons by ordinary citizens frightened by the collapse of law and order and growing insecurity following the revolution, especially during the short-lived Morsi government. As one commentary in 2014 noted, "Egyptians now worry about violence ranging from politically motivated shootings and bombings to random street crime."[149] Moreover, after 2011 there was a dramatic increase in violent crime: homicides rose from 774 in 2010 to 2,144 in 2012; home invasions increased from 7,368 in 2010 to 11,699 in 2012, while armed robberies increased more than tenfold with 233 in 2010 and 2,807 in 2012.[150] Against this background, the desire for some form of protection led to a surge in the demand for weapons—and the inevitable increase in prices. "A Russian-made Kalashnikov that would have been purchased for $500 in 2011" by early 2014 would "cost nearly $5,000 on the black market."[151] As one arms dealer commented, "business is better now than ever before. People are panicked. When there is a lack of government, people start looking for their own way of protecting themselves."[152] It is hardly surprising, then, that several Facebook groups went on to deal guns online.[153]

One group that has long had an affinity for weapons are the Saeedis who make up much of the population in southern Egypt.[154] Highly tribal and conservative, with a penchant for revenge killings, the Saeedi have embraced weapons as a key part of their culture.[155] And acquisition of weapons has never been easier. During the revolution, the Saeedis benefited from the looting of police stations.[156] This was followed by the Libyan bonanza. Consequently, "firearms are now rampant across southern Egypt to the point the south could field a small army if they ever wanted to, with weapons ranging from RPGs, M2 Browning's, DShKs, and a multitude of small firearms from different origins. Not to mention the heavier arsenal such as Mi-24/35 Hind's rocket pods."[157]

Given its nature far beyond the reach of the government in Cairo, the Sinai is the ideal location for smuggling networks to take root. The Sinai served as a key transit site for the movement of arms originating from Iranian-linked brokers, moved into Sudan, transferred to Egypt, ultimately destined for Hamas in Gaza—likely involving Bedouin and Sinai's nomadic populations as facilitators. In addition to Sudan, Iran also smuggles arms to Hamas via Yemen before moving to Gaza.[158] Since Bedouins and nomads have maintained a traditional culture, which involved unregulated trade, the area has become, in effect, "both a haven and a crossing point for smuggling fighters, weapons and illicit goods" between Egypt and the Maghreb.[159] Israel has major concerns about weapons smuggling in the Sinai, since the region has been a key conduit for Hamas and other groups, including more recently violent Salafists, to bring in weapons and ammunition via underground tunnels.[160] Since taking power, the Sisi government in Egypt tightened security along the Gaza border, shut down many of Hamas's tunnels (flooding some of them with sewage), and even harassed Gazan fishermen that stray into Egyptian waters. This loss of sanctuary initially provided Hamas with a serious logistical challenge, especially considering how critical these tunnels are for smuggling goods (including weapons) and infiltrating fighters into Israel. But as the attacks of October 7, 2023, demonstrated, with Iranian help, Hamas found a way to smuggle in weapons and rockets unbeknownst to Egyptian or Israeli authorities.

The ready availability of arms was also a boon for the ISIS insurgency in the Sinai. Although it has its roots in the alienation and marginalization of the Bedouin tribes and their exclusion from anything to do with the tourism industry, the insurgency—at least in its early stages—saw an opportunistic alliance between the tribes and Islamist groups, most notably Ansar Bayt al-Maqdis (ABM), which subsequently became an Islamic State affiliate known as Islamic State–Sinai Province (IS-SP) or Wilayat Sinai (WS).[161] IS-SP also cooperates with Hamas in Sinai, although Hamas seems to keep the organization at a distance in Gaza itself—interesting dynamics that could change in the wake of the October 7 Hamas attacks and subsequent conflict with Israel. For the Bedouin, it is a result of many years of suppression and victimization. "Historically, Bedouin under both Israeli and Egyptian rule have been disenfranchised by the state through denial of identification and property papers, withholding of state services, such as running water and electricity, understaffed schools and hospitals, and Bedouin home demolitions by the state."[162] In parts of Sinai, Bedouin are not even allowed to own homes.[163] Even so, the relationship between the tribes and Wilayat Sinai has not always been smooth. Moreover, Egyptian security forces eventually reached out to the tribes, pursuing a wedge-driving strategy that, while not as dramatic or successful as the Anbar Awakening in Iraq, has created more positive and collaborative relationships with some of the tribes, at least. Clashes occurred between Wilayat Sinai and the Tarabin tribe from 2015 onward. Moreover, "some elements of some tribes began to take a more active role in security issues, seeking to align with the state. On May 10, 2015, the Sinai Tribes Union, an unofficial organization which claims to coordinate activities among Sinai's 24 tribes, offered 11 recommendations to the Egyptian government related to counter-terrorism, linking increased security cooperation with increased state integration."[164] Yet intertribal rivalries remain, and many of the tribes retain a high degree of skepticism about the Egyptian government, which is viewed as an expansive and exclusive patronage network for the elites that continue to pay fealty to the Sisi regime.

For years, Wilayat Sinai has displayed remarkable resilience in its struggle against the Egyptian state, increasing the tempo of its attacks in 2013 in response to Morsi's removal and the "suppression of Islamist groups."[165] The following year it pledged allegiance to Islamic State, which was then at the height of its power. In some respects, this was a calculated effort to obtain more resources. As one study has noted,

> financial, logistical, and manpower factors also influenced ABM's turn toward IS. Ansar Bayt al-Maqdis needed funds at a time when IS was overloaded with cash and revenues after it swept over and gained control of a third of Iraq and Syria. Since joining IS, WS has also received logistical support from IS in Iraq and Syria and assistance from the IS franchise in Libya. Islamic State leaders in Syria have called on WS's supporters to join WS for jihad against the Egyptian army. Wilayat Sinai has expanded its numbers to around 1,250 fighters, almost a 30 percent increase from when it was organized as ABM.[166]

Yet the decision to become an Islamic State franchise also reflected the increased hostility toward a government that, at that point, was adopting an almost exclusively repressive approach to the insurgency in Sinai. IS affiliates and franchise groups tend to ebb and flow, in response to counterterrorism efforts and other factors on the ground. But in many of the areas and regions where counterterrorism has been repressive, the Islamic State has won new recruits, bringing in military-aged males whom an overmilitarized government approach has radicalized.

The emergence and growth of IS-SP presented new opportunities for weapons trafficking and arms smuggling throughout the Sinai. As IS-SP grew more tenacious in its operations, targeting Egyptian military personnel, civilians, and infrastructure, its demand for small arms to outfit its personnel and initiate kinetic operations rose. The group looked to develop business relationships with Bedouin traffickers engaged in smuggling activities to act as consumers of arms or to supply weapons for future financing efforts. Elements of the Bedouin are known to have engaged in arms acquisition and trafficking activities in the past, notably with Hamas. As the Bedouin acted as facilitators for the Sinai's smuggling markets, IS-SP, in return, acted as both mediators and arms traffickers, driving arms acquisition activity on the peninsula. The Sinai remains an ungoverned territory, now used by jihadist organizations to smuggle weapons from looted arsenals in Libya.[167] In response to growing lawlessness in the Sahel, which Cairo has long feared will spill over throughout the region and impact criminal groups with ties to Egypt, the government has looked to sign bilateral agreements with countries in Africa to jointly combat the growing risks of organized crime.[168] As of 2024, Egypt has made progress against IS-SP, relying on tribal engagement to reduce jihadist attacks. But subpar efforts on development and human rights leave open the possibility of an IS-SP resurgence in the future.[169]

Ansar Bayt al-Maqdis and then Wilayat Sinai benefited enormously from the flow of arms out of Libya and into Egypt. Although this pipeline has diminished, if not dried up completely, Wilayat Sinai has been able to obtain weapons after successful attacks on Egypt's security forces.[170] This has allowed the organization to replenish its weapons. At its apex, the operational tempo of attacks suggests that Wilayat Sinai has sufficient arms to sustain a protracted insurgent campaign. "Between late 2014 and July 2018, IS claimed 955 attacks in the Sinai Peninsula. In recent years, high-profile attacks on civilian targets have included the bombing of a Russian passenger jet in October 2015 and an attack on a Sufi mosque in November 2017. In 2017 and 2018, Wilayat Sinai carried out fewer attacks, but the number of fatalities has risen. This may indicate that the group is planning attacks more strategically and with the goal of maximizing casualties."[171] After the Egyptian military's Comprehensive Operation Sinai 2018 wound down, militant attacks resumed, and from October 2019 to October 2020, "Wilayat Sinai, has claimed 222 attacks and 699 casualties."[172] It is hard, therefore, to disagree with the assessment that Wilayat Sinai remains "a persistent threat for Egypt," albeit in 2024 this threat has been attenuated significantly, along with the din of ISIS franchises in Libya, Yemen, Somalia, and Southeast Asia.[173] Israel's war in neighboring Gaza could serve to resuscitate militant activity in the Sinai, particularly given the high casualty count among civilians, especially children, which is having a radicalizing effect on Arabs and Muslims throughout the region.

Cigarette Smuggling

When it comes to cigarette smuggling in Egypt, the country is, first and foremost, a transshipment country. It is one of the early destinations and transit countries for cigarettes produced in the United Arab Emirates. Yet, it is a support player to cigarette smuggling into and through Libya rather than a major and independent player. Cigarettes move through Egypt "after flowing across the Arabian Peninsula or directly from the Red Sea."[174] Indeed, "illicit cigarette flows from the United Arab Emirates to Egypt were three times as large in 2017 compared to the annual average in 2008–2012. Using this new route, traders smuggle cigarettes towards the European Mediterranean countries, mainly France, Italy, and Malta."[175] As discussed in the the Chapter 5, the Egyptian-Libyan border remains porous, with the Awlad Ali tribes playing an enormous role in cross-border smuggling of various commodities, including counterfeit and illicit cigarettes. Moreover, the flows go both ways and "about 0.3 billion illicit cigarettes originating from Libya were smoked in the Egyptian market" in 2017.[176]

According to a 2013 commentary, one of the major distribution points for illicit cigarettes was the Beb El-Bahr street market in Bab Al-Shaareyah, a historic Cairo neighborhood.[177]

> At the middle of the market, vendors selling peculiar cigarette packages start to appear off the sides of the street. The further you walk, the more vendors you find up until you reach what seems to be a wholesale cigarette market. Under a number of improvised tents, towers of cigarette packages are displayed on nearly every street corner, adorned with placards of prices. Although those packages of cigarettes may look familiar, a closer look shows that their brands are unknown. These are smuggled cigarettes, and Bab El-Bahr street market is their home."[178]

Many of the illicit cigarettes are from China, with "brands of their own, such as Capital, Pine, L&J, Malimbo, and Golden Eagle" as well as counterfeit Marlboros.[179] Although these cigarettes contain unknown and potentially dangerous chemical ingredients, their low price makes them attractive. Their attraction was increased when the government imposed taxes on normal cigarettes, increasing their price by about 70 percent.[180] The result was that "the illicit cigarette market share in Egypt rose from 2% in 2009 to 19% in 2013, leading to a loss of government revenue."[181] It is perhaps not surprising, therefore, that since 2018, Egypt has been working with the World Health Organization to combat the trade in illicit cigarettes. In January 2021, President Sisi promulgated Law No. 170 of 2020 to ratify the protocol to eliminate illicit trade in tobacco products.[182]

Antiquities Smuggling

Egypt has always been a looters' paradise, whether the looters were the imperial powers who acquired Egyptian antiquities during the colonial era, criminal organizations specializing in trafficking of antiquities, poor Egyptians who saw antiquities as a potential source of subsistence, or corrupt officials who treated antiquities as a means of personal enrichment. After the Arab Spring and the ouster of President Mubarak, the problem assumed a new dimension. As Katie Paul of the Antiquities Coalition noted, the "uprisings also served as the catalyst for cultural racketeering, or the systematic theft of art and antiquities by organized criminal syndicates."[183] By collecting media and social media reports of antiquities theft and looting over a three-year period, Paul and her colleagues were able to collate the data and analyze it for emerging trends and patterns. What they found was disturbing: "the graphic analysis demonstrated that both individuals and groups seeking to steal Egypt's cultural patrimony are not selective or prone to single attacks; they undertake their efforts repeatedly and at a variety of places with clear evidence of recurring patterns and cycles."[184] Without a dedicated and well-resourced campaign to deter this activity, it is likely to continue unabated, dealing not just an economic blow, but also having serious deleterious cultural impacts.

Although the emphasis was on organized crime, the analysis focused broadly on heritage crimes and their varying forms, such as cultural destruction and cleansing, "illegal excavation carried out by individuals as well as at the gang and mafia level; criminally organized looting on an industrial scale like that carried out by gangs and mafia, also known as cultural racketeering; damage and looting of heritage sites as a result of land encroachment for development, agriculture, or squatting . . . and museum and facility looting."[185] To one degree or another, all of these factors are presently at play in Egypt. At the same time, there is a growing professionalization about much of the looting and theft. As Paul once again noted, "Illicit antiquities trafficking—or cultural racketeering—is like a virus. It infects a particular population, and as news circulates of the riches available in archaeological finds, the virus spreads."[186] Imitation and emulation become the order of the day—a trend that is magnified if it becomes clear that some of those involved are making substantial profits, despite the risks. Consequently, "what began as a local gang trade in many regions gave way to industrialized antiquities trafficking operations."[187] This evolution was possible largely because the potential supply of antiquities in Egypt, although not infinite, remains vast. Although the similarities should not be overdrawn, in some ways, the prevalence of antiquities, together with limited control mechanisms and lack of knowledge about what is in various storage sites, is not altogether different from the situation in the former Soviet Union during the 1990s with loose nuclear and radiological materials.[188]

There are several major sources of antiquities. The first and most important are the archeological sites. As a study by Sarah Parcak and her colleagues noted, in Egypt "sites range in size from a simple scatter of potsherds to a 42km^2 area such as the region of Luxor (Ancient Thebes), which contains hundreds of individual components (e.g. palaces, housing, temples, shrines and tombs)."[189] The same study, which provided the first systematic, country-scale archaeological assessment for Egypt, identified 1,100 sites that were surveyed for damage using satellite imagery and subsequently some selective site visits.[190] The findings, which covered the period from 2002 to 2013, were revealing and included the following highlights:

- Of the 1,100 sites surveyed for damage, 267 (or 24.3 percent) revealed evidence of looting pits and/or encroachment from buildings and cemeteries.[191]
- "The percentage of total looting damage during the years 2002–2008 shows a slight upward trend, especially from 2006–2008, but this pales in comparison to the increase in the years 2009–2013."[192]
- During 2009 there were 15,889 new looting pits, and another 18,634 in 2010, accounting for more than 34,500 new pits over the two-year period. In 2008 only 3,247 pits were visible.[193]
- The increase in looting in 2009–2010 was attributed to the economic downturn associated with the global financial crisis. More specifically, Egypt suffered from a rise in the consumer price index from 40 to 150, a massive drop in tourism, and high levels of unemployment—reaching 36 percent of those fifteen to twenty-four years old.[194]
- Pit looting and encroachment from 2002–2008 accounted for only 5.4 percent of the total damage visible from 2002 to 2013, while 2009–2010 accounted for 22.2 percent and 2011–2013 accounted for 72.3 percent.[195]
- "Compared to the period from 2002–2008, looting levels doubled in 2009–2010, and then doubled again in 2011–2013."[196] The initial doubling of looting was a response to economic crisis, while the second doubling reflected continued economic crisis combined with the new opportunities resulting from the political crisis in Egypt, and especially the collapse of the police and the withdrawal of protection from the sites.

Another source of antiquities was the storage warehouses scattered through the country. One commentary suggested there were "at least 72 archaeological warehouses in Egypt" while acknowledging that other estimates were as high as 200.[197] There is also diversity among the warehouses. Of the 72, "35 are museum warehouses, 20 are expedition warehouses and 17 are smaller on-site warehouses spread across Egypt. Only 14 warehouses out of 72 have ever been inspected."[198] The dearth of inventories means there is no baseline from which to assess whether items have been stolen. It also seems likely that at least some of the warehouses are vulnerable to looting, although in August 2017 "an attempt to smuggle 124 objects from a Ministries of Antiquities (MA) storage facility in Maadi was foiled."[199] Nevertheless, some warehouses were likely targeted after 2011 in the belief they contained gold and other valuables.[200]

The other potential source of antiquities is Egypt's museums. These too are vulnerable to theft, although they have at least kept records of the items in their possession, making thefts easier to track. Part of the problem is that the decline in tourism has meant less funding for the museums, as well as for protecting their treasures. According to one analysis, heritage and ecological tourism has fallen by 95 percent since 2011.[201] "Revenues fell from 3bn Egyptian pounds in 2010 to a projected 125m Egyptian pounds in 2014. The drop has left the MA—which derives most of its income from tourist revenues—struggling to pay the 44,000 staff on its books, let alone embark on grand projects of reform."[202] Moreover, under Morsi little attention was given to antiquities, as relatively few of them were Islamic.[203] After his overthrow, revenge attacks on cultural property became more frequent.[204] These included a 2013 attack on the Mallawi National Museum, approximately 200 miles south of Cairo, where gunmen ransacked the museum and in the process of doing so destroyed or stole 1,050 objects out of a total of 1,089 items.[205] Some were recovered, but many were irrevocably lost and were never recovered. Even under the military government, antiquities are not a high priority, especially given the economic and security challenges facing Sisi. It is also possible that there are emerging parallels with the Mubarak regime, with officials becoming complicit in the looting and smuggling of antiquities, as bribery and corruption become far more commonplace. There is also disregard for more recent but nonetheless historic buildings. Indeed, "it appears that there are few mobile items that are safe from the attention of looters. Architectural ornaments—from doorknobs to entire doors, ceilings, and pulpits—are routinely ripped out and sold, usually overseas in markets such as Qatar and Abu Dhabi."[206]

Although the antiquities trade can be understood as a mix of strategic, well-planned criminality on the one side, and opportunistic crime on the other, there are discernible patterns. Paul's focus on patterns and trends has revealed that theft and looting at archeological sites peaked in March in each year from 2011 to 2013.[207] "One explanation for this could be the favorable weather between the months of November and April. Incidentally, this is also one of the reasons why these months are often popular during tourist season. Taking into consideration the typical months of Egypt's tourism season indicates another potential reason for increased activity during these months, which could result from the significantly decreased presence at sites due to the major drops in tourist attendance after 2011."[208] The concomitant of this was the annual "repetition of increased incidents involving customs officials between March and May, typically in the month of April. The increase in sites affected is followed by a rise in incidents occurring at customs points."[209]

An estimated 3 billion to 6 billion US dollars' worth of Egyptian antiquities have been smuggled out of the country since 2011.[210] According to one study,

> there are several potential smuggling routes departing Egypt, some via Libya (and then across the Mediterranean), others traversing the Eastern Desert to Port Safaga. Removal of objects via tunnels to Gaza is another possibility, but northeast Sinai is heavily policed. The detected looting corridors suggest that the looted goods end up in port cities (Alexandria and Port Said) for easier shipping; a police operation in Spain found 2,200 objects hidden in vases in a shipping container from Alexandria.[211]

Reports suggest that families that own or control some of the tunnels to Gaza kept trying to reopen them.[212] Efforts were made by Israel, Egypt, and Hamas to stop this—not least because there was an established crossing point between Egypt and Gaza at Rafah that was opened in February 2021.[213] But with the war between Israel and Hamas in Gaza that kicked off following Hamas's October 7, 2023, terrorist attack into southern Israel, there is more scrutiny on what is passing through these tunnels than at any time in recent memory. In January 2024, Israel pressed Egypt to cut off Hamas smuggling routes, with Israeli authorities complaining to Cairo that Hamas has used the Philadelphi Corridor to smuggle weapons and people through underground tunnels.[214] Between 2021 and 2023, smuggling across Israel's border with Egypt (and Jordan), primarily involving drugs or guns, increased significantly.[215]

One case that gained international attention was the 2012 seizure of two Egyptian sarcophagi that turned up in an antiquities shop in Jerusalem. "The painted wooden sarcophagi, described as 'breathtaking' by the Israel Antiquities Authority, had been sawed in half so they could be smuggled in a suitcase. . . . The objects were returned to Egypt in 2016 by Israeli authorities, just two of several dozen repatriated by Israel since the 2011 revolution."[216] It is difficult to know if this kind of vandalism in the trafficking process is widespread. It is perhaps more prevalent in the lower ends of the market where the emphasis is on getting it out of the country rather than protecting its value and maximizing the profit. Certainly, as Paul observed, "large scale items . . . take immense effort and resources to move under the radar, often making their way through transit countries like Israel, Qatar, and the UAE, or to major market regions like the U.S., U.K., and Western Europe."[217] In this connection, the United States now accounts for 43 percent of "the global art and antiquities market," making it a very attractive final destination for many of these rare items.[218]

At the same time, it bears emphasis that participants in the illicit antiquities market vary enormously—in knowledge, resources, connections, and motives. In some cases, it is as simple as people excavating in their homes in the hope that they will find something valuable. At the other end of the spectrum in terms of sophistication are the large-scale organizations and networks that are able not only to acquire items of value, but also to export them to countries where they can be sold at an enormous profit. At this stage, antiquities trafficking is simply the illegal variation of legitimate trade. As such it requires that the commodities themselves are laundered—that is, that they appear to be legitimate and not the result of theft, looting, or other illicit acquisition. The more sophisticated antiquities traffickers and brokers are also able to provide false provenance of one kind or another through connections to document forgery. This laundering process, as conceptualized by A. J. G. Tijhuis, is similar to the mechanism of a lock in shipping: "a lock bridges the gap between two levels, and . . . is . . . a metaphor for the gap between the legitimate and illicit market. These two markets do not collide but smoothly connect through the lock. And the lock itself cannot be pinpointed to belong to either the legal or illegal domain."[219] Moreover, "this transformation is either facilitated by certain unique individuals, legitimate organizations, or jurisdictions. In many cases these three are combined to bridge the gap between illicit and legitimate."[220] As a result, stolen or looted antiquities are provided with a false provenance and integrated into the legal market, making them difficult, if not impossible, to recover and return to the rightful owner or owners.

Social media also facilitates the trafficking of antiquities. As one organization noted, "social media has facilitated the explosive growth of the illegal antiquities trade. A global web of traders, traffickers, and even terrorists use platforms like Facebook and WhatsApp to buy and sell looted antiquities."[221] One counter-trafficking project is "tracking more than 120 groups on Facebook with a combined membership of more than two million members where plundered artifacts are marketed and traded."[222] There have also been some recent seizures and arrests that provide interesting snapshots into the trafficking process as a whole:

- In 2017, Ladislav Otakar Skakal, Italy's former honorary consul in Luxor, attempted to smuggle 21,855 artefacts—including 21,000 golden coins, "151 miniature figurines, five mummy masks, 11 pottery vessels, three ceramic tiles dating to the Islamic period and a wooden sarcophagus"—in a container from Alexandria to Salerno.[223] The container was supposedly under diplomatic auspices but was seized by Italian authorities. In January 2020, Skakal was sentenced in absentia to fifteen years' imprisonment.[224] It was also discovered that "the antiquities were smuggled with the aid of Raouf Ghali, the brother of former Hosni Mubarak–era finance minister Youssef Ghali."[225] The items were returned to Egypt by the Italian authorities.
- In January 2019, a cartouche of King Amenhotep I, was retrieved from an auction house in Britain after being discovered on an international auction website. "Steps were then taken to stop the sale and withdraw the listing."[226] It was not clear when the cartouche had been smuggled out of Egypt and into Britain.
- In July 2020, Ashraf Omar Eldarir, a US citizen from Brooklyn, was indicted for smuggling Egyptian cultural property into the United States. As an Immigration and Customs Enforcement release noted, "on Jan. 22, 2020, Eldarir arrived at JFK from Egypt with three checked suitcases" and a false declaration that he had only 300 dollars-worth of goods.[227] The suitcases actually contained "590 bubble and foam-wrapped Egyptian antiquities. When the protective wrapping was opened, loose sand and dirt spilled out, and some of the items smelled of wet earth, indicators that the artifacts had been recently excavated."[228] The items included "gold amulets from a funerary set; a relief with the cartouche of a Ptolemaic king that was, originally part of a royal building or temple; wooden tomb model figures with linen garments adhering dating to approximately 1900 BCE, and two complete Roman period funerary stelae of the type found at Kom abu Bellou in Egypt."[229]
- In June 2021, France returned 114 artifacts smuggled from Egypt.[230] Egyptian police arrested a former Mubarak-era member

of parliament, Alaa Hassanin, whom they believed had been responsible for the illegal export of the pieces.[231] The authorities also seized 201 Pharaonic, Greek, and Roman artifacts, including "two wooden tablets engraved with hieroglyphics, 36 statues of various lengths, 52 copper coins believed to be from the Greek and Roman periods . . . three black basalt plates" that were in a Cairo warehouse.[232] A few days later they also arrested a major businessman, Hassan Rateb, and seventeen others.[233] Reportedly, Rateb had funded illegal excavations carried out by Hassanin and his people.[234]

- In September 2022, investigators in New York City seized twenty-seven antiquities from the Metropolitan Museum of Art (Met), valued at more than $13 million. The items passed through the custody of known antiquities traffickers; six of these artifacts will be returned to Egypt, with the rest being sent back to Italy.[235] In September 2023, German art dealer Serop Simonian, the alleged leader of a suspected Egyptian antiquities trafficking ring, was arrested and sent to France.[236] Simonian is believed to be responsible for trafficking a gold sarcophagus and other antiquities to the Met, as well as antiquities that were smuggled to the Louvre Abu Dhabi.
- In September 2023, it was revealed that the British Museum purchased an ancient Egyptian artifact from a dealer with a conviction for smuggling antiquities out of the country. The museum allegedly bought a *shabti*, a figurine found in ancient Egyptian tombs, from Mousa Khouli, the operator of a New York–based auction house. According to *The National*, Khouli pleaded guilty to buying and smuggling Egyptian antiquities, including coffins, funerary boats, and limestone figures, according to the US Attorney's Office for the Eastern District of New York.[237]

As these cases suggest, there are arrests, some of them of relatively prominent people who have become involved in antiquities smuggling. In 2019 the government arrested 930 people for looting.[238] Although this might appear to be a step forward, one commentary suggested that it was in part a diversionary tactic indicating "an increased interest on the part of the government to highlight looting for objects as the cause of site destruction, rather than the equally widespread destruction of sites through unauthorized and unchecked building and road construction."[239] In this sense, the situation is very similar to that in Libya, where building has posed real problems for the protection of cultural heritage. Still, even with a limited capacity, the Egyptian government is attempting to make progress. Over the past decade, Egypt has signed bilateral agreements that have helped recover antiquities with countries such as Chile, Cyprus, Ecuador, Guatemala, Greece, Italy, Jordan, Lebanon, Peru, Saudi Arabia, Spain, and Switzerland.[240]

Illicit Financial Flows

It is relatively easy to find broad details about illicit financial flows (IFFs) out of Egypt; it is much more difficult, however, to drill down and peel back the myriad layers of opacity. Yet some points are very clear. "Egypt stands out in the magnitude of illicit flows. IFFs from Egypt are estimated to have reached US$105.2 billion, constituting 14.7 percent of the total illicit outflows from Africa."[241] Indeed, "Egypt ranked third in Africa, after Nigeria and South Africa for the exportation of illicit capital in the period of 1980–2."[242] Egypt also topped the ranking among North African countries for illicit outflows and, along with Algeria, accounted for 66 percent of the illicit outflows from North Africa.[243] This reflected the nature of authoritarian governments and their tendencies towards kleptocracy. Mubarak and his family and cronies were perhaps less blatant in their corruption than Ben Ali and his family and entourage in Tunisia, but they nevertheless exploited control of the state apparatus in much the same way, amassing personal fortunes, significant portions of which were moved outside the country. The Mubarak government operated with impunity, controlling the organs of the state and accountable to no higher power, thus enabling corruption among the leadership's inner circle. Some of these outflows were moved into offshore tax havens and bank secrecy jurisdiction. According to one report, the outflows between 1970 and 2013 to the top five recipient jurisdictions were, perhaps unsurprisingly, as follows:

- Cayman Islands, US$5,818 million
- British Virgin Islands, US$2,738 million
- Panama, US$1,358
- Luxemburg, US$1,037 million
- Bahamas, US$ 276 million[244]

Although some of this might have been corporate funds, it is hard to avoid the conclusion that much of it derived from corruption and kleptocracy. Unfortunately, efforts to curtail these flows and recover assets that have been moved from Egypt are hindered by several factors, including limited political will and technical capabilities, the absence of a clear and effective strategy for systematic asset recovery, and the lack of access to tax information from the free zones discussed below.

The other forms of financial flows that typically require consideration are laundering the proceeds of crime and the financing of terrorism. Somewhat surprisingly, there is not much concern over these issues. Egypt was not even included in part of the 2019, 2020, or 2021 International Narcotics Control Strategy Report (INCSR) dealing with money laundering. Whether this was a political decision or simply that Egypt was not on the US radar in terms of money laundering is uncertain. The 2018 INCSR observed that although Egypt was not considered a regional financial center or a major hub for money laundering, it did have vulnerabilities.[245] The report noted that "Egypt remains vulnerable by virtue of its large informal, cash-based economy. There are estimates that as much as two-thirds of the population does not have bank accounts, and the informal economy accounts for approximately 40 percent of the GDP. Consequently, extensive use of cash is common."[246]

A second vulnerability comes from the prevalence of the illicit markets in drugs, people, organs, antiquities, and arms discussed above. Although it is impossible to offer a ballpark assessment, let alone a precise figure regarding the proceeds of criminal activities in Egypt, the amount is clearly substantial. A third potential vulnerability that is little discussed is the hawala system, which facilitates private, unregulated, informal financial transfers outside the formal banking system. A fourth vulnerability is what the IMF described as onshore or domestic tax havens that in Egypt are known as free zones and operate largely outside the remit of the Egyptian Tax Authority.[247] The zones facilitate tax avoidance and, because the companies operating within them have both discretion and opacity, could readily be used for trade-based money laundering. The final vulnerability is that "the Egyptian military owns business enterprises that are in almost every sector and produce an extremely wide area of services and goods. It runs hotels, sea resorts, and apartment buildings, along with lavish villas. It owns cement, steel, jeep, fertilizer, home appliances, pasta, and other factories; runs gas stations; and constructs toll highways."[248] Moreover, in some respects, the military is privileged with nearly 600 properties exempt from real estate taxes.[249] The military is omnipotent and this, combined with the lack of oversight or transparency, provides a fertile environment for corruption and associated money laundering.

Although there is an anti-money-laundering system in place, these structural factors almost certainly minimize or undermine its effectiveness.

Moreover, the system itself has several weaknesses—especially in terms of prosecutions and convictions.[250] The low number of convictions in particular means that there is little to deter money laundering[251]—which is even more significant given the scope of illicit markets in Egypt. Although Egypt has made serious efforts to meet Financial Action Task Force requirements and standards, the US Department of State really does need to include the country in future INCSRs on money laundering.

Conclusion

Egypt has a major problem with organized crime and illicit markets, some of which are highly coercive and exploitative. Yet it seems to be doing little about them apart from adopting highly repressive approaches that, in many respects, are counterproductive. According to some scholars, the social contract in Egypt is in danger of failing, and for many it has failed already. Expectations after the Arab Spring raised political consciousness without materially improving the lives of the vast majority of Egyptians.[252] Sisi's stranglehold over the apparatus of the state, including the economy, continues to benefit his direct patronage network while failing ordinary Egyptians, pushing many into the shadows.

The state, with both highly criminalized security forces and a powerful military, is part of the problem rather than part of the solution. State-embedded criminal actors are perhaps more powerful than the Organized Crime Index acknowledges. The issue, therefore, is how long the military dictatorship will endure if the repressive government continues to face economic constraints. It is certainly feasible that it will increasingly seek to rely on the proceeds of crime as a way of sustaining itself and maintaining regime legitimacy.

Notes

1. Stacher, *Watermelon Democracy*, p. xiv.
2. Ibid., p. xvii.
3. Ibid.
4. Bertelsmann Transformation Index (BTI), *Egypt Country Report 2020*, p. 3.
5. Ibid., p. 4.
6. Ibid.
7. ENACT, *Organized Crime Index 2019—Egypt*, p. 1.
8. Ibid.
9. Ibid.
10. Revkin, "Egyptian State Unravels."

11. Ibid.
12. Anonymous interview of Sinai-based Egyptian journalist conducted by Jason M. Blazakis, March 19, 2021.
13. Bertelsmann Transformation Index (BTI), *Egypt Country Report 2022*.
14. Interview conducted by authors.
15. Interpol and ENACT, *Illicit Goods Trafficking*, p. 15.
16. Ibid.
17. Ibid.
18. Library of Congress Country Studies and CIA *World Factbook*, "Egypt Drug Trafficking."
19. Ibid.
20. Ibid.
21. Ibid.
22. Narconon, "Drug Addiction in Egypt."
23. Ibid.
24. Ibid.
25. Schwartzstein, "Egypt's New Drug Addiction."
26. Ibid.
27. Ibid.
28. Curnow, "Tramadol Addiction Sweeping Egypt."
29. Ibid.
30. Ibid.
31. UNODC, *World Drug Report: 2021—Booklet 3*, p. 91.
32. Ibid.
33. UNODC, *World Drug Report: 2021—Booklet 5*, p. 47.
34. France 24, "Voodoo and Strox."
35. Ibid.
36. Ibid.
37. Ibid.
38. UNODC, *World Drug Report: 2021—Booklet 5*, p. 47.
39. Interpol and ENACT, *Illicit Goods Trafficking*, p. 16.
40. Ibid.
41. Ibid.
42. Ibid.
43. Micallef, *Shifting Sands*, p. 18.
44. Ibid., p. 6.
45. Ibid., p. 18.
46. New Arab, "Egypt Navy Busts 170kg."
47. Ibid.
48. Egypt Today, "Interior Ministry Foils Attempt."
49. Al-Youm, "Heroin Trafficker Arrested in Sharqiya."
50. Ahram Online, "Egypt Foils Attempt to Smuggle."
51. Al-Youm, "Heroin Trafficker Arrested in Sharqiya."
52. Ibid.
53. Xinhua, "Egypt Seizes Foreign Ship."
54. Ibid.
55. Ibid.
56. Fabian, "IDF Seizes $2.5 Million."
57. Levitt and Von Thaden, "Guns, Drugs, and Smugglers."
58. The claim is made in Interpol and ENACT, *Illicit Goods Trafficking*, p. 15.
59. Ayesh, "Arabic Press Review."

60. Ibid.
61. Ibid.
62. Ibid.
63. El-Din, "Egyptian Judge Sentenced to Life."
64. Cairo Scene, "Confessions of an Egyptian Drug Dealer."
65. Perry, "Looking for Hashish in Cairo?"
66. Ibid.
67. ENACT, *Organised Crime Index–Africa 2019.*
68. Perry, "Looking for Hashish in Cairo?"
69. Ibid.
70. Ibid.
71. Ibid.
72. Ibid.
73. Ibid.
74. El-Dine, "Eastern and Western Egyptian Borders."
75. Rittel and Webber, "Dilemmas in a General Theory of Planning."
76. Columb, *Trading Life*, pp. 65–66.
77. Ibid., p. 74.
78. Yahya, *Irregular Migration or Human Trafficking?*
79. Human Rights Watch, *World Report 2021*, p. 225.
80. Ibid., p. 225.
81. Van Reisen, Estefanos, and Reim, "Human Trafficking in the Sinai," p. 21.
82. Ibid.
83. Ibid., p. 28.
84. Ibid.
85. Ibid., p. 20.
86. Ibid.
87. Quoted in ibid., p. 36.
88. Ibid.
89. Ibid.
90. Quoted in ibid., p. 37.
91. Ibid., p. 38.
92. Ibid., p. 39.
93. Ibid., pp. 39–40.
94. Ibid., p. 47.
95. Ibid., p. 49.
96. Ibid.
97. Ibid.
98. Columb, *Trading Life*, p. 86.
99. Ibid., pp. 86–87.
100. Operational Data Portal, "Mediterranean Situation."
101. Bird, "Human Smuggling in Africa," p. 19.
102. Colomb, *Trading Life: Organ Trafficking*, p. 86.
103. Ibid., p. 87.
104. Bird, "Human Smuggling in Africa," p. 20.
105. Ibid.
106. Columb, *Trading Life*, p. 92.
107. Völkel, "Livin' on the Edge."
108. Columb, *Trading Life*, p. 99.
109. Ibid.
110. Völkel, "Livin' on the Edge."

111. Ibid.
112. Ibid.
113. Bird, "Human Smuggling in Africa," p. 46.
114. Al-Masry Al-Youm, "Illegal Immigration from Egypt."
115. Bird, "Human Smuggling in Africa," p. 47.
116. Ibid.
117. Ibid., p. 48.
118. US Department of State, "2023 Trafficking in Persons Report: Egypt."
119. See Columb, *Trading Life*.
120. Ibid., p. 2.
121. Ibid., p. 5.
122. Ibid.
123. Ibid., p. 7.
124. Ibid., p. 12.
125. Ibid., p. 52.
126. Ibid., pp. 14–15.
127. Ibid., p. 19.
128. Ibid., p. 75.
129. Ibid., p. 36.
130. Ibid., p. 48.
131. Ibid., pp. 57–58.
132. Ibid., p. 61.
133. Ibid., p. 113.
134. Ibid.
135. Ibid.
136. Ibid., p. 116.
137. Ibid.
138. Ibid., p. 117.
139. Ibid., p. 118.
140. Ibid.
141. Interview conducted by authors.
142. Quoted in Marsh, "Brothers Came Back with Weapons," p. 86.
143. Ibid., p. 86.
144. Ibid.
145. Quoted in ibid.
146. Ibid.
147. *Times of Israel*, "Egypt Confiscates Weapons."
148. Hadid and Nassar, "As Egypt Floods Gaza."
149. Frenkel, "Egypt's Gun Boom."
150. Ibid.
151. Ibid.
152. Ibid.
153. Ibid.
154. Adham, "Arms Smuggling Hub of Egypt."
155. Ibid.
156. Ibid.
157. Ibid.
158. Amer, "How Iran Smuggles Arms."
159. Raghavan, "Militant Threat Emerges."
160. Clarke, "Salafism's Rise Threatens Gaza."
161. Jumet and Gulmohamad, "Reframing the Campaign."

162. Ibid., p. 6.
163. Ashour, "Sinai's Insurgency," p. 557.
164. Tahrir Institute for Middle East Policy, "Sinai Tribes in Egypt's War," p. 1.
165. Mapping Militants Project, "Islamic State—Sinai Province."
166. Jumet and Gulmohamad, "Reframing the Campaign," p. 14.
167. Byman, "Is Hamas Winning?" p. 67.
168. Abu Zaid, "Egypt Steps Up Support."
169. Levy, "Egypt's Counterinsurgency Success in Sinai."
170. Ashour, "Sinai's Insurgency," p. 546.
171. Mapping Militants Project, "Islamic State—Sinai Province."
172. McManus, "Army Is Not the Winner."
173. McManus, "ISIS in the Sinai."
174. Meneghini and Milani, "Maghreb Route," p. 12.
175. Ibid., p. 25.
176. Ibid., p. 14.
177. Sarah El Masry, "Smoke and Mirrors: Smuggled Cigarettes."
178. Ibid.
179. Ibid.
180. Ibid.
181. See World Health Organization Regional Office for the Eastern Mediterranean, "Egypt: Tobacco."
182. Iraq, "Egypt Signs Protocol."
183. Katie A. Paul, "Cultural Racketeering in Egypt," p. 21.
184. Ibid.
185. Ibid.
186. Ibid.
187. See, for example, Williams and Woessner, "Real Threat of Nuclear Smuggling."
188. Parcak et al., "Evidence of Archaeological Site Looting," p. 190.
189. Ibid., pp. 191, 198.
190. Ibid., p. 191.
191. Ibid., p. 193.
192. Ibid., p. 195.
193. Ibid., pp. 199–200.
194. Ibid., p. 196.
195. Ibid.
196. Fitz Gibbon, "Egypt's Brutal Regime."
197. Ibid.
198. Ibid.
199. On the more general beliefs about gold and antiquities, see ibid.
200. Tassie, De Trafford, and van Wetering, "Egypt's Heritage in Times of Conflict," p. 40.
201. Ibid.
202. Ibid., p. 17.
203. Ibid., p. 33.
204. Ibid., pp. 33–34.
205. Ibid., p. 25.
206. Paul, "Cultural Racketeering in Egypt," p. 23.
207. Ibid., p. 26.
208. Ibid.
209. Tassie, De Trafford, and van Wetering, "Egypt's Heritage in Times of Conflict," p. 34.

210. Parcak et al., "Evidence of Archaeological Site Looting," p. 200.
211. Jalal, "Despite Egyptian Campaign, Gaza."
212. Ibid.
213. Said and Keller-Lynn, "Israel Presses Egypt."
214. Levitt and Von Thaden, "Guns, Drugs, and Smugglers."
215. Paul, "Repatriating the Past."
216. Ibid.
217. Ibid.
218. Tijhuis, "Trafficking Problem: A Criminological Perspective," p. 89.
219. Ibid.
220. See Alliance to Counter Crime Online, "Plundered Heritage."
221. Ibid.
222. France 24, "Ex-minister's Brother Jailed."
223. Al Arabiya News, "Egypt Jails Ex-Italian Diplomat."
224. Ibid.
225. BBC News, "Egypt Recovers Smuggled Artefact."
226. US Immigration and Customs Enforcement, "Brooklyn Man Indicted."
227. Ibid.
228. Ibid.
229. Reuters, "Authorities Recover 114 Smuggled Antiquities."
230. Nation Press Services, "Former Egypt MP Held
231. Ibid.
232. Ahram Online, "Renowned Egyptian Businessman Arrested."
233. Ibid.
234. Mashberg and Bowley, "Investigators Have Seized 27 Antiquities."
235. Azimi, "Louvre Abu Dhabi."
236. Tahir, "British Museum Bought Artefact."
237. Fitz Gibbon, "Egypt's Brutal Regime."
238. Ibid.
239. El Sawy, Mahmoud, and Aldroubi, "Stealing from History."
240. Khodary, *Illicit Financial Flows*, p. iii.
241. Ibid.
242. Ibid.
243. Ibid., p. 5.
244. US Department of State, *International Narcotics Control Strategy Report*, Volume 2 (March 2018), p. 99.
245. Ibid.
246. Khodary, *Illicit Financial Flows*, p. 5.
247. Abul-Magd, "Egypt's Military Business."
248. Iraq, "Egypt Signs Protocol."
249. Khodary, *Illicit Financial Flows*, p. 16.
250. MENAFATF, *Anti-Money Laundering: Egypt*, pp. 4, 7.
251. Ibid., p. 7.
252. Ibrahim, "Dynamics of Egyptian Social Contract."

7

The Mediterranean Connection: Governance and Crime

DESPITE ASPIRATIONS FOR REFORM AMONG THE CITIZENS OF NORTH AFRICAN countries, the promise of the Arab Spring has wholly dissipated, only to be replaced by disillusionment, resignation, and a high degree of apathy. Citizens in the five countries we examined have few rights or freedoms, while economic opportunities are minimal, and prospects for the future remain dismal. Yet, this is not due simply to organized crime and illicit economies. The fundamental problems in North Africa are political and economic, not criminal; above all else, the key issue is governance or, rather, the lack thereof. The daunting and unfortunate reality is that no North African state is good at governance or provides the resources necessary to enhance or improve its record. As such, it is not just about a lack of capabilities but also a seeming absence of political will. Accordingly, this chapter initially offers a comparative summary of criminal networks and illicit economies in Morocco, Algeria, Libya, Egypt, and Tunisia. It then looks at issues of governance and social contracts across North Africa before offering a brief and, unfortunately, bleak assessment of the prospects for the future of this pivotal region.

Analyzing criminal economies is challenging because criminal activities are intended to be surreptitious. Unlike terrorist groups, which promote their ideologies and use attacks as a form of propaganda, criminal organizations seek to operate clandestinely, obfuscating the various nodes within local and transnational networks. Similarly, research on illicit economies attempts to highlight transactions and flows that deliberately reside in the shadows. To overcome such challenges, this study relied on a broad range of sources, including those produced by international organizations and specialized nongovernmental organizations—

especially the Global Initiative Against Transnational Organized Crime, whose analysts consistently provide exceptional scholarly ethnographic research conducted at the national and local levels. Their work is inspirational and informative, and we draw heavily on it in the current study. Moreover, we leverage community access to detailed articles reporting from on the ground, piecing together a kaleidoscope that provides insights into the complex drivers, facilitators, and inhibitors of criminal behaviors and illicit economies.

Accordingly, this comparative analysis structured each country section similarly, with an introductory overview that explores state capacity and resilience and provides a foundation for understanding the inhibitors and the facilitators of smuggling and trafficking. One of the overarching findings is that while the five North African countries face some common challenges in terms of organized crime and illicit economies, there are also important variations. The countries vary in terms of which illegal markets are most prominent, which commodities are smuggled or trafficked, and the extent to which corruption is an important facilitator. There are also variations in the capacities of the governments concerned to combat these activities. The activities themselves are summarized in Table 7.1.

The table highlights both similarities and differences among the five countries in North Africa. Morocco is a transit country, a destination country for irregular migrants, as well as a point of origin for others. As elsewhere in the region, economic and social issues are significant drivers of Moroccans attempting to flee the country for Europe. Morocco is the only country in North Africa that directly borders Europe through the Spanish enclaves of Ceuta and Melilla. Following the storming of the Melilla border fence in June 2022, the European Union and Morocco announced a joint anti-trafficking collaboration to strengthen cooperation between their government agencies tasked with border security.[1] Morocco is the only country in the region that is both a major drug producer and exporter with bicoastal access to enable smuggling and trafficking. An astonishing 80 percent of hashish consumed in Europe transits through the Strait of Gibraltar. Cigarette smuggling, however, is not nearly as pervasive in Morocco as in other North African countries, including neighboring Algeria. Nor is Morocco plagued by arms trafficking networks, as is the case in Libya. It does, however, struggle with making progress in combating money laundering.

Illegal gold mining and oil smuggling are among the most lucrative criminal markets in Algeria, along with the drug trade (especially cannabis) and arms trafficking, which became a much more germane

Table 7.1 Summary of Trafficking Activities per Country

Country	Drugs	Humans	Arms	Other	Illicit Financial Flows
Morocco	Major producer of cannabis/hashish; transshipment point for cocaine	Point of origin; transit country; destination for migrants; routes through Ceuta and Melilla and to the Canary Islands	Limited arms smuggling and trafficking	Illegal sand extraction; stolen vehicles	Some money laundering and bulk cash smuggling
Algeria	Transshipment points for European Union; domestic consumption of cannabis, cocaine, synthetics, and pharmaceuticals	Significant levels of human smuggling/trafficking of irregular migrants; strategic gateway for migrants to European Union and throughout North Africa	Impacted by spillover of arms, weapons, and ammunition from Libya	Producer of licit cigarettes that are smuggled; major node in illicit cigarette smuggling networks	Low-level and high-level corruption; growing problem with money laundering
Libya	Transshipment country for cannabis, cocaine, and pharmaceuticals, including tramadol	Supply side for human smuggling is competitive; growing problem with detention of migrants and kidnapping for ransom (KFR)	Epicenter for arms smuggling and trafficking of small arms and light weapons in the region	Rampant oil smuggling; cigarette smuggling "on steroids"; and antiquities, looting, and smuggling	Ongoing civil war and governance challenges exacerbate illicit economic flows

continues

Table 7.1 continued

Country	Drugs	Humans	Arms	Other	Illicit Financial Flows
Egypt	Important transit hub for European-bound heroin; growing domestic consumption market; proliferation of counterfeit pharmaceuticals	Smuggling and trafficking of humans intersects and overlaps; natural magnet for migrants from Sudan, South Sudan, Eritrea, Ethiopia, and Somalia	Bordered by Libya on one side and Gaza on the other; Bedouin smuggling culture; high demand for weapons in Sinai Peninsula	Industrial-scale antiquities theft and smuggling; growing illicit transplant market for organs	Corruption and kleptocracy remain major issues; ineffective anti-money-laundering efforts
Tunisia	Cannabis is most prevalent, while cocaine and heroin less so; growing market for pharmaceuticals	Proximity to Sicily makes Tunisia an attractive human smuggling destination; facilitated by fishermen; government struggles to prosecute or convict traffickers and smugglers	Arms trafficking is less of an issue in relative terms but a definite challenge in absolute terms	Due to significant arbitrage opportunities and high levels of poverty, contraband smuggling is rampant	Trade-based money laundering; widespread corruption within government and political elites

issue following the collapse of Libya as sophisticated weapons flowed in all directions across Libya's borders. Areas of weakness include the judicial system and the country's anti-money-laundering system, which suffers from glaring gaps and shortcomings. Cigarette smuggling is a dominant issue in Algeria, with the illicit trade benefiting terrorist groups, including those linked to al-Qaeda, who are paid to provide armed protection to smugglers. In the summer of 2022, the United States called upon Algeria to dedicate more resources to curbing human smuggling.[2] This includes greater transparency from Algeria's law enforcement entities that stand accused of corruption and malfeasance, including the mistreatment of migrants. Even Algeria's focus on securing the border and deporting migrants back to Mali and Niger is unlikely to be enough to stem the tide of migrants in the future. Ongoing instability throughout the Sahel, including an uptick in violence perpetrated by Jama'at Nusrat al-Islam wal-Muslimin and Islamic State in the Greater Sahara, sometimes referred to as Islamic State Sahel Province, could lead to problems in Algeria, if spillover violence emanating from Mali continues to spread across the region's relatively porous borders.

Tunisia is no longer the poster child for the Arab Spring. Since coming to power in October 2019, Kais Saied has implemented some disastrous policies and made migrants from sub-Saharan Africa into scapegoats for the ills currently plaguing the country.[3] Terrorist attacks on the Bardo Museum and the Sousse resort damaged the tourism trade, as did the Covid-19 pandemic. An attack in May 2023 targeting a synagogue in Djerba, Tunisia, further added to safety concerns.[4] Tunisia remains under pressure from both the European Union and the International Monetary Fund, dealing with austerity measures and the resulting complications. These measures have led to further growth in the informal economy, which already accounted for a significant portion of the country's gross domestic product. Drug trafficking and human smuggling both remain prevalent, and given the dire economic conditions, authorities frequently look the other way rather than cracking down on those participating in the shadow economy. Permitting illicit economic activity relieves pressure on the government, attenuates social violence, and retards the rural exodus. Illicit economies reduce unemployment and offer sources of income to people living in parts of the country suffering from a dearth of public investment. Many of these areas, including Ben Gardane, have become hubs for foreign fighters, which inevitably breeds further instability and violence.

Libya is still divided between rival administrations with no internationally recognized government. Both centers of power maintain close ties to a range of violent nonstate actors, including militia groups and criminal networks. Accordingly, both the Libyan National Army (LNA) and the Government of National Unity continue to clash. The LNA's leader, Khalifa Haftar, maintains connections to the Wagner Group and the Rapid Support Forces in Sudan and is tied to a range of illicit activities, including arms trafficking.[5] Haftar has also been backed by Saudi Arabia and the United Arab Emirates in his quest to consolidate control over the country. The political process in Libya is deeply interconnected with organized crime, with criminal proceeds and government finances often indistinguishable from one another. Arms trafficking is paramount, with the initial diffusion of arms to neighboring countries followed by arms coming into the country as outside states vie for influence. The criminal methods employed by illicit networks vary depending on direction and terrain. Mafia-style militia groups and competing warlords are deeply embedded in criminal markets beyond arms, including drug trafficking, human smuggling, human trafficking, cigarette smuggling, and illicit oil smuggling. Since 2015, the European Union has provided hundreds of millions of dollars for Libya to stem the flow of migrants coming from the country. According to the Brookings Institution, "the EU approach has empowered both state and 'hybrid' militias to kill and torture migrants with impunity."[6] Militias run brutal detention centers throughout the country, which serve as a shadow immigration system funded by the European Union. The system repeatedly victimizes vulnerable migrants from sub-Saharan Africa[7] while empowering and enriching militias, exacerbating corruption, and contributing to widespread human rights abuses.[8]

Egypt, too, is a destination and transit country for irregular migrants from across Africa, including Sudan, Eritrea, South Sudan, Ethiopia, and Somalia—especially given the enduring conflicts and instability in these countries. Fighting in Sudan, which erupted in April 2023 and continued unabated, has only exacerbated the refugee flow to surrounding countries. By June 2023, Egypt had already taken in over 150,000 Sudanese fleeing from fighting between the Rapid Support Forces and the Sudanese military;[9] by the end of December 2023, UNHCR estimated that 409,000 Sudanese had fled to Egypt.[10] This dispossessed population also creates an expanded set of targets for illegal kidney transplants. Furthermore, given its history and wealth of historic commodities, Egypt is and will remain, a major source of antiquities smuggling. Highly valuable and increasingly vulnerable antiquities and cultural heritage sites have been plundered over the years, facilitated by rampant corruption and bribery. Illegal excavation is carried out by individuals, gangs, and mafia-style groups. Such looting on an industrial scale has even been labeled cultural racketeering. One area where Egypt remains under the radar, however, is in the smuggling and trafficking of drugs. In an interview undertaken for this book, as noted in Chapter 6, Egypt has become "a key hub for trafficking drugs coming from Asian countries like Afghanistan bound for Europe using sea routes."[11] In addition, locally grown marijuana and derivative products (hashish) are smuggled to Europe using the same routes, while the synthetic drugs trade in Egypt is also expanding.

In sum, the countries of North Africa have problems with organized crime and illicit economies that are significant and substantial but—except for Libya—not overwhelming. Yet, this is not a problem of overtly weak or fragile states, as is the case, for example, in Central and South America. Four of the five countries—to one degree or another—have a "fierce state," while in the outlier, Libya, the fierce state under Muammar Gaddafi has been replaced by fierce factions. Competing militias and rival power groups engage in both instrumental and anomic violence as they seek to claim the mantle of statehood and the access to state resources that go with it.[12] For their part, Egypt and Algeria superficially appear very different: the Mubarak regime was overthrown in Egypt, whereas Bouteflika survived until 2019 and was only forced to step down by the military because of the Hirak. Nevertheless, both countries, in essence, are military dictatorships, with the key difference being that one is blatant, and the other is more covert and subtle in its control over the country. In this connection, Algeria's reform of press freedoms in late 2023 is an example of change that is cosmetic at best. Presented by members of the government as allowing independent journalism, it does not prevent the government from punishing critics of the regime even while ostensibly allowing them independence. As one commentary noted, "in reality, the new media regulations will probably amount to little more than a public relations maneuver."[13] Indeed, Algeria has managed to maintain a façade of civilian rule and a thin veneer of reform but ultimately remains a coercive and corrupt state in which disaffection is high, and many people are voting with their feet by trying to leave.

Ironically, the fierce states in North Africa are directing much of their fierceness toward immigrants who are seeking to enter and stay in the countries or to use the country as a springboard to Europe. The problem for North Africa—as discussed in Chapter 1—is that it has become an extended buffer state and even a forward defense for Fortress Europe—a process encouraged by European Union states, especially Italy and Spain. In fact, the migration issue has all the characteristics of a "wicked problem" that is resistant to solutions.[14] European governments have restricted opportunities for legal migration, asylum seekers coming to Britain have been sent to Rwanda, and irregular migrants who have made it to Europe are increasingly being returned to North Africa. Migrants from sub-Saharan Africa already in North Africa face the prospect of being rounded up, incarcerated, and brutally expelled into the badlands of the Sahel. Migrant deaths at sea have become common, but so have deaths on land. Moreover, leaders in both Algeria and Tunisia have used inflammatory language against migrants, encouraging hatred and even violence. There are few safe spaces for migrants in North Africa. Morocco is probably the most hospitable, but even in Morocco, migrants face hardship and risk.

Fierceness is one thing; legitimacy is quite another. For states to be legitimate, there must be a common agreement between rulers and ruled on the principles and procedures that frame political life and the exercise and transfer of both power and authority. In addition, states must meet the needs of their citizens and engage in efficient and effective economic management if they are to elicit and maintain the loyalty of their citizens. They must also be inclusive rather than exclusive and provide for the security of their populations. As Troy Thomas and Stephen Kiser observed, "citizens desire safety and security, a relatively equal application of justice, and a generally legitimate distribution of goods and resources. When these are not delivered, the state loses legitimacy . . . the first step in the failure of governance is taken."[15] In a similar vein, although autocratic states are cosmetically strong, according to Robert Rotberg, they also have underlying weaknesses in terms of their inability to provide public goods for their citizens.[16] Indeed, Nazih Ayubi, author of *Overstating the Arab State*, drew an important distinction between fierce states and strong states, arguing that many Arab states are fierce states in that they can resort to raw coercion to preserve themselves but lack both infrastructure power and ideological legitimacy and therefore, in essence, are weak states.[17] Such states are prone to develop alliances with criminal organizations.

Rent-seeking and the construction of patronage networks by government elites meshes with the use of corruption by criminal and drug trafficking organizations seeking to extend their influence into law enforcement agencies and the higher reaches of government. Corruption is used by criminals to obtain support and protection as well as information and knowledge, and thereby to neutralize the instruments of social control. Put in systemic terms, drug trafficking and criminal organizations flourish where state capacity is weak or nonexistent—and despite outward appearances, the fierce states of North Africa have weak foundations. Moreover, criminals maintain a vested interest in ensuring that the state is willing to acquiesce in their activities. For its part, the political elite, anxious to continue enjoying the mutual benefits these links provide, wants them to remain private. Seen from this perspective, the tendency of autocratic governments to limit the degree of openness is intensified by the desire of individual members of the government apparatus—who are benefiting from corruption and/or links with criminal organizations—to ensure that their activities do not become the focus of public and media scrutiny. Where organized crime is deeply embedded, and organic relations exist between criminals and government officials, the entrenched interests in limiting the emergence of democratic forms of governance are enormous. Organic relationships of this kind not only pose a challenge to the integrity of state structures but also have a corrosive impact on society, eroding faith in government, increasing alienation of the population, and stunting the development of a civil society based on the rule of law.

Closely linked to this is a process identified by William Reno in which individual interests are given precedence over the collective interests of the polity.[18] These individual interests take various forms, including corruption, which seeks to use public office for private gain and diverts resources from the state to key individuals or groups—a process that has a corrosive effect on authority and legitimacy. In this connection, Robert Jackson noted that the state in Africa is regarded primarily as "an exploitable treasure trove devoid of moral value. . . . Corruption is integral rather than incidental to African politics. Self-enrichment and personal or factional aggrandizement constitute politics."[19] Moreover, mechanisms of participation and accountability are neutralized by patrimonial structures and practices and by forms of personal rule that reduce political life to connections and money.[20] Principles and policies are irrelevant, and citizen participation in political action is rendered meaningless. William Reno has compellingly highlighted the corrosive impact of all this. As he noted, corruption erodes well-functioning state institutions, thereby often provoking domestic criticism. To counter this, leaders seek loyalty through patronage relationships, typically at the expense of neglecting public goods for society.[21]

As Sarah Chayes has pointed out, however, weakness is not always what it appears. In some instances, the dominance of a predatory elite does not result in conflict but simply in a state that is weak in terms of the provision of services but both strong and adept at the extraction of rents and corrupt payments. This is most likely when there is both structured corruption and centralized control, with a high degree of consolidation at the top of the pyramid.[22] In such states, the dominance of the elites is often self-perpetuating and inhibits the emergence of powerful state institutions. State structures, processes, and activities—such as low levels of direct taxation on income or wealth—that are sometimes interpreted as evidence of state weakness are often a consequence of choices made by elites whose primary concern is with extending and perpetuating their own wealth and privilege. As Chayes argued, "acute corruption should be understood not as a failure or distortion of government but as a functioning system in which ruling networks use selected levers of power to capture specific revenue streams. This effort often overshadows ordinary activities routinely connected with running a state."[23] Under Abdelaziz Bouteflika, Algeria certainly fit this model, and it is not clear that the successor government led by Abdelmadjid Tebboune has moved far away from it. Similarly, in Egypt, the model of military capitalism lends itself to the same kind of self-serving politics. In Tunisia, in contrast, allegations and charges of political corruption have become a major instrument of the increasingly authoritarian government of Saied, which seems to be harkening back to the bad old days of the Ben Ali regime. As Saied consolidates his rule, therefore, it would not be surprising if he also sought personal wealth through the looting of the state.

Another useful way of thinking about all this is through the lens of social contracts between the government and the governed. Most scholars agree that the social contract involves an agreement on rights and obligations between the state and society: the society implicitly and explicitly provides consent to be governed in return for certain kinds of deliverables from the state. One study suggested that these typically involve three Ps: protection, provision, and participation.[24] In Libya, with Gaddafi's removal, any semblance of the social contract disappeared. Most citizens live in fear as localized militias rule their territories by repression and coercion. While aspirations for a new social contract remain, this is likely to be unattainable so long as major powerbrokers continue to strive for supremacy.

In Algeria, the social contract has been dependent on oil revenues, and as revenues fell from 2014 to 2020, the social contract frayed at the edges. Higher oil and gas prices in 2022 and 2023 made it possible once more to meet demands for provision in the short term, but an effective social contract for the long term could prove more elusive. Morocco holds greater hope. While both participation and provision remain modest, and substantial reforms are still required, King Mohammad's ability to exercise soft rather than hard power—based on the longevity and the aura of the monarchy—provides a cushion of legitimacy that helps to hold the social contract together.[25] For their part, Tunisian citizens—against a backdrop of poor economic performance and stalemated democratic institutions—have placed less emphasis on participation in the hope and expectation of greater provision. The difficulty, however, is that the government's limited resource base will set limits to this, thereby increasing the possibility of further instability.

Egypt scores well on protection but more modestly on provision and extremely poorly on participation. In January 2011, the demand was for a new social contract promoting "bread, freedom, and social justice."[26] After the chaos surrounding the short-lived presidency and military ouster of Mohamed Morsi in 2013, however, Egyptians were offered a "more exclusionary" social contract.[27] "Blaming the uprisings for the political turmoil and economic crises, deprived communities were therefore willing to accept a new social contract that not only denies their basic political rights but also undermines the socio-economic benefits guaranteed under the old populist social contract. They thus tolerated the state's failure to fulfil these socio-economic rights in exchange for political stability."[28] Indeed, the military government cut subsidies and increased energy prices while peoples' aspirations for employment remained unfulfilled. Not surprisingly, therefore, Solava Ibrahim has contended that the failures in health care and education that broke the social contract under Mubarak have still not been resolved, while economic crises have particularly hurt poor "female-headed households in urban areas and young informal workers—both suffering from high inflation and unemployment."[29] As Solava Ibrahim suggests, some reversion to a more comprehensive social contract is essential.[30] Failing this, the military regime could ultimately find itself in a situation almost identical to that which faced Mubarak.

The prognosis for the five countries of North Africa is not good. Climate change in the region itself will likely have all sorts of directly disruptive consequences, although Morocco appears to be well-situated to exploit the move to renewable energy. Both climate change and conflicts in the Sahel and sub-Saharan Africa will continue to drive the exodus of people northward, many of them in the largely futile hope of reaching Europe. The governments of North Africa are being paid by the European Union and by individual EU members to stop irregular migrants crossing the Mediterranean. Even the harsh, highly repressive approach that several of these governments have adopted, however, has not been sufficient to deter those who are already in desperate straits and are willing to take enormous risks to reach countries where they might have increased opportunities. Indeed, it is probably time to rethink irregular migration and human smuggling as criminal activities, particularly with the emergence of self-smuggling. Failing this, the exodus can only result in a massive humanitarian catastrophe that goes far beyond the deaths, drownings, and despair that are already so clear.

Notes

1. AFP/Reuters, "EU, Morocco Joint Anti-trafficking Effort."
2. *North Africa Post*, "Human Trafficking."
3. Soufan Center, "Tunisian President's Incendiary Comments."
4. Kourdi and Alam, "At Least Five Killed."
5. Soufan Center, "Haftar's Growing Criminal Enterprise."
6. Dhingra, "US Migration Policy."
7. Urbina, "Secretive Prisons Keep Migrants Out."
8. Burke and Yayboke, "Addressing Fragility in Libya."
9. Soufan Center, "Looming Disaster: Sudan's Refugees."
10. See UNHCR, "Sudan Emergency."
11. Interview conducted by authors.
12. The notion of the "fierce" state is discussed in Ayubi, *Overstating the Arab State*, especially chapter 12.
13. Serrano, "Tebboune's Media 'Reforms.'"
14. Rittel and Webber, "Dilemmas in General Theory of Planning."
15. Thomas and Kiser, *Lords of the Silk Route*, p. 45.
16. Ibid., p. 5.
17. Ayubi, *Over-stating the Arab State*.
18. Reno, "Protectors and Predators."
19. Robert H. Jackson, "Quasi-States, Dual Régimes," p. 527.
20. Flanary, "The State in Africa," p. 184.
21. Reno, "Warfare in Collapsed States."
22. Chayes, "Unrecognized Threat to International Security."
23. Ibid.
24. Loewe, Zintl, and Houdret, "Social Contract as Tool of Analysis."
25. Ibid.
26. Ibrahim, "Dynamics of Egyptian Social Contract," p. 11.
27. Ibid., p. 1.
28. Ibid., p. 11.
29. Ibid., p. 1.
30. Ibid., p. 11.

Bibliography

Abdelmoula, Mohamed Rami. "Natural Resources in Tunisia Between Scarcity, Abundance, and Waste." *As-Safir Al-Arabi*, April 9, 2022. https://assafirarabi.com/en/44453/2022/04/09/natural-resources-in-tunisia-between-scarcity-abundance-and-waste/.

Abderrahim, Tasnim. *Morocco: Irregular Migration Ebbs as Rabat Cracks Down on Human Smuggling*. Geneva: Global Initiative Against Transnational Organized Crime, July 2023.

———. *Tunisia: Increased Fragility Fuels Migration Surge*. Global Initiative Against Transnational Organized Crime, July 2023.

Abderrahmane, Abdelkader. "Curbing Tunisia's Crippling Illicit Financial Flows." Institute for Security Studies, July 6, 2022. https://issafrica.org/iss-today/curbing-tunisias-crippling-illicit-financial-flows.

———. "Illegal Sand Extraction Threatens Morocco's Tourism Economy." ENACT Africa, April 27, 2021. https://enactafrica.org/enact-observer/illegal-sand-extraction-threatens-moroccos-tourism-economy.

———. "Plunder of Algeria's Red Gold." Institute for Security Studies, January 31, 2023.

———. "Trade and Counterfeit Goods: What Will It Take To Stub Out North Africa's Illegal Tobacco Trade?" ENACT, December 14, 2022. https://enactafrica.org/enact-observer/what-will-it-take-to-stub-out-north-africas-illegal-tobacco-trade.

Abouzzohour, Yasmina. "Coping with COVID-19's Cost: The Example of Morocco." Brookings Institution, December 23, 2020.

Abouzzohour, Yasmina, and Nejla Ben Mimoune. "Algeria Must Prioritize Economic Change Amidst COVID-19 and Political Crisis." Brookings Institution, December 2, 2020.

Abul-Magd, Zeinab. "Egypt's Military Business: The Need for Change." Middle East Institute, November 9, 2015.

Abu Zaid, Mohammed. "Egypt Steps Up Support for Campaign Against Terror, Crime Groups in Sahel Region." *Arab News*, August 25, 2021.

Adenwala, Ali, Massinissa Benlakehal, and Mina Chiang. *Determinants of Anti-Trafficking Efforts Case Study: Algeria*. British Institute of International and Comparative Law, June 2022.

Adham, S. "The Arms Smuggling Hub of Egypt: The South." *Silah Report*, November 26, 2018. https://silahreport.com/2018/11/26/the-arms-smuggling-hub-of-egypt-the-south/.

Adimoha, Ronald. "Moroccan Police Seize 27.3 Tonnes of Cannabis Resin." *News Central Africa*, July 8, 2019. https://newscentral.africa/2019/07/08/moroccan-police-seize-tonnes-cannabis/.

AFP/Reuters. "EU, Morocco announce joint anti-trafficking effort." July 8, 2022.

AfricaNews. "Moroccan Opponent Maati Monjib Arrested for Money Laundering." December 29, 2020.

———. "Record Seizure of Over 31 Tonnes of Cannabis in Morocco." April 28, 2022.

———. "Tunisia: President Saied Dismisses Economy Minister." October 19, 2023.

African Network of Centers for Investigative Reporting. "Algerian Gas Deals Linked to Massive Bribery." 2016. https://panamapapers.investigativecenters.org/algeria/.

Agence France-Presse. "Algeria Jails Former Energy Boss." Voice of America: Africa, November 15, 2022.

———. "Tunisia Fishermen Become Lifesavers of the Mediterranean." Voice of America, June 16, 2019. https://www.voanews.com/africa/tunisia-fishermen-become-lifesavers-mediterranean.

Agence de Presse Africaine. "Moroccan Parliament Passes Anti-Money Laundering Bill." APA News, April 21, 2021. http://apanews.net/en/news/moroccan-parliament-passes-anti-money-laundering-bill.

Agencia EFE. "Spaniards Arrested After Police in Morocco Uncover Largest Ever Cocaine Stash." October 4, 2017. https://www.efe.com/efe/english/world/spaniards-arrested-after-police-in-morocco-uncover-largest-ever-cocaine-stash/50000262-3398928.

Agenzia Nazionale Stampa Associata (ANSA). "Arrest Warrant for Italian in Libya." August 20, 2015.

———. "Libya Extradites Italian Arms Trafficker." April 1, 2019.

Ahmed, Hamid Ould. "Algeria Blighted by Youth Unemployment Despite Recovering Oil Prices." Reuters, September 12, 2018.

Ahmed, Massood. "Bringing the Informal Sector into the Fold." *IMF Blog*, November 16, 2011.

Ahram Online. "Algeria Sentences Ex-Energy Minister to 20 Years in Prison." January 19, 2023. https://english.ahram.org.eg/News/484568.aspx.

———. "Egypt Foils Attempt to Smuggle 72 kgs of Heroin." October 1, 2018. https://english.ahram.org.eg/News/312558.aspx.

———. "Renowned Egyptian Businessman Arrested over 'Funding Excavation of Antiquities.'" June 29, 2021. https://bit.ly/2WA82qk.

Al Arabiya News. "Egypt Jails Ex-Italian Diplomat for Smuggling Antiquities." January 22, 2020. https://bit.ly/3kC7Qiz.

———. "Morocco Police Seizes 5.4 Tonnes of Cannabis, Haul of Cocaine." April 23, 2023.

Alarm Phone. "Shocking Number of Deaths, But Also Growing Struggles on the Ground." AlarmPhone.org, January 29, 2021. https://bit.ly/3B5BCD5.

Alberici, Emma, and Giulia Sirignani. "In a Ruined City on the Italian Coast, the Nigerian Mafia Is Muscling In on the Old Mob." ABC News Australia, March 16, 2020. https://www.abc.net.au/news/2020-03-17/castel-volturno-is-headuarters-for-nigerian-mafia-in-italy/12033684.

Al-Dayel, Nadia, Aaron Anfinson, and Graeme Anfinson. "Captivity, Migration, and Power in Libya." *Journal of Human Trafficking* 9, no. 3 (2023): 280–298.

Algeria Press Service. "Army Arrests Three Drug Traffickers in Tlemcen, 39 Illegal Gold Miners in Southern Country." June 12, 2019.

———. "Illizi: Artisanal Gold Mining in South, 'Added Value' to Economy." September 27, 2020.

———. "Nine Drug Traffickers Arrested, 2500 kg of Cannabis Seized." May 26, 2021.

———. "Over 25 Tonnes of Cannabis Resin Seized in Four Months." June 25, 2021.

———. "South: Young People Can Form Cooperatives to Prospect for Gold." July 16, 2020.

———. "23 Illegal Gold Miners Captured in Tamanrasset, Djanet." August 12, 2019.

Algiers Herald. "Cocaine Trafficker Linked to President's Son Sees Jail Sentence Halved." June 16, 2020. https://www.algiersherald.com/cocaine-trafficker-linked-to-son-of-algerias-president-sees-jail-sentence-halved/.

Alioua, Ahmed. "The Flow of Cigarettes from Algeria to France Decreased by 78%." *Echorouk El Yawmi*, June 26, 2021. https://www.echoroukonline.com/the-flow-of-cigarettes-from-algeria-to-france-decreased-by-78.

Aliriza, Fadil. "How Tunisia's Crooked Cops Are Undermining the Revolution." *Foreign Policy*, February 9, 2016.

Al Jazeera. "Algeria's FLN Wins Most Seats in Parliament." June 15, 2021.

———. "Morocco Scolds Spain over Virus Help for Independence Leader." April 25, 2021.

———. "Tunisia Completes Barrier Along Libya Border." February 7, 2016.

AllAfrica. "Tunisia: Attempt to Smuggle 1049g of Heroin At Tunis-Carthage Airport, Foiled." September 11, 2020. https://allafrica.com/stories/202009110840.html.

———. "Tunisia: Inflation Rate Up to 5.7 Percent in June 2021." July 6, 2021. https://allafrica.com/stories/202107060597.html.

———. "Tunisia: Medenine—Border Post of Ras Jedir Reopened for Goods Transport." June 12, 2021. https://allafrica.com/stories/202106140694.html.

All Arab News. "Libyan Antiquities in Grave Danger from Ongoing Militia Class, Looting, Smuggling." July 24, 2022. https://allarab.news/libyan-antiquities-in-grave-danger-from-ongoing-militia-clash-looting-smuggling/.

Alliance to Counter Crime Online. "Plundered Heritage: The Antiquities Trade on Social Media." 2020. https://www.counteringcrime.org/plundered-heritage-antiquities-trade-on-social-media.

Al Marsad. "Tunisian Investigation: Ghannouchi Receives US$30 Million in Commission for Smuggling Weapons to Libya." March 27, 2021. https://almarsad.co/en/2021/03/27/tunisian-investigation-ghannouchi-receives-us30-million-in-commission-for-smuggling-weapons-to-libya/.

Alpers, Philip, and Marcus Wilson. *Guns in North Africa: Small Arms Policy, Firearm Injury and Gun Law*. Sydney School of Public Health, University of Sydney. GunPolicy.org, October 1, 2014. https://www.gunpolicy.org/firearms/region/north-africa.

Altai Consulting. *Leaving Libya: Rapid Assessment of Municipalities of Departures of Migrants in Libya*. Report prepared for Embassy of the Netherlands to Libya, June 2017.

Altman, Steven, and Caroline Bastian. *DHL Global Connectedness Index 2022*. DHL in Partnership with NYU Stern, March 2023.

Alvi, Hayat. *The Political Economy and Islam of the Middle East: The Case of Tunisia*. Cham, Switzerland: Palgrave MacMillan, 2019.

Al-Youm, Al-Masry. "Heroin Trafficker Arrested in Sharqiya." *Egypt Independent*, January 18, 2019.

———. "Illegal Immigration from Egypt to Europe down to Almost Zero: IOM Chief." *Egypt Independent*, January 19, 2020.

Amara, Tarek. "Tunisia Finishes Libya Border Fence Intended to Keep Out Militants." Reuters, February 6, 2016.

Amer, Adnan Abu. "Report Outlines How Iran Smuggles Arms to Hamas." Al-Monitor, April 9, 2021.

American Society of Overseas Research (ASOR). *The State of Illicit Trade and Looting off Libyan Antiquities: 2011–2020*. December 31, 2020.

Amezian, Ibtissam. "Morocco's Civil Society Sounds Alarm over Crack-Cocaine 'Pouffa' Prevalence to Curb a Looming Epidemic." Hespress English, July 25, 2023.

Amrani, Iman. "Why Don't We Think of North Africa as Part of Africa?" *Guardian*. September 9, 2015.

Andreas, Peter. "Criminalizing Consequences of Sanctions: Embargo Busting and Its Legacy." *International Studies Quarterly* 49, no. 2 (June 2005): 335–360.

Anesi, Cecilia, Lorenzo Bagnoli, and Giulio Rubino. "Malta, a Modern Smugglers' Hideout." Organized Crime and Corruption Reporting Project, Daphne Project, October 10, 2018.

Anesi, Cecilia, Margherita Bettoni, and Giulio Rubino. "'Armed and Dangerous': Inside the 'Ndrangheta's Intercontinental Cocaine Pipeline." Organized Crime and Corruption Reporting Project, August 5, 2021.

———. "The 'Ndrangheta's 'Little Kiss': Inside an Organized Crime Clan That Moved Cocaine Across Europe." Organized Crime and Corruption Reporting Project, June 30, 2021.

Arab News. "Cronies, Corruption: How Algeria's Auto Sector Hit the Wall." February 14, 2021.

Arab Observer. "Tunisian Newspaper Reveals Huge Fortune of Rached Ghannouchi." March 27, 2021. https://www.arabobserver.com/tunisian-newspaper-reveals-the-huge-fortune-of-rached-ghannouchi/.

Arab Weekly. "Arab Migrants in Tunisia Willing to Risk Lives to Cross to Europe." May 3, 2021.

———."Growing Number of Algerians Tempted by Illegal Migration to Europe." June 27, 2020.

———. "Tunisian TV Series Highlights Illegal Migrants Plight." April 27, 2021.

Arieff, Alexis. *Crisis in Mali*. Washington, DC: Congressional Research Service. January 14, 2013.

Arieff, Alexis, Christopher M. Blanchard, Lauren Ploch Blanchard, and Andrew S. Bowen. *Russia's Wagner Group in Africa: Key Issues for Congress*. Washington, DC: Congressional Research Service. August 3, 2023.

Ashour, Omar. "Sinai's Insurgency: Implications of Enhanced Guerilla Warfare." *Studies in Conflict & Terrorism* 42, no. 6 (2019): 541–558.

Associated Press. "Spain Arrests 89 for Speedboat Smuggling of Migrants, Drugs." AP News, March 7, 2020.

———. "Spain to Ban Speedboats Used by Drug, Migrant Traffickers." AP News, October 26, 2018.

Atoussi, S., I. Razkallah, I. N. Ameziane, A. Boudebbouz, M. Bara, Z. Bouslama, and M. Houhamdi. "Illegal Wildlife Trade in Algeria, Insight Via Online Selling Platforms." *African Journal of Ecology* 60 (2022): 175–181.

Atoussi, Sadek, Imane Razkallah, Rabah Zebsa, Mouslim Bara, and Zinette Bensakhri. "Corruption and Poaching in Algeria." In "Contemporary Wild Meat Hunting, Consumption, and Trade in Africa," edited by Katharine Abernethy. Special issue, *African Journal of Ecology* 60, no. 2 (June 2022).

Attkisson, Sharyl. "Thousands of Libyan Missiles from Qaddafi Era Missing in Action." CBS News, March 25, 2013.

Aublanc, Alexandre. "Moroccan Political and Business Leaders Caught Up in International Drug Trafficking Case." *Le Monde*, December 31, 2023.

Ayadi, Lotfi, Nancy Benjamin, Sami Bensassi, and Gaël Raballand. "An Attempt to Estimating Informal Trade Across Tunisia's Land Borders." *Articulo: Journal of Urban Research* 10 (2014).

Ayesh, Mohammad. "Arabic Press Review: Egyptian Judge Accused of Running Drug-Trafficking Network." Middle East Eye, February 23, 2021.

Ayubi, Nazih N. *Over-stating the Arab State*. London: Tauris, 1995.

———. *Overstating the Arab State: Politics and Society in the Middle East*. New York: I. B. Tauris, 1996.

Aziani, Alberto. "The Heterogeneity of Human Smugglers: A Reflection on the Use of Concepts in Studies on the Smuggling of Migrants." *Trends in Organized Crime* 26 (2023): 80–106.

Azimi, Roxana. "Louvre Abu Dhabi: A Twist in the Antiquities Trafficking Case?" *Le Monde*, October 31, 2023.

Babchinetskaya, Izabella. "FATF Concludes Fourth Plenary on Money Laundering and Terrorist Financing Risks."JD Supra, July 1, 2021. https://www.jdsupra.com/legalnews/fatf-concludes-fourth-plenary-on-money-5504483/.

Babuta, Alexander, and Cathy Haenlein. *Commodity Smuggling in the Maghreb: A Silent Threat*. Policy Brief. Rabbat, Morocco: OCP Policy Center, May 2018. https://www.policycenter.ma/sites/default/files/OCPPC-PB1814.pdf.

Badran, Sammy Zeyad. "Demobilising the February 20 Movement in Morocco: Regime Strategies During the Arab Spring." *Journal of North African Studies* 25, no. 4 (2020): 616–640.

Bajec, Alessandra. "Cashing in on Misery: Despite Covid-19, North Africa's Human Traffickers Are Thriving." New Arab, February 15, 2021. https://bit.ly/3go9MtI.

Balay, Sophie. "Italy Cracks Migrants and Cigarette Smuggling Ring." Organized Crime and Corruption Reporting Project, June 7, 2017. https://www.occrp.org/en/daily/6558-italy-cracks-migrants-and-cigarette-smuggling-ring.

BBC News. "Activist Abdurraouf Eshati Admits £18.6m Arms Plot Role." October 26, 2015.

———. "Algeria Siege: 37 Foreigners Died, PM Says." January 21, 2013.

———. "Black Axe Mafia: Italian Police Arrest 30 Nigerian Suspected Gang Members." April 26, 2021.

———. "Egypt Recovers Smuggled Artefact from UK Auction." January 6, 2019.

———. "Gaddafi Wants EU Cash to Stop African Migrants." August 31, 2010.

———. "Islamist PJD Party Wins Morocco Poll." November 27, 2011.

———. "Italy Smashes 'Jihadist' Tunisian Speedboat Trafficking Gang." April 10, 2018.

———. "Mokhtar Belmokhtar Charged over Algeria Gas Plant Siege." July 19, 2013.

———. "Profile Mokhtar Belmokhtar." June 15, 2015.

———. "Spain Drug Bust: 'Speedboat Smugglers' Arrested." April 3, 2021.

———. "Turkish Police Seize Radioactive Material in Anti-Smuggling Raid." March 19, 2018.

Beinin, Joel, Bassam Haddad, and Sherene Seikaly, eds. *A Critical Political Economy of the Middle East and North Africa*. Palo Alto, CA: Stanford University Press, 2020.

Benazizi, Aya. "Spain Reports Increase in Irregular Migration from Algeria." *Morocco World News*, September 16, 2022.

Bencharif, Sarah-Taissir. "EU Parliament Scandal: The Morocco Connection." *Politico*, December 16, 2022.

Benlarabi, Naima. "Human Trafficking in African Women: Case of Trafficking in Sub-Saharan Women in Morocco." In *Dynamics of Inclusion and Exclusion in the MENA Region: Minorities, Subalternity, and Resistance*, edited by Hamza Tayebi and Jochen Lobah, 169–197. Morocco: Hanns Seidel Foundation, September 2019.

Bergin, Daniel, Sadek Atoussi, and Siân Waters. "Online Trade of Barbary Macaques *Macaca sylvanus* in Algeria and Morocco." *Biodiversity and Conservation* 27 (2018): 531–534.

Bertelsmann Transformation Index (BTI). *Algeria Country Report 2020*.

———. *Algeria Country Report 2022*.

———. *Egypt Country Report 2020*.

———. *Egypt Country Report 2022*.

———. *Libya Country Report 2020*.

———. *Libya Country Report 2022*.

———. *Morocco Country Report 2020.*

Bertoluzzi, Giulia. "Tunisian Fishermen on the Frontline of the Migrant Tragedy." Middle East Eye, November 12, 2017.

Bianchi, Andrea Prada, and Pesha Magid. "Decolonization's Last Stand in the Sahara." *Foreign Policy*, June 24, 2023.

Bird, Lucia. "Human Smuggling in Africa: The Creation of a New Criminalised Economy?" Continental Report 04, ENACT, July 2020. https://bit.ly/2V0jBGP.

Birnbaum, Michael. "Smuggling Refugees into Europe Is a New Growth Industry." *Washington Post*, September 3, 2015.

Black, Ian. "WikiLeaks Cables Accuse Moroccan Royals of Corruption." *Guardian*, December 6, 2010.

Blazakis, Jason M. "Interview via Zoom of Nick Snaith." The Soufan Group, March 15, 2021.

———. "Interview via Zoom with Samuel Juett." The Soufan Group, February 24, 2021.

Blickman, Tom. *Morocco and Cannabis: Reduction, Containment or Acceptance*. Drug Policy Briefing 49. Amsterdam: Transnational Institute, March 2017.

Bobin, Frédéric. "A Troubling New Wall Arises at the Tunisia-Libya Border." *Le Monde* (English edition), August 31, 2015, https://bit.ly/2UVDWNA.

Bobin, Frédéric, and Philippe Jacqué. "In the European Parliament, Suspected Moroccan Corruption Sparks Backlash." *Le Monde*, January 21, 2023.

Bonfiglio, Ayla, Ana-Maria Murphy-Teixidor, Simon Nissling, and Vanessa Leigh. "Smuggling Networks Along the Central Mediterranean Route (CMR)." Migration Data Portal, November 22, 2020.

Bongarra, Francesco. "Tunisia Reiterates Commitment to Combating Illegal Migration." Arab News, August 2, 2021.

Bouanani Soumia, and Chaib Bounoua. "Analyzing the Informal Economy in Algeria from an Institutional Perspective." *Revue d'études sur les institutions et le développement* 7, no. 2 (2022): 60–75.

Boukhars, Anouar. "Barriers Versus Smugglers: Algeria and Morocco's Battle for Border Security." Carnegie Endowment for International Peace, March 19, 2019.

———. "The Potential Jihadi Windfall From the Militarization of Tunisia's Border Region With Libya." *CTC Sentinel* 11, no.1 (January 2018).

Boussel, Pierre. "The War Against Human Traffickers in Libya." Carnegie Endowment for International Peace, August 10, 2023.

Brachet, Julien, and Judith Scheele. "Captives at Large: On the Political Economy of Human Containment in the Sahara." *Politics & Society* 50, no. 2 (2021): 1–24.

Brahimi, Alia. "Libya's Political Impasse and the $6 Billion Question." *MENASource*, February 1, 2023. https://www.atlanticcouncil.org/blogs/menasource/libyas-political-impasse-and-the-6-billion-question/.

Bremner, Michael. "The Melilla Massacre: How a Spanish Enclave in Africa Became a Deadly Flashpoint." *Guardian*, August 29, 2023.

Bromley, Mark, Giovanna Maletta, and Kolja Brockmann. *Arms Transfers and SALW Controls in the Middle East and North Africa: Mapping Capacity-Building Efforts*. SIPRI Background Paper. Stockholm International Peace Research Institute, November 2018.

Bryant, Lisa. "As Algeria Prepares for Legislative Elections, Authorities Crack Down on Dissent." Voice of America, June 3, 2021.

Burke, Lauren, and Erol Yayboke. "Addressing Fragility in Libya Means Protecting Migrant Rights." Center for Strategic and International Studies, February 27, 2023. https://www.csis.org/analysis/addressing-fragility-libya-means-protecting-migrant-rights.

Byman, Daniel. "Is Hamas Winning?" *Washington Quarterly* 36, no. 3 (Summer 2013): 63–76.

Cairo Scene. "Confessions of an Egyptian Drug Dealer." January 17, 2015. https://cairoscene.com/LifeStyle/Confessions-of-Egyptian-Drug-Dealer-cairo.

Calandra, Francesca. "Between Local and Global: The 'Ndrangheta's Drug Trafficking Route." *International Annals of Criminology* 55, no. 1 (2017): 78–98.

Callimachi, Rukmini, and Lorenzo Tondo. "Scaling Up a Drug Trade, Straight Through ISIS Turf." *New York Times*, September 13, 2016.

Caminando Fronteras. "Missing: 47 Men Who Disappeared on the Algerian Route." November 2022. https://caminandofronteras.org/en/missing-47-migrant-men-who-disappeared-on-the-algerian-route/.

Carbone, Giovanni. "Nigeria and Contemporary African Migration." In Torelli, *Great Mediterranean Challenge*, 43–56.

Carter, Humphrey. "33 Illegal Immigrants Intercepted in Mallorcan Waters." *Majorca Daily Bulletin*, May 12, 2022.

Castells, Manuel. "Grassrooting the Space of Flows." *Urban Geography* 20, no. 4 (1999): 294–302.

Caulderwood, Kathleen. "Drugs and Money in the Sahara: How the Global Cocaine Trade Is Funding North African Jihad." *International Business Times*, June 5, 2015.

Cengiz, Mahmut. "Amped in Ankara: Drug Trade and Drug Policy in Turkey from the 1950s Through Today." Working Paper on Improving Global Drug Policy: Comparative Perspectives Beyond UNGASS 2016, Brookings Institution, Washington, DC, April 2017.

Cengiz, Mahmut, and Kutluer Karademir. "The Impacts of Authoritarianism on Organized Crime in Turkey." *Small Wars Journal*, November 8, 2020. https://smallwarsjournal.com/jrnl/art/impacts-authoritarianism-organized-crime-turkey.

Center for Insights in Survey Research. *Public Opinion Survey: Residents of Tunisia, September 24–October 11, 2020*. International Republican Institute, 2020. https://www.iri.org/sites/default/files/2020-10_iri_tunisia_report_-_final.pdf.

Chama, Brian. *Anti-Corruption Tabloid Journalism in Africa*. Gewerbestrasse, Switzerland: Palgrave Macmillan, 2019.

Chamekh, Mohamed. "Illegal Migration in Tunisian Rap." *Athens Journal of Mediterranean Studies* 7, no. 1 (January 2021).

Chaouali, Nadia, Bilel Moslah, Kamel Ben Salem, Dorra Amira, Abderazzek Hedhili, and Nabil Ben Salah. "Illicit Substances Identified in the Urine of 11.170 Suspected Drug Users in North Tunisia." *Pan African Medical Journal* 38, article 20 (January 2021).

Chauzal, Gregory, and Sofia Zavagli. *Post-revolutionary Discontent and F(r)actionalisation in the Maghreb: Managing the Tunisia-Libya Border Dynamics*. Clingendael Report, Netherlands Institute of International Relations, August 2016.

Chayes, Sarah. "Corruption: The Unrecognized Threat to International Security." Working Group on Security and Corruption Paper, Carnegie Endowment for International Peace, Washington, DC, June 6, 2014.

Cherif, Rahma Ouled. "SIPRI: Morocco Was 17th Biggest Importer of Trafficked Guns 2009–2018." *Moroccan World News*, March 15, 2019.

Chikhi, Lamine. "Algerian Ex Oil Executives on Trial on Corruption Charges." Reuters, March 15, 2015.

China Daily. "Spain Seizes Over 900 Kilos of Cocaine, Arrests 10." May 22, 2018. https://www.chinadaily.com.cn/a/201805/22/WS5b0383baa3103f6866ee9d57.html.

China Global Television Network Africa. "93 African Children Freed in Algeria from Human Trafficking Networks." November 19, 2018. https://africa.cgtn.com/93-african-children-freed-in-algeria-from-human-trafficking-networks/.

Chouvy, Pierre-Arnaud. *The Supply of Hashish to Europe*. Report prepared for the European Monitoring Centre for Drugs and Drug Addiction (EMCDDA), July 2015.

CIA. "Morocco." *The World Factbook*, 2021. https://www.cia.gov/the-world-factbook/countries/morocco/.

Clarke, Colin P. "How Salafism's Rise Threatens Gaza." *Foreign Affairs*, October 11, 2017.

———. "If Your Country Is Falling Apart, the Wagner Group Will Be There." *New York Times*, August 11, 2023.

Coastal Care. "Beach Sand Mining Defaced Algeria's Eastern Coastal Region." April 25, 2014. https://coastalcare.org/2014/04/le-pillage-du-sable-a-lest-detruit-la-region-algerie/.

———. "Environmental Concern: Sand Mining Goes Unabatted! Oran, Algeria." https://coastalcare.org/2014/04/atteinte-a-lenvironnement-le-pillage-de-sable-continue-oran-algeria/.

———. "470,000 US Dollars' Worth of Illegally Mined Sand Seized in 2019, Algeria." May 17, 2020. https://coastalcare.org/2020/05/470000-us-dollars-worth-of-illegally-mined-sand-seized-in-2019-algeria/.

———. "The Unsustainable Harvest of Coastal Sands—*Science*." Excerpt. December 12, 2023. https://coastalcare.org/2023/12/the-unsustainable-harvest-of-coastal-sands-science/.

Cochrane, Allan, and Kathy Pain. "A Globalizing Society?" In *A Globalizing World? Culture, Economics, Politics*, edited by David Held, pp.5–46. London: Routledge, 2004.

Coggio, Tessa. "Europe's Tackling of 'Root Causes' of African Migration Has a Mixed Record." Migration Policy Institute, May 6, 2021.

Collas, Aurélie. "Morocco: Two Years After Cannabis Law, Farmers in the Rif Still 'in the Dark.'" *Le Monde*, May 8, 2023.

Collins, Larry, and Dominique Lapierre. "The French Connection—In Real Life." *New York Times*, February 6, 1972.

Columb, Sean. *Trading Life: Organ Trafficking, Illicit Networks and Exploitation*. Stanford, CA: Stanford University Press, 2020. Kindle.

Conflict Armament Research. *Investigating Cross-Border Weapons Transfers in the Sahel*. London: Conflict Armament Research, November 2016.

Coppola, Gian Franco. "The Incredible Story of Giulio Lolli." *Libya Tribune*, December 2, 2019. https://en.minbarlibya.org/2019/12/02/the-incredible-story-of-giulio-lolli/.

Cordall, Simon Speakman, and Lorenzo Tondo. "'Entire Families Are Arriving at Our Shores': Covid Drives Tunisian Exodus." *Guardian*, August 12, 2020.

Cornish, Derek. "The Procedural Analysis of Offending and Its Relevance for Situational Prevention." *Crime Prevention Studies* 3 (1994): 151–196. Downloaded from Center for Problem-Oriented Policing. https://www.popcenter.org/sites/default/files/library/crimeprevention/volume_03/06_cornish-2.pdf.

CSO Alliance. "Has Algeria Joined Africa's New 'Cocaine Coast'?" January 30, 2019. https://pfsoalliance.com/news/has-algeria-joined-africas-new-cocaine-coast-8914.

Cuddy, Alice. "Mediterranean Is World's Most Overfished Sea: Report." Euronews, September 7, 2018. https://www.euronews.com/2018/07/09/mediterranean-is-world-s-most-overfished-sea-report.

Cullinane, Susannah. "Man Gets 6 Years After $28.5 Million Invoice for Ammunition Found on Phone." CNN, October 27, 2015.

Curnow, Walt. "Tramadol Abuse Addiction Sweeping Egypt as Part of the World's Growing Opioid Crisis." ABC News Australia, May 4, 2018. https://ab.co/3DwiT5F.

Daily Sabah. "Turkey Becomes Favorite Destination for Foreign Criminals." July 31, 2014. https://www.dailysabah.com/turkey/2014/07/31/turkey-becomes-favorite-destination-for-foreign-criminals.

Dandurand, Yvon. "Thinking Globally, Acting Locally: The Criminality-Resilience Nexus." Global Initiative Against Transnational Organized Crime, May 13, 2022. https://globalinitiative.net/analysis/resilience-ocindex/.

Danssaert, Peter. "States Gather to Tackle Illicit Trade in Small Arms and Light Weapons." International Peace Information Service (IPIS), July 11, 2022. https://

ipisresearch.be/weekly-briefing/states-gather-to-tackle-illicite-trade-in-small-arms-and-light-weapons/.
Daoud, Kamel. "The Algerian Exception." *New York Times*, May 29, 2015. https://www.nytimes.com/2015/05/30/opinion/the-algerian-exception.html.
Davis, Gabriel. "Democracy or Dependence? The Future of Algeria in a Rentier Economy." *NewArab comment* (blog on Medium), April 21, 2020. https://bit.ly/3iN37ex.
de Georgio, Andrea. "West Africa: Economic and Socio-Political Dynamics." In Torelli, *Great Mediterranean Challenge*, 57–66.
de Haas, Hein. *Irregular Migration from West Africa to the Maghreb and the European Union: An Overview of Recent Trends*. Geneva: International Organization for Migration, September 2008. https://www.unhcr.org/49e479ca0.pdf.
Deknatel, Frederick. "New Drug Routes Through Lawless Libya Raise Questions About ISIS' Role." *World Politics Review*, September 23, 2016.
Delia, Julian. "Just Four EU Countries Seized More Cannabis Than Malta in 2018." *Times of Malta*, September 24, 2020.
Delpuech, Aida. "Italian Waste. Part 2: The New Protagonists from Italy." Inkyfada, May 7, 2021. https://inkyfada.com/en/2021/05/07/italian-waste-tunisia-investigation-2/.
Delpuech, Aida, and IrpiMedia. "Italian Waste: The Vast Corruption Network Behind the Environmental Scandal." Inkyfada, March 9, 2021. https://inkyfada.com/en/2021/03/09/investigation-waste-corruption-italy-tunisia/.
De Lugo, Lucia Bird Ruiz-Benitez. *North-West Passage: The Resurgence of Maritime Irregular Migration to the Canary Islands*. Human Smuggling and Trafficking Ecosystems—North Africa and the Sahel 2022 Series. Geneva: Global Initiative Against Transnational Organized Crime, December 2022.
Demuynck, Meryl, Tanya Mehra, and Reinier Bergema. *ICCT Situation Report: The Use of Small Arms and Light Weapons by Terrorist Organisations as a Source of Finance in the Middle East and North Africa*. The Hague: International Centre for Counter-Terrorism (ICCT), 2020.
Deutsche Welle. "Should the EU Help Legalize Cannabis Farms in Morocco?" April 28, 2021.
Devereux, Charlie. "Trouble in Spanish Africa." *New European*, July 17, 2021.
Dhaouadi, Rim. "Crime and Excessive Punishment in Tunisia." Project Syndicate, November 19, 2019, https://bit.ly/3xm5Yiy.
———. "New Hope for Tunisia's Human Trafficking Victims." ENACT, July 30, 2019. https://enactafrica.org/enact-observer/new-hope-for-tunisias-human-trafficking-victims.
———. "Social Media and the Sale of Arms in Libya." ENACT, April 12, 2019. https://enactafrica.org/research/trend-reports/social-media-and-the-sale-of-arms-in-libya.
———. "Tunisia Must Put Its Human Trafficking Laws to Work." Institute for Security Studies, January 16, 2020. https://issafrica.org/iss-today/tunisia-must-put-its-human-trafficking-laws-to-work.
Dhingra, Reva. "US Migration Policy and Nonstate Groups: Lessons from Libya." Brookings Institution, February 15, 2023.
Dillman, Bradford. "Introduction: Shining Light on the Shadows: The Political Economy of Illicit Transactions in the Mediterranean." *Mediterranean Politics* 12, no. 2 (July 2007): 123–139.
Dridi, Manel. "Tunisia's Informal Employment Crisis." Carnegie Endowment for International Peace, February 14, 2023.
Dubuis, Anna, and Emily Pennink. "Muslim Preacher Jailed After Cops Find Invoice for £18 Million of Ammunition on His Mobile Phone." *Mirror*, October 27, 2015. https://www.mirror.co.uk/news/uk-news/muslim-preacher-jailed-after-cops-6716460.
Dunya News. "Spain Busts Money Laundering Network." May 9, 2013. https://dunyanews.tv/en/Crime/173067-Spain-busts-money-laundering-network.

DZ Breaking. "Algeria: A Cache of Weapons and Ammunition Discovered in Bordj Badji Mokhtar—Statement." August 21, 2017. https://www.dzbreaking.com/2017/08/21/algeria-cache-weapons-ammunition-discovered-bordj-badji-mokhtar-statement-2/.

Eaton, Tim. *Libya's War Economy: Predation, Profiteering and State Weakness*. London: Chatham House, 2018.

Eaton, Tim, Renad Mansour, Lina Khatib, Christine Cheng, Jihad Yazigi, and Peter Salisbury. *Conflict Economies in the Middle East and North Africa*. Chatham House Report. London: Royal Institute of International Affairs, 2019.

Echorouk El Yawmi. "Annaba-Sardinia: New Crossing Point for Syrian Refugees in Algeria Towards Italy." October 18, 2015. https://bit.ly/3iZYKwo.

———. "Mafia of Illegal Exploration Drains the Algerian Desert's Gold." May 8, 2021. https://www.echoroukonline.com/ma%EF%AC%81a-of-illegal-exploration-drains-the-algerian-deserts-gold.

Economist. "Trafficking in North Africa: Boom Boom." August 17, 2013.

Economist Intelligence Unit. *Democracy Index 2020: In Sickness and in Health?* London: Economist Group, 2021.

ECPAT International and Amane. *Sexual Exploitation of Boys—Morocco Report*. Bangkok: ECPAT International, 2022.

Ede, Andrew. "Illegal Migration to Mallorca Is 'Unfortunately a Profitable Business.'" *Majorca Daily Bulletin*, March 26, 2023.

Egypt Today. "Interior Ministry Foils Attempt to Smuggle Heroin in Red Sea." December 10, 2017.

El-Din, El-Sayed Gamal. "Egyptian Judge Sentenced to Life in Prison for Possession of 68kg of Cannabis." Ahram Online, April 1, 2017. https://bit.ly/2Y6QqD7.

El-Dine, Ahmed Shihab. "The Eastern and Western Egyptian Borders: "All Is Allowed! Anything Goes!" *As-Safir Al-Arabi*, June 12, 2019. https://bit.ly/3BuWfsn.

Eljechtimi, Ahmed. "Informal Labour Accounts for Two-Thirds of Morocco Jobs, Statistics Agency Reports." Reuters, May 30, 2023.

———. "Morocco's Bill to Legalise Cannabis Divides Growers." US News & World Report (Reuters), March 18, 2021. https://www.usnews.com/news/world/articles/2021-03-18/moroccos-bill-to-legalise-cannabis-divides-growers.

El Kamouni-Janssen, Floor. *Only God Can Stop the Smugglers: Understanding Human Smuggling Networks in Libya*. The Hague: Clingendael Institute, February 2017.

El Masry, Sarah. "Smoke and Mirrors: Smuggled Cigarettes." *Daily News Egypt*, July 24, 2013.

El Sawy, Nada, Sinan Mahmoud, and Mina Aldroubi. "Stealing from History: Inside the Multimillion-Dollar Illegal Trade in Artefacts from the Middle East" *National*, May 20, 2022.

El Watan (Algiers). "Libya-Linked Gun Trafficking Ring Dismantled in Algeria [FR]." May 23, 2016. Taken from GunPolicy.org.

———. "More Than 300 Guns Seized from Terrorists in Algeria [FR]." April 19, 2016. Taken from GunPolicy.org.

EMCDDA. *Overview of Drug Markets in the European Neighbourhood Policy-South Countries*. Lisbon: European Monitoring Centre for Drugs and Drug Addiction, 2022.

ENACT. *Organised Crime Index—Africa 2019*. https://bit.ly/3gN0NTd.

———. *Organized Crime Index 2019—Libya*. https://ocindex.net/country/libya.

———. *Organized Crime Index 2019—Algeria*. https://ocindex.net/assets/downloads/ocindex_profile_algeria.pdf.

———. *Organized Crime Index 2019—Egypt*. https://ocindex.net/assets/downloads/ocindex_profile_egypt.pdf.

———. *Organized Crime Index 2019—Morocco*. https://ocindex.net/assets/downloads/ocindex_profile_morocco.pdf.

———. *Organized Crime Index 2019—Tunisia*. https://ocindex.net/assets/downloads/ocindex_profile_tunisia.pdf.

Erlanger, Steven. "Earthquake Puts Morocco's Elusive King in Spotlight." *New York Times*, September 12, 2023.

Eurobsit. "Libyan Oil Fueled Organized Crime in Malta." Blog on Medium, October 2, 2018. https://medium.com/@Eurobsit/smuggled-libyan-oil-fueled-organized-crime-in-malta-4462f927d836.

EuroMed Rights. "Migrants and Refugees in Algeria." On the Move—Latest Migration News, April 13, 2021–April 26, 2021. https://bit.ly/3DfYn94.

Euronews. "Malta's Government Responsible for Murder of Journalist Daphne Caruana Galizia, Inquiry Finds." July 29, 2021. https://bit.ly/3yGU1Fy.

Euronews with AP. "Hundreds of Migrants Attempt in Vain to Enter the Spanish Enclave of Melilla." March 8, 2022. https://www.euronews.com/2022/03/08/hundreds-of-migrants-attempt-in-vain-to-enter-the-spanish-enclave-of-melilla.

European Environment Agency. "Mediterranean Sea Region Briefing—The European Environment—State and Outlook 2015." February 18, 2015. https://www.eea.europa.eu/soer/2015/countries/mediterranean.

European Monitoring Centre for Drugs and Drug Addiction. "Opioid Trafficking Routes from Asia to Europe." June 4, 2015.

European Public Prosecutor's Office. "Counterfeit Cigarette Trafficking Scheme Between North Africa and Italy: 12 Arrests and Seizures in Italy." November 30, 2021. https://www.eppo.europa.eu/en/news/counterfeit-cigarette-trafficking-scheme-between-north-africa-and-italy-12-arrests-and.

———. "First Verdict in EPPO Case in Italy: 10 Convictions for Tobacco Smuggling." December 22, 2022. https://www.eppo.europa.eu/en/news/first-verdict-eppo-case-italy-10-convictions-tobacco-smuggling.

European Training Foundation. "Algeria: Education, Training and Employment Developments 2020." 2020. https://bit.ly/3znrFQY.

Europol. *OCTA 2011: EU Organised Crime Threat Assessment*. The Hague: Europol, April 28, 2011.

———. *OCTA 2007: EU Organised Crime Threat Assessment*. The Hague: Europol, April 1, 2007.

———. "Trash Worth Millions of Euros." September 18, 2019. https://www.europol.europa.eu/newsroom/news/trash-worth-millions-of-euros.

Fabian, Emanual. "IDF Seizes $2.5 Million Worth of Drugs on Egypt Border." *Times of Israel*, July 3, 2022.

Fabrizio, Natale, Silvia Migali, and Rainer Münz. *Many More to Come? Migration from and within Africa*. Luxembourg: Publications Office of the European Union, 2018.

Faiola, Anthony. "The Racist Roots of the Rise in Migration to Europe This Year." *Washington Post*, June 30, 2023.

Fairbanks, Waylon. "Lebanon's Fuel Oil Scandal." *MEES* 63, no. 36 (September 4, 2020).

Farolfi, Sara, and Stelios Orphandes. "Cyprus Records Shed Light on Libya's Hidden Millions." Organized Crime and Corruption Reporting Project, July 25, 2018.

Farrah, Raouf. *Algeria's Migration Dilemma: Migration and Human Smuggling in Southern Algeria*. Geneva: Global Initiative Against Transnational Organized Crime, December 2020.

FishAct. "Investigating Illegal Bottom Trawling in the Gulf of Gabes, Tunisia." 2018. https://fishact.org/2018/12/investigating-illegal-bottom-trawling-in-the-gulf-of-gabes-tunisia/.

Fitz Gibbon, Kate. "Egypt's Brutal Regime Wants to Renew US Blockade on Art; Claims to Protect Heritage & Culture." Cultural Property News, March 10, 2021.

Fitzgibbon, Will. "Algeria Launches Money Laundering Probe on Back of Panama Papers." International Consortium of Investigative Journalists, September 10, 2018.

Flanary, Rachel. "The State in Africa: Implications for Democratic Reform." *Crime, Law and Social Change* 29, no. 2–3 (1998): 179–196.

Fondation Selles. "Morocco." Excerpt from the book, *Sexual Exploitation: New Challenges, New Answers*. 5th Global Report. Paris: Fondation Selles, 2019. https://fondationscelles.org/pdf/RM5/MOROCCO_Excerpt_5th_Global_Report_Fondation_SCELLES_2019.pdf.

Fonseca, Joseph R. "'Intra-Mediterranean Container Trades' Update." MarineLink, November 3, 2014. https://www.marinelink.com/news/intramediterranean-trades380085.

Ford, Alessandro. "Libya, North Africa Emerge as Cocaine Transit Hubs." Insight Crime, January 20, 2021. https://insightcrime.org/news/analysis/libya-north-africa-cocaine-transit/.

Foroudi, Layli. "'The Sea is Dead': How Fishing and Migration Collide on Tunisia's Shores." New Humanitarian, September 14, 2020.

Fortuna, Gerardo, and Sarantis Michalopoulos. "OLAF: Up to France to Request Help on Genuine Cigarettes Smuggled from Algeria." Euractiv, September 17, 2018. https://bit.ly/2Wh5P38.

France 24. "'Europe or Death': West Africans Risk All to Leave Tunisia." May 3, 2021. https://www.france24.com/en/live-news/20210503-europe-or-death-west-africans-risk-all-to-leave-tunisia.

———. "Ex-minister's Brother Jailed for Smuggling Egyptian Antiquities." February 15, 2020. https://www.france24.com/en/20200215-ex-minister-s-brother-jailed-for-smuggling-egypt-antiquities.

———. "Five Things to Know About Italy's 'Ndrangheta Mafia." January 11, 2021. https://www.france24.com/en/live-news/20210111-five-things-to-know-about-italy-s-ndrangheta-mafia.

———. "Voodoo and Strox: The Synthetic Drugs Wreaking Havoc in Cairo." July 23, 2018. https://observers.france24.com/en/20180723-voodoo-strox-drugs-cairo-egypt.

Frenkel, Sheera. "Egypt's Gun Boom." BuzzFeed News, January 6, 2014.

Friedman, Thomas L. *The Lexus and the Olive Tree*. New York: Farrar, Straus and Giroux, 1999.

Gall, Carlotta. "Corruption Crackdown Intensifies in Tunisia, and People Cheer." *New York Times*, June 25, 2017.

Gallien, Max. "Informal Institutions and the Regulation of Smuggling in North Africa," *Perspectives on Politics* 18, no. 2 (2018): 492–508.

———. "Smugglers and States: Illegal Trade in the Political Settlements of North Africa." PhD thesis, London School of Economics, January 2020. http://etheses.lse.ac.uk/4116/1/Gallien__Smugglers-and-states.pdf.

Gamella, Juan Francisco, and Maria Luisa Jiménez Rodrigo. "Multinational Export-Import Ventures: Moroccan Hashish into Europe Through Spain." In *A Cannabis Reader: Global Issues and Local Experiences*, edited by Sharon Rödner Sznitman, Börje Olsson, and Robin Room. Monograph Series 8, Volume 1. Lisbon: European Monitoring Centre for Drugs and Drug Addiction, 2008.

Ganot, Steven. "Morocco Intercepts Over 1.4 Tons of Cocaine in Major Anti-Drug Operation." The Media Line, January 3, 2024.

Gaye, Serigne Bamba. *Connections Between Jihadist Groups and Smuggling and Illegal Trafficking Rings in the Sahel*. Dakar-Fann, Senegal: Friederich Ebert Stiftung Peace and Security Centre of Competence Sub-Saharan Africa, 2018. https://library.fes.de/pdf-files/bueros/fes-pscc/14176.pdf.

Ghanem, Dalia. *Algeria's Borderlands: A Country unto Themselves*. Beirut: Carnegie Middle East Center, May 2020. https://carnegieendowment.org/files/Ghanem-Algeria-Tunisia.pdf.

———. "Specter of Jihadism Continues to Haunt Maghreb." Middle East Institute, September 14, 2018.

Ghanem, Dalia, and Omar Benderra. "A Looming Crisis." *Diwan—Middle East Insights from Carnegie* (blog), August 5, 2019. https://carnegie-mec.org/diwan/79624.

Ghebouli, Zine Labidine. "Algerians' Clandestine Exodus: A Complex National Tragedy." Middle East Institute, October 19 2022.

Ghilès, Francis. "Tunisia Is the Sick Man of North Africa," *CIDOB Notes Internacionals* 223 (January 2020).

Gibraltar Chronicle. "Police and Customs Fish 2.4 Tonnes of Cannabis Resin from the Sea." February 27, 2017.

Global Alliance for Incinerator Alternatives. *Illegal Shipments of Italian Municipal Waste to Tunisia*. 2021. https://www.no-burn.org/wp-content/uploads/2021-03-03-Italy-Tunisia-short-report.pdf.

Global Detention Project. "Libya: Overview." n.d. Accessed September 2023 https://www.globaldetentionproject.org/countries/africa/libya.

Global Initiative Against Transnational Organized Crime. Africa Organised Crime Index 2021—Morocco. 2021. https://africa.ocindex.net/assets/downloads/2021/english/ocindex_summary_morocco.pdf.

Gorman, Sophie. "Tunisian NGOs Triumph in David-vs-Goliath Toxic Waste Battle with Italy." France 24, February 21, 2022.

Hamad, Fatma Ben. "The Daredevil Drivers Smuggling Fuel and Household Goods into Tunisia." France 24, *Observers*, February 7, 2023. https://observers.france24.com/en/tv-shows/the-observers/20230207-tunisia-smuggling-tiktok-knatria-fuel-police.

Horsley, Rupert. *Libya: Sophisticated Smugglers Thrive as Libyan Governance Stagnates*. Geneva: Global Initiative Against Transnational Organized Crime, September 2023.

Horsley, Rupert, and Jessica Gerken. *Libya: Stability Fuels Rebound in Human Smuggling*. Human Smuggling and Trafficking Ecosystems—North Africa and the Sahel 2022 Series. Geneva: Global Initiative Against Transnational Organized Crime.

Human Rights Watch. "Tunisia: African Migrants Intercepted at Sea, Expelled." October 10, 2023.

Global Organized Crime Index. "ENACT Index—Africa." Global Initiative Against Transnational Organized Crime, 2021 and 2023. https://ocindex.net/.

———. *Algeria 2023*. https://ocindex.net/assets/downloads/2023/english/ocindex_profile_algeria_2023.pdf.

———. *Libya 2021*. https://ocindex.net/assets/downloads/2021/english/ocindex_profile_libya_2021.pdf.

———. *Libya 2023*. https://ocindex.net/assets/downloads/2023/english/ocindex_profile_libya_2023.pdf.

———. *Morocco 2023*. https://ocindex.net/assets/downloads/2023/english/ocindex_profile_morocco_2023.pdf.

———. *Tunisia 2023*. https://ocindex.net/assets/downloads/2023/english/ocindex_profile_tunisia_2023.pdf.

Gnes, Davide. *Maghnia: Crossing the Uncrossable Border—Mission Report on the Vulnerability of Sub-Saharan Migrants and Refugees at the Algerian Moroccan Border*. Copenhagen: Euro-Mediterranean Human Rights Network, December 2013. https://www.refworld.org/pdfid/5315886c4.pdf.

Gómez-Céspedes, Alejandra. "Spain: A Criminal Hub." In *Corruption and Organized Crime in Europe: Illegal Partnerships*, edited by Philip Gounev and Vincenzo Ruggiero. London, New York: Routledge, 2012.

Gormezano, David. "Dutch PM Under Protection as the "Mocro Mafia' Drug Cartel Sows Fear in the Netherlands." France 24, February 10, 2021. https://www.france24

.com/en/europe/20211002-dutch-pm-under-protection-as-the-mocro-mafia-drug-cartel-sows-fear-in-the-netherlands.

Government of France. "Two Operations Against Drug Trafficking Produce Exceptional." March 3, 2020. https://www.gouvernement.fr/en/two-operations-against-drug-trafficking-produce-exceptional-results.

Government of Isle of Man. "Financial Sanctions: Libya." Gov.im (Official Isle of Man Government Website), June 15, 2018. https://www.gov.im/news/2018/jun/15/financial-sanctions-libya/.

Guarascio, Francesco. "Europe Flooded with Cocaine Despite Coronavirus Trade Disruptions." Reuters, April 30, 2020.

Guardian. "Coastguard Seizes Half a Tonne of Cocaine Floating off Algeria Coast." June 28, 2021.

Gulraj, Priya. "Cannabis Bales Worth £14m Wash Up on Gibraltar Shoreline." *Gibraltar Chronicle*, February 1, 2019.

Gun Policy. "Algeria—Gun Facts, Figures and the Law." Accessed September 2023. https://www.gunpolicy.org/firearms/region/algeria.

Hadid, Diaa, and Wissam Nassar. "As Egypt Floods Gaza Tunnels, Smugglers Fear an End to Their Trade." *New York Times*, October 7, 2015.

Hamaizia, Adel, and Yahia H. Zoubir. "Algeria's Perfect Storm: COVID-19 and Its Fallout." Chatham House, May 6, 2020.

Hamamouchi, Abdellatif El. "Morocco: A Brewing Crisis of Governance." Carnegie Endowment for International Peace, July 11, 2023.

Hamann, Jasper. "Morocco Accused of Pervasive Money Laundering, Placed On 'Grey List.'" *Morocco World News*, February 27, 2021.

Hand, Marcus. "Tangier Med Takes Mediterranean Top Container Port Crown in 2020." Seatrade Maritime News, March 17, 2021

Hanlon, Querine, and Matthew M. Herbert. *Border Security Challenges in the Grand Maghreb*. Peaceworks no. 109. Washington, DC: United States Institute of Peace, 2015. https://bit.ly/3DdMdxK.

Harchaoui, Jalel. "Too Close for Comfort: How Algeria Faces the Libyan Conflict." Security Assessment in North Africa Briefing Paper. Small Arms Survey, July 2018. http://www.smallarmssurvey.org/fileadmin/docs/T-Briefing-Papers/SAS-SANA-BP-Algeria-Libya.pdf.

Harvard Health Blog. "Is Tramadol a Risky Pain Medication?" June 14, 2019. https://www.health.harvard.edu/blog/.

Heine, Jorge, and Ramesh Thakur, eds. *The Dark Side of Globalization*. Tokyo: United Nations University Press, 2011.

Hekking, Morgan. "From Fuel to Amphetamines: The Worrisome Evolution of Morocco's Black Markets." *Morocco World News*, July 14, 2019.

Herbert, Matthew. "From Contraband to Conflict: Links Between Smuggling and Violence in the Borderlands of Meso-America and North Africa." PhD diss., Fletcher School of Law and Diplomacy, Tufts University, April 2019.

———. "Just Across the Sea: The Changing Politics of Irregular Migration From and Through Morocco and Tunisia." In Torelli, *Great Mediterranean Challenge*, pp. 89–104.

———. *"La Mal Vie": The Routes, Drivers and Politics of North African Irregular Migration*. Pretoria: Institute for Security Studies, 2019.

———. *Losing Hope: Why Tunisians Are Leading the Surge in Irregular Migration to Europe*. Global Initiative Against Transnational Crime, January 2022.

———. *Tunisia: Growing Irregular Migration Flows Amid Worsening Political Fragility*. Global Initiative Against Transnational Crime, July 2022.

Herbert, Matt, and Max Gallien. *Divided They Fall: Frontiers, Borderlands, and Stability in North Africa*. North Africa Report 6. Pretoria: Institute for Security Studies, December 2020. https://issafrica.s3.amazonaws.com/site/uploads/nar-6.pdf.

———. *A Rising Tide: Trends in Production, Trafficking and Consumption of Drugs in North Africa*. Geneva: Global Initiative Against Transnational Organized Crime, May 2020.

Herbert, Matt, Rupert Horsely, and Emadeddin Badi. *Illicit Economies and Peace and Security in Libya*. UN Security Council Illicit Economies Watch 2023 Series. Geneva: Global Initiative Against Transnational Organized Crime, July 2023.

Hinnant, Lori, Jerome Delay, and Bram Jansenn. "Algeria Forces 13,000 Migrants into the Desert, Some to Their Deaths." Associated Press, July 6, 2018.

Human Rights Watch. "Algeria: Migrants, Asylum Seekers Forced Out." October 9, 2020.

———. "Italy: Halt Abusive Migration Cooperation with Libya." February 12, 2020.

———. "Italy-Libya Connection." September 23, 2009.

———. *World Report 2021: Events of 2020*. New York: Human Rights Watch, 2021. https://www.hrw.org/sites/default/files/media_2021/01/2021_hrw_world_report.pdf.

Husken, Thomas. "The Practice and Culture of Smuggling in the Borderland of Egypt and Libya." *International Affairs* 93, no. 4 (2017): 897–915.

Ibrahim, Solava. "The Dynamics of the Egyptian Social Contract: How the Political Changes Affected the Poor." *World Development* 138 (February 2021): 1–15. https://www.sciencedirect.com/science/article/pii/S0305750X20303818.

ICIJ. "Oceano Blu Trading Limited." International Consortium of Investigative Journalists Offshore Leaks Database. https://offshoreleaks.icij.org/nodes/55053510.

Immigration and Refugee Board of Canada. "Algeria: Treatment of Failed Refugee Claimants Returned to Algeria; Whether Low-Ranking Police Officers or Members of the Security Forces Would Be Subject to Any Reprisals from State Authorities 2007-July 2014." August 11, 2014. https://www.refworld.org/docid/540428854.html.

Impicciatore, Roberto, and Alessandro Rosina. "Europe and Africa: Demographic Dynamics and Migratory Flows." In Torelli, *Great Mediterranean Challenge*, 19–30.

InfoMigrants. "53% of Migrants Lost Jobs in Tunisia in COVID-19 Lockdown." May 8, 2020.

———. "More Than 190 Migrants in 13 Boats Rescued Off Spain's Balearic Islands." September 23, 2020.

International Crisis Group. "Breaking Algeria's Economic Paralysis." Report no. 192, November 19, 2018.

———. *Libya Turns the Page*. Middle East/North Africa Report no. 222, May 21, 2021. https://www.crisisgroup.org/middle-east-north-africa/north-africa/libya/222-libya-turns-page.

———. *Reform and Security Strategy in Tunisia*. Middle East/North Africa Report no. 161, July 23, 2015.

———. *Tunisia's Borders: Jihadism and Contraband*. Middle East/North Africa Report no. 148, November 28, 2013.

International Organization for Migration. *Baseline Study on Trafficking in Persons in Tunisia: Assessing the Scope and Manifestations*. Tunis: International Organization for Migration (IOM) Tunisia, 2013. https://bit.ly/3rJJeYq.

———. *Migration in Malta: Country Profile 2015*. Geneva: IOM, 2016.

Interpol. "Hazardous Materials Seized in Largest Global Operation Against Illegal Waste." August 8, 2017.

———. "INTERPOL Operation Targets Illegal Trade of E-Waste in Europe, Africa." February 25, 2013.

———. "Massive Drug Seizures in Twin Operations Across Africa and Middle East." May 17, 2021.

———. "Operation Weka II: Nearly 700 Human Trafficking Victims Rescued." June 29, 2022.

Interpol and ENACT. *Illicit Goods Trafficking Via Port and Airport Facilities in Africa*. In collaboration with ENACT, June 2020.

———. *Overview of Serious and Organized Crime in North Africa*. September 30, 2018. https://bit.ly/2WkjIOb.

Iraq, Maryam. "Egypt Signs Protocol to Eliminate Illicit Trade in Tobacco Products." HG.org, n.d. https://bit.ly/3t8MTQf.

Islam, Zyma. "Workers Tricked, Trafficked: Sold in Algeria, Waiting for Rescue." *Daily Star*. February 26, 2001. https://bit.ly/3sHdmnM.

Jackson, Robert H. "Quasi-States, Dual Régimes, and Neoclassical Theory: International Jurisprudence and the Third World." *International Organization* 41, no. 4 (Autumn 1987): 519–554.

Jacquemet, Marco. "Transidioma Afloat: Communication, Power, and Migration in the Mediterranean Sea." *History and Anthropology* 31, no. 1 (2020): 138.

Jalal, Rasha Abou. "Despite Egyptian Campaign, Gaza Border Tunnels Resume Smuggling Activity." Al-Monitor, April 27, 2021. https://bit.ly/3DvyNNz.

Jenzen-Jones, N. R., and Ian McCollum. *Web Trafficking: Analyzing the Online Trade of Small Arms and Light Weapons in Libya*. Small Arms Survey, April 15, 2017. http://www.smallarmssurvey.org/fileadmin/docs/F-Working-papers/SAS-SANA-WP26-Libya-web-trafficking.pdf.

Jlassi, Asma, Sofiane Mahjoub, and Valerio Crespi. "Preliminary Analysis of the Impact of COVID-19 on the Fishery and Aquaculture Sectors in Tunisia." *FAO Aquaculture Newsletter* 62 (October 2020). http://www.fao.org/3/cb1550en/cb1550en.pdf.

Jumet, Kira, and Zana Gulmohamad. "Reframing the Campaign: From Egypt's Ansar Bayt al-Maqdis to Wilayat Sinai, Islamic State's Sinai Province." *Studies in Conflict & Terrorism* 46, no. 8 (2023): 1464–1490.

Kahneman, Daniel, and Amos Tversky. "Prospect Theory: An Analysis of Decision Under Risk." *Econometrica* 47, no. 2 (March 1979): 263–292.

Kartas, Moncef. "On the Edge? Trafficking and Insecurity at the Tunisian-Libyan Border." Working Paper 17, Small Arms Survey, Geneva, December 2013. http://www.smallarmssurvey.org/fileadmin/docs/F-Working-papers/SAS-WP17-Tunisia-On-the-Edge.pdf.

Kasraoui, Safaa. "DGSN Annual Report: Morocco Seized Over 217 Tonnes of Cannabis in 2020." *Morocco World News*, December 24, 2020.

———. "Moroccan Police Seize 3 Tonnes of Cannabis in Larache Port." *Morocco World News*, September 27, 2023.

———. "Morocco Arrests Moroccan, Algerian Nationals for Drug Trafficking." *Morocco World News*, February 6, 2020.

———. "Morocco's BCIJ Seizes 7 Tons of Cannabis in Casablanca." *Morocco World News*, April 12, 2019.

———. "The Tale of the Desert Escobar Case: As It Happened." *Morocco World News*, December 26, 2023.

———. "12 Tons of Cannabis Resin Seized at Tanger-Med Port in 2 Days." *Morocco World News*, October 30, 2019.

Kasturi, Charu Sudan. "Why Libya's Future Is a Haze of Cigarette Smoke." Ozy. https://www.ozy.com/around-the-world/why-libyas-future-is-a-haze-of-cigarette-smoke/87184/.

Keefe, Patrick Radden. "The Geography of Badness: Mapping the Hubs of the Illicit Global Economy." In Miklaucic and Brewer, *Convergence: Illicit Networks*, 2013.

Kemp, Walter. *Transnational Tentacles: Global Hotspots of Western Balkan Organized Crime*. Geneva: Global Initiative Against Transnational Organized Crime, July 2020.

Kemper, Steve. *A Labyrinth of Kingdoms: 10,000 Miles Through Islamic Africa*. New York: W. W. Norton and Company, 2012.

Khaldi, Nazim. Statement of First Secretary, Permanent Mission of Algeria, to the United Nations, at the Eighth Biennial Meeting of States to Consider the Implementation of the Programme of Action to Prevent, Combat and Eradicate the Illicit Trade in Small Arms and Light Weapons in All Its Aspects. New York, June 27–July 1, 2022. https://docs-library.unoda.org/Programme_of_Action_on_Small_Arms_and_Light_Weapons_-EightBiennial_Meeting_of_States_(2022)/ALGERIA-STATEMENT-BMS8-AGENDA-ITEM-8.pdf.

Khan, Mohsin, and Karim Mezran. "Aftermath of the Arab Spring in North Africa." Issue Brief, Atlantic Council, Washington, DC, October 2016.

Khodary, Yasmin. *Illicit Financial Flows and Tax Reforms in Egypt: Mapping of the Literature and Synthesis of the Evidence*. Nairobi: Partnership for African Social and Governance Research (PASGR), August 2018.

Khoury, Nasser. "On the Algerian Involvement in the Case of Fuel Oil Fraud in Lebanon." Beirut Today, May 11, 2020.

Kilavuz, M. Tahir, and Sharan Grewal. "Algerians Have Been Protesting for a Year. Here's What You Need to Know." *Washington Post*, February 22, 2020.

Kingsley, Patrick, and Sara Creta. "The Ship That Stopped 7,000 Migrants, and Smuggled 700,000 Cigarettes." *New York Times*, September 28, 2020.

Kirchgaessner, Stephanie, Lorenzo Tondo, and reporters for the Daphne Project. "Malta 'fueling Libya instability' by failing to tackle oil smuggling." *Guardian*, May 9, 2018.

Kirechu, Peter. "Profiteers, Vultures, and the Defeat of the UN Embargo on Libya." War on the Rocks, January 12, 2021.

Kisambe, Samuel. "Morocco: Massive Cocaine Smuggling Attempt Foiled in Casablanca." CGTN Africa, February 12, 2018. https://africa.cgtn.com/2018/02/12/morocco-massive-cocaine-smuggling-attempt-foiled-in-casablanca/.

Klein, David. "Italy Arrests Dozens of Suspected Nigerian Mafia Members." Organized Crime and Corruption Reporting Project, November 4, 2020. https://www.occrp.org/en/daily/13348-italy-arrests-dozens-of-suspected-nigerian-mafia-members.

Klitgaard, Robert. "International Cooperation Against Corruption." *Finance & Development* 35, no. 1 (March 1998): 3–7. https://www.imf.org/external/pubs/ft/fandd/1998/03/pdf/klitgaar.pdf.

———. "Three Levels of Fighting Corruption." Carter Center Conference on Transparency for Growth in the Americas, Carter Center, Atlanta, May 3, 1999. https://www.cartercenter.org/news/documents/doc1193.html.

KnowYourCountry. "Morocco: Risk & Compliance Report." March 2018. http://www.knowyourcountry.info/files/moroccoamlreportaug14_6.pdf.

Kourdi, Eyad, and Hande Atay Alam. "At Least Five Killed in Attack Near Synagogue in Tunisia." CNN, May 10, 2023.

Kozlowski, Nina. "Morocco: Spain Plans to End the Crisis in Ceuta and Melilla." *Africa Report*, July 9, 2021.

KPMG. *Illicit Cigarette Consumption in the EU, UK, Norway, Switzerland, Moldova and Ukraine: 2022 Results*. June 28, 2023. https://www.pmi.com/resources/docs/*default*-source/itp/kpmg-report—-illicit-cigarette-consumption-in-the-eu-uk-norway-switzerland-moldova-and-ukraine—-2022-results.pdf.

Kuschminder, Katie, and Anna Triandafyllidou. "Smuggling, Trafficking, and Extortion: New Conceptual and Policy Challenges on the Libyan Route to Europe." *Antipode* 52, no.1 (2020): 206–226.

Kutub, Adam. "What Happens in Morocco: Israelis Flock to Flourishing Sex Tourism." Ynet News, September 30, 2023. https://www.ynetnews.com/magazine/article/bjf4ljxlt.

Kuwait News Agency. "Algerian Police Seize Arms Workshop." February 22, 2014. https://bit.ly/3mtszb8.

Lahlou, Mehdi. "Migration Dynamics in Play in Morocco: Trafficking and Political Relationships and Their Implications at the Regional Level." Middle East and North Africa Regional Architecture (MENARA) Working Papers no. 26, November 2018. https://www.iai.it/sites/default/files/menara_wp_26.pdf.

Laoubi, Khaled, and Masahiro Yamao. "The Challenge of Agriculture in Algeria: Are Policies Effective?" *Bulletin of Agricultural and Fisheries Economics* 12, no. 1 (March 2012): 65–73.

Lebovich, Andrew. "AQIM and Libya's Missing Weapons." *Al-Wasat*, April 4, 2011. https://thewasat.wordpress.com/2011/04/04/aqim-and-libyas-missing-weapons/.

Leggewie, Claus, and Rachid Ouaissa. "Algeria's Gramscian Situation." *International Politics and Society*, June 11, 2021. https://www.ips-journal.eu/topics/democracy-and-society/algeria-a-neglected-partner-5237/.

Le Matin d'Algérie. "Gun Trafficking Gangs Arrested in Algeria [FR]." May 5, 2016. Taken from GunPolicy.org, https://www.gunpolicy.org/firearms/search/?q=&l=Algeria.

Lensari, Mokhtar Ahmed, and Sid Ahmed Bellal. "Illegal Migration from the Sahel Countries to Europe: Tamanrasset Is an Algerian City with Sahelian Characteristics." *Arab World Geographer* 22, no. 3 (2019): 212–213.

Levi, Michael. "Money for Crime and Money from Crime: Financing Crime and Laundering Crime Proceeds." *European Journal on Criminal Policy and Research* 21, no. 2 (2015): 275–297.

Levitt, Matthew. "Contending with the PKK's Narco-Terrorism." *Washington Institute for Near East Policy*, December 8, 2009.

Levitt, Matthew, and Lauren Von Thaden. "Guns, Drugs, and Smugglers: A Recent Heightened Challenge at Israel's Borders with Jordan and Egypt" *CTC Sentinel* 16, no. 7 (July 2023).

Levy, Ido. "Egypt's Counterinsurgency Success in Sinai." Washington Institute for Near East Policy, PolicyWatch 3555, December 9, 2021.

Lewis, David, and Adama Diarra. "Special Report: In the Land of 'Gangster-Jihadists.'" Reuters, October 24, 2012.

Library of Congress Country Studies and CIA *World Factbook*. "Egypt Drug Trafficking." December 1990. https://bit.ly/3zwzHHr.

LibyaMohammed. "12 Stolen Artifacts Smuggled into Spain Recovered." *Libya Observer*, 27 November 2023.

The Local. "Italian Police Bust Migrant Trafficking Ring in Sicily," June 6, 2017. https://www.thelocal.it/20170606/italian-police-bust-migrant-trafficking-ring-in-sicily/.

Loewe, Markus, Tina Zintl, and Annabelle Houdret. "The Social Contract as a Tool of Analysis: Introduction to the Special Issue on 'Framing the Evolution of New Social Contracts in Middle Eastern and North African Countries.'" *World Development* 145 (September 2021).

Lopez-Acevedo, Gladys, Gordon Betcherman, Ayache Khellaf, and Vasco Molini. *Morocco's Jobs Landscape: Identifying Constraints to an Inclusive Labor Market*. Washington, DC: International Bank for Reconstruction and Development and World Bank, 2021.

Loudis, Jessica. "The Cartel, the Journalist and the Gangland Killings that Rocked the Netherlands." *Guardian*, October 6, 2022.

Lounnas, Djallil. "The Links Between Jihadi Organizations and Illegal Trafficking in the Sahel." Middle East and North Africa Regional Architecture (MENARA) Working Papers no. 25, November 2018. https://www.iai.it/sites/default/files/menara_wp_25.pdf.

Luck, Taylor. "'Break the Silence': In Tunisia, Rappers Keep the Revolution Alive." *Christian Science Monitor*, July 16, 2020.

Mabrouk, Mirette F. "Egypt's Sizeable Informal Economy Complicates Its Pandemic Response." Middle East Institute, June 22, 2020.

Mackie, Kyle. "Italian Police: Mafia and Nigerian "Vikings" Gang Collaborating in Palermo." Organized Crime and Corruption Reporting Project. June 28, 2017.

Mahyou, Sania. "'Outlaws': Morocco's Rif Provides Refuge for Cannabis Farmers." Al Jazeera, July 28, 2023.

Mainwaring, Cetta. *At Europe's Edge: Migration and Crisis in the Mediterranean.* Oxford, UK: Oxford University Press, 2019.

Majorca Daily Bulletin. "Migrant Route from Algeria Has Become 'Permanent.'" December 1, 2020.

Malakooti, Arezo. *The Political Economy of Migrant Detention in Libya: Understanding the Players and the Business Models.* Geneva: Global Initiative Against Transnational Organized Crime and Clingendael Institute, April 2019.

Malakooti, Arezo, and Chiara Fall. *Migration Trends Across the Mediterranean: Piecing Together the Shifting Dynamics.* Global Initiative Against Transnational Organized Crime and Clingendael Institute, February 2020.

Malta Independent. "AFM Intercepts Vessel Spilling Oil at Sea; 28 Questioned by Police." July 2, 2013.

Malta National Focal Point for Drugs and Drug Addiction. *National Report on The Drug Situation and Responses in Malta 2021.* 2021. https://cdn-others.timesofmalta.com/8e3de911c65f47ddd5495cf27ff6417f04b3b736.pdf.

Mancuso, Marina, and Francesca Maldi. "Does Human Smuggling Converge with Other Transnational Crimes in North Africa and the Mediterranean Area?" In *The Evolution of Illicit Flows: Displacement and Convergence Among Transnational Crime*, edited by Ernesto U. Savona, Rob T. Guerette, and Alberto Aziani, 140–172. Cham, Switzerland: Springer, 2022.

Mangan, Fiona. *Illicit Drug Trafficking and Use in Libya: Highs and Lows.* Peaceworks no. 161. Washington, DC: United States Institute of Peace, May 2020.

Manisera, Sara, Davide Mancini, and Ariana Poletti "Illegal Trawling Ravages Tunisian Seagrass Meadows Crucial for Fish." *Mongabay Series: Oceans*, May 24, 2023.

Mapping Militants Project. "Islamic State—Sinai Province (Wilayat Sinai)." Stanford University Center for International Security and Cooperation, Mapping Militant Organizations, December 2018. https://cisac.fsi.stanford.edu/mappingmilitants/profiles/islamic-state-sinai-province.

Maritime Herald. "The New Drug Route from Morocco to Europe with a Stopover in Spain, UN Report." August 20, 2020. https://www.maritimeherald.com/2020/08-20-the-new-drug-route-from-morocco-to-europe-with-a-stopover-in-spain-un-report-drug-trafficking-ports-covid-19.

Marks, Jon. "The Maghrib Economies: A Perpetual Search for Relevance and Reform." In *Routledge Handbook on the Modern Maghrib*, edited by George Joffe, 568–597. London: Routledge, 2023.

Marsh, Nicholas. "Brothers Came Back with Weapons: The Effects of Arms Proliferation from Libya." *PRISM: The Journal of Complex Operations* 6, no. 4 (2017): 78–97.

Martin, Maria, and Claudi Perez. "Tensions Rising in Spain's Canary Islands over Irregular Immigration." *El País* (English), February 1, 2021.

Masbah, Mohammed, and Rachid Aourraz. *COVID-19: How Moroccans View the Government's Measures?* Rabat: Moroccan Institute for Policy Analysis, March 2020.

Mashberg, Tom, and Graham Bowley. "Investigators, Citing Looting, Have Seized 27 Antiquities from the Met." *New York Times*, September 2, 2022.

Mbiyozo, Aimee-Noel. "Pressure Grows on Africa to Take Back Its Migrants." ReliefWeb, June 10, 2019.
McDermott, Jeremy, James Bargent, Douwe den Held, and Maria Fernandez Ramírez. *The Cocaine Pipeline to Europe*. Geneva: Global Initiative Against Transnational Organized Crime, February 2021.
McDougall, James. "The Fall of Abdelaziz Bouteflika." *Foreign Affairs*, April 10, 2019.
McGrath, Rachel. "Conflict and Crime: Smuggling to Turkey from Iraq and Syria." *Pitt Policy Journal* 11 (Spring 2020).
McManus, Allison. "The Army Is Not the Winner in Border Battlefields." Italian Institute for International Political Studies, December 6, 2020.
———. "ISIS in the Sinai: A Persistent Threat for Egypt." Newlines Institute for Strategy and Policy, June 23, 2020.
Meddeb, Hamza. *Leveraging Lives: Serbia and Illegal Tunisian Migration to Europe*. Malcolm H. Kerr Carnegie Middle East Center, March 2023.
———. *Precarious Resilience: Tunisia's Libyan Predicament*. Middle East and North Africa Regional Architecture, Future Notes no 5., April 2017. https://bit.ly/3xflqfa.
———. *The Volatile Tunisia-Libya Border: Between Tunisia's Security Policy and Libya's Militia Factions*. Malcolm H. Kerr Carnegie Middle East Center, September 2020.
———. *Young People and Smuggling in the Kasserine Region of Tunisia: Stories of Dispossession and the Dynamics of Exclusion*. London: International Alert, May 2016.
Meers, Jelter. "Italy: After Cosa Nostra, Nigerian Black Axe New Foe for Police." Organized Crime and Corruption Reporting Project, May 17, 2018.
Melgar, Patricia, Guiomar Merodio, Elena Duque, and Mimar Ramis-Salas. "'Petites Bonnes' Minors Sex Trafficked in Morocco and Spain." *Children and Youth Services Review* 120 (January 2021).
MENAFATF. *Anti-Money Laundering and Counter-Terrorist Financing Measures: The Arab Republic of Egypt*. Mutual Evaluation Report. Manama, Bahrain: Middle East and North Africa Financial Action Task Force, May 2021. https://www.fatf-gafi.org/media/fatf/documents/reports/mer-fsrb/MENAFATF-MER-Egypt-2021-English.pdf.
———. *Anti-Money Laundering and Counter-Terrorist Financing Measures: Tunisia*. Mutual Evaluation Report. Manama, Bahrain: Middle East and North Africa Financial Action Task Force, May 2016. https://www.fatf-gafi.org/media/fatf/documents/reports/mer-fsrb/Tunisia_MER_2016_EN.pdf.
———. *Kingdom of Morocco Mutual Evaluation Report: Anti-Money Laundering and Counter-Terrorist Financing Measures*. Manama, Bahrain: Middle East and North Africa Financial Action Task Force, April 2019.
———. *Mutual Evaluation Report of the People's Democratic Republic of Algeria: Anti-Money Laundering and Combating the Financing of Terrorism*. Middle East and North Africa Financial Action Task Force, December 1, 2010.
———. *Mutual Evaluation Report, 7th Follow-Up Report for Algeria: Anti-Money Laundering and Combating the Financing of Terrorism*. Middle East and North Africa Financial Action Task Force, April 27, 2016.
Meneghini, Cecilia, and Riccardo Milani. "Maghreb Route—Mapping Cigarette Trafficking Along the Maghreb Route." Booklet 4 in *ITTP NEXUS in Europe and Beyond*, edited by Alberto Aziani and Marco Dugato. Milano: Transcrime–Università Cattolica del Sacro Cuore, 2019.
Mersch, Sarah. "The Panama Papers Arrive in Tunis" Carnegie Endowment for International Peace, May 11, 2016.
Micallef, Mark. *Shifting Sands—Libya's Changing Drug Trafficking Dynamics on the Coastal and Desert Borders*. Background paper commissioned by the EMCDDA for the EU Drug Markets Report, 2019.

Micallef, Mark, Raouf Farrah, Alexandre Bish, and Victor Tanner. *After the Storm: Organized Crime Across the Sahel-Sahara Following Upheaval in Libya and Mali.* Geneva: Global Initiative Against Transnational Organized Crime, 2019.

Micallef, Mark, Matt Herbert, Rupert Horsley, Alexandre Bish, Alice Fereday, and Peter Tinti. *Conflict, Coping and Covid: Changing Human Smuggling and Trafficking Dynamics in North Africa and the Sahel in 2019 and 2020*. Geneva: Global Initiative Against Transnational Organized Crime, April 2021.

Micallef, Mark, Rupert Horsley, and Alexandre Bish. *Human Conveyor Belt Broken: Assessing the Collapse of the Human-Smuggling Industry in Libya and the Central Sahel.* Geneva: Global Initiative Against Transnational Organized Crime, March 2019.

Michalopolous, Sarantis. "Tobacco Smuggling: Marseille's Illicit Secret." Euractiv, July 22, 2018. https://bit.ly/3iNuXXP.

Middle East Eye. "Pandora Papers: Morocco King Mohammed VI's Sister Used Shell Company." October. 4, 2021.

———. "Tunisia's Rached Ghannouchi Wins Libel Case in UK High Court" May 29, 2020.

Middle East Monitor. "Algeria's Energy-Giant Sonatrach Launches Digital Platform to Report Corruption." September 11, 2023. https://www.middleeastmonitor.com/20230911-algerias-energy-giant-sonatrach-launches-digital-platform-to-report-corruption/.

———. "Ecuador Seizes over Half a Ton of Cocaine Destined for Tunisia in Banana Container." January 12, 2022.

Middle East Online. "Foreign Cannabis Keeps Moroccan Crop Stable." October 10, 2019. https://middle-east-online.com/en/foreign-cannabis-keeps-moroccan-crop-stable.

Miklaucic, Michael, and Jacqueline Brewer, eds. *Convergence: Illicit Networks and National Security in the Age of Globalization*. Washington, DC: National Defense University Press, 2013.

Military Africa. "Algeria Embarks on Manufacturing Heavy Chinese Weaponry." June 28, 2023.

Miller, Alyssa Marie. "Shadow Zones: Contraband and Social Contract in the Borderlands of Tunisia." PhD diss., Department of Cultural Anthropology, Duke University, 2018. https://dukespace.lib.duke.edu/dspace/bitstream/handle/10161/18205/Miller_duke_0066D_14698.pdf?sequence=1&isAllowed=y.

Moiseienko, Anton, Alexandria Reid, and Isabella Chase. *Improving Governance and Tackling Crime in Free-Trade Zones*. Occasional Paper. London: Royal United Services Institute for Defence and Security Studies (RUSI), October 2020. https://www.a-cg.org/media/publications/2020/10/20/114.pdf.

Molina, Irene Fernandez. "The Monarchy vs. the 20 February Movement: Who Holds the Reins of Political Change in Morocco?" *Mediterranean Politics* 16, no. 3 (November 2011): 435–441.

Monitoring the 21st Century Asian Arms Race. "Cheap Chinese Assault Rifles Are Made in Algeria." July 7, 2022. https://21stcenturyasianarmsrace.com/2022/07/07/cheap-chinese-assault-rifles-are-made-in-algeria/.

Monzini, Paola. *Smuggling of Migrants into, through and from North Africa: A Thematic Review and Annotated Bibliography of Recent Publications*. New York: United Nations Office on Drugs and Crime, 2010.

Morocco Latest News. "Algeria, a Hub for Hard Drugs in North Africa." MoroccoLatest-News.com, June 30, 2021.

Morocco World News. "Police in Fez Seize 1.675 Tons of Cannabis Resin." March 5, 2019.

Morris, Sarah, Anaïs Guerard, and Rosa Perez Mas. "Strait of Gibraltar: A Gateway for Drug Smugglers." France 24, July 24, 2020. https://www.france24.com/en/europe/20200724-gibraltar-a-gateway-for-drug-smugglers.

Mundy, Jacob. *Imaginative Geographies of Algerian Violence*. Stanford, CA: Stanford University Press, 2015. Kindle.

Nacer, Idriss Hadj. "From Rags to Riches to Rags Again: Deconstructing the Narratives of Crony Capitalism and Neoliberal Ideology Through the Example of Algeria." Working Paper No. 1632, Economic Research Forum, Giza, Egypt, April 2023.

Naceur, Sofian Philip. "Ruthless, Illegal, and Dangerous: Algeria's Unprecedented Mass Deportations Are Creating a Humanitarian Emergency in Niger." Rosa Luxemburg Stiftung, March 29, 2023. https://www.rosalux.de/en/news/id/50203.

Nadeau, Barbie Latza. "Italian Mob Trades Weapons for Looted Art from ISIS in Libya." *Daily Beast*, October 18, 2016.

Narconon. "Drug Addiction in Egypt." n.d. https://www.narconon.org/drug-information/egypt-drug-addiction.html.

Nation Press Services. "Former Egypt MP Held over Looted Relics." June 26, 2021. https://thenationpress.com/en/news-114018.html.

Ndikumana, Léonce, and James K. Boyce. "Capital Flight from Africa: Updated Methodology and New Estimates." PERI Research Report, Political Economy Research Institute, University of Massachusetts–Amherst, June 2018.

Nefzi, Samir. "Drugs to Suit all Tastes in Tunisia," Institute for War and Peace Reporting, November 21, 2013. https://www.refworld.org/docid/528f29f14.html.

New Arab. "Egypt Navy Busts 170kg of Heroin on Iranian Boat." December 19, 2016. https://english.alaraby.co.uk/news/egypt-navy-busts-170kg-heroin-iranian-boat.

New Humanitarian. "Syrians Seeking Refuge in Libya." May 23, 2013.

News Desk. "NGO Report Claims over 4,400 Migrants Died Trying to Reach Spain During 2021." *Spain in English*, January 3, 2022.

NISAT. "Researcher's Database: Imports to Morocco from All Countries in 2019." Norwegian Initiative on Small Arms Transfers, 2020. http://nisat.prio.org/Trade-Database/Researchers-Database/.

North Africa Post. "French Court Frees TunisAir Flight Attendant Convicted for Smuggling." March 26, 2021.

———. "Human Trafficking: U.S. Calls on Algeria to Take Urgent Action Against Smugglers." July 22, 2022.

———. "Morocco's Police Seize Over 4.8 Tons of Cannabis & 6 kg of Cocaine." July 21, 2020.

———. "Tunisian Forces Kill One Citizen in Buffer Zone with Libya." May 26, 2021.

———. "Tunisia: Security Forces Bust Arms Smuggling Operation from Turkey to Libya," January 9, 2020.

Nuclear Threat Initiative. "Eight Persons Caught Smuggling Nuclear Materials." September 7, 1998. https://www.nti.org/analysis/articles/eight-persons-caught-smuggling-nuclear-materials/.

Nugent, Paul, and A. I. Asiwaju, eds. *African Boundaries: Barriers, Conduits and Opportunities*. London: Pinter, 1998.

Operational Data Portal. "Mediterranean Situation." October 2023. https://data2.unhcr.org/en/situations/mediterranean.

Organized Crime and Corruption Reporting Project (OCCRP). "Joseph Muscat: 2019 Person of the Year in Organized Crime and Corruption." 2020. https://www.occrp.org/en/poy/2019/.

Orsini, Giacomo, and Anna Sergi. "The Emergency Business: Migrants Reception, Mafia Interests, and *Glocal* Governance: From Lampedusa to Rome." In *The Janus-Faces of Cross-Border Crime in Europe*, edited by Petrus C. van Duyne, Tomáš Strémy, Jackie H. Harvey, Georgios A. Antonopoulos, and Klaus von Lampe. The Hague: Eleven International Publishing, 2018.

Ouali, Aomar, and Paul Schemm. "Algeria Reels from Tales of Oil Sector Corruption." Associated Press, March 3, 2013.

Pacific Logistics Group. "Top 5: The Busiest Container Ports in the Mediterranean." June 24, 2022. https://pacificlt.com/en/2022/06/24/top-5-the-busiest-container-ports-in-the-mediterranean/.

Packaging Insights. "Activists Call for Justice Over Italian Waste Management Corruption Scandal in Tunisia." May 5, 2021. https://bit.ly/2VnBSxG.

Palm, Anja. "The Italy-Libya Memorandum of Understanding: The Baseline of a Policy Approach Aimed at Closing All Doors to Europe?" *EU Immigration and Asylum Law and Policy*, October 2, 2017. https://eumigrationlawblog.eu/the-italy-libya-memorandum-of-understanding-the-baseline-of-a-policy-approach-aimed-at-closing-all-doors-to-europe/.

Paoli, Letizia. "The Decline of the Italian Mafia." In *Organized Crime: Culture, Markets, and Policies*, edited by D. Siegel and H. Nelen, 15–28. New York: Springer, 2008.

Parcak, Sarah, David Gathings, Chase Childs, Greg Mumford, and Eric Cline. "Satellite Evidence of Archaeological Site Looting in Egypt: 2002–2013." *Antiquity* 90, no. 349 (February 2016): 188–205.

Parker, Claire. "Economic Fallout from Coronavirus Leads to Surge in Tunisians Leaving for Europe." *Washington Post*, September 24, 2020.

Partridge, Matthew. "Book Review: *The Force of Obedience: The Political Economy of Repression in Tunisia* by Béatrice Hibou," *Africa at LSE* (blog), April 17, 2014. https://bit.ly/3zynxNy.

Passas, Nikos. "Global Anomie, Dysnomie, and Economic Crime: Hidden Consequences of Neoliberalism and Globalization in Russia and Around the World." *Social Justice* 27, no. 2 (2000): 16–44.

———. "Globalization, Criminogenic Asymmetries, and Economic Crime." *European Journal of Law Reform* 1, no. 4 (1999): 399–423.

Paul, Katie A. "Cultural Racketeering in Egypt—Predicting Patterns in Illicit Activity: Quantitative Tools of the 21st-Century Archaeologist." In *The Future of the Past: From Amphipolis to Mosul, New Approaches to Cultural Heritage Preservation in the Eastern Mediterranean*, edited by Konstantinos Chalikias, Ariel Pearce, and Steve Renette. Proceedings of the "The Future of the Past" Conference held at UPenn Museum, April 10–11, 2015. https://bit.ly/2YcrTgh.

———. "Repatriating the Past: Filling the Holes in Egypt's History Left by Looting." HeritageDaily, December 14, 2016. https://bit.ly/3zvWxij.

The Paypers. "EUR 4 Million Seized in Large Money-Laundering Bust in France." November 16, 2020.

Pelham, Nicholas. "The Mystery of Morocco's Missing King." *1843 Magazine*.

Perry, Alex, and Connie Agius. "Migrants and the New Mediterranean Mafia." *Newsweek*, June 10, 2015.

———. "The Long Read: The Evil Genius Behind the Migrant Crisis." *Irish Examiner*, July 4, 2015. https://www.irishexaminer.com/lifestyle/arid-20340621.html.

Perry, Mark. "Looking for Hashish in Cairo? Talk to the Police." *Foreign Policy*, August 23, 2013.

Pilkey, Orrin H., Norma J. Longo, William J. Neal, Nelson G. Rangel-Buitrago, Keith C. Pilkey, and Hannah L. Hayes. *Vanishing Sands: Losing Beaches to Mining*. Durham, NC, and London: Duke University Press, 2022.

Pope, Henry. "Spain's National Police Arrest Network of Human Traffickers." Organized Crime and Corruption Reporting Project, August 11, 2021. Preussen, Wilhelmine. "Record Amount of Cocaine Seized in Antwerp in 2022." *Politico*, January 10, 2023.

Price, Roz. "Illicit Financial Flows in North Africa (Algeria, Egypt, Libya, Morocco and Tunisia)." K4D Helpdesk report 630, Institute for Development Studies, Brighton, UK, June 25, 2019. https://bit.ly/3zfEmx6.

Public Eye and Trial International. *Libyan Fuel Smuggling: A Swiss Trader Sailing Through Troubled Waters*. March 2020.
Quillen, Stephen. "Forest Fires, Wilting Crops, and Dwindling Shorelines: How Scorching Temperatures Are Destroying Tunisia's Natural Resources." New Arab, August 22, 2023. https://www.newarab.com/features/scorching-temperatures-destroy-tunisias-natural-resources.
Raghavan, Sudarsan. "Militant Threat Emerges in Egyptian Desert, Opening New Front in Terrorism Fight." *Washington Post*, March 14, 2018.
Rahhou, Jihane. "Moroccan Banks Dominated West Africa's Banking Market in 2021." *Morocco World News*, August 20, 2022.
Rahim, Zamira, and Stephanie Halasz. "Half a Ton of Cocaine Found Floating off Algerian Coast." CNN, June 29, 2021.
Raineri, Luca. "The Malta Connection: A Corrupting Island in a 'Corrupting Sea'?" ECPR Studying Group on Organised Crime, 2019. https://standinggroups.ecpr.eu/sgoc/wp-content/uploads/sites/51/2020/01/the-malta-connection-a-corrupting-island-in-a-corrupting-sea-1.pdf.
Ramzi, Walid. "Algeria Thwarts Mali Arms Smuggling." Derechos, April 16, 2013. http://www.derechos.org/peace/mali/doc/mali293.html.
Rangel-Buitrago, Nelson, and William Neal. "The Unsustainable Harvest of Coastal Sands," *Science* 382, no. 6675 (December 2023): 1116–1118.
Rastello, Luca. *I Am the Market: How to Smuggle Cocaine by the Ton, in Five Easy Lessons*. New York: Faber and Faber, 2009.
Ratcliffe, Verity, Souhail Karam, and Salma El Wardany. "Algeria's Oil and Gas Exports Plummet." Al Jazeera, February 8, 2021.
———. "An Oil Country No More? Algerian Energy Exports Sink Rapidly." Al Jazeera, February 8, 2021.
Réalités (Tunisia). "Algeria Seizes Many Guns at Tunisian and Libyan Borders [FR]." November 16, 2016. Taken from GunPolicy.org.
ReliefWeb. "Detailed Findings of the Independent Fact-Finding Mission on Libya." UN Report A/HRC/52/CRP.8, Human Rights Council. https://reliefweb.int/report/libya/detailed-findings-independent-fact-finding-mission-libya-ahrc52crp8.
———. "UNHCR Tunisia Operational Update—30 November 2020." Situation Report, December 15, 2020. https://reliefweb.int/report/tunisia/unhcr-tunisia-operational-update-30-november-2020.
Reno, William. "Protectors and Predators: Why Is There a Difference Among West African Militias?" In *Fragile States and Insecure People?* edited by Louise Andersen, Bjorn Moller, and Finn Stepputat, 99–122. New York: Palgrave Macmillan, 2007.
———. "Warfare in Collapsed States and Special Problems of Conflict Resolution." *Global Dialogue* 6 (July 2001).
Resa-Nestares, Carlos. "Transnational Organized Crime in Spain: Structural Factors Explaining Its Penetration." In *Global Organized Crime and International Security*, edited by Emilio C. Viano. Aldershot, UK: Ashgate, 1999.
Resta, Valeria. *Tunisia and Egypt After the Arab Spring: Party Politics in Transitions*. New York: Routledge, 2023.
Reuters. "Algeria's Foreign Exchange Reserves Drop to $44 Billion." July 25, 2021.
———. "Egyptian, French Authorities Recover 114 Smuggled Antiquities—Statement." June 23, 2021.
———. "Hundreds of Migrants Scale Fence in Spain's Melilla Enclave for Second Day." March 3, 2022.
———. "Morocco Seizes 1.37 Tons of Cocaine Concealed in Frozen Fish." October 20, 2023.
———. "Over 200 Migrants Scale Fence into Spain's Melilla Enclave." July 22, 2021.

———. "Tunisia Closes Libya Border Post After Smugglers Kill Soldier." March 11, 2013.

"Tunisia Seizes Three Arms Caches Near Libyan Border." November 14, 2016, https://www.reuters.com/article/idUSKBN139131/

Revkin, Mara. "The Egyptian State Unravels: Meet the Gangs and Vigilantes Who Thrive Under Morsi." Yale Law School News, June 27, 2013.

Reynolds, Paul. "Over 20 Tonnes of Cannabis Resin Seized in Canary Islands." Raidió Teilifís Éireann, June 5, 2021.

Rittel, Horst, and Melvin Webber. "Dilemmas in a General Theory of Planning." *Policy Sciences* 4 (June 1973): 155–169.

Ritter, Karl. "Explainer: Spain's Migrant Crisis in North Africa." AP News, May 19, 2021.

Rizk, Joelle. "Exploring the Nexus Between Armed Groups and the Trafficking and Smuggling of Human Beings in the Central Sahel and Libya." *Studies in Conflict and Terrorism* (November 2021): 1–21.

Rubenfeld, Samuel. "Algeria, Angola, Panama Removed from FATF Blacklist." *Wall Street Journal*, February 19, 2016.

Rubino, Giulio, Cecilia Anesi, and Lorenzo Bagnoli. "Death in a Smugglers' Paradise." Organized Crime and Corruption Reporting Project, May 3, 2018.

Saadi, Dania. "Algeria's 2020 Hydrocarbons Production to Shrink to 8% Year-on-Year: Energy Minister." S&P Global, December 20, 2020.

Sabrihomuglu, Lale. "Turkey Detects Nuclear Material Trafficking." *Jane's Intelligence Review*, August 1, 2001.

Sadiki, Larbi. "Tunisia's Migration to the North." Brookings, January 17, 2019.

Sahan Foundation and IGAD. *Human Trafficking and Smuggling on the Horn of Africa–Central Mediterranean Route*. February 2016.

Said, Summer, and Carrie Keller-Lynn. "Israel Presses Egypt to Better Secure Borderland Against Hamas Smugglers." *Wall Street Journal*, January 7, 2024.

Saidani, Mongi. "Tunisia: Interior Ministry Seizes Turkish Weapons Smuggled from Libya." *Asharq Al-Awsat*, January 9, 2020.

Saleh, Mariam. "Population Below the Poverty Line in Tunisia, 2018–2021." Statista.com, April 28, 2021.

Sanchez, Gabriella, Kheira Arrouche, Matteo Capasso, Angeliki Dimitriadi, and Alia Fakhry. *Beyond Networks, Militias and Tribes: Rethinking EU Counter-Smuggling Policy and Response*. EuroMeSCo Policy Study no. 19. Barcelona: European Institute of the Mediterranean, April 2021.

Sanchez, Nacho. "Spanish Police Seize Large Drone Used to Carry Drugs from Morocco." *El País* (English), July 15, 2021

Sands, Jennifer. "Organized Crime and Illicit Activities in Spain: Causes and Facilitating Factors." *Mediterranean Politics* 12, no. 2 (2007): 211–232.

Santini, Ruth Hanau. *Limited Statehood in Post-revolutionary Tunisia: Citizenship, Economy and Security*. Cham, Switzerland: Palgrave Pivot, 2018.

Saudi Gazette. "Tunisian Coastguard Tackles High-Speed Smugglers." April 28, 2017.

Schaer, Cathrin, and Tarak Guizani. "To Get to Europe, Tunisian Migrants Turn To 'Self-Smuggling.'" Deutsche Welle, August 11, 2021.

Schwartzstein, Peter. "Egypt's New Drug Addiction." Daily Beast, April 14, 2017.

The Sentry. *Libya's Kleptocratic Boom*. Washington, DC: November 2023.

Sergi, Anna. "Nigerian Gangs Partner with Sicilian Mafia." *Jane's Intelligence Review*, August 3, 2016.

———. "Policing the Port, Watching the City. Manifestations of Organised Crime in the Port of Genoa." *Policing and Society* 31, no. 6 (2021): 639–655.

———. *The Port-Crime Interface: A Report on Organized Crime & Corruption in Seaports*. Self-published, Amazon, 2020.

Serra, Mattia. "Beyond Migration: Assessing Libya's Smuggling Sector." Jadaliyya, April 8, 2021. https://www.jadaliyya.com/Details/42588.

Serrano, Francisco. "Higher Oil Prices Are Giving Algeria's Regime Breathing Room." Middle East Institute, May 25, 2022.

———. "Tebboune's Media 'Reforms' Won't Unmuzzle Algeria's Press." World Politics Review, December 22, 2023.

Shaw, Mark, and Fiona Mangan. *Illicit Trafficking and Libya's Transition: Profits and Losses*. Peaceworks no. 96. Washington, DC: United States Institute of Peace, 2014.

Shaw, Mark, and Tuesday Reitano. *The Political Economy of Trafficking and Trade in the Sahara: Instability and Opportunities*. Sahara Knowledge Exchange, World Bank, December 2014.

Shelley, Louise. *A Hazy Crisis: Illicit Cigarette Smuggling in the OSCE Region. Hearing Before the United States Commission on Security and Cooperation in Europe*. 115th Congress, July 19, 2017. Statement of Louise Shelley. https://www.csce.gov/sites/helsinkicommission.house.gov/files/Shelley%27s%20Testimony.pdf.

———. "Money Laundering into Real Estate." In Miklaucic and Brewer, *Convergence: Illicit Networks*, 2013.

Simpara, Mahamadou. "Morocco Seizes Nearly 363 Kilograms of Cocaine in El Guergarate." *Morocco World News*, January 3, 2024.

Small Arms Survey. *Libya Ranked 40 in the World in 2007 for Gun Ownership per Hundred People*. Chapter 4, annex 2, 2007. https://www.smallarmssurvey.org/sites/default/files/resources/Small-Arms-Survey-2007-Chapter-02-annexe-4-EN.pdf

Small Arms Survey and African Union. *Weapons Compass. Mapping Illicit Small Arms Flows in Africa*. Geneva: Small Arms Survey, Graduate Institute of Development Studies, January 2019. http://www.smallarmssurvey.org/fileadmin/docs/U-Reports/SAS-AU-Weapons-Compass.pdf.

Soto, Alonso. "Record Cocaine Busts Signal West Africa Is Transit Hub Again." Bloomberg, March 13, 2019.

Soufan Center. "Algeria Positioned to Help Europe in Ukraine Crisis." IntelBrief, February 11, 2022.

———. "Haftar's Growing Criminal Enterprise in Libya." IntelBrief, July 29, 2019.

———. "A Looming Disaster: Sudan's Refugees Face Dire Humanitarian Conditions in Chad." IntelBrief, May 26, 2023.

———. "Tunisian President's Incendiary Comments Lead to Backlash Against Sub-Saharan Migrants." IntelBrief, April 7, 2023.

Stacher, Joshua. *Watermelon Democracy: Egypt's Turbulent Transition*. New York: Syracuse University Press, 2020.

Statista.com. "Algeria: Youth Unemployment Rate from 1999 to 2019." May 2021. https://bit.ly/3zntoFW.

Strazzari, Francesco, and Simone Tholens. "'Tesco for Terrorists' Reconsidered: Arms and Conflict Dynamics in Libya and in the Sahara-Sahel Region." *European Journal of Crime Policy Research* 20 (2014): 343–360.

Strazzari, Francesco, and Francesca Zampagni. "Illicit Firearms Circulation and the Politics of Upheaval in North Africa." In *Triggering Terror: Illicit Gun Markets and Firearms Acquisition of Terrorist Networks in Europe*, edited by Nils Duquet and Kevin Goris, 435–460. Brussels: Flemish Peace Institute, 2018.

Summers, Chris. "You Dopes! Drug Smugglers Throw £4MILLION of Cannabis Overboard As They Flee from Police Boats in High-Speed Chase in the Bay of Gibraltar." *Daily Mail*, January 5, 2017.

Tahir, Tariq. "British Museum Bought Ancient Egyptian Artefact from Convicted Antiquities Smuggler." *National*, September 25, 2023.

Tahrir Institute for Middle East Policy. "Sinai Tribes in Egypt's War on Terror." November 28, 2018. https://timep.org/wp-content/uploads/2018/11/SinaiTribesIssueBrief.pdf.

Taipei Times. "Tunisia Detains Ex-official Over Italy Waste Scandal." December 24, 2020. https://www.taipeitimes.com/News/world/archives/2020/12/24/2003749314.

Talan. "Hannibal: 1st Regtech That Puts the Blockchain at the Service of the Compliance Authorities (AML/CTF)." May 25, 2021. https://talan.com/en/our-news/detail/news/hannibal-1st-regtech-that-puts-the-blockchain-at-the-service-of-the-compliance-authorities-aml-t/.

Talani, Leila Simona, and Roberto Roccu, eds. *The Dark Side of Globalisation*. London: Palgrave Macmillan, 2019.

Tassie, G. J., A. De Trafford, and J. van Wetering. "Egypt's Heritage in Times of Conflict and Crisis." In *The Management of Egypt's Cultural Heritage*, Volume 2, edited by F. A. Hassan, G. J. Tassie, L. S. Owens, A. De Trafford, J. van Wetering, and O. El Daly, 14–47. London: ECHO and Golden House Publications, 2015.

Terrorism, Transnational Crime and Corruption Center. *Research Findings: Illicit Hubs, Tobacco Trade and Convergence with Illicit Commodities*. Arlington, VA: TraCCC, April 23, 2019.

Thomas, Troy, and Stephen Kiser. *Lords of the Silk Route*. Institute for National Security Studies Occasional Paper 43. Colorado Springs, CO: US Air Force Academy, May 2002.

Tijhaus, A. J. G. "The Trafficking Problem: A Criminological Perspective." In *Crime in the Art and Antiquities World: Illegal Trafficking in Cultural Property*, edited by Stefano Manacorda and Duncan Chappell, 87–97. New York: Springer, 2011.

Tika, Ali Abduallah. "The Role of the Informal Economy in Libya's Development: A Case Study of the Informal Food Sector in Misrata." PhD thesis, University of the Western Cape, 2018.

Times of Israel. "Egypt Confiscates Weapons Smuggled from Libya to Gaza." June 29, 2012.

Times of Malta. "'Malta Has Become a Crossroad of Illegal Trafficking'—Italian Police." October 10, 2018.

Tinasti, Khalid. "View from the Ground—Harm Reduction, Drug Policy and the Law in the Maghreb: Focus on Morocco and Algeria." Global Drug Policy Observatory, Swansea University, October 2016. https://bit.ly/3DnARHg.

Tognini, Giacomo. "A New Migrant Gateway on Algeria's Western Border." Worldcrunch, April 10, 2018.

———. "Border Row Is Bad News for Moroccan Workers in Algeria." Worldcrunch, May 28, 2018.

Tondo, Lorenzo. "Libya Releases Man Described As One of World's Most Wanted Human Traffickers." *Guardian*. April 13, 2021.

———. "Puglia Crimewave Points to Emergence of 'Fifth' Italian Mafia." *Guardian*, May 19, 2020.

Torelli, Stefano M., ed. *The Great Mediterranean Challenge: What Pushes People from Africa Northwards*. Milan: Reset Dialogues on Civilizations, 2019.

———. "Introduction." In Torelli, *Great Mediterranean Challenge*, 11–16.

Toub, Ben. "An Absurd Case of Mistaken Identity Draws to a Close." *New Yorker*, July 13, 2019.

Transparency International. "Corruption Perceptions Index: Algeria." 2020. https://www.transparency.org/en/cpi/2020/index/dza.

———. "Corruption Perceptions Index: Egypt." 2020. https://www.transparency.org/en/cpi/2020/index/egy.

———. "Morocco: Glaring Gaps Revealed by Response to the Coronavirus Pandemic." *Transparency Maroc* (blog), February 12, 2021. https://www.transparency.org/en/blog/morocco-glaring-gaps-revealed-by-the-management-of-the-coronavirus-pandemic.

Triandafyllidou, Anna, and Marie McAuliffe, eds. *Migrant Smuggling Data and Research: A Global Review of the Emerging Evidence Base*, Volume 2. Geneva: International Organization for Migration, 2018.

Tyson, Luke. "Spanish Police Uncover Submarine Designed to Traffick Cocaine from Morocco." *Morocco World News*, March 16, 2021.

UNCTAD. *Tackling Illicit Financial Flows for Sustainable Development in Africa*. Economic Development in Africa Report 2020. New York: United Nations Conference on Trade and Development, 2020.

UNDP. "Scaling Fences: Voices of Irregular Africa Migrants to Europe." United Nations Development Program Report, October 2019. https://scalingfences.undp.org/en/.

UNECA. *Illicit Financial Flows: Report of the High-Level Panel on Illicit Financial Flows from Africa*. United Nations Economic Commission for Africa, Commissioned by the AU/ECA Conference of Ministers of Finance, Planning and Economic Development, 2015. https://bit.ly/3zowolC.

UNHCR. "Italy Weekly Snapshot (11 Dec–17 Dec 2023)." 2023. https://reliefweb.int/report/italy/italy-weekly-snapshot-11-dec-17-dec-2023.

———. "Key Facts and Figures." January 2024. https://www.unhcr.org/us/?gad_source=1&gclid=EAIaIQobChMImKaslNDCgwMVgimtBh1PzQGpEAAYASAAEgKfifD_BwE.

———. *Mixed Migration Trends in Libya*. Report prepared for UNHCR by Altai Consulting, 2017. https://reliefweb.int/sites/reliefweb.int/files/resources/LIB-HCR-MAS-Final-Report.pdf.

———. "Operational Data Portal, Spain." November 2023. https://data.unhcr.org/en/country/esp.

———. "Sudan Emergency." n.d. https://www.unhcr.org/eg/sudanemergency.

UNICEF. "Algeria—MENA Generation 2030 Country Fact Sheet." Regional Office for the Middle East and North Africa, February 2019. https://www.unicef.org/mena/media/4176/file.

UNICRI. *Illicit Financial Flows and Asset Recovery in the State of Libya*. United Nations Interregional Crime and Justice Research Institute Research Paper, 2021.

UNODC. *Firearms Trafficking in the Sahel*. United Nations Office on Drugs and Crime Transnational Organized Crime Threat Assessment. New York: United Nations, 2022.

———. *Fuel Trafficking in the Sahel*. New York: United Nations, 2022.

———. *Global Report on Cocaine 2023: Local Dynamics, Global Challenges*." New York: United Nations, March, 2023.

———. *Global Study on Firearms Trafficking 2020*. New York: United Nations, March 2020. https://bit.ly/3kgQcAN.

———. *Illicit Trafficking in Firearms, Their Parts, Components and Ammunition to, from and across the European Union*. Vienna: United Nations, 2020.

———. *Organized Crime and Irregular Migration from Africa to Europe*. Vienna: United Nations Office on Drugs and Crime, July 2006. https://www.unodc.org/pdf/research/Migration_Africa.pdf.

———. *Smuggling of Migrants into, through and from North Africa*. New York: United Nations, 2010.

———. *Transnational Organized Crime in West Africa: A Threat Assessment*. Vienna: United Nations Office on Drugs and Crime, 2013. https://www.unodc.org/documents/data-and-analysis/tocta/West_Africa_TOCTA_2013_EN.pdf.

———. *World Drug Report: 2021—Booklet 5. Covid-19 and Drugs: Impact Outlook.* Vienna: United Nations Office on Drugs and Crime, 2021. https://www.unodc.org/res/wdr2021/field/WDR21_Booklet_5.pdf.

———. *World Drug Report 2021—Booklet 3. Drug Market Trends: Cannabis Opioids.* Vienna: United Nations Office on Drugs and Crime, 2021. https://www.unodc.org/res/wdr2021/field/WDR21_Booklet_3.pdf.

UN Security Council. "Ermias Ghermay." June 7, 2018. https://www.un.org/securitycouncil/sanctions/1970/materials/summaries/individual/ermias-ghermay.

———. S/2013/99. *Final Report of the Panel of Experts Established Pursuant to Resolution 1973 (2011) Concerning Libya.* March 9, 2013. https://www.undocs.org/S/2013/99.

———. S/2016/209. Letter dated 4 March 2016 from the Panel of Experts on Libya established pursuant to resolution 1973 (2011) addressed to the President of the Security Council.

———. S/2017/466. Letter dated 1 June 2017 from the Panel of Experts on Libya established pursuant to resolution 1973 (2011) addressed to the President of the Security Council.

———. S/2018/812. Letter dated 5 September 2018 from the Panel of Experts on Libya established pursuant to resolution 1973 (2011) addressed to the President of the Security Council.

———. S/2019/914. Letter dated 29 November 2019 from the Panel of Experts on Libya established pursuant to resolution 1973 (2011) addressed to the President of the Security Council.

———. S/2021/229. Letter dated 8 March 2021 from the Panel of Experts on Libya established pursuant to resolution 1973 (2011) addressed to the President of the Security Council.

———. S/2023/673. *Final report of the Panel of Experts Established Pursuant To Resolution 1973 (2011) concerning Libya.* September 14, 2023. https://www.securitycouncilreport.org/un-documents/document/s-2023-673.php.

———. "Violence, Hatred, Piracy, Cross-Border Crime Pose Dire Threat to Mediterranean Stability, Secretary-General Tells Security Council." Security Council 8106th Meeting (PM), November 17, 2017. https://www.un.org/press/en/2017/sc13073.doc.htm.

Urbina, Ian. "The Secretive Prisons That Keep Migrants Out of Europe." *New Yorker*, November 28, 2021.

US Department of Labor. *2015 Findings on the Worst Forms of Child Labor.* Washington, DC: Bureau of International Labor Affairs, September 2016. https://bit.ly/3AUk90j.

US Department of State. *International Narcotics Control Strategy Report*, Volume 1. *Drug and Chemical Control.* Bureau of International Narcotics and Law Enforcement, March 2021. https://www.state.gov/wp-content/uploads/2021/02/International-Narcotics-Control-Strategy-Report-Volume-I-FINAL-1.pdf.

———. *International Narcotics Control Strategy Report*, Volume 1. *Drug and Chemical Control.* Bureau of International Narcotics and Law Enforcement, March 2022. https://www.state.gov/wp-content/uploads/2022/03/22-00767-INCSR-2022-Vol-1.pdf.

———. *International Narcotics Control Strategy Report*, Volume 2. *Money Laundering.* Bureau of International Narcotics and Law Enforcement Affairs, March 2018.

———. *International Narcotics Control Strategy Report*, Volume 2. *Money Laundering.* Bureau of International Narcotics and Law Enforcement, March 2021. https://www.state.gov/wp-content/uploads/2021/02/21-00620-INLSR-Vol2_Report-FINAL.pdf.

———. *International Narcotics Control Strategy Report*, Volume 2. *Money Laundering.* Bureau of International Narcotics and Law Enforcement, March 2022. https://www.state.gov/2022-incsr-volume-ii-money-laundering-as-submitted-to-congress/.

———. *Money Laundering and Financial Crimes Country Database*. International Narcotics Control Strategy Report, June 2016. https://2009-2017.state.gov/documents/organization/258726.pdf.
———. "Trafficking in Persons Report." 2021. https://www.state.gov/reports/2021-trafficking-in-persons-report/.
———. "Trafficking in Persons Report 2023: Morocco." 2023. https://www.state.gov/reports/2023-trafficking-in-persons-report/morocco/.
———. "2018 Trafficking in Persons Report: Algeria." Office to Monitor and Combat Trafficking in Persons, June 2018. https://www.state.gov/reports/2018-trafficking-in-persons-report/algeria/.
———. "2019 Trafficking in Persons Report: Algeria." Office to Monitor and Combat Trafficking in Persons, June 2019. https://www.state.gov/reports/2019-trafficking-in-persons-report-2/algeria/.
———. "2020 Trafficking in Persons Report: Algeria." Office to Monitor and Combat Trafficking in Persons, June 2020. https://www.state.gov/reports/2020-trafficking-in-persons-report/algeria/.
———. "2020 Trafficking in Persons Report: Tunisia." Office to Monitor and Combat Trafficking in Persons, June 2020. https://www.state.gov/wp-content/uploads/2020/06/2020-TIP-Report-Complete-062420-FINAL.pdf.
———. "2021 Trafficking in Persons Report: Algeria." Office to Monitor and Combat Trafficking in Persons, June 2021. https://www.state.gov/reports/2021-trafficking-in-persons-report/algeria/.
———. "2021 Trafficking in Persons Report: Cote d'Ivoire." Office to Monitor and Combat Trafficking in Persons, June 2021. https://www.state.gov/reports/2021-trafficking-in-persons-report/cote-divoire/.
———. "2021 Trafficking in Persons Report: Libya." https://www.state.gov/reports/2021-trafficking-in-persons-report/morocco/.
———. "2021 Trafficking in Persons Report: Morocco." Office to Monitor and Combat Trafficking in Persons, 2021. https://www.justice.gov/eoir/page/file/1415456/download.
———. "2021 Trafficking in Persons Report: Tunisia." Office to Monitor and Combat Trafficking in Persons, June 2021. https://www.state.gov/reports/2021-trafficking-in-persons-report/tunisia/.
———. "2022 Trafficking in Persons Report: Algeria." Office to Monitor and Combat Trafficking in Persons, 2022. https://www.state.gov/reports/2022-trafficking-in-persons-report/algeria/.
———. "2022 Trafficking in Persons Report: Tunisia." Office to Monitor and Combat Trafficking in Persons, 2022. https://www.state.gov/reports/2022-trafficking-in-persons-report/tunisia/.
———. "2023 Trafficking in Persons Report: Algeria," Office to Monitor and Combat Trafficking in Persons, 2023. https://dz.usembassy.gov/wp-content/uploads/sites/236/2023-Trafficking-in-Persons-Report-Algeria.pdf.
———. "2023 Trafficking in Persons Report: Egypt." Office to Monitor and Combat Trafficking in Persons, 2023. https://www.state.gov/reports/2023-trafficking-in-persons-report/egypt.
———. "2023 Trafficking in Persons Report: Libya." Office to Monitor and Combat Trafficking in Persons, 2023. https://www.state.gov/reports/2023-trafficking-in-persons-report/libya/.
———. "2023 Trafficking in Persons Report: Tunisia." Office to Monitor and Combat Trafficking in Persons, 2023. https://www.state.gov/reports/2023-trafficking-in-persons-report/tunisia/.
———. "The United States Designates ISIS Financial Facilitators." Press Statement. https://www.state.gov/the-united-states-designates-isis-financial-facilitators/.

US Department of the Treasury. "Guidance to Financial Institutions Based on the Financial Action Task Force Publication on Anti-Money Laundering and Counter-Terrorist Financing Risks." Financial Crimes Enforcement Network Advisory FIN-2011-A014, November 15, 2011. https://bit.ly/3BdR1kJ.

———. "Treasury Sanctions International Network Smuggling Oil from Libya to Europe." Press Release, February 26, 2018. https://home.treasury.gov/news/press-releases/sm0298.

———. "Treasury Sanctions Supporters of the Kurdistan Workers Party (PKK) Tied to Drug Trafficking in Europe." Press Release, February 1, 2012. https://home.treasury.gov/news/press-releases/tg1406.

———. "Treasury Targets Two Politically Connected Brothers in Lebanon for Profiting from Public Corruption." Press Release, April 4, 2023. https://home.treasury.gov/news/press-releases/jy1384.

US Embassy. "2023 Trafficking in Persons Report: Algeria." 2023. https://dz.usembassy.gov/wp-content/uploads/sites/236/2023-Trafficking-in-Persons-Report-Algeria.pdf.

US Immigration and Customs Enforcement. "Brooklyn Man Indicted on Cultural Artifacts Smuggling Charges." July 6, 2020. https://www.ice.gov/news/releases/brooklyn-man-indicted-cultural-artifacts-smuggling-charges.

US Securities & Exchange Commission. "SEC Charges Honeywell with Bribery Schemes in Algeria and Brazil." Press Release, December 19, 2022. https://www.sec.gov/news/press-release/2022-230.

van Reisen, Mirjam, Meron Estefanos, and Lena Reim. "Human Trafficking in the Sinai: Mapping the Routes and Facilitators." In *Human Trafficking and Trauma in the Digital Era: The Ongoing Tragedy of the Trade in Refugees from Eritrea*, edited by Mirjam Van Reisen and Munyaradzi Mawere. Mankon, Bamenda, Cameroon: Langaa RPCIG, 2017.

Vella, Matthew. "Customs' Drug Bust: 10 Tonnes of Cannabis Resin Worth €28.5 Million Inside Container Ship." *Malta Times*, September 18, 2018.

———. "Italians Arrest Ex-Malta Footballer Darren Debono in Lampedusa on Fuel Smuggling Suspicions." *Malta Today*, October 21, 2017.

Viorst, Milton. "Algeria's Long Night." *Foreign Affairs* (November/December 1997): 86–99.

Völkel, Jan Claudius. "Livin' on the Edge: Irregular Migration in Egypt." Middle East Institute, April 12, 2016.

Volpi, Frédéric. "Algeria Versus the Arab Spring." *Journal of Democracy* 24, no. 3 (July 2013): 104–115.

Walsh, Declan. "Coast to Coast, a Corridor of Coups Brings Turmoil in Africa." *New York Times*, July 29, 2023.

"Gibraltar Detains a Spanish and a Portuguese with 825 Kilos of Hashish." January 13, 2021. https://www.gibraltarpanorama.gi/174310?format=print.

Weekly Standard. "Whose Convenience? Hurd's Bank, July 2015." Hudson Institute, December 12, 2016. https://www.hudson.org/research/13146-whose-convenience.

Wehrey, Frederic. *Tunisia's Wake-Up Call: How Security Challenges From Libya Are Shaping Defense Reforms*. Washington, DC: Carnegie Endowment for International Peace, March 2020.

Williams, Phil. *Criminals, Militias and Insurgents: Organized Crime in Iraq*. Carlisle, PA: US Army War College, 2009.

———. "The Global Crisis of Governance." In *Beyond Convergence: World Without Order*, edited by Hilary Matfess and Michael Miklaucic, 21–45. Carlisle, PA: National Defense University and Peacekeeping and Stability Institute, US Army War College, 2016.

Williams, Phil, and Paul N. Woessner. "The Real Threat of Nuclear Smuggling." *Scientific American* 274, no. 1 (January 1996): 40–44.

Willis, Michael J. *Algeria*. New York: Oxford University Press, 2022.

Winfield, Nicole. "Italy Confirms Higher Cancer, Death Rates From Mob's Dumping of Toxic Waste." *Washington Post*, January 2, 2016.

Woody, Christopher. "Police in Peru Took Down an International Drug Ring Hiding Cocaine in Vegetables." Business Insider, January 13, 2017.

———. "Spanish and Moroccan Police Seized 5,700 Pounds of Cocaine in the Middle of a High-Seas Trafficking Corridor." Business Insider, December 6, 2016.

World Bank. "The World Bank in Tunisia." May 30, 2023. https://www.worldbank.org/en/country/tunisia/overview.

Worldcrunch. "Algeria to Sardinia, A New Migrant Route to Europe." November 13, 2017.

WorldECR. "OFAC Acts to Disrupt Libya-Europe Oil Smuggling Network." March 1, 2018.

World Health Organization Regional Office for the Eastern Mediterranean. "Egypt: Tobacco." n.d. http://www.emro.who.int/egy/programmes/tobacco-free-initiative.html.

World Port Source. "World Ports by Country." August 9, 2021.

Xinhua. "Egypt Seizes Foreign Ship with 2 Tons of Heroin at Red Sea." April 5, 2019. http://www.xinhuanet.com/english/2019-04/05/c_137950839.htm.

———. "Italy Busts 14-Member Migrant and Tobacco Smuggling Ring." January 16, 2019. http://www.xinhuanet.com/english/2019-01/16/c_137746409.htm.

Yahia, Jihane Ben. "In Morocco, Is Cocaine the New Cannabis?" ENACT, April 11, 2018.

Yahia, Jihane Ben, and Raouf Farrah. "Algerian Cocaine Bust Points to Alarming Trends." ENACT Observer, December 10, 2018.

Yahya, Abdelmageed M. *Irregular Migration or Human Trafficking? The Realities of Cross-Border Population Mobility in Western Sudan*. Sudan Brief no. 1. Bergen, Norway: Chr. Michelsen Institute, 2020. https://www.cmi.no/publications/7174-irregular-migration-or-human-trafficking.

Yale Environment 360. "Amid Coronavirus Lockdown, a Spike in Illegal Logging in Tunisia." May 7, 2020. https://e360.yale.edu/digest/amid-coronavirus-lockdown-a-spike-in-illegal-logging-in-tunisia.

Yeager, Matthew G., Randall G. Shelden, and Alyssa Holden. "The Political Economy of Corporate Bribery: SNC-Lavalin Group as a Case Study." *International Criminology* 1 (December 2021): 341–355.

Yee, Vivian. "Years of Graft Doomed 2 Dams in Libya, Leaving Thousands in Muddy Graves." *New York Times*, September 27, 2023.

Yousef, Lubna, and Tim Eaton. "The Dual Face of Migrant Smuggling in Libya." New Arab, March 30, 2023.

Zagaria, Valentina. "The Morally Fraught *Harga*: Migration Blame Games in a Tunisian Border Town." *Cambridge Journal of Anthropology* 37, no. 2 (Autumn 2019): 57–73.

Zaitseva, Lyudmila. "Illicit Trafficking in the Southern Tier and Turkey Since 1999: A Shift from Europe?" *Nonproliferation Review* (Fall–Winter 2002): 168–182. https://www.nonproliferation.org/wp-content/uploads/npr/93zait.pdf.

Zardo, Federica, and Chiara Loschi. "EU-Algeria (Non)Cooperation on Migration: A Tale of Two Fortresses." *Mediterranean Politics* 27, no. 2 (2022): 148–169.

Zeidan, Adam. "Kais Saied, President of Tunisia." *Britannica*, December 27, 2023. https://www.britannica.com/biography/Kais-Saied.

Zouiten, Sara. "Police Abort International Drug Trafficking Operation in Casablanca Port." *Morocco World News*, June 9, 2022.

Index

About the Book

SMUGGLING AND TRAFFICKING ACTIVITIES HAVE INTENSIFIED THROUGHOUT North Africa in recent years, threatening both fragile economies and human security. The authors of *The Mediterranean Connection* examine the nature of these illicit flows and the routes that they take across Algeria, Egypt, Libya, Morocco, Tunisia, and beyond. As they explore the practices of criminal networks and what allows them to thrive in the region, they open a window to the dark underbelly of the global economy.

Phil Williams is professor of political science and Posvar Chair for International Security Studies at the University of Pittsburgh. **Jason M. Blazakis** is professor of practice in nonproliferation and terrorism studies at the Middlebury Institute of International Studies at Monterey. **Colin P. Clarke** is director of research and senior research fellow at the Soufan Group.